Jews & Gender

RESPONSES TO OTTO WEININGER

Inscription on Otto Weininger's tombstone (composed by his father, Leopold) in the Matzleinsdorf Protestant Cemetery (Vienna), Group 14, Grave No. 126:

"This stone marks the resting place of a young man whose spirit found no peace in this world. When he had delivered the message of his soul, he could no longer remain among the living. He betook himself to the place of death of one of the greatest of all men, the Schwarzspanierhaus in Vienna, and there destroyed his mortal body."

Jews

& Gender

RESPONSES TO OTTO WEININGER

Edited by Nancy A. Harrowitz
and Barbara Hyams

TEMPLE
UNIVERSITY
PRESS
Philadelphia

Temple University Press, Philadelphia 19122
Published 1995

Frontis photograph by Konstanze Zinsler. Reprinted from
Jacques Le Rider, *Der Fall Otto Weininger*, p. 49, by kind
permission of the publisher, Löcker Verlag, Vienna, Austria
(© 1985). Translation of the inscription is by David
Abrahamsen, *The Mind and Death of a Genius* (New York:
Columbia University Press, 1946), p. 207.

Printed in the United States of America

Library of Congress Cataloging-in-Publication Data

Jews & gender : responses to Otto Weininger / edited by Nancy A.
   Harrowitz and Barbara Hyams.
      p.   cm.
   Includes bibliographical references and index.
   ISBN 1–56639–248–9. — ISBN 1–56639–249–7 (pbk.)
   1. Weininger, Otto, 1880–1903. 2. Antisemitism. 3. Sexism.
I. Harrowitz, Nancy A. (Nancy Anne), 1952– . II. Hyams, Barbara.
III. Title: Jews and gender.
B3363.W54J48   1995
193—dc20   94-31741

For Arthur Zeiger,
without whose inspiration
and knowledge about Otto Weininger
this volume would not have been conceived

Contents ✦

III   WEININGER AND MODERN LITERATURE

Acknowledgments ✦

Nancy A. Harrowitz would like to thank Arthur Zeiger, Jeffrey Mehlman, Katherine O'Connor, and Steven Beller for their provocative conversations about Weininger and his influence. I would also like to thank Kristie Foell, Barbara Spackman, Keala Jewell, Fiora Bassanese, and Melissa Zeiger for their advice regarding different aspects of this project. My thanks to Boston University for a research grant that included privileges at Widener Library, Harvard. My husband, Craig Haller, deserves special thanks for his computer expertise, which greatly facilitated the project, and for his drollness and patience. I would like to especially thank my co-editor, Barbara Hyams, for her painstaking research, her tireless efforts to improve this volume, and her friendship and good humor through it all.

Barbara Hyams would like to thank the Mellon Foundation for a grant to attend a workshop at Rice University on "Biology and the Study of Women"; the National Endowment for the Humanities for a grant to attend a summer seminar at Stanford University on "The Woman Question in European and American Thought, 1750–1950"; Boston University for a seed grant that included library privileges at Harvard University's Widener Library; the Fulbright Commission for a Research Fellowship at the University of Innsbruck, Austria; and the librarians of the Memorial House of the Wannsee Conference (Berlin) and the Institute for Anti-Semitism Research at the Technical University of Berlin for friendly assistance with their respective collections. Individuals deserving special thanks in connection with my research include Linda Adair, Susan Clark, Elisabeth Long, Karen Offen, Peter R. Frank, Sara Lennox, Katherine Arens, Werner M. Bauer, Elfriede Pöder, Allan Janik, Sigurd Paul Scheichl, Erika Weinzierl, Hannelore Rodlauer, Robert Skloot, Annegret Ehmann, Wolfgang Benz, Antje Gerlach, and Wulf Hopf. I would especially like to thank the members of the Women in German Boston Study Group for reading drafts of my work and for always asking the right questions: Kay Goodman, Ritta Jo Horsley, Luise Pusch, Monika Totten, Margaret Ward, and Christiane Zehl-Romero. For additional good advice, many thanks to Harry Zohn, Gerda Lederer, and the Brandeis Faculty

Study Group (David Gil, Eugene Goodheart, Michael Harris, Robert Maeda, Alan Mintz, and Hugh Pendleton). Loving thanks to my husband, Mark R. Eaton, for his patience, encouragement, and sense of humor during my work on this project. Last but never least, thanks to my co-editor and friend, Nancy Harrowitz, for countless hours of hard work, great wit, and perseverance.

I ✦
Introduction

1 ✦

A CRITICAL INTRODUCTION TO THE HISTORY OF WEININGER RECEPTION

Barbara Hyams and Nancy A. Harrowitz

In 1903 Otto Weininger, a Viennese Jew who converted to Protestantism the day he became a doctor of philosophy,[1] published a book entitled *Geschlecht und Charakter* (Sex and Character). In his book Weininger set out to prove the moral inferiority of "the woman" and "the Jew" by way of a dogmatic neo-Kantianism, a theory of human bisexuality, and an explanation of gender roles based on a kind of sociobiology and a racist psychology of "Jewishness." Weininger was almost immediately immortalized by his culture as the young genius who had brought these elements together under one title. He sensationalized their urgency as well through his suicide at age twenty-three in the room where Beethoven had died. A companion volume of short texts and aphorisms, *Über die letzten Dinge* (On Last Things), appeared in Dec. 1903, just a few months after his death (Weininger 1904).[2]

Sex and Character is an attempt to define and understand what Weininger calls *"M"* and *"W"*: male and female traits, respectively, apparent in every person of either sex. Weininger tries to avoid equating *"W"* directly with women, but this effort ultimately fails because he elides *"W"* with *das Weib* (woman) on more than one occasion in the text. Weininger's book is flamboyant, full of pseudoscientific claims about male genius and female character deficits. It may well be described as an apotheosis of misogyny that is exacerbated by a penultimate chapter asserting that Jewish male behavior is essentially effeminate. In this chapter, Weininger presents an analysis of what is Jewish, laid out along the same lines as his definitions of *"M"* and *"W"*: He claims that there is no causal relationship between Jewish qualities and Jews, yet states that Jewish qualities are to be found most often in Jews. His essentialist definitions of women and Jews blatantly contradict his claim to be describing poles of behavior, or "character," to which real men's and women's gender identities and levels of spirituality correspond to varying degrees.

Weininger's assessment of Jews within the framework of gender is responsible for much of the interest, both positive and negative, that his text has generated and continues to generate. The question that this twinning raises is still compelling: Why represent Jews and women together, as two sides of the same coin?[3]

The prevailing image of Jewish male sexuality at the turn of the century in Central Europe was closely linked to images of the *femme fatale* and the women's emancipationist.[4] The culture as a whole harbored fears of Jewish reproduction, since Jews were assimilating so well that their representation in the professions far outnumbered their percentage of the population. By vilifying Jews as more lascivious than non-Jews, the Christian host culture also expressed fears that the emancipation of the Jews had unleashed a competitive labor force and a rival cultural voice. By likening male Jews to sexually or politically aggressive non-Jewish women, the patriarchal dominant culture insulted male Jews by underscoring their relative powerlessness as a social group.

More in tune with his culture than he may have realized, Weininger vehemently disavowed the emancipation movements for Jews and women, respectively, that had gained momentum in the course of the nineteenth century. A number of Weininger scholars, such as Jacques Le Rider and Gerald Stieg, have noted the apparent fear of sexuality and Judaism that is coupled in Weininger's thought. Weininger was repulsed by cultural openness about sexuality. He despised both those who celebrated the pleasure of sex and those who valued the propagation of one's own kind as life's most sacred duty. He believed that sexuality was only one aspect of life for men, for whom intellectual genius and spiritual transcendence were the crowning achievements, while he thought that women, whom he deemed amoral, intellectually inferior, and incapable of transcendence without male guidance, were innately obsessed with sexuality. Hence his claim that his era had become "feminized" was an indictment of his culture's frank approach to human sexuality.

Nonetheless, despite the move toward sexual openness, women in Weininger's day who acknowledged sexual pleasure while shirking the duties of motherhood were still seen as embodying the culture's worst fears about the meaning of women's emancipation. But Weininger himself went further than condemning female libido. He was equally critical of the impulse to reproduce. In this respect, he was truly monklike,[5] for he was repulsed by the flesh and by what he perceived as a base act of desperation to find meaning in the production of further generations of human beings. Thus, his "solution to the Woman Question" was to urge men to cease having intercourse with women in order to prepare the human soul for immortality.

When Weininger refers to Jews or Jewish character, the male is assumed to be the subject, not the female.[6] In this respect, he invokes patriarchal assumptions about the predominance of male subjectivity in both Christian and Jewish cultures. When Weininger does turn his attention—in passing—to the female Jew, he derives her definition from that of the male Jew. Because the Jewish man lacks a feeling for the "transcendent," Weininger reasons, the Jewish woman is "sexually complemented and spiritually impregnated" at an extremely low metaphysical level, and thus represents the two earthbound poles of femininity (i.e., mother and prostitute) even more fully than does the "Aryan" woman (Weininger 1903, 429). The crucial parallel between "Aryan" mothers and male Jews, according to Weininger, lies in the extent to which male Jews encourage matchmaking as a means to the end of reproducing their "race."

Weininger's hatred for his fellow Jews thus focuses on the reproduction of Jewish families. On a personal level, Weininger's stance may well have involved homoerotic feelings and rebellion against his family's expectation that he would marry and have a family of his own. Weininger, the apostate Jew and anti–family man, used his constructions of both Jew and gender to exacerbate the crisis of identity felt throughout the culture as a whole.[7] What Weininger defined as gender roles in *Sex and Character* is therefore inextricably linked with the Jewish/sexuality conundrum whose constraints he sought to escape.

The impact of Weininger's *Sex and Character* and "On Last Things" on his own generation and the next was widespread. His slim body of work is still significant because of the extent of its influence on the most important thinkers and writers of Weininger's time—Ludwig Wittgenstein, Karl Kraus, Elias Canetti, Sigmund Freud, Franz Kafka, Hermann Broch, James Joyce, D. H. Lawrence, and Gertrude Stein among them— many of whom will be discussed in this volume of essays on Weininger's influence and his reception in Western culture. Weininger's name is no longer a household word, but his voice is still heard in texts by familiar authors who helped form modern and postmodern culture. His text has rendered any boundaries between genre, nationality, or discipline obsolete; his influence, stemming from a work that today might be called "popular science," has been felt in literature, philosophy, science, and history.

An examination of the effect that Weininger and his texts had on some of the most influential writers of this century is important for several reasons. A study of Weininger reception during his own period helps us understand the incipient ideology of the Third Reich in regard to male Jews and "Aryan" women. A close look at the history of the reception (*Wirkungsgeschichte*) of Weininger's thought in well-known texts also demonstrates the ways in which his transmission of low regard for women and Jews still plays a part—albeit a less virulent one—in Western culture.

In approximately the past 15 years, there has been a resurgence of interest in Weininger that seeks to understand the reasons behind his pervasive influence on some of the best minds of the twentieth century. Contemporary scholars who specialize in modern European and Israeli literature and history have contributed to an understanding of Weininger reception. The reception of Weininger's texts raises issues pertinent to our understanding of how literature interacts with nonliterary texts. The contributors to this volume all explicitly or implicitly examine the concept of influence. Many of Weininger's most renowned readers have interacted with *Geschlecht und Charakter* and *Über die letzten Dinge*, whether in the original German or in translation, by rewriting them as parts of their own texts. The fictional qualities of Weininger's ostensibly nonliterary texts aside (cf. Iser 1993), writers of modernist and post-Holocaust fiction have given voice to their understanding of Weininger's "Woman" and Weininger's "Jew."

Our knowledge of the Holocaust as well as fascism's manipulation of sexuality and gender roles in the twentieth century leads to unavoidable questions. Do we view the reception of Weininger by Nazi ideologues in the same way as his reception by James Joyce, who subsequently disseminated Weininger's ideas not only through his own work but also by introducing Weininger's work to Italo Svevo? Does a more intimate knowledge of Weininger's thought put into jeopardy our reading of the important writers who were affected by him and who translated his ideas in their works? If Weiningerian ideas are part of what we define as greatness in certain texts, such as Joyce's *Ulysses*, does that elevate Weininger to the level of a genius or cast aspersions on our definition of greatness?[8] One thing is clear: Weininger has survived as a powerful catalyst for twentieth-century thought. Perhaps we come closest to the essence of his appeal in Wittgenstein's paradoxical remark to G. E. Moore: "It is his enormous mistake which is great."[9]

The methodological differences in the secondary literature, discussed more fully in the next section, allow us to grasp the complexity of the issues at stake. There are basically two approaches. The first approach insists on what may be called a cultural relativist position, which seeks to reconstruct the conditions, proclivities, and contradictions of a past era. The other approach emphasizes the position of the reader (critic) in her or his own era and therefore looks at anti-Semitism, misogyny, and homophobia from late twentieth-century perspectives. The former approach can be faulted for appearing to discount or even forgive bigotry and for failing to take into account the diachronic effect of prejudice. The latter approach can be faulted for not fully appreciating the historical period that produces a given text and thus for failing to understand fully either the text's inception or its initial reception. Not all approaches to Weininger fall neatly into one or the other, but most do lean in one of these two directions.

This essay will first survey the ground covered since the appearance of Weininger's texts, and then discuss the contribution of this volume of essays to Weininger scholarship and to the larger questions that an examination of Weininger's influence generates.

THE HISTORY OF WEININGER RECEPTION

The history of Weininger reception falls naturally into two historical periods: before and after World War II. The first period encompasses his immediate contemporaries, the modernist generation; the second, those who must necessarily view him from a post-Holocaust perspective. Critical commentary on Weininger has grown parallel to postwar research on modernist literature. Three other fields of scholarship of particular relevance to Weininger reception—psychoanalysis, research on anti-Semitism, and gender studies—have also seen tremendous growth in the postwar era.

Initial Weininger reception was marked by direct, forceful affirmation or refutation of his ideas, in some cases by authors who knew him personally. The early years of Weininger reception included defenses of his integrity in Karl Kraus's periodical *Die Fackel* ([The Torch], 1903, 1904, 1906, 1907, 1921). There were evaluations by feminists such as Grete Meisel-Hess (1904) and Rosa Mayreder (1905; see also Bubeniček 1986) in Austria and Charlotte Perkins Gilman (1906) in the United States; Emil Lucka's memorial (1905); Wilhelm Fliess's (1906) attack on Weininger as a plagiarist;[10] André Spire's (1913) study in French of three controversial Jews; and a number of philosophical treatises, including Bruno Sturm's (1912) alternative solution to the problem of morality.

If Weininger himself has been a relatively obscure figure to English-speaking readers, so too have those Austrian female intellectuals to whom he attributed an overabundance of male attributes and whose aspirations for social and legal equality (including the vote) were anathema to Weininger (Troll-Borostyáni 1893, 1903; Popp 1909, 1929; Anderson 1992). Rosa Mayreder's (1905 and 1913) work, for example, highlights the intensity with which male and female intellectuals of the era struggled with issues of gender identity, of the individual versus the masses, of ethical questions in an increasingly technological society. Some of Mayreder's ideas anticipate European intellectual developments later in the century (e.g., those of Deleuze, Kristeva, Cixous).[11]

Sigmund Freud was the first to read an early draft of Weininger's dissertation, entitled "Eros and Psyche," probably in the fall of 1901, which was more than six months before Weininger submitted it to the University of Vienna as "Geschlecht und Charakter: Eine biologische und psychologische Untersuchung" (Sex and Character: A Biological and Psychological Investigation). Weininger had gone to him for advice on finding a publisher and was sorely disappointed by Freud, who found his work "too speculative and too boldly deductive with regard to the scientific treatment of the main subject" (Swoboda 1923; Abrahamsen 1946). The manuscript that Freud saw contained "no depreciatory *[sic]* words about the Jews and much less criticism of women" (Abrahamsen 1946, 208). Freud's subsequent reaction to Weininger's book *Sex and Character* appears in a footnote to his case history of "Little Hans" (1909). According to Freud, the "unconscious root" of both anti-Semitism and the male sense of superiority over women lies in the castration complex: "Weininger (the young philosopher who, highly gifted but sexually deranged, committed suicide after producing his remarkable book, *Geschlecht und Charakter* [1903]), in a chapter that attracted much attention, treated Jews and women with equal hostility and overwhelmed them with the same insults. Being a neurotic, Weininger was completely under the sway of his infantile complexes; and from that standpoint what is common to Jews and women is their relation to the castration complex" (Freud 1955–74, vol. 10, 36n).[12] Albeit from a different perspective, Freud too saw a compelling logic to pairing Jews and women as two sides of the same coin.

Bruno Sturm's vitalistic philosophy was both anti-Weininger and antifeminist. He answered Weininger's charge that sexual relations can never be moral by distinguishing between "happy" eroticism and "unhappy" sexuality. Weininger was unable to appreciate the benefits of organic pleasure, according to Sturm, because he damned all forms of sexual behavior "a priori" (Sturm 1912, 54). Weininger's transcendental philosophy doomed him to a negation that would never be compatible with earthly reality. In short, Weininger tried to build a science of characterology and totally transcendental religion on the shaky foundation of his own subjective unhappiness. Significantly, Sturm elected to interpret Weininger's extreme form of Kantian religion without even mentioning his pronouncements on "Jewishness." For his part, Sturm affirmed the joy of sex with no intention of restructuring social, political, and economic opportunities for women, thereby demonstrating his affinity with Karl Kraus's attitudes toward erotic freedom (Zohn 1971, 42–47; Wagner 1981): Women need only be released from fear of their strongly erotic nature. He ascribed total blame for the "nervousness of our age"—a term popularized by Hermann Bahr's *Die Überwindung des Naturalismus* (The Overcoming of Naturalism)[13] of 1891—to the "barbarous dogmas of society" that stifle human nature (Sturm 1912, 77).

Weininger's intellectual status was on the rise in the interwar years.[14] His book had gone through twenty-five editions in roughly as many years. Elias Canetti gives the flavor of Weininger's popularity in the mid-1920s in this passage from his memoirs, *Die Fackel im Ohr* (The Torch in My Ear):

"Other boys whom I met in this circle indulged in the arrogance of higher literature: if not Karl Kraus, then Otto Weininger or Schopenhauer. Pessimistic or misogynous utterances were especially popular, even though none of these boys was a misogynist or misanthrope. . . . However, the severe, witty, scornful statements were viewed by these young people as the cream of intellect" (Canetti 1982a, 77). In the same vein, philosophy students wrote doctoral dissertations comparing Weininger's thought to that of Kant (Zunzer 1924; Biró 1927; Thaler 1935) and Nietzsche (Rosenberg 1928).

No Jewish writer of the period did more to secure Weininger's reputation as a self-hating Jew than did Theodor Lessing in his famous book of 1930, *Der jüdische Selbsthaß* (Jewish Self-Hatred). Featured in one of six case studies, Weininger emerges as a "Jewish Oedipus" who cursed his mother's blood (Lessing 1930, 82). According to Lessing, Weininger became obsessed with the belief that spirit is superior to nature, such that "woman" and "Jew" became synonymous with the "depths of nature" he feared and avoided. While Lessing pointed correctly to the tragic effect of Weininger's extremely polarized philosophy, he himself was caught up in the inflammatory racial rhetoric of his era. His most unfortunate pronouncement was that "no human being has ever freed himself from the constraints of his blood. No categorical imperative has ever obscured the voice of blood" (Lessing 1930, 91), which Nazi propagandists used to their best advantage (Kohn 1962; Janik 1987).

During this phase, both Weininger as a personality and his works became an increasingly suitable topic for literature. From the works of Kafka to Broch to Joyce to Svevo, Weiningerian characters populate many modernist novels throughout Europe. Weininger's eccentric pursuit of immortality lent itself particularly well to fiction.

To some minds, Weininger belonged as much in the realm of literature as in those of philosophy or psychology. In the early 1920s, for example, Oskar Baum wrote an essay on Weininger for an anthology of contemporary Jewish writers of German literature, edited by Gustav Krojanker (Baum 1922). Krojanker and Baum's rationale for including an essay on Weininger in a volume pertaining to literature was that "his type of spirit, the content of his thought and finally, his fate, are so characteristic of a certain social stratum of Western Jews, that a generic concept seems to be embodied here in its purest form" (Baum 1922, 138). From Baum's vantage point, Weininger, who was not raised in a religious Jewish household and did not educate himself about Eastern Jews, Hasidism, the Kabbalah and the Talmud, described "Jewishness" with gross inaccuracy but showed profound insight into the plight of assimilated Western Jews. Despite Weininger's methodological looseness and emotional stake in irrevocable dualisms, Baum respected the antimechanistic cultural critique he saw at the core of Weininger's thought and memorialized him as a "forerunner of the new age" (Baum 1922, 135).

In numerous anti-Semitic tracts and treatises, Weininger's thought was quoted out of context by Nazi ideologues, like their *völkisch* precursors, as one of many "confessions" by Jews that they belonged to an inferior race. Male exponents of Nazi ideology for the most part ignored Weininger's views on the "Aryan woman" but shared his virulent critique of female emancipation. They promoted motherhood as the ideal occupation for women. Weininger, who had sought the aid of all men in helping women to overcome the "female" in themselves, implicitly fostered Nazi men's delusions of male superiority, but interfered philosophically with the will to propagate the "Aryan race" and hence with the Nazi program of selective breeding.[15]

The science of characterology coexisted with and survived the Nazi era. An interesting case in point is Hubert Rohracher, an Austrian professor of psychology who published five editions of a standard text on characterology between 1934 and 1948. In his study of sex-based differences between men and women, Rohracher maintained throughout this period that the mental ability to produce original work in philosophical, artistic, and technical areas is "totally absent" in women. He believed that this "fact" should serve as a starting point for a psychology of women as well as a challenge for researchers to find out why it is the case. Rohracher faulted Weininger's "metaphysics of the sexes" for its "not strictly scientific methods" based on general observations and historical examples whose validity depends largely on the "character and experiences of the person evaluating them" (Rohracher 1948, 224–28). While Rohracher implicitly exposed the androcentric bias of late nineteenth- and early twentieth-century characterology, his own method betrays an essentialist, ahistorical approach to mental ability in women.[16]

In the postwar years, Weininger reception initially shifted from any kind of direct engagement with his ideas to sociological, psychological, and historical explanations of why he came to have such thoughts. This was not simply a matter of historical distance. His thesis rubbed salt in the wounds of humanists and social scientists writing after the Holocaust as well as those of new generations of feminists. As critical editions of the works of modernist writers became available (both in their original languages and in translation) and as psychoanalytic interpretation, critical theory, and feminist interpretations gained credence in literary criticism, renewed interest in the legacy of Otto Weininger was inevitable.

Just after the end of the war, Viola Klein (1946), a student of Karl Mannheim, and David Abrahamsen (1946), a professor of psychiatry at Columbia University, contributed to Weininger reception in England and the United States. Their respective methodologies were a sociological analysis of the history of "feminine character" as an ideology[17] and psychiatric psychology.[18] Hans Kohn's (1962) monograph on Karl Kraus, Arthur Schnitzler, and Weininger as Jews of *fin-de-siècle* Vienna ushered in a decade of research on Weininger in relation to such diverse writers as Hermann Broch (Durzak 1967), Emil Lucka (Krizmanic 1969), and Günter Grass (Blomster 1969).

Blomster (1969) demonstrates how Grass used Weininger's *Sex and Character* as "documentary material" in his postwar novel about German history from 1917 to 1957, *Hundejahre* ([*Dog Years*], 1963; 1989). Weininger and his text served a two-fold function in Grass's novel: first, by providing "a means for self-definition in the hands of Eddi Amsel and his father," and second, by contributing "certain perspectives to Grass's investigation of the love-hate and blood brotherhood of Nazi and Jew" (Blomster 1969, 135). The elder Amsel tries to "overcome" his Jewish background by participating in the church choir, by joining the athletic club, and by reading Weininger. The younger Amsel looks to Weininger's chapter on "Jewishness" as a guideline in his quest for essence, or *Sein* (Blomster 1969, 133). The "complex relationship between Amsel and his enemy-friend, Walter Matern," becomes more understandable in light of Weininger's theory of anti-Semitism. By invoking Weininger, Grass "has given an example of bad faith and its machinations in the every-day world" (Blomster 1969, 138).

Germaine Greer helped to make a new generation of English-speaking women's liberationists aware of the broad outlines of Weininger's thought, albeit in brief, in the "Womanpower" chapter of her well-known book *The Female Eunuch* (1970). She interpreted Weininger's critique of "female thinking" as an exemplary denial by a young male intellectual that the mind-body split in Western culture could or should be healed. In the course of the 1970s and 1980s and continuing into the 1990s, German, Austrian, French, Italian, British, and American academic studies have appeared on Weininger.[19] In 1978 Weininger's younger brother, Richard, published an autobiography in English, *Exciting Years*, which unfortunately provided no insights into Otto Weininger's life or works.

Jehoshua Sobol, Israel's most prominent and controversial playwright, created a Weininger for the stage in his 1982 play, *Nefesh Yehudi: Ha-Layla Ha-Aharon shel Otto Weininger* (The Soul of a Jew: The Death of Otto Weininger; Weininger's Last Night [n.d]). It ran for five consecutive seasons in Haifa and gained international attention in the 1980s.[20] Several critics have noted the inherent shifts in context and implications when the play is performed outside of Israel (Feldman 1987; Rokem 1989 [abridged in this volume as Chapter 19]).

The Hungarian sociologist and novelist Miklós Hernádi has also fictionalized Weininger's death in the form of a mystery novel entitled *Otto*

(Hernádi 1990), in which Chief Inspector Barner of the State Police undertakes a criminal investigation of the sociological and psychological factors that contributed to Weininger's alleged suicide and possible murder. In this literary tour de force, the detective becomes one with the research scholar. The novel's translation into German in 1993 made it available to a wider audience and thereby contributed to the popular dissemination of the Weininger legend.

In the past decade, there has been an ongoing methodological war between Jacques Le Rider and a number of literary scholars and historians, including Sigurd Paul Scheichl, a Kraus scholar. Le Rider is a crucial figure in Weininger studies; he published the first full-length scholarly monograph on Weininger since Abrahamsen (1946). A revised Sorbonne dissertation, it appeared first in French (Le Rider 1982) and within three years was translated into German in an expanded, further revised edition (Le Rider 1985). The book is a thorough investigation of Weininger's life and the early controversies surrounding Weininger, including Wilhelm Fliess's plagiarism charge (Fliess 1906). Unlike Abrahamsen's traditional psychoanalytic analysis of Weininger, Le Rider's book problematizes the convergence of anti-Semitism and antifeminism in *fin-de-siècle* Vienna.

Taking issue with Le Rider's portrayal of Weininger as anti-Semitic, Scheichl insists on making a historical distinction between political anti-Semitism (represented by forerunners of the Nazis such as Georg von Schönerer and Karl Lueger) and conservative *Kulturkritik* (culture criticism) as practiced by Kraus and Weininger. *Kulturkritik*, Scheichl argues, "is part of their rhetoric against the modern age, but they do not call for any political or social change to the disadvantage of the Jews.[21] Weininger, for instance, insists upon his not wishing to pave the way for any persecution of the Jews.... We know that, nevertheless, Weininger's writings would later be used to justify anti-Semitic persecutions; but in spite of that there is no reason to doubt the subjective honesty of his words" (Scheichl 1987, 94).

Scheichl's insistence on a "multi-layered image" of the "climate of intolerance" in *fin-de-siècle* Vienna leads him to reflect on the hermeneutic nature of the task: "Auschwitz has finally made us recognize the common features of all hostility towards Jews, and we know that the anti-Semitic mass movements would not have been possible without personal prejudice and without the theories of *Kulturkritik*." And yet, Scheichl adds, the historian must also ask: "Is it fair not to ask what people have thought in their time but only what has become of their thought in our time?" (Scheichl 1987, 108). Scheichl argues for the use of different terms to distinguish between different historically specific attitudes toward Jews, not in an effort to whitewash the past nor to justify genocide, but to give complexity its due.

Le Rider also co-edited an anthology of critical articles in German with

Norbert Leser (Le Rider and Leser 1984). A number of Leser's points in the introductory essay, "Otto Weininger und die Gegenwart," coincide with those of Allan Janik, another major Weininger scholar, although Leser writes as an Austrian who was personally inspired by Weininger's work in the early stages of his own development. Both Leser and Janik contend that Weininger's thought *and* suicide should not be explained (i.e., dismissed) as the outgrowth of an aberrant personality. They assert that Weininger did not despise women or Jews (including himself *as* a Jew), but expressed their respective plights in terms designed to shock them out of complacency.

Janik is Le Rider's most outspoken critic, for Janik believes that in his monograph on Weininger Le Rider "failed to be sufficiently radical in his critique of Weininger by being *insufficiently contextual* in his approach." Janik contends that Le Rider "exposes" Weininger's anti-Semitic and sexist thinking in order to "disagree" with it. However, if a reader "simply rejects Le Rider's liberal, feminist perspective," Janik reasons, he may never gain any understanding of Weininger as a "historical curiosity" (Janik 1985, 97).

Looking at Weininger in context, Janik argues, shifts our focus away from the "sensational and controversial aspects of Weininger's thoughts" (Janik 1985, 115) not in order to suppress controversy, but as part of a hermeneutic enterprise to locate what may seem sensational to us, or even what was sensationalized at the time, in its complete setting.[22] The danger in Janik's approach is that, in its desire to read Weininger contextually, it may appear to lend dignity to all aspects of Weininger's program. Janik knows that his criticism of Le Rider can be interpreted as contentious toward feminists and Jews.

Taking a quite different approach to the problem of Weininger interpretation, Janik insists that rationality has come to be measured by how it is accomplished rather than what conclusions it draws, for "each and every scientific allegation must be evaluated independently on the basis of the reasoning which went into it and not simply on the basis of what is claimed." (Janik 1986, 76)[23] Many scholars with political agendas, he thinks, tend to ignore this shift in the model of rationality and to make judgments about the past and about contemporary foreign cultures solely on the basis of substance. It remains an open question whether Weininger's thought might be rational without being substantively true, such that its rationality could have contributed to its appeal.[24]

JEWS AND GENDER: RESPONSES TO OTTO WEININGER

Since much of the discussion about Weininger has taken place in German, French, and Italian, this volume aims to provide a broad, interdisciplinary representation of the Weiningerian legacy in English as well as many new readings of the issue. The essays are exemplary of Weininger studies in the past few years, and include works by both Le Rider and Janik so as to bring together these two major strands in Weininger scholarship. The first section of this book introduces readers to Weininger research and provides new biographical information on Weininger.

The first essay, by Le Rider, is in part a retrospective on Weininger scholarship since the publication of the German translation of his Weininger monograph in 1985. Le Rider stresses the centrality of the crisis of male sexuality among Weininger and his contemporaries (Le Rider 1990a, 1990b, 1993) and takes issue with recent critical approaches to early twentieth-century European history that differentiate between anti-Semitism and hostility toward Jews (Scheichl 1987; Janik 1987).

Hannelore Rodlauer (1990) has transcribed and edited an early draft of Weininger's previously lost doctoral dissertation,[25] upon which *Sex and Character* was based, as well as heretofore unpublished letters. Her contribution to our volume is a translation of part of the introduction to her collection of rediscovered primary literature. Rodlauer's work is of particular consequence to Weininger studies because of ongoing debates regarding Weininger's relationship to scientific and philosophical theories of his time; for example, Janik's claim that Weininger was on the cutting edge of contemporary thought can be better understood through an examination of Weininger's education and his dissertation.

The second part of our book, "In Context," focuses on Weininger in the context of his contemporaries. Allan Janik, in his essay written for this volume, considers the concept of "influence" in regard to one of Weininger's intellectual heirs, Ludwig Wittgenstein. Janik calls for a "robust understanding" of what constitutes influence, and uses this as a starting point for his remarks regarding affinities between Wittgenstein and Weininger. In his discussion of Weininger and how he could have influenced Wittgenstein, Janik describes what he sees as Weininger's challenge of the clichéd role of the sexes in his effort to go beyond these facile and limiting categorizations. Janik's essay is thought-provoking as it looks at Weininger's agenda from a very different perspective than that of many other Weininger scholars. In attempting to define "influence" as a "structuring of problems" rather than the "details of their solutions," Janik adds to our understanding of what the relationship between context and legacy might mean.

Nancy A. Harrowitz examines the concept of "influence" in regard to one of Weininger's late nineteenth-century forerunners, Cesare Lombroso, who examined the "faults" of women by using a culturally biased logic similar to that Weininger applied to Jews. Lombroso ultimately conflates the two groups, and what is at stake in his confusion of categories begins to emerge. Harrowitz's approach is to some degree at odds with that of Janik. The tension between these two essays lies in Harrowitz's attempt to establish a delicate middle ground between an overly apologetic stance toward the text, generated by perhaps too much sympathy for the historical conditions in which Lombroso found himself and fostered as well by a certain blindness to the overt perniciousness of the writing, and a naive horror that does not take into account at all the conditions that produced the text. Janik's stance, in Harrowitz's view, tends toward the former, and has been fostered by a reaction against a reading based solely on substance.

In "Weininger as Liberal?" Steven Beller argues that European liberalism "exerted immense pressure for the 'stranger' to conform not only to a lowest common denominator of social norms, but also to the whole set of social and cultural-national values and standards of the community concerned." Beller takes Weininger to be "an extreme case of a particular form of liberal theory," and demonstrates how this can be read in light of the realities of Jewish assimilation. In the last part of his essay, Beller describes the difficulties inherent in Weininger's labels *"M"* and *"W,"* and concludes that the confusing nature of these categories has obfuscated the meaning of Weininger's text.

Beller's explanation of liberalism as an ethos of assimilation augments our synchronic picture of Weininger as an apostate Jew. His reading is essentially in agreement with Janik's: contextual in a way that is provocative because it appears to minimize the pernicious elements of Weininger's thought. Yet his reading is generated by an understanding of the political and social tensions of the day that is indispensable. Beller sees Weininger as an extreme case, but not as an anomaly.

While David Abrahamsen and Jacques Le Rider laid the foundation for our historical understanding of Freud's reaction to Weininger, Sander L. Gilman asserts in "Otto Weininger and Sigmund Freud: Race and Gender in the Shaping of Psychoanalysis" that the meaning of Freud's representation of the "creative" can be understood in the context of his role as both a scientist and a Jew in *fin-de-siècle* Vienna. Freud's particular definitions of the interrelated concepts of "creativity," "genius," and "madness" are integral to his argument for the universality of the human psyche. Gilman describes Weininger's indebtedness to an ongoing discourse of race and gender, and then looks at Freud's relation to these concepts. His detailed account of Freud's debt to Weininger, while accounting for other figures important to the period such as Otto Rank and Cesare Lombroso, at the same time provides a rich contextual understanding of Weininger's work. Gilman also points out in clear terms Weininger's anti-Semitism and self-hatred, viewing these phenomena as distinguishable despite his assessment of the context in which they arose. Implicitly countering Janik's objection that Le Rider sensationalized aspects of

Weininger's thought, Gilman demonstrates that an understanding of context does not necessarily soften the impact of prejudice.

Katherine Arens's essay traces the sources of characterology back to two divergent scientific traditions that provided the backdrop for Weininger's work as the first text to introduce the notion of scientific racism to a popular Viennese readership. In order to understand the reception of Weininger's text in his day, Arens also looks at the work of the biologist Paul Kammerer and the physician and psychoanalyst Karen Horney. As she explores the mechanism of scientific paradigms and the popular reception of science, Arens affords an approach similar to Gilman's, situating Weininger's work as a continuation of intellectual trends already present in *fin-de-siècle* Vienna.

In "Otto Weininger and the Critique of Jewish Masculinity," John M. Hoberman asserts that the origins of Weininger's self-hatred have been little studied, and he traces the ways in which the Jewish male was figured as weak and effeminate through images and stereotypes prevalent at the time. Weininger's textual response to the feminization of the Jewish male is then traced through a close examination of passages from *Sex and Character*. Hoberman's analysis demonstrates the problems inherent in the assumption that the adjective "Jewish" implicitly refers to male Jews. His study of the "myth of Jewish effeminacy" lends another aspect to the historical dimension of Weininger's views on gender and "race."

Although the Nazi view of Weininger was mostly a straightforward matter of exploiting "Jewish self-hatred," Weininger proved to be a problematic figure for Nazi ideologues, because *Sex and Character* was primarily about gender, not "race," and its low opinion of women made manifest what was covert in Nazi ideology. In her essay, Barbara Hyams analyzes Nazi reception of Weininger. Nazi men's reception of Weininger until 1943 ignored Weininger's negative assessment of female character and motherhood while exploiting his condemnations of Jewish character by developing the pernicious *völkisch* genre of "Jewish self-revelations." Since a number of Weininger's theses about women and motherhood contradicted Nazi myths about the family, it eventually became opportune for Nazi men to discredit Weininger's sexism. After the German military disaster in Stalingrad, gestures were made to increase women's sense of comradeship with men, including a brochure in which Weininger's "dangerous definitions of women" are assaulted for robbing mothers of their dignity. By accentuating Weininger's "arrogant Jewish" rejection of equal social status for women and men, Nazi ideologues laid the blame for social tension between the sexes at the door of the Jews in order to obscure the sexist principles of the Third Reich.

The final section of this volume looks at Weininger in relation to modernist belles-lettres and post-Holocaust theater. We have translated

Gisela Brude-Firnau's often-cited feminist analysis of Weininger's influ-ence on the German novel and Gerald Stieg's reading of Weiningerian elements in Kafka's *The Castle*. Marilyn Reizbaum has thoroughly revised her study of Weininger and James Joyce. Freddie Rokem has also revised and abridged an earlier essay on Jehoshua Sobol's play *The Soul of a Jew*. In addition, there are new articles, written expressly for this volume, by Jeffrey Mehlman on Guillaume Apollinaire, Alberto Cavaglion on Italo Svevo, Elfriede Pöder and Natania Rosenfeld on James Joyce, and Kristie A. Foell on Elias Canetti.

Brude-Firnau discusses the way in which Weininger's work can be seen as a contentious response to the women's movement. She sees Weininger's quest to define the essence of female character as an "early attempt to formulate a scientific understanding of woman." Brude-Firnau notes the discrepancies in Weininger's method as he often begins a thought using the abstract category "*W*" for woman, yet ends it by shifting to empirical statements about all women with the term *das Weib* (woman). In her discussion of Weininger's influence on the German novel using the examples of Franz Kafka, Hermann Broch, Robert Musil, and Günter Grass, Brude-Firnau furnishes a guide to understanding the scope of Weininger's impact within any given literary text, thus branching across the scientific disciplines discussed in the first part of this book to the literary ones that comprise its second half.

Jeffrey Mehlman focuses on the bisexual aspect of Weininger's theories by demonstrating the intersection of anti-Semitic motifs and bisexuality in one of Apollinaire's major poems, "La Chanson du mal-aimé" (The Song of the Ill-Loved Lover), written in 1903, the year in which *Sex and Character* was first published in German. Mehlman distin-guishes a moment in Apollinaire's poem in which "the anger against a woman is quirkily actualized as a fury against Jews." Thus the same kind of affinity Weininger asserts between women and Jews is reproduced in Apollinaire. Mehlman's analysis of the Apollinaire poem and the similari-ties to Weininger's thought embedded within it further shows the extent to which Weininger's ideas were part of the literary culture of the time, even when their influence was only indirect.

Calling Weininger's book the "philosophical best seller of the first third of the century," Gerald Stieg closely examines a relationship between Kafka and Weininger that goes beyond any textual response to Weininger's ideas found in Kafka's novels. Stieg asserts that the two shared certain fundamental attitudes toward Jewishness and sexuality as well as a "monkish sacralization of writing," which Stieg identifies as a component of Viennese modernism. Using an intertextual approach based on a close reading of Kafka and Weininger, Stieg analyzes the effect of cultural attitudes toward Jews and sexuality that influenced both authors.

The position of woman is deeply affected by this conflation of Jews and sexuality, as she is the "other" that must be avoided. In order to demonstrate these affinities, Stieg analyzes sources as diverse as Kafka's diary entries, a poem by Weininger, Weininger's interpretation of *Parsifal*, and Kafka's novel *The Castle*, calling Kafka a "Weininger in private." Stieg's essay moves between the private and the public, combining examinations of biographical resources such as diaries with analyses of works intended by their authors for publication.

The great impact of Weininger on James Joyce has been noted by several scholars. We have selected three essays on Weininger and Joyce for this volume, so that this issue could be examined from more than one point of view.

Marilyn Reizbaum's argument is based on the "Jewish self-hatred" hypothesis. The Jew, who is metaphorically linked to the female both by Weininger in *Sex and Character* and by Joyce in *Ulysses,* through the character of Bloom, represents negative qualities. In her essay, Reizbaum states that "the kinds of connections between race and sex that Weininger makes appear most prevalently and climactically in the 'Circe' chapter of Ulysses, [which] dramatizes the psychodynamic of self-hatred, linked here with gender and race." Reizbaum suggests that by exploring the model of Weiningerian self-hatred, Joyce could confront self-hatred in himself and perhaps through his art exorcise those elements of Weininger's thought that were irreconcilable with his own.

In "James Joyce's Womanly Wandering Jew," Natania Rosenfeld describes the influence that Weininger's theories had upon Joyce, specifi-cally expressed in his characterizations of Molly, a "Weiningerian" woman, and Bloom in *Ulysses*. Delineating this influence as both misogy-nistic and anti-Semitic, she contextualizes her close literary reading of *Ulysses* with theories regarding Zionism and Jewish assimilation prevalent at the time. According to Rosenfeld's analysis, Molly and Bloom end up playing out the tensions in Joyce's attitude toward Weininger's theories, and it ultimately becomes clear that Joyce is subverting Weininger while still rejecting Zionism.

Elfriede Pöder concentrates on female representation in "Molly *Is* Sexuality: The Weiningerian Definition of Woman in James Joyce's *Ulysses*." Pöder demonstrates the degree to which Joyce's Molly is Weinin-gerian theory incarnate, and claims that the resemblance is so strong as to make us suspect that Joyce deliberately set out to create a blueprint of Weininger's theories in the character of Molly. To illustrate her claim, she points out, for example, that Molly's mode of thinking is irrational, associative, disconnected; her flow of thoughts a superficial "tasting," a "sliding and gliding through subjects" only; yet, her mind is perfectly capable of consistency, exactness, and accuracy when recalling sexual experiences. Like Rosenfeld, Pöder describes an important difference between Weininger and Joyce in her conclusion, where in a crucial reversal, she asserts that Joyce sought to establish a feminine identity for his characters that was opposed to that theorized by Weininger.

In his essay "Svevo and Weininger (Lord Morton's Mare)," Alberto Cavaglion traces the appearance of Weininger's thought in Italo Svevo's novel, *La coscienza di Zeno* (The Confessions of Zeno), and cites other moments in Italian literature influenced by the legacy of Weininger. Svevo's use of Weiningerian concepts is heavily ironized and satirized through the comic persona of Zeno. Cavaglion demonstrates how this comic filtering makes it difficult to understand the precise nature of Svevo's debt to Weininger, until Svevo's debt to the scientific concept of telegony, the effect of the first mating on all future progeny, is uncovered. Telegony was a notion to which Weininger subscribed and to which he makes reference in *Sex and Character*. Weininger's interest in the scientific discourse of his time, such as telegony and Darwinism, is made clear by the complicated cultural genealogy we find explored in Cavaglion's essay. The ability of Weininger's text to disseminate this interest across disciplines into literary spheres is apparent as well through Joyce's interest and through Joyce's publicizing of Weininger to Svevo.

In "Whores, Mothers, and Others: Reception of Otto Weininger's *Sex and Character* in Elias Canetti's *Auto-da-Fé*," Kristie A. Foell analyzes the tension between Canetti's satirical style (Pöder 1985), his use of Weiningerian concepts, and his own disclaimers of either misogyny or affinity for Weininger. Foell uses the two characters of Therese and Kien as examples of a Weiningerian interplay in Canetti. Situating them within Weininger's ideological framework, Foell questions whether these two characters were created as a textual response to Weininger's ideas. Interweaving her literary analysis of Canetti's novel with Weininger's ideology regarding *"W"* and *"M,"* Foell discusses the short distance between reality and fiction that Canetti espoused as a further twist to the Canetti/Weininger relationship. Her analysis bears a resemblance to Stieg's in its ability to look at different kinds of literary and extraliterary sources in order to survey the extent and types of influence found in literature.

In this volume's concluding essay, Freddie Rokem discusses the dynamic tension between history and memory in Jehoshua Sobol's play *The Soul of a Jew*, and its reception in Israel and abroad. He highlights the controversial metaphors in Sobol's work in the context of its 1982 premiere in Israel and comments at length on its performances in Europe. If Weininger is a metaphor in Israel for the "torn Jewish soul" in light of Israel's 1982 war with Lebanon and the difficulties of realizing a Jewish state, the ground shifts radically, for example, in German-speaking countries and most particularly in Vienna. The specter of a self-hating Jew on a

Viennese stage on the fiftieth anniversary of the November 1938 Pogrom evoked a different, although not unrelated, complex of issues for Austrian society in relation to its own past and present. Particularly in light of renewed violence in the 1990s against foreigners, the desecration of Jewish cemeteries and memorials to Jews who were persecuted during National Socialism, and renewed debates over what constitutes assimilation into German or Austrian society, German-speaking performances of the play raise difficult questions about the extent to which theater (and film) can jar audiences into a confrontation with the present.

The essays in this volume explore the interrelation of influence and bigotry, the subtle interplay between scientific paradigms and literature, and the construction of gender, both male and female. These works thus engage in debates that go beyond even the tremendous influence of the writing of Otto Weininger and its effect on prejudice against Jews of both genders and against women of all cultural and ethnic backgrounds in the twentieth century.

2 ✦

"THE OTTO WEININGER CASE" REVISITED

Jacques Le Rider

Translated from the French
by Kristie A. Foell

Otto Weininger's *Sex and Character* gathers up the Western tradition of misogyny and brings it to its paroxysm. Weininger's works may be interpreted as symptoms of a repressive and authoritarian civilization, founded on the principle of male superiority—a reading that dominates the monograph I have dedicated to this book (Le Rider 1982, 1985).[1]

But doesn't *Sex and Character* say as much about the male as it does about the female? Doesn't it tell us as much about the anxieties of the masculine as it does about the "inferiority" of the feminine? Weininger's antifeminist diatribes betray a crisis of the masculine that his suicide pathetically illustrates. *Sex and Character* is a cry of distress and a confession of weakness. Weininger only hates Woman (the feminine) because he is afraid of femininity—or because he retains a repressed nostalgia for it. He trumpets forth the laws of patriarchy at a time when he thinks he sees a new, triumphant matriarchy imposing itself. He celebrates the ceremonies and parades of the masculine with pomp and circumstance in order to indict the decadence of modern manhood by contrast. He ends up by clinging to the ideal of the Genius, which could have extricated him from the impasse of *Sex and Character* by putting him back in harmony with life, but which finally reveals itself as contrary to nature. This is what I attempt to demonstrate in my *Modernité viennoise et crises de l'identité* (Le Rider 1990a, Eng. trans. 1993), in which Weininger is again one of the central figures.

August Strindberg considered Weininger as a brother genius. In a letter to Artur Gerber, an intimate friend of Weininger's, in 1903, Strindberg writes: "the cynicism of life had become unbearable for him [Weininger]."[2] Weininger refuses the compromise of the idealist ethic whose "amorous ideal takes the form of a marriage of the heart, where the corporeal element is accepted as an 'expression' of the passion of the soul. But this ideal finds itself constantly undermined by a 'quasi-realism'. This tension renders the bourgeois man particularly receptive to cynical sexual jokes, dirty key-hole-peeping realism and pornography. This is why he wears such a cynical leer on his lips."[3] Weininger denounces the hypocrisies of Kantian morality; Kant had already experienced the greatest difficulty in integrating into his ethic conjugal sexuality, which he tolerated as a remnant of animal nature in the age of practical reason. Weininger thinks the "angelic" tendency of the Kantian ethic through to its logical conclusion, which is to say to the point of absurdity. His mystical quest is a quest for purity.

In this sense, Otto Weininger resembles Antonin Artaud, the "madman" who spat on woman when he encountered a representative of the sex in the corridors of the asylum at Rodez, crossing himself ostentatiously as he spat. One finds in these two men's works (particularly Weininger's *Über die letzten Dinge* [1904]) the same fascination with astrology, alchemy, occultism; the same search for the unity of things, which would lead to an original androgyny, to a state that, as Artaud writes in *Héliogabale*, "brings together once again man and woman, the hostile poles, the ONE and the TWO, and marks the end of contradictions" (Artaud 1967, 105ff.). The Weiningerian Genius is "the Father-man, neither man nor woman," of which Artaud dreams (Artaud 1979, 13).

The experience of totality attributed to the Genius microcosm in Weininger's thought leads back to an experience of emptiness, of death in life; it leads to what Artaud calls "the appetite for not being": "The Hermit has avenged the Evil come from the shadows of Woman by the power which he has just reinvented. The force which he has used to detach himself has given back to him an inverse force./And it was a force of death./The Destiny of each one of us is a Destiny of Death. A cycle of the World is accomplished."[4] To refuse Woman, for Artaud as for Weininger, is to refuse to acknowledge that there could be in me "something horrible which rises and which comes not from me, but from the shadows I have within me. . . . And soon this is all that will be there: this obscene mask which sneers forth from between sperm and shit."[5] To spiritualize the flesh, to reconstruct the masculine, to deny one's relationship with father and mother, to scrape away at the body until it is a clean, pure body with neither sex nor organs: All this means that "a *Superior Initiation* will be the fruit of this Death and that everything which has its origin in sexuality will be consumed by flames in this Superior Initiation, its fire changed into the process of Initiation. The absolute Supremacy of Man will be reestablished everywhere."[6]

Weininger's "metaphysical" misogyny recalls Franz Kafka as much as it does Artaud—a comparison supported this time by biography, for it is known that Kafka was influenced by his reading of *Sex and Character*.[7] The horror of sexuality is expressed in his diary of 1913: "Coitus as a punishment for the happiness of living together. To live as ascetically as possible, more ascetically than a bachelor, that is the only possible way for me to endure marriage. But her?"[8] A letter to Milena from 1920 even establishes a Weiningerian comparison between sexuality and Jewishness in Kafka's thinking: "My body, often quiet for years, would then be shaken to an unbearable degree by this longing for a certain small act of baseness, for something slightly disgusting, embarrassing, dirty: even in the best part of what I had here, there was still something of this longing, some bad smell, a bit of sulfur and brimstone, a bit of hell. This drive had about it something of the eternal Jew, meaninglessly pulled, meaninglessly wandering through a meaninglessly dirty world."[9] A "monkish" leaning (cf. Stieg 1987, Chap. 13, this volume) is expressed in Kafka's notes dated August 20, 1916, in which he outlines the comparative merits of the married man and the celibate: the latter remains "pure," as he preserves his energies and concentrates on his work (Kafka 1976, n. 11, 173). In Kafka's stories and novels, Woman is given the role of incarnating the temptations and menaces of sexuality that bring about the fall of Man (cf. Stach 1987).

Sex and Character develops a metaphysics of the masculine in which the male principle is identified to the point of absurdity with figures of intellect, creativity, liberty, and will, while cutting itself off ever more deeply from the body, instinct, life, and nature. The realization of the masculine imperative leads finally to a sort of death that is not a nothingness but an absolute. Just like Daniel Paul Schreber's *Denkwürdigkeiten eines Nervenkranken*, Weininger's treatise communicates the (no doubt typically masculine!) sentiment that it is a thousand times easier to be a woman than to be a man. The realization of a feminine destiny, according to Weininger, consists of a simple abandonment to the calls of nature, of the flesh, of the drives to passivity, to forgetfulness, to sleep of the spirit, to the will of the world, to procreation. Fulfilling a masculine destiny, on the other hand, demands a prodigious and painful effort whose maxim is "Become a genius!"

In *Sex and Character*, everything begins with bisexuality. The first part of the book describes the extraordinary original confusion of masculine and feminine in every individual. The smallest cell, the smallest globule of the human being, can be broken down into one formula: $xM + yF$. Weininger expounds the idea of a fundamental hermaphroditism with such panache that many of his contemporaries attributed this "discovery" to him, which caused a violent polemic between Weininger (posthumously!), Swoboda, Fliess, and Freud. As late as 1924, Freud himself felt he had to offer the following clarification: "Among non-specialists the notion of human bisexuality is often attributed to Otto Weininger, a philosopher who died young, and who took this idea as the basis of a fairly ill-considered book. . . . This claim is poorly founded, as the above evidence should demonstrate."[10]

J. B. Pontalis has emphasized the major role that bisexuality plays for the dissidents or marginal figures of psychoanalysis: Fliess, Adler, Jung, Groddeck, Ferenczi.[11] But their dissident views on bisexuality often go hand in hand with serious divergences on the subject of femininity. *Woman is the first sex, the strong sex*, is the concept that emerges from behind the proclaimed male chauvinist intentions of *Sex and Character*. The task of becoming masculine, according to Weininger, is truly the *via difficilior*, while the woman (at least the woman who does not trouble to "emancipate herself from her own femininity," as Weininger says) has but to persevere in her passive (non)-existence. Bisexuality thus has a different meaning for man and woman. Masculine or feminine sexual identity does not result from the mere accentuation of one of the two sexes present in original bisexuality. The ontogenesis and psychogenesis of the male and the female do not follow simply homologous and parallel paths. Feminization is the result of a passive process; masculinization, of an active process (Sullerot 1978, esp. 27–218).

The extraordinary demands Weininger makes of men would surely seem intolerable to most of them. Weininger has no illusions on this point: "It may seem to many that I have given 'men' the better portion in the preceding investigation. This reproach seems to me unjustified. I did not set out to idealize men in general, but to show the best powers and possibilities that lie hidden in every man. However, as we have seen, there are men who have become women or who never ceased being women."[12] On this subject, Weininger agrees with Freud, who observed that, given the bisexual constitution of individuals, "most men also remain far beneath the masculine ideal."[13] By pushing the consequences of Weininger's theory to an extreme, one may say that all human beings are at first (psychologically) women, and that the majority of them never detach themselves from this blissful, but morally inferior, original state. In the process of becoming masculine, the individual passes through a phase of "masculine protest" (to use Alfred Adler's expression); masculinity is never a definitive acquisition. Virility constantly has to be conquered afresh, on pain of regressing toward femininity, which always stands ready to reclaim its territory.

The fear of feminine sexuality that inspires Weininger's theories is expressed by homosexual themes and behaviors. Must one therefore talk about the homosexuality of Weininger (cf. Puff-Trojan 1986) or Kafka? Many recent critical studies have taken this leap and analyse with serious arguments the homosexuality that expresses itself between the lines of Kafka's work (cf. Mecke 1982; Mendoze 1986; Beck 1986). But this diagnostic system seems too reductive. The goal of this article is not to make pronouncements on this or that case, but to examine the deconstruction of the masculine that seems so closely bound up with the idea of modernity itself.

Already in Charles Baudelaire one encounters a similar hatred of "normal" sexuality, which "strongly resembles a method of torture or a surgical act" (Baudelaire 1975a, 651 ff.), as well as a violent misogyny combined with a nostalgia for the *mundus muliebris* of childhood. As Gerd Mattenklott has shown with regard to the painter Aubrey Beardsley and the poet Stefan George (Mattenklott 1985), homosexuality is but one of the names one may use to designate that revolt against the "natural" givens of sexuality, and that feminization of art and literature, which characterized modernity around the turn of the century.

It is a fact that the novelist David Herbert Lawrence, the author of *Women in Love* and *Lady Chatterley's Lover*, had read Otto Weininger's works (cf. Delavenay 1969, 1984). Lawrence also, even if only through the mediation of Frieda Weekley (nee von Richthofen), had contact with certain currents of German *Lebensphilosophie*, in particular with the Schwabing circles (cf. Green 1974). The novels and essays of D. H. Lawrence develop a coherent metaphysics of sexuality and of masculinity/femininity[14] in which several major aspects of the "modern crisis" of sexual identities can be found. A parallel between Weininger and Lawrence can be ascertained, for the two authors share similar intuitions; they open themselves to the vision of evil and battle to rediscover innocence, to make grace descend to earth once again.

Lawrence described the destructive face-off between man and woman just as cruelly as Weininger. In Lawrence's novels, the men who symbolize the coming of a new, virile race pass through a stage of antifeminism. In *Women in Love*, Birkin flings stones at the reflection of the moon in the lake while heaping curses upon Cybele, "the cursed Syria Dea," the personification of woman's aggressive desire. He doubts heterosexual love and at times prefers the "Walt-Whitmanian" camaraderie among men (symbolized by the boxing scene between Birkin and Gerald). The scourge of modernity is the bisexualization of culture and the confusion of sexual characteristics. The men in Lawrence's books who successfully transcend the battle of the sexes in order to reach cosmogonic eroticism do so only by passing through an extreme crisis. Birkin painfully disengages himself from his destructive relationship with Hermione when he meets Ursula. The game warden has undergone formidable ordeals and at first refuses Constance Chatterley's advances. *The Man who Died:* this Lawrence title summarizes the belief that life is an initiation that requires us to pass through an encounter with death before coming to life again on a higher plane.

For Lawrence as for Weininger, the sin that always accompanies human life is the loss of original unity and the cleft between subject/object or masculine/feminine. How can one rediscover the reconciled world that existed before the sins that the Bible designates with the single verb "to know"? Weininger's "wisdom" consists in living in the mode of geniality ("in Genius, the world and the I have become one") (Weininger [1903] 1980, 221 n. 19); the wisdom of Lawrence is to recognize that "nothing about me is isolated or absolute, so that my individuality is really an illusion" (Lawrence 1946, 200). It is the superficial (and typically feminine, Weininger would say) affirmation of the individual and the individual's petty egocentric whims that provokes the disunion of subject and world as well as the battle of the sexes.

The Lawrencian hero's limit experience, close to death, strongly recalls the interior experience described by Bataille: "We can hardly stand the situation which yokes us to chance individuality, to the mortal individuals we are. Even while we nourish the anguished desire that this mortal being might continue its life, we are also obsessed with a primary continuity, something before our individual being which connects us with Being. . . . This nostalgia governs the three forms of eroticism in all men" (Bataille 1957, 22).[15] Bataille thus makes a distinction between the eroticism of the body, the eroticism of the heart, and finally sacred eroticism.

Otto Weininger, in his nostalgia for primary continuity, sought the path of sacred eroticism. "Our hearts fail at the thought that the discontinuous individuality which is in us will be suddenly annihilated," Bataille writes in the passage quoted above; "as trivial as our beings may be, we cannot imagine putting the Being in them at risk without violence." During the summer of 1903, Weininger went through an overwhelming mystical crisis, the traces of which can be read in *Über die letzten Dinge* (Weininger 1904) and in the fragments of the *Taschenbuch* (Weininger 1919). This crisis was characterized by brutal interruptions of symbols and a radical questioning of the same "I" that *Sex and Character* naively placed at the center of the universe: "There is no I, there is no soul. The intelligible I is nothing but vanity."[16] This mental shipwreck, which could have extricated Weininger from the impasse of *Sex and Character*, finally led him to suicide. Rather than a philosophical death, this was an initiation cut short.

More fundamentally than a union between man and woman, eroticism, according to Lawrence, is union with the All, with the flow of life, with the divine. In the course of developing his thoughts about genius, Weininger seemed close to similar conclusions. But his entire error, and his unhappiness, consisted in not wanting to distinguish between the sexuality he denied and eroticism, a superior form of acceptance of life, the affirmation of an individuality freed from illusions of individuation. This difficult break with an existence dominated by the ego and governed by the cerebral functions (which, in its ultimate consequences, risks ending in suicide) is necessary if the masculine destiny is to find some harmony with the immanent sense of life, on pain of transforming the masculine/feminine dialogue into a battle of Thanatos against Eros.

◆ There is a second theme that seems closely, perhaps even indissociably, tied to that of the crisis of masculine identity: the crisis of Jewish identity at the end of a century of emancipation, at the moment when the assimilation that appears almost completed finds itself brutally called into question by anti-Semitism. The close relationship between these two themes, the crisis of sexual identity and the crisis of Jewish identity, manifests itself most forcefully in Otto Weininger's work. Weininger's entire oeuvre is a search for Unity: unity of the individual and the *Volk*, unity of the knowing subject with the world, its object, unity of the soul and the body, unity of life with the higher plane of being. In Weininger's work, the intrusion of evil is translated into figures of tearing and splitting. Contemporary individualism atomizes society into floating subjectivities, technology and science cut off human beings from their sense of belonging in the universe, sexuality transforms the flesh into a "foreign body." Since he rejects life lived in the rhythm of decadence, Weininger can approve of existence only as a stage to be passed through, leading to conversion and rebirth. The forces of evil are those that present an obstacle to such progress. In *Sex and Character*, they assume the faces of the eternal feminine and the Jew.

In his last fragments and aphorisms, Weininger lucidly wrote that "the hatred of woman is always only the hatred, not yet overcome, of one's own sexuality."[17] In the same way, the anti-Semitism of Weininger, the Jew, crystallizes all that he hates in himself, since his Jewishness calls into question the Wagnerian, *völkisch* authenticity to which he aspires. From the masochistic violence that he projects onto his objects of "scientific" knowledge (the bio-characterology of women and Jews) he draws a feeling of intense guilt, which he assuages by vituperating against "Jewish science" (that is, his *own* science) and against the evils of "the Jewish spirit" (his *own* spirit), which analyze and dissect reality instead of seeking to comprehend and respect it.

The partial homology of the ensembles of antifeminism and anti-Semitism in Weininger's work makes for the originality of his texts. However, this homology is not unique in its genre. It can be found in Arthur Schopenhauer or in D. H. Lawrence with an analogous significance.[18] In Schopenhauer, evil is affirmed in the will to live, but it is possible that something beyond this will is turned toward the world, a reality prior to sin: we are at the juncture of two worlds. Human knowledge can place itself at the service of the will to live, but it can also open the redemptive path that passes through the abolition of the will to live: through aesthetic contemplation or the experience of sorrow, which leads to pity for the absurd sufferings of life. Access to this "third kind of knowledge," however, is endangered through the fault of women, who "fundamentally only exist in order to propagate the species and whose vocation is entirely subsumed in this task."[19] Woman guarantees the perpetuity of the will to live; she hearkens to an obscure necessity that perpetually recycles the vital impulse. Similarly, according to Schopenhauer, "the fundamental characteristics of Judaism are *realism and optimism*, which same are closely related and are necessary preconditions of *theism*."[20] Realism naively confuses phenomena and noumena, forbidding itself any intuition of the highest level of being (Weininger would similarly say that the Jew cannot progress from contemplation to Genius). Optimism inspires as much disgust in Schopenhauer as procreation (for Weininger, the Jew and the woman are the two zealous missionaries of the empty idea of progress). Finally, theism postulates a creator to whom human beings owe servile gratitude: Schopenhauer has nothing but disdain for this kind of "good girls' " piety.

In Baudelaire's work, we find a somewhat similar scheme. Woman seems to be made to remind man constantly of the identity of life and desire. The poet's "misogyny" expresses his refusal of the natural conditions of existence, which he experiences as a perpetual fall from grace, against the spontaneous materialism of woman, who "does not know how to separate the soul from the body. She is simplistic as the animals" (Baudelaire 1975b, 694). The God of the Church, the author of this creation in which evil perpetuated by the desire of love reigns, himself appears effeminate: he is "the most prostituted being" (Baudelaire 1975b, 692) declares Baudelaire, who speaks "of the Church's femininity as the reason for its omnipotence" (Baudelaire 1975b, 650). The ideology of progress fills him with nothing but disgust: "I understand by progress the progressive diminution of the soul and the progressive domination of matter" (Baudelaire 1976, 581).[21] In "Mon Coeur mis à nu" (My heart laid bare), one finds this strange chain of thoughts: "Of the infamy of printing, great obstacle to the development of the Beautiful./A pretty conspiracy to organize for the extermination of the Jewish Race./The Jews, *Librarians* and witnesses of *Redemption*" (Baudelaire 1975b, 706 n. 37).[22] Claude Pichois insists, in his note to this passage, that "all charges of anti-Semitism [in Baudelaire's writings] are to be dismissed" (Baudelaire 1975b, 1511 n.). Perhaps, but in Schopenhauer, Baudelaire, and Weininger, misogyny and anti-Semitism are articulated according to an analogous "logic."

Schopenhauer, Baudelaire, and Weininger fling the blame for all that they hate, and especially what they hate in themselves, back onto the Jew. The woman and the Jew are two forms of the same temptation: that of "resigning oneself to exile, of taking root in a land of disgrace, of coming to terms with a fallen nature, accommodating oneself to a minor destiny" (Lévy-Valensi 1962, 626 n. 34). From this perspective, there is as much chance as necessity in the games of pairing that structure the triangle masculine/feminine/Jew. Thus Georg Groddeck, in his essay "Das Zwiegeschlecht des Menschen (Human Bisexuality) (1931), says of the Jews: "There is no other people on earth as decidedly masculine as the Jews" (Groddeck 1966, 258). The arrangement of the triangle (with the masculine now on top, as in Weininger, now on the bottom, as in Groddeck; and with the Jew *invariably* at the bottom) depends on the particular personality distortion through which observations are filtered. Weininger is dominated by the phantasm of an excess of femininity, Groddeck (after the fashion of Otto Gross) by his obsession with a lack of femininity.

What matters is that the Jew is always identified with that which poses an obstacle: an obstacle, in the last analysis, to an aspiration that tends to deny and pass over the insufficiencies of the human condition. Groddeck interpreted the symbolism of Jewish circumcision in these terms:

> The foreskin is cut away in order to remove everything feminine from the emblem of masculinity; for the foreskin is feminine, it is the vagina in which the masculine gland is hidden. . . . Things are different with the Jews: when they cut away the foreskin . . . , they thereby eliminate the bisexuality of the man, they take away the feminine characteristics of the masculine. In so doing, they defer to the bisexual Godhead by renouncing their own innate godlike nature; through circumcision, the Jew becomes only a man.[23]

With the expression "masculine," Groddeck means nothing heroic, nor even positive:

> If one takes a man for what he is, a needy, unfree being, fettered in a thousand ways by the monotonous daily round, a being capable of being elevated only once in a while, and that only for the short duration of the excitation, whose abiding force lies not in excitement, but in subordination to the law, one comes to the conclusion that the Jew has repressed the feminine as far as is humanly possible.[24]

Otto Weininger affirmed exactly the opposite viewpoint, for in his mind the evil was not the repression of the feminine but an excess of femininity. Still, Groddeck and Weininger have in common their refusal of the "human, all too human," and their demand for the "superman." According to Roger Lewinter, who has elucidated Groddeck's point of view while criticizing his implicit anti-Semitism, circumcision effectively represses every sign of femininity in the man: it signifies the human being's renunciation of the bisexual play that would be sacrilege, a phantasmatic rivalry with God. The distance that separates the creature from the creator and that defines the two cannot be transgressed. "Judaism is in fact a sort of humanism: a possible way of existing in this world from which the superhuman—bisexuality—has been banished" (Lewinter 1973, 199ff.)

What creates the strongest tie between the feminine and the Jew in Freudian psychoanalysis is the gaze of the anti-Semite, whose phobia, like that of the misogynist, arises from the castration complex. If one bears in mind the hypothesis of psychological bisexuality, then masculine antifeminism signifies nothing other than men's hatred of the feminine that they find within themselves. Can one go as far as to conceive of a psychological Jew/non-Jew duality that, like bisexuality, would be common to all individuals? Otto Weininger seems to have been close to this hypothesis. At the beginning of *Sex and Character*, he specifies that he will speak not of men and women but of masculine and feminine *substances*, of "ideas" of masculinity and femininity. Similarly, in Chapter 13 of the second part of his book, Judaism becomes an "idea in the Platonic sense," and Weininger states that "there are Aryans who are more Jewish than many Jews."[25]

Weininger thus arrives at a new explanation of anti-Semitism: those who hate Jewishness the most are those who are most suffused by it. Only philo-Semites are perfectly pure, free of all Jewishness: they know not of what they speak, says Weininger. Richard Wagner thus must have had a large amount of the Jew in him in order to have developed such a noble anti-Semitic rage (similarly, Weininger explains, Wagner drew the inspiration that permitted him to create the character Kundry from the secret folds of femininity in his own temperament). "This explains why the most virulent anti-Semites are found among the Jews,"[26] concludes Weininger. Nietzsche himself had not hesitated, in 1888, to accept responsibility for the rumors circulating in Germany about Wagner's mysterious Jewish ancestry (Nietzsche 1980, 41).

Around 1900, the designation "Jew" was called into service for the most arbitrary word plays. For example, Carl Dallago styles Hermann Bahr a "cosmopolitan Jew."[27] And Bahr himself defined the Viennese as "Judaicized," which is not to be considered a compliment. The "true" Jew, Bahr explains (without explaining what he means by this), has no power over the city of Vienna. This is regrettable, Bahr adds, for the Viennese could use the Jew's sense of hard work, of enterprise, of the seriousness of life (one is inclined to think that Bahr has in mind the Eastern European Jews [*Ostjuden*], poor workers who remained faithful to Jewish orthodoxy).

> All that is productive, grand, powerful in Judaism is not liked [in Vienna]. But the Jew who no longer wants to be one, the traitor to his race, which he forsakes, the actor who pretends to belong to a different race—this Jew is a blood relative of Vienna. The artificiality of these uprooted existences that, emptied of all history, are anxious to pump into themselves every present and

every future, who are only skins that inflate themselves in a different form each day, not capable of being anything, but able to appear to be everything, has always allured the Viennese. He sees himself in this type of Jew. In this sense, one can say that the Viennese is Judaicized through and through—and he was so even before the first Jew arrived.[28]

According to Bahr, just as there is a typically Viennese self-hatred (*Wiener Selbsthaβ*) comparable to Jewish self-hatred (*jüdischer Selbsthaβ*), there is also a resemblance between the decadence of the modern Viennese and the "fallen state" of the assimilated Jew.

Freud's work contains several germs of a theory close to Weininger's, which would place the Jew/non-Jew dualism at the very heart of the Jewish psychological constitution and which would make anti-Semitism the hatred of the individual for the quotient of Jewishness present in oneself. Did not Freud introduce this duality in the personality of Moses by maintaining that Moses was an Egyptian? Freud appears to start down Weininger's path by interpreting anti-Semitism as an internal conflict of the Jew when he writes to Arnold Zweig, on August 18, 1933: "We defend ourselves against castration in every form, and perhaps a bit of opposition against our own Jewishness is slyly hidden here. Our great leader Moses was, after all, a vigorous anti-Semite, and he makes no secret of this. Perhaps he was really an Egyptian."[29]

It would be tempting to go a bit further with Weininger's intuition that all anti-Semitism derives from a subjective antagonism between Jewishness and non-Jewishness within the individual, just as all antifeminism can be traced back to a protest of the male against his own femininity. Hitler himself wanted German citizens to go back to the third generation to assure themselves that there was no Jewish ancestor hidden in their genealogy who could have contaminated the race, and this obsession with racial purity reveals itself as indissociable from the fear of woman, who is capable of all treachery against German blood: "Woman introduced sin into the world," declared Hitler, "and the ease with which she gives way to the salacious artifices of the inferior man, close to animality, is the principle cause of the pollution of Nordic blood."[30] One of the constitutive phantasms of the anti-Semitic phobia could well be the fear of discovering oneself a Jew, just as the misogynist trembles to see himself unmasked as a woman.

Seen in this light, the discussion Allan Janik has carried on since the appearance of the French version of my book in 1982 rests on several fundamental misunderstandings. According to the point of view supported by Janik, Weininger was "not really" an antifeminist, nor an anti-Semite, but at most evidenced a "theoretical and nuanced" misogyny and an "animosity towards the Jews" (*Judenfeindschaft*) quite different from racist anti-Semitism.[31] Janik claims that a fair interpretation of Weininger has to situate *Sex and Character* in the context of the scientific research and philosophical discussion of his time in order to allow his "scientificity" and his theoretical "plausibility" to come to light. It is not necessary for me to repeat here my previously published arguments against Janik (Le Rider 1983, 1985). Let me emphasize only that the discussion of the apparent or real antifeminism of *Sex and Character* (a reality evident to this observer) is beside the point if one considers this book from the position of the *crisis of masculine identity*, which seems to be its main theme.

Let me also highlight the fact the debate about *Judenfeindschaft/ Antisemitismus* rests on an error of valuation. This argument implicitly affirms that anti-Semitic racism is not evident *stricto sensu* until the presence of a biological modality of thought is incontestable. However, as Pierre-André Taguieff has shown in his treatise *La Force du préjugé. Essai sur le racisme et ses doubles* (The Power of Prejudice: An Essay on Racism and Its Doubles), we cannot hold to "the belief that racism is essentially a theory of distinct and unequal races, defined in biological terms, and engaged in an eternal battle for world domination" (Taguieff 1988, 12).[32] Taguieff emphasizes that, in the twentieth century, racism presents itself primarily as a system of norms, values, and imperatives, as an overvaluation of difference ("heterophobia") understood in culturalist terms of individual and collective identity. If one accepts this idea, then "the word 'race' can no longer be taken as the exclusive or preeminent sign of racist methods at work" (Taguieff 1988, 105).[33] To say that Weininger contests the biological theory of races in no way permits the conclusion that he is neither a racist nor an anti-Semite. Taguieff cites Hitler's striking observation: "We are speaking of the Jewish race out of linguistic convenience, for, properly speaking, and from the genetic point of view, there is no Jewish race. . . . The Jewish race is above all a mental race" (Taguieff 1988, 168).[34,35] Given such a definition of race, it should be possible to write, without linguistic abuse, that Weininger's work stems from racism and anti-Semitism, which does not make him less worthy of our critical attention but in fact *more* worthy.

As to Otto Weininger's supposed scientificity, I believe I have amply demonstrated that it in fact masks a pseudoscientific procedure using an amalgamation of scientific "facts," arbitrarily selected from the most disparate realms in order to construct an apparatus of authoritative arguments that is entirely governed by a few fundamental obsessions.[36] In this light, Weininger's so-called scientific discourse really derives from a phobic delusion. The recent rediscovery of his first manuscripts, preserved at the Academy of Sciences in Vienna and published by Hannelore Rodlauer,[37] confirms that Weininger's main "scientific" talent lay in placing at the service of his *Weltanschauung* a vertiginous compilation of bits of information gleaned from different university disciplines and glued together with incontestable rhetorical force.

The most convincing realization of Otto Weininger's personality is, in my opinion, the one presented in the Israeli Joshua Sobol's play *Weiningers Nacht (The Soul of a Jew: Weininger's Last Night)*, the most finished version of which is the *Wiener Fassung*, presented at the Vienna Volkstheater in 1988–89.[38] For Sobol, there is no doubt that the true context of Weininger's short biography was Karl Lueger's Vienna, shaken by anti-Semitism and by the first Zionist movements. On the stage, Weininger, played by the excellent actor Paulus Manker, was transformed into a Woody Allen, more sad than funny, oppressed by the personality of his father. Sobol presents Weininger in a rather troubled light,[33] only imperfectly separated from the maternal bosom, a young student mired in a project of immoderate proportions that is ruining his mental and physical health, tormented by pubescent sexual anxieties and by his Jewish identity, against which he rebels. Both grotesque and pathetic, engaging and repulsive, genial and lamentable, Weininger as revived by Sobol remains a living presence in the gallery of familiar Viennese personalities of 1900, not only as a theoretical challenge but as a *cas humain*.

3 ✦
FRAGMENTS FROM WEININGER'S EDUCATION (1895–1902)

Hannelore Rodlauer

Translated from the German by Kristie A. Foell and Nancy Chadburn

THE GYMNASIUM STUDENT

From quite an early age, Otto Weininger demonstrated a decided gift for foreign languages. The records of the Royal and Imperial State Gymnasium at the Piarist Cloister in Vienna attest to his consistently "excellent" achievements in his major subject, Greek, as well as in English and French, which he took as electives; he had mostly above-average marks in Latin, German, philosophical propaedeutics (logic and empirical psychology), history, and geography; lesser achievements in (Jewish) religion; and distinct weaknesses in the natural sciences; the fact that he received a "very satisfactory" diploma verifies that he exerted himself to overcome the last. The reasons why Weininger was nevertheless refused a "certificate of graduation with distinction" apparently lie in his personality: "Because he continually disrupted lessons," he so provoked his teachers that, for years, in spite of his academic success, they could not agree to show him leniency in particular instances, such as his final grade for physical education, in which his performance was always poor—an indication of the disharmony between body and mind that had existed in Weininger from the first as well as of his refusal to conform. "My pleasure in 'hell-raising' in class is my *pleasure in chaos*," Weininger noted in his pocket notebook in 1903 (Weininger 1903).[1]

In the spring of 1896, when he was barely sixteen, Weininger wrote an etymological treatise on an adjective that appears in this form of speech only in Homer; the meaning of the word remains unknown even today. Probably on the suggestion of his Greek teacher, he submitted his article to the highly respected philological journal *Indogermanische Forschungen* (Indo-European Research). His conviction that he was right remained unaffected by the editor's rejection; in a further piece this schoolboy analyzed the arguments that might have led to the rejection and made an emphatic case for his position, concluding: "Nonetheless I adhere fully to my interpretation of νῶποψ"[2] Here is early evidence of the dogmatic stubbornness that would later astonish and offend Weininger's professors and friends during his student years. In the school year 1896–97 the outstanding historical philologist, Germanist, and academic philosopher Wilhelm Jerusalem took over the instruction of Weininger's Greek class and saw the students through to their matriculation examination in the summer of 1898 (Rodlauer 1990, 70 n. 40). The annual reports of the school record that all pupils read Demosthenes; Homer's *Odyssey;* Plato's *Apology, Euthyphro,* and *Crito;* and Sophocles' *Oedipus Tyrannus.*[3] In a lecture before the professional society Mittelschule, Jerusalem defended the educational value of teaching ancient languages in response to calls for the reduction or elimination of Latin and Greek instruction in favor of "more realistic" subjects of study:

> In order to possess the ability required to master reading and thinking assignments, the young minds of today must be taught better than ever, and therefore formal education, and an intensive formal education at that, is among the most imperative claims of the present. . . . It is my conviction—a conviction strengthened by many years of teaching experience as well as theoretical reflection—that the educational value of Greek lies in the formal, the aesthetic, and not least the ethical aspect. . . . The elaborate and often not easily comprehensible sentences of Demosthenes and Plato repay the effort of struggling with their painstaking, often pedantic analysis, for important thoughts, valuable all one's life, emerge. . . . Our pupils can understand the general maxims of Demosthenes, Plato, and Sophocles, whereas Schiller's philosophical verse and Goethe's *Faust* are too difficult for many. . . . In Demosthenes . . . the ethical element is always foregrounded; and how much more so in Plato, for here the figure of Socrates is, of course, always the most significant. Therefore it makes quite good sense if one chooses from among Plato's writings the *Apology, Crito,* and the last chapters of *Phaedo,* and thus limits oneself to the *mediation of Socratic ethics,* which acquire such irresistible power through the sage's martyrdom. For me the treatment of the *Apology* belongs to the greatest pleasures that Greek instruction offers. Here one finds natural opportunities to touch on general ethical questions; indeed the discussion of these is essential to full comprehension of this immortal work. . . . The famous passage on loyalty to duty and especially on the obligation imposed by one's chosen profession; dicta such as those asserting that life without constant self-examination is not worth living, that one must not move a judge to pity, that for a good man there is no evil either in life or in death, these must surely, if thoroughly discussed and understood, leave some trace in the hearts of the pupils (Jerusalem 1903, 7, 13, 18, 21, 29 [emphasis added]).

In consideration of the imperfect maturity of most seventeen- and eighteen-year-olds, however, Jerusalem doubts the value of assigning readings from Plato's purely metaphysical dialogues:

Up to now I have not dared to read one of the truly philosophical dialogues, such as *Phaedo, Gorgias, Phaedrus,* or the *Symposium,* or the first *Book of the State,* in school. . . . The doctrine of ideas is certainly very interesting for the historian of philosophy, but one can no longer argue its actual truth, and it is much too difficult to make its psychological origin and historical significance clear. Thus we will probably have to content ourselves with presenting Plato to pupils as an artist, and only in very exceptional circumstances attempt to delve more deeply into his philosophy (Jerusalem 1903, 30).

All of Weininger's works, not least the study *Eros und Psyche* (Eros and Psyche), document the formative effect on his thinking of these very Platonic dialogues. It is not very likely that Jerusalem's star pupil first became acquainted with them as a university student; the literature excluded from school lessons was probably especially intriguing to him. Certainly Weininger also obtained access to the well-stocked faculty library at his school. Theoretically he had already had the opportunity to acquaint himself with numerous works of the belletristic, philosophical, and psychological literature from which he later quoted, for besides its regular acquisitions, the library was augmented by books donated by authors like Wilhelm Jerusalem and Weininger's future university professors. Doubtless Weininger owes the deep impression that Plato and Socratic ethics left on him to Jerusalem's pedagogical commitment; it is a mark too little noted, not only in *Sex and Character,* but especially in the posthumous cultural-critical essay "Wissenschaft und Kultur" ("Science and Culture") (Weininger 1904, 142–82). It remains uncertain whether Jerusalem also found the opportunity in the context of his Greek instruction to give his pupils an introduction to contemporary philosophical developments. As a psychologist he explicitly used psychology as a tool for grammar and interpretation (Jerusalem 1896). In 1895 his work *Die Urteilsfunktion: Eine psychologische und erkenntniskritische Untersuchung* (The Function of Judgment: A Psychological and Cognitive-Critical Treatise) appeared. As Jerusalem emphasizes in another passage, this book "takes its bearings from Kant and is intended to carry Kant further, but from a biogenetic point of view"; however, Kant's theory of the a priori nature of space and time, as well as his system of the concepts of pure reason, laid down in the "table of categories," could "no longer be upheld in view of the results of modern sensory physiology" (Jerusalem 1904, 43).

Wilhelm Jerusalem was the only member of the Philosophical Society of the University of Vienna on the Gymnasium faculty, and was also a close friend of the physicist, sensory physiologist, and cognitive theoretician Ernst Mach. In Jerusalem, Weininger found a mentor who, by sheer force of personality and example, influenced his future choice of studies and helped him make the transition to academic life.

Weininger passed the *Matura* and graduated in the summer of 1898; he listed his "chosen profession" as "philosopher with a humanistic bent."[4] "Immediately after completing his *Gymnasium* studies" he applied for "membership in the Philosophical Society," where he found an exciting atmosphere for the free development of his intellectual gifts (Philosophical Society 1902–3, 5). In principle, the Society placed him on an equal footing with prominent scholars. In the discussions of the lectures given during the Society's meetings (held weekly from November through June), "the young man's unusually broad intellectual preparation, displayed in extensive papers and experimental independent work, amazed all the members and gave them great hopes for the development of his ability and industry" (Philosophical Society 1902–3, 5).

THE STUDENT AND THE PHILOSOPHICAL SOCIETY

Weininger began his studies at the University of Vienna in the fall of 1898. His early writings (*Frühschriften*) attest to the encyclopedic interests that helped the philosophy student to acquire an extremely broad education in a mere four years (eight semesters) of study.[5] Weininger attended lectures by Jodl, Müllner, Höfler, and Stöhr on the history of philosophy, logic, psychology, pedagogy, and the emerging field of experimental psychology, which at the time was so new that only Leipzig had a separate institute devoted to the subject. The hard sciences that earlier had given Weininger trouble in school—math, physics, chemistry—complemented his philosophical training; he studied these subjects with such significant scholars as Mertens, Boltzmann, Lieben, and Franz Exner, as well as young assistants like Anton Lampa, who would later achieve prominence. In addition, he sought insight into all the life sciences, such as biology, zoology, and human medicine. The names Sigmund Exner, Heinrich Obersteiner, Krafft-Ebing, and Wagner-Jauregg offer only a sampling of Weininger's teachers from the faculty of medicine ("Curriculum vitae," Rodlauer 1990, 210–11). Weininger, who wanted to be a psychologist, was especially impressed by the latter two, who represented the world-famous Vienna Medical School's trend toward psychiatry. The Viennese weekly *Die Zeit*[6]—an international and culturally progressive forum in which the twenty-year-old Weininger himself wanted to be heard (Rodlauer 1990, 64–65)—commented on this trend in August 1899: "A change is once again taking place in modern psychology. Just as Helmholtz's progress in the physiology of the senses once blazed the trail from 'psychophysics' to physiological psychology, so today does another medical discipline, *psychiatry*, seem to be gaining in importance for psychology. . . . The field of psychology stands at the threshold of its third period, the psychopathological period, which has been introduced almost exclusively by the publications of the Heidelberg psychiatrist Emil Kraepelin" (Gystrow 1899, 133).

The first lecture Weininger could possibly have attended at the Philosophical Society was held in the fall of 1898 by the world-famous nerve pathologist Heinrich Obersteiner (Rodlauer 1990, 211 n. 11; Lesky 1978, 386). As early as 1893—the year in which Freud and Breuer published their "preliminary report" *Über den psychischen Mechanismus hysterischer Phänomene* (On the Psychic Mechanism of Hysterical Phenomena)—the hypnosis specialist Obersteiner had reported on the path-breaking findings of the distinguished neurophysiologist Josef Breuer (himself an active member of the Philosophical Society) and his young friend Sigmund Freud, who had returned to Vienna from his Paris studies with Charcot. Breuer's and Freud's *Studien über Hysterie* (Studies on Hysteria), as well as Freud's independent works on hysteria and other neurotic phenomena, exerted an ongoing influence on Weininger.

In December 1898, Weininger became aware of a peculiar personality who would exercise an equally long-lived influence on him when Houston Stewart Chamberlain, the English writer and cultural philosopher who was then living in Vienna, held a lecture on Richard Wagner's philosophy ("Letters," Rodlauer 1990, 80 n. 62). Weininger, already a devoted Wagnerian, may have been one of the most attentive members of Chamberlain's audience. The more infamous chapters of the main body of *Sex and Character* owe many of their essential impulses to the anti-Semite Chamberlain.

One of the most stellar representatives of the Vienna Medical School held the next lecture at the Philosophical Society: the physiologist Sigmund Exner, a teacher of Weininger's. One of his central concerns was to investigate the physiology of the retina as well as the nerve structure of the larynx (Lesky 1978, 541).

In February 1899, Weininger was able to hear his philosophy teacher Friedrich Jodl lecture to the Society. The Munich native Jodl attached great importance to the literature of the Enlightenment insofar as it was "a critical ferment" contradicting "all metaphysical construction and all theologizing philosophy" (Meinong 1914, 446–52), according to Alexius von Meinong, a student of Franz Brentano and a member of the Philosophical Society, despite the fact that he lived in Graz ("Letters," Rodlauer 1990, 60–61 n. 11, 12; 92 n. 83; 159 n. 14). Almost every representative of the "Brentano School" belonged to the Philosophical Society; Brentano himself had also been a member until he left Austria (Rodlauer 1990, 159 n. 14). Brentano, a former priest who vehemently rejected German idealism, left Vienna in 1895. Ernst Mach was called from Prague to replace him "under heavy clerical protest."[7] Jodl had succeeded in obtaining a teaching post in Prague with the first volume of his *Geschichte der Ethik*

(History of Ethics); after publishing his *Lehrbuch der Philosophie* (Philosophy Textbook), he was called to Vienna (shortly after Mach). At the same time, the cleric Laurenz Müllner was named a full professor of the Philosophical Faculty as a "healthy antidote" against the liberal, anticlerical Jodl (Jodl 1920, 172; Rodlauer 1990, 59 n. 5). Christian von Ehrenfels, a student of Meinong's from Graz, succeeded to Jodl's post in Prague; he was a "member at large" of the Philosophical Society (Weininger 1990, 92 n. 83). In Vienna, Jodl began work on his edition of the writings of the philosopher Ludwig Feuerbach. Jodl's widow Margarete remembered those times:

> In the early years of his teaching in Vienna, he set up discussion hours for his advanced students who wanted a more specialized professional training. . . . He rejected in principle the notion of forming a unanimous opinion or school of thought among his students and auditors. To bring to life the "ingenium philosophicum, *independent thinking*, a deep sense of the *manifold forms of truth*" among his students seemed to Jodl a great advantage to his students. Jodl thought "that freedom and liberation from such one-sided coercion were especially needed by thinkers in Austria, where, since the university reform, philosophy had already been forced into provincial isolation (when Herbart and Brentano left Vienna along with their schools)" (Jodl 1920, 181 [emphasis added]).

One of Jodl's students, the same age as Weininger, deserves special attention: Victor Josef Kraft.[8] Kraft, a member of the Philosophical Society, was later a member of the Vienna Circle (*Wiener Kreis*) and the last holder of the Chair for History and Philosophy of the Inductive Sciences, which had been created for Mach in Vienna. At the meetings of the Society, Weininger also met Hermann Swoboda, who had devoted himself to psychology after becoming a doctor of jurisprudence, as well as Moriz Rappaport and Oskar Friedländer (pseudonym Ewald), Stefan Zweig, and the young lawyer Otto Stoessl, who became known as a short-story writer and *Fackel* author.

During the winter semester 1899–1900, the focal points of the Society were two discussions on solipsism and a series of meetings on vitalism. Swoboda's lecture, "Is There Evidence Against Solipsism?" (November 22 and 29, 1899), introduced the first set of discussions, which Ludwig Boltzmann repeatedly and temperamentally dominated. The Viennese biologist and pediatrician Max Kassowitz's[9] lecture, "Vitalism Old and New" (December 14, 1899), introduced the sequence of lectures, which occasioned a lively debate. Kassowitz, as a representative of the mechanical-causal position, and Swoboda, as an empiricist, naturally treated both vitalism and solipsism skeptically. Erna Lesky (1978) has found neo-vitalist tendencies in the Vienna Medical School. One of the staunchest opponents of both solipsism and vitalism *in science* was Ernst Mach, who was also a member of the Philosophical Society (Rodlauer 1990, 60 n. 10). Mach had been paralyzed on one side by a stroke in the summer of 1898; not only could he scarcely fulfill his teaching duties, but it was also difficult for him to take part in the meetings of the Society. Nonetheless, Weininger wrote to Swoboda on December 26, 1899: "I finally decided to write to Mach, and I was with him for forty-seven minutes today! Won't you be curious! But my bank balance isn't enough to pay for the postage it would take to mail you a written report of everything that was said. So you'll just have to be patient until we see each other again, hopefully soon!" (Rodlauer 1990, 62) Weininger's urgent desire to speak to Mach may well have arisen from the discussions of solipsism and vitalism at the Society. What must this visit have been like: the nineteen-year-old and the sixty-year-old, who has been described as kindly, full of humor, and open to other opinions? It is possible that Weininger, who had studied almost all of Mach's writings, asked the scholar about that exemplary page from Mach's *Analyse der Empfindungen* (The Analysis of Sensations), in which he wrote that "anyone who has once been under Kant's influence and taken up an idealistic viewpoint, anyone who has not rid himself of the last shreds of the idea of the thing in itself [*Ding an sich*], will surely retain a certain tendency to solipsism." After making distinctions between the approaches of philosophy and the natural sciences to the problem of identity and ego, Mach concludes that "the physical underpinnings of the ego, the body, provide points of departure that introspective psychology cannot give so satisfactorily" (Mach 1922, 292). In 1902 this position of Mach's would become the bone of contention that distanced Weininger from his "empiriocritical phase" and that provided the impetus for his departure from Swoboda's viewpoint.

✦ Mach, operating from the stance of the physicist striving for "economy of thought" for natural science research, rejects the idea of a metaphysical "life force," as he wrote in his *Principles of Thermodynamics* of 1896: "The living human or animal body differs from the dead as the electrical body differs from the unelectrical. Thus it is no wonder that the "soul" was likewise conceived of as matter, especially considering the belief that one perceived it in isolation in dreams and so forth. When *animistic* ideas influence physical theories, the latter belong, as already noted [in "Die ökonomische Natur der physikalischen Forschung" (The Economic Nature of Physical Research), 1882], to the sphere of fetishism" (Mach 1900, 428).

The Philosophical Society continued the discussion in the direction of Darwinism-Lamarckism-teleology in 1901–2. In the course of the conversations in January and February 1900, Weininger had very likely contributed a lecture of his own, a revised written version of which he offered for publication to *Die Zeit* in early October 1900. His article was not published. In November he evidently discussed the rejection with Müllner (who, although never a member of the Society, participated in the meetings) (letter of November 30, 1900, Rodlauer 1990, 66). After this Weininger turned to a methodologically "mechanistic" experiment, the result of which would bear the title *Eros und Psyche*. In March 1902, he declared his adherence to the "neo-vitalist" position with his sketch "Toward a Theory of Life."

In March 1900, by popular request Josef Breuer gave a lecture on the German physicist, philosopher, and psychologist Gustav Theodor Fechner's *Ideen zur Schöpfungs- und Entwicklungsgeschichte der Organismen* (Ideas on the Creation and Development of Organisms) of 1873. In April 1901, a special lecture by Alois Höfler commemorated the one-hundredth birthday of Fechner, whose work was of great importance to Mach, among others. Weininger's numerous references to Fechner's writings testify to their formative value.[10] Without mentioning him by name, Weininger proceeds from Fechner's vitalistic position at the beginning of "Toward a Theory of Life." With respect to Fechner's *Ideas on the Creation and Development of Organisms* and Wilhelm Preyer's *Hypothesen über den Ursprung des Lebens* (Hypotheses on the Origin of Life) ("Cosmozoic Theory"), Weininger wrote the following in his final published version [in *Sex and Character*]:

> Surely, however, the organic can never be explained through the inorganic, but rather the latter through the former. There is no doubt that Fechner and Preyer are correct when they say the dead is generated by the living and not vice-versa. Which we see occurring daily in individual life . . . while no one has ever seen anything living generated by something dead—this should also be applied to inorganic matter in its entirety, in the sense of the "biogenetic" parallelism between ontogenesis and philogenesis. If the theory of spontaneous generation has had to retreat from so many of its outposts, from Swammerdam to Pasteur, it will likewise give up its last hold, of which it seems to have so many in its monistic need, if that need can be satisfied by other and better means. The equations for dead phenomena will perhaps emerge someday, through the application of certain current values, as borderline cases of the equations of living phenomena; but it will never be possible to represent, conversely, the living through the non-living. The efforts to create a homunculus are foreign to Faust; Goethe did not without reason reserve them for Wagner, the famulus. Truly, only the excrement of the living can be approached by means of chemistry; the dead is after all itself only an excretion of life. The chemical approach places the organism on the same level with its refuse and secretions. How else could one explain notions such as the belief that one can influence the sex of an unborn child by a greater or lesser consumption of sugar? (Weininger 1903)

This philosophically legitimate rejection of the mechanical-causal view of life, which dominated the thinking and research of the time, escalated into a passionate hatred of "Jewry." Weininger claimed that a conspicuous number of Jews supported this antimetaphysical, unmystical ideological view in the biological sciences. Weininger continues:

> The *unchaste approach* to the things that the Aryan in the depths of his soul regards as *providence* first entered natural science through the Jews. The time of the deeply religious scientists, for whom their object shared, if only in small part, in a transcendental dignity, for whom there were secrets, who scarcely recovered from their astonishment at what they felt they had been *favored* to discover, the time of a Copernicus and Galileo, a Kepler and Euler, Newton and Linné, Lamarck and Faraday, Konrad Sprengel and Cuvier seems to be past. Today's freethinkers, who, because they are devoid of spirit, can no longer believe in the immanent revelation of something higher in the totality of nature, cannot—perhaps for that very reason—really replace and equal those men, even in their particular scientific provinces.

Viewed from the perspective of the final version, in the notorious chapter "Jewry," Weininger's rough draft already reveals the capital logical fallacy, the reason for his use of Fechner's (as well as Hering's, discussed below) ideas as the basis for this characterology of "Jewishness" (and of the typical "female").

The pursuit of the good, or the just life (at first in thought *and*—scientific—action) presents itself to Weininger from 1902 as the pursuit of the just *view* of the world. It must on principle judge energetic action as immoral—in politics, for example, as well as experimental psychology and medical therapy—as intrusions upon an autonomous subject that is thereby degraded to an object. Even before obtaining his doctorate, Weininger no longer considered himself a scientist but rather a "mystic," and hoped that his exercises in musical composition would lead him to a career as both a philosopher *and* an artist.[11]

After completing his studies Weininger went on an extended summer trip: his pilgrimage took him to the country of Hamsum and Ibsen, he experienced Wagner's *Parsifal* in Bayreuth, and he visited Wilhelm Wundt's Institute for Experimental Psychology in Leipzig—which he had originally chosen as the site of further studies but later belittled. In August 1902, Weininger wrote from Dresden of seeing Gustav Klimt's faculty picture *Philosophy* (rejected by the University of Vienna) at the international painting exhibition. Weininger showed interest in aesthetic questions; the lectures and discussions organized by the aesthetics section of the Philosophical Society appear in his writings, especially in the chapter "Erotics and Aesthetics" in *Sex and Character*.

After the unofficial exhibition of Klimt's *Philosophy* and its departure "from the prophet's fatherland" (*Die Zeit*, no. 288, April 7, 1900, 12), the art historian Franz Wickhoff held the legendary lecture "What Is Ugly?" at the Philosophical Society on May 5, 1900. The cultural battle unleashed in Vienna by Klimt's *Philosophy* corresponds to the ideological controversies existing within the sciences, which Weininger, as a student of philosophy and psychology, fought out within himself. In him the *Zeitgeist* hardens into a sort of bizarre crystal. Carl E. Schorske's well-known description of the affair of Klimt's "university pictures" vividly conveys this "spirit," within which and in opposition to which Weininger's education was completed (Schorske 1982, chap. 5, esp. 213–28).

When Klimt's faculty picture *Medicine*, unofficially exhibited in spring 1901, caused feelings to run high, Weininger was working on the first version of his psychobiological study *Eros und Psyche*. The same theme links Weininger's study and Klimt's *Medicine:* the androgynous (spiritual) constitution of human beings.

THE "DISCREET CHARM" OF THE ECONOMIC PRINCIPLE

In August 1900, Weininger accompanied Swoboda to the Fourth International Psychology Conference in Paris; Josef Clemens Kreibig, an instructor of ethics and psychology and one of the founding members of the Philosophical Society, was also with them (Rodlauer 1990, 61 n. 12). In the discussion after a lecture by the French psychologist Paul M.-J. Joire, the twenty-year-old Weininger emphasized the value of introspection for gaining insights in psychology ("Letters," Rodlauer 1990, 77 n. 57). In the high value he placed on introspection as a method, Weininger's position thus diverged from the physiological psychology of a Mach or Avenarius, in whose empiriocriticism he had become interested as a result of a conversation with Swoboda in late June 1899. In his famous lecture "The Economic Nature of Physical Research," held at the meeting of the Imperial Academy of Sciences on May 25, 1882, Mach had set forth his position on this question: "It appears certain that only the physical method is appropriate to psychological physiology. . . . We will never get to know this intellectual field through self-observation alone. Self-observation in concert with physiological research, which searches for physical connections, can display this field clearly before our eyes, and will thereby truly reveal our inner person for the first time" (Mach 1882, 316 ff.).

Impressed by the conference, Weininger sought to carve himself a reputation as a *psychologist:* "The revolution which 'natural science and technology' have brought about in the past century will have to hide its face before the revolution that psychology is about to introduce; we stand at the very beginning of its development and must therefore struggle through its childhood diseases," he wrote to Swoboda on October 10, 1900

(Rodlauer 1990, 65). Weininger may have already staked out his future field of research around this time, for on October 6 he had written that he had submitted his article on vitalism to the journal *Die Zeit.*

The public prosecutor Lino Ferriani also published an article on "Decadent Parents" (*Die Zeit*, no. 282, February 2, 1900, 118), in which he blamed mothers for a greater proportion of child abuse than fathers, who, he said, were only "morally complicit." To back up his claims, he referred to Lombroso's criminological and anthropological work, which, he said, demonstrated "the preponderance of craftiness, weakness and cruelty of the criminal woman" (Lombroso and Ferrero 1894).[12] On June 30, 1900, *Die Zeit* (no. 300, 205) published a review of the first two volumes of Magnus Hirschfeld's *Jahrbuch für sexuelle Zwischenstufen* (Annual for Sexual Hybrids), which drew attention to a petition for the repeal or weakening of Paragraph 175 (the sodomy law) of the German Criminal Code, which had been printed in the first volume (1899). One of the main authors of the annual, the Berlin psychiatrist Albert Moll, wrote a defense of women's emancipation, "Die angebliche Minderwertigkeit des Weibes" ("The So-Called Inferiority of Women"), which appeared in *Die Zeit* on October 6, 1900 (no. 314, 5). Two weeks earlier, the Viennese social hygienist Max von Gruber had spoken out in the journal on behalf of the admission of women to the medical and pharmaceutical professions. On October 27, the journal published "Eine Anregung zur Erziehungsfrage" ("A Suggestion on Child Rearing") by the Berlin feminist Hedwig Dohm: "The notion that mothers are the natural and necessary rearers of their children is one of those lies that are common currency. . . . Most mothers have absolutely no idea of their children's character, a situation that calls forth both astonishment and pity" (*Die Zeit* no. 317, October 27, 1900; 53; discussed in nos. 325 and 327). Dohm called for the "education and self-education of mothers," and believed that children should be turned over to tutors "such as the young Greek may have found in Plato and Socrates"; finally, she demanded that children be "saved from the arbitrary whims of parents."

All these thoughts are repeated in Weininger's *Eros und Psyche*, which he began conceiving around this time, often in the same style or even in the same wording of the original author. Most of the views and source citations collected in Weininger's manuscript were probably taken from the *Annual for Sexual Hybrids* and the *Die Zeit* articles cited above. For example, the bisexual constitution of the human being, which became an important theme for Weininger, was one of the arguments brought forth in the petition published in the 1899 *Annual:*

> The scientific research that has concerned itself with the question of homosexuality, especially during the last twenty years in German-, English-, and French-speaking areas . . . has unanimously confirmed the view of the first scholars who devoted their attention to this subject, namely, that there must

be a deep, inner constitutional predisposition for this phenomenon, which recurs in all times and places. It is presently as good as proven that the causes of this phenomenon, so puzzling at first glance, have developed in relationship to the *original bisexual constitution* of man. It therefore follows that no one whose feelings are so constituted is to be considered morally culpable (Hirschfeld 1899, 239).

Among the many signers of the petition were Weininger's teachers Richard von Krafft-Ebing and Heinrich Obersteiner, as well as the authors Hermann Bahr (at this time still one of the publishers of *Die Zeit*) and Arthur Schnitzler.

In October 1900, Swoboda sought out Sigmund Freud; whether as patient or student remains unclear on the basis of Freud's contradictory statements. He learned from Freud about the generally bisexual constitution that explained and helped in the treatment of certain neuroses. Ever since Freud had heard about constitutional bisexuality and periodicity from his close friend Wilhelm Fliess, who kept him informed of developments in these areas, these ideas had greatly influenced his thinking and his medical work. As early as August 1, 1899, he had written to Fliess: "Bisexuality! You are certainly right about this. I am getting used to viewing *every sexual act as an occurrence between four individuals*" (Freud 1985, 356 [emphasis added]).

Freud's recounting of events seems to confirm the reconstruction of some of the influences on Weininger's *Eros und Psyche* that I have attempted above. Only Freud's version remains due to the quarrel over the "discovery" of bisexuality that Fliess initiated after reading *Sex and Character* after Weininger's death. On July 23, 1904, Freud answered Fliess's suspicion "that Weininger received knowledge of my ideas through you" as follows: "I too believe that the late Weininger was a burglar with a key he picked up. Here is everything I know about it. Swoboda, who was an intimate friend of his and who had learned about bisexuality (which comes up in every treatment) from me, mentioned the word "bisexuality"—as he tells it—when he found Weininger preoccupied with sexual problems. Whereupon Weininger clapped his hand to his forehead and rushed home to write his book" (Freud 1985, 464).

Swoboda's recounting in his defense of Weininger, *Die gemeinnützige Forschung und der eigennützige Forscher* (Research for the Common Good and the Self-Serving Researcher, Swoboda 1906), is very similar to Freud's, but Swoboda denies that the name Fliess was ever mentioned in his conversation with Freud (Freud 1985, 465). The fact that Freud already counted bisexuality as one of the cornerstones of his psychoanalytic practice probably helped Weininger to decide on his field of psychological research. Weininger had a lively interest in Freud's publications and would later draw on his *Studies on Hysteria* (written with Josef Breuer) to support his own antifeminist theses. Weininger began to organize his material against the background of the Platonic myth, which is explicitly used in the introduction to *Sex and Character* as testimony to the venerable age of the problematics of gender, on which he is about to shed the first "scientific light" (Weininger 1903). Plato's "explanation" of adultery in the *Symposium* led Weininger to make associations with Goethe's novel of adultery, *Elective Affinities* (Rodlauer 1990, 171 n. 28). Goethe based the conception of his great novel on a comparison between certain chemical phenomena ("elective affinities") and empirically occurring human behaviors. The young researcher was motivated to explore the natural laws underlying the phenomenon of erotic attraction, inspired by the scientific discoveries on human bisexuality and similar observations in plants and animals that had been published not by Fliess but rather by Krafft-Ebing and Havelock Ellis. Using a model of psychophysical parallelism, Weininger wanted to portray the rules governing psychic life by using the methods and formulaic expressions of physics. Just as the poet and scientist Goethe had portrayed a parallel between psychic and chemical phenomena almost as a parable, Weininger attempted to solve the riddles of erotic attraction using scientific methods. He was "proud" to have confirmed Goethe with his "law of love" (Weininger 1903, 48, 50); but he insisted that he was supporting neither adultery nor "free love." Rather, Weininger intended to support the marriage of love, which was only possible when the proportions of male and female vital "substance" of the two partners combined to form a whole man and a whole woman.

In the first part of *Sex and Character*, Weininger reveals with a single word the method he used to arrive at his mathematical formula for sexual attraction: "The first formula was only an *'economic'* summary of the regularity of all cases of sexual attraction of ideal force" (Weininger 1903, 44). Those familiar with the work of Mach and Avenarius will immediately realize that the "economic principle" is at work here. Avenarius had formulated this principle in 1876 under the title *Philosophie als Denken der Welt nach dem Prinzip des kleinsten Kraftmaßes* (Philosophy as Thinking the World According to the Principle of the Smallest Possible Force). Mach developed his thoughts on the subject in his 1882 Academy lecture, "Die ökonomische Natur der physikalischen Forschung" ("The Economic Nature of Physical Research"); in his *Analyse der Empfindungen und das Verhältnis des Physischen zum Psychischen* (Analysis of Sensations and the Relationship of the Physical to the Psychic), he referred to his agreement with Avenarius (originally published 1886). In "The Economic Nature of Physical Research" Mach writes:

> Scientific communication always contains a description, i.e., an imitation of a thought experience, which is meant to *replace* the experience and spare us the

trouble of having it again. The *summarizing* description was invented in order to spare us the trouble of teaching and learning itself. The laws of nature are no different . . .

All our efforts to reflect the world in our thoughts would be fruitless if we did not succeed in finding some enduring qualities in the diverse, changing world. Hence the striving for the *concept of substance, whose source is no different from the modern idea of conservation of energy* (Mach 1882, 301, 306 [emphasis added]).

The second edition of Mach's *Principien der Wärmelehre, historish-kritisch entwickelt* (Principles of Heat Theory) appeared in 1900. Among Weininger's manuscripts, which the Vienna City and State Library acquired from Swoboda, is a faithful transcription of Mach's foreword to this edition, dated August 1899.[13] When compared with Weininger's letters, the handwriting points to the time *before* the first, handwritten draft of *Eros und Psyche*. Weininger had apparently devoted special attention to the transcription.

Weininger's study *Eros und Psyche* begins with the assumption of two "ideal" substances, M and W (for male and female, respectively), which are polar opposites and which combine to complete not only the individual but also his/her protoplasm, a concept analogous to Boyle-Mariotte's Law. A comparison of Weininger's thought process with Mach's exposition of the "concept of substance" in his *Heat Theory* makes it appear likely that Weininger followed Mach in arriving at his "law of love" (Mach 1900, 423–31; Rodlauer 1990, 146, 161, 163, nn. 3, 4, 15, 17).

The series of lectures and discussions on Nietzsche in the Philosophical Society, which followed his death on September 25, 1900, may have been partially responsible for the misogynistic tone of Weininger's study. Nietzsche's influence may also have contributed to Weininger's suppression of the profeminist viewpoints of many of the writers whose works on bisexuality and homosexuality he cites (especially the leading authors of the *Annual for Sexual Hybrids*). All of *Eros und Psyche*'s enthusiastic humanitarian positions on education, homosexuality, and women's liberation (which meant, for Weininger, the liberation of those "manwomen" born with a disproportionately high M quotient) could easily have been taken from the early volumes of the *Annual for Sexual Hybrids* or from *Die Zeit*. Where, then, is the "originality" that Weininger's dissertation adviser, Jodl, saw in the expanded version of *Eros und Psyche*? (letter of February 15, 1902, Rodlauer 1990, 106, and document of dissertation, 213–14)?

Jodl was probably unfamiliar with Weininger's sources; in the first part of *Sex and Character*, which is the final version of the physiological portion of *Eros und Psyche*, Weininger only refers to the volumes of the *Annual* he consulted in two footnotes. This could create the impression that he gathered the huge amount of literature he cites himself. As the letters to Swoboda imply, it seems that Weininger's teachers were easily impressed by large bibliographies. The official evaluations of his dissertation confirm this. Weininger's theoretical stance and his methods *are* original. His independent, courageous approach to explosive societal problems is astonishing. Weininger's *intention* to develop a theoretical basis from which to "solve" these problems (as odd as the particulars sometimes turned out), as well as his humanitarian engagement, probably appealed to a champion of autonomy and enlightenment like Jodl, who had gone through the school of English empiricists such as David Hume.[14]

In the spring of 1901, Weininger, with Swoboda's assistance, began looking for a title that would "draw." Because he hoped his work would effect social change, he also wanted to publish it as quickly as possible. He planned to ask a prominent scholar for a foreword that could give his first work more weight in the public eye; first he considered the Viennese social hygienist Max von Gruber and the psychiatrist and thyroid specialist Wagner-Jauregg, Krafft-Ebing's successor, whose view that sexual inversion was a decadent phenomenon Weininger firmly rejected (Rodlauer 1990, 69 nn. 37–39). The search for a pithy title seems to have ended after his first conversation with Rudolf Kassner, on April 23, 1901. After completing his dissertation on "the eternal Jew in literature" in 1896, Kassner had published two books, *Die Mystik, die Künstler und das Leben* (Mysticism, Artists, and Life), in 1900, and *Indischer Idealismus* (Indian Idealism), in 1902–3. He turned to various translation projects, including the dialogues of Plato. When Weininger visited him, Kassner was working on a translation of the *Symposium* and on a series of parables about Eros in the style of the Platonic dialogues, which appeared in 1902 under the title *Der Tod und die Maske* (Death and the Mask). In the first of these parables, "Psyche und der Faun," Psyche asks the Faun, "Then you have never heard of the king of Arcadia and his three daughters, and how Eros, the gods' son, courted me, Psyche, the youngest daughter?" (Kassner 1902, 9). The two authors certainly would have discussed the progress of their respective works on Eros, and Weininger's poetic, ambivalent title for his psychobiological study may have been born in this way.

Now that Weininger had found a title that satisfied him, he hurried to write an abstract of his intellectual experiment, which he deposited in a sealed envelope at the Imperial Academy of Sciences on June 4, in order to assure his claim to originality. He spent the summer vacation in Purkersdorf, a town in the Vienna forest (*Wienerwald*) west of the city, where, in a garden pavilion, he wrote down his thoughts for the planned publication in great detail, with only sporadic source citations. Several factors may have inspired Weininger to write a separate chapter on hysteria: Albert Moll's discussion, in the second *Annual for Sexual Hybrids*, of the frequency of hysterical (and epileptic) symptoms in homosexuals;[15] Charcot's similar observations; and several works on hysteria by Charcot's students Janet and Freud (both alone and with Breuer). Since Freud felt that hysterical phenomena could be traced back to a defense against or a "forgetting" of unbearable thoughts or experiences (Freud 1894), Weininger decided that hysteria belonged to the psychology of the "feminine."

Swoboda suggested that Weininger show his manuscript to Freud, who would be able to find him a publisher. Weininger had already paid a call on Deuticke, Freud's publisher, who had scared him off with cost-sharing demands that far exceeded Weininger's means. Weininger was not unknown to Freud, as Swoboda's comment in a letter of August 12, 1901, "You visited him once!" shows; this is a fact not previously known (Rodlauer 1990, 81–82). Whether Weininger's visit was as patient or student remains unknown. The collection of Freud's notes kept by the Sigmund Freud Society contains no further information.

In August 1901 Freud wrote to Fliess:

> As far as I can see, my next work will be called "Human Bisexuality." It will go to the root of the problem and say the last word it may be granted me to say—the last and the most profound. For the time being I have only one thing for it: the chief insight which for a long time now has built itself upon the idea that repression, my core problem, is possible only through reaction between two sexual currents. I shall need about six months to put the material together and hope to find that it is now possible to carry out the work. But then I must have a long and serious discussion with you. The idea itself is yours. You remember my telling you years ago, when you were still a nose specialist and surgeon, that the solution lay in sexuality. Several years later you corrected me, saying that it lay in bisexuality—and I see that you are right. So perhaps I must borrow even more from you; perhaps my sense of honesty will force me to ask you to coauthor the work with me; thereby the anatomical-biological part would gain in scope, the part which, if I did it alone, would be meager. I would concentrate on the psychic aspect of bisexuality and the explanation of the neurotic. That, then, is the next project for the immediate future, which I hope will quite properly unite us again in scientific matters as well (Freud 1985, 448).[16]

Fliess had spent years working on a book about his discoveries on bisexuality and periodicity, which did not appear until 1906 under the title *Der Ablauf des Lebens* (The Course of Life). One can recognize how much Freud's announcement must have irritated him even in Freud's next letter of September 19, 1901:

> I do not comprehend your answer concerning bisexuality. It is obviously very difficult to understand each other. I certainly had no idea of doing anything but working on my contribution to the theory of bisexuality, elaborating the thesis that repression and the neuroses, and thus the independence of the

unconscious, presuppose bisexuality. You will by now have seen from the relevant reference to your priority in "Everyday Life" that I have no intention of expanding my role in this insight. But the establishment of some link to the general biological and anatomical aspects of bisexuality would be, after all, indispensable in any such work. Since almost everything I know about it comes from you, all I can do is cite you or get this introduction entirely from you. Right not I am not at all eager to appear in print. Meanwhile we will no doubt have a chance to discuss it. One cannot simply say, "The conscious is the dominant, the unconscious the underlying sexual factor," without grossly oversimplifying the very much more complicated matter, even though that is of course the basic fact (Freud 1985, 450–51).

We can see how fragile the friendship had become through the competition resulting from the two men's intentions to publish on the subject of bisexuality. Freud's ambivalent attitude, even his shock at the project Weininger gave him to read at precisely *this* moment, is thus understandable. On the one hand he could not deny him his honest admiration, as Weininger reported to Swoboda; on the other hand, his self-interest did not allow him to go so far as to declare the manuscript ready for publication. It had to be suppressed. Under pressure from Fliess, Freud later admitted that "the manuscript shown to me, though, had an entirely different wording than the printed book; I was also quite alarmed by the chapter on hysteria, which was written *ad captandam benevolentiam meam* [to capture my favor], but the underlying theme of bisexuality was of course recognizable, and I must have regretted at the time that via Swoboda, as I already knew, I had handed over your idea to him. In conjunction with my own attempt to rob you of your originality, I better understand my behavior toward Weininger and my subsequent forgetting" (Freud 1985, 466). As it now appears, Swoboda's communication to Weininger of Freud's ideas on bisexuality probably did not give Weininger his initial idea, but only the final impetus actually to carry out his research.

After Freud's friendly dismissal of his work, Weininger submitted his manuscript to his teachers Jodl and Müllner in an attempt to win a scholarship. This time he received the Leopold Trebisch Scholarship, for which he had previously applied unsuccessfully. On Saint Stephen's Day (December 26), 1901, exactly two years after Weininger's visit to Mach's residence, Jodl received Weininger for a conference. After reading the study, Jodl gave Weininger to understand that he would accept the piece as a dissertation after a few corrections, and suggested the unambiguous title *Geschlecht und Charakter* instead of the poetic *Eros und Psyche,* which disappointed Weininger. Jodl also indicated that he would recommend the revised work to a publisher if Weininger revised it according to his suggestions (letters of December 27, 1901, and January 1, 1902, Rodlauer 1990, 100–104).

This unexpected possibility of earning his doctorate sooner because of Jodl's recognition of *Eros und Psyche* made Weininger revise his plan of following Swoboda to Leipzig, where the latter had received a postdoctoral fellowship to study at Wilhelm Wundt's Institute for Experimental Psychology.

In the weeks following this interview with Jodl, Weininger unexpectedly fell prey to a deep depression. He became increasingly preoccupied with other topics. In the fall of 1901 he had had another talk of several hours with Kassner, probably about Houston Stewart Chamberlain's anti-Semitic work of cultural philosophy, *Die Grundlagen des* 19. *Jahrhunderts* (*The Foundations of the Nineteenth Century*). (Kassner was a friend of Chamberlain's.)[17] *Die Zeit* had published a series of thorough and rather negative reviews of Chamberlain's work as each volume appeared.[18] As the chapter on "Judaism" in *Sex and Character* shows, Chamberlain's ability "to make the world comprehensible from one particular standpoint"[19] made him Weininger's most important authority.

In the winter of 1901–2, Weininger immersed himself in Ibsen's Nordic Faust drama, *Peer Gynt;* its protagonist's lifelong search for his true self occasioned deep distress in the seeker, Weininger. His inner crisis kept him from writing down his thoughts about *Peer Gynt*, but also made it impossible for him to continue his work on *Eros und Psyche*, now entitled *Geschlecht und Charakter*, according to his earlier paradigm.

At the end of November 1901, Max Kassowitz's lecture on "The Crisis of Darwinism" had reintroduced the Philosophical Society's continuing debate on vitalism. The lecture coincided, both in timing and in content, with Weininger's intellectual crisis. With the "teleological argument," he now tried to develop his psychology of the sexes (which had been indebted to psychophysical parallelism) into a "differential" psychology, that is, a philosophical psychology of man and a scientific-biological psychology of woman.

From his teleological standpoint, Weininger now began to settle accounts with the natural sciences. In his posthumous cultural critique, "Wissenschaft und Kultur" ("Science and Culture"), he disparages his own work in the service of science:

> Our time has proclaimed science itself to be a means to an end. This "philosophy" [here Weininger cites Mach's works on the economic principle] resulted from the *general economic understanding* of things that once occupied a higher place in the scale of values. Historical materialism destroys the entire value of the human past by attributing no further meaning to history than the struggle for food and foraging areas; in the same way, the understanding of science as a method of saving work was the most enormous degradation of the human thirst for knowledge that the world has ever seen. This viewpoint was cleverly presented, to be sure, and *drew more than one person into its sphere of*

influence through the discreet charm of its presentation, although many of those it drew were destined to remain only a short while. It did not lack for the biological ostentation so common today, either. But the biological viewpoint, as it is presently understood, is nothing other than utilitarian (Weininger 1904, 172 [emphasis added]).

In the winter of 1902, the "discreet charm" vanished. "Zur Theorie des Lebens" (On the Theory of Life), drafted over the course of a few days in March, shows a different Weininger.

"BACK TO KANT!"

In March 1902, Weininger had another conversation with Rudolf Kassner. Although in the previous autumn Kassner had still been able to inspire Weininger, the changed young man was now "greatly displeased" with Kassner's undifferentiated evaluation of Ibsen, Kant,—and Paul Lindau ("Letters," Rodlauer 1990, III n. 103). Weininger's extreme remarks about Kassner in his letters to Swoboda should not, however, lead us to discount the role of this man of letters, philosophist, and physiognomist as a sort of midwife for Weininger's thinking and writing. Weininger often wrote letters to friends asking them to meet personally with him so that he could develop his thoughts through conversation. In addition to criticism, Kassner gave numerous and diverse suggestions for further reading. Kassner's personal friendship with Chamberlain meant, however, that the fruitful discussions between the two young men also offered a danger of Weininger's being ideologically seduced by the English philosopher. (A year before Weininger began his studies, Chamberlain had given a lecture on "Indian Thought" in the Philosophical Society; a year later, he again spoke on "Richard Wagner's Philosophy.") Kassner recalled decades later that

> Chamberlain was an anti-Semite and dedicated his "Foundations of the Nineteenth Century" to a racially pure Jew. He claimed that Jews were incapable of creative genius, and only called Weininger, the author of *Sex and Character*, a genius because Weininger had himself desperately denied Jews genius and, himself a Jew, was nonetheless an anti-Semite. Weininger had visited me several times before the publication of his later famous book. Never in my life have I met such a gifted person, a person gifted in so many different areas, who at that same time was not at all what one would call a personality, who exuded so little fascination or power. If one may say so, Weininger looked and carried himself like a deeply disturbed young man from the business world (Kassner 1938, 155).

In March 1902, Weininger drafted the "vitalistic" theory of biology and psychology mentioned above, with the Platonic dialogue *Phaido* as implicit background. As he had done with *Eros und Psyche*, he deposited his

raw sketch with the Academy of Sciences to ensure his rights of author-
ship. The first pages of this manuscript demonstrate a close relationship to
the discussions of Darwinism, Lamarckism, and the "teleological argument" in the Philosophical Society (Breuer 1902). Weininger begins with a
reference to Ewald Hering's lecture at the Academy, "Über das Gedächtniss als eine allgemeine Function der organisirten Materie" (On Memory
as a Common Function of Organic Matter), which was based on Lamarck's
theses. Hering attempts

> to relate a large number of apparently unrelated phenomena, partly from
> conscious, partly from unconscious organic life, and to perceive them as
> expressions of one of the same basic capacity of organized matter, namely as
> functions of its *memory* or *ability to reproduce.* Often one thinks of memory only
> as the ability to reproduce ideas or series of ideas intentionally. But is it not
> also memory when the forms and events of past days arise in our consciousness
> unbidden? We have a perfect right to expand the concept of memory to
> include all unintentional sensations, ideas, feelings, and aspirations, and no
> sooner have we done this, than *memory* becomes a *primeval ability, which is the*
> *source of and simultaneously the tie that binds together our entire conscious life* (Hering
> 1870, 268; cited in Rodlauer 1990, 193 [emphasis added]).

On the basis of "Hering's memory," Weininger now conceived his
"differential" psychology of the sexes. He also based his new insights on
the thesis (after Lamarck) of the teachability of organic life and the
inheritability of learned traits in the sense of a qualitative higher development (as opposed to anorganic matter, which was subject to unchangeable
laws). Some of the thoughts Weininger first sketched out in his *Theory of
Life* would develop into the "principal"—that is, ethical—investigation of
sexual difference, proceeding from biological, determining facts in the
book version of *Sex and Character.* He wrote, for example, that "*W* has no
ego; hence her untruthfulness; the female has no soul; it *lives in moments;*
for the absolute female there would be no *principium contradictionis.*
Undine! Hence absolute lack of a sense of responsibility! Incomprehen-
sion in the face of the question: why did you do that? *Lack of memory and
continuity. The female lives in moments, the man in a continuum.* Therefore it is
true: 'females have no character' " (Rodlauer 1990, 201 [emphasis added]).

Since, in Weininger's characterology, "the absolute female" has no
memory, he concludes that it is not really an organic being—not a formed,
indivisible individual—but rather anorganic matter without memory, and
therefore without soul or ego. This is an almost logical conclusion based on
Hering's treatise "On Memory as a Common Function of Organized
Matter." Matter—material—materialistic (in practical life as in science):
here is the connection between "woman" and "Jew." Weininger yoked
church fathers and philosophers into the service of his argumentation.

Swoboda compares Weininger's affect-driven formation of ideas after his crisis of 1901–2 with the psychological mechanisms Freud uncovered in *The Interpretation of Dreams* and *Jokes and Their Relation to the Unconscious.*

Presumably Friedrich Jodl would have liked to tone down or remove many things in Weininger's dissertation, which was essentially completed in late April (letter of April 25, 1902, Rodlauer 1990, 116). As far as one can tell by comparing Jodl's comments in his official evaluation and the book version of *Sex and Character,* Weininger seems to have undertaken only those changes that would not weaken the ethical substance of his work. Changes were limited to such peripheral matters as, for example, the characterology of the "ego-person" as a typical "masochist" and the "world-person" as a typical "sadist" (terms Krafft-Ebing had introduced to describe sexual perversions), Weininger's first attempts at an "animal psychology," and the weight he gave to the notion of periodicity (an idea taken from Swoboda) as an explanation of psychological and characterological variations.

The historical aspect of the criteria for a dissertation and for scholarly work in general should not be underestimated. Only those who ignore the historical perspective will be offended by the very positive evaluation Weininger's dissertation received. After Weininger's suicide in October 1903, Jodl felt called upon to make the following statement in a Viennese newspaper: "Weininger's dissertation, which earned him a Ph.D. from the University of Vienna at the age of twenty-four, was an exceptional achievement even from the perspective of scholarly knowledge. Weininger then devoted another year of intense work to his topic, and published his work as a book last summer under the title *Sex and Character.* In that year, he wrote most of the second, more deductive section of the book, the part that primarily gave offense, and on which his teachers could not possibly have exercised any direct influence" (Jodl 1903).[20]

Weininger's tendency to treat ethical questions must have pleased a president of the Ethical Society, and this may have been one reason why Jodl allowed Weininger his freedom of thought despite his fantastic tangents. Having once approved Weininger's ethical framework, Jodl could not do much against Weininger's attacks on those he held responsible for the decline in values, namely, women, Jews, and the positive (that is, antispiritual) sciences (represented by Mach and Wundt); for Weininger, such attacks were inextricably related to his ethical stance. When Jodl first met Weininger, the latter had been a "convinced adherent" of empiriocriticism; according to Swoboda, Weininger was "delighted" with Mach's "Antimetaphysical Introduction" to his *Analysis of Sensations* with its relativistic conception of ego ("The apparent persistence of the ego consists primarily in continuity, in its slow rate of change. . . . The ego cannot be rescued" [Swoboda 1923, XI]). As his letters show, Weininger had also considered continuing his studies at Wundt's Leipzig Institute for Experimental Psychology, where Swoboda studied after receiving his Ph.D. in Vienna. Wundt's institute was considered the most progressive research group of its time; his psychology was a "psychology without a soul."[23] By the time Weininger could have carried out this plan, however, the two friends had already become estranged, or, rather, Weininger had become estranged from his own previous world view. In May 1902, Weininger wrote to Swoboda that he was now frequenting the literary circle of the erstwhile Café Griensteidl; his new friends represented the Young Vienna [*Jung-Wien*] movement, and their discussions were always "about art" (letter of May 19, 1902, Rodlauer 1990, 117 n. 110). He also wrote that he was working on his essay about Ibsen, probably influenced by the German premiere of *Peer Gynt;* he found the time for this project while waiting for Jodl to return his dissertation for revision.

It was in the Young Vienna circle that the reaction to Mach's "Antimetaphysical Introduction" bore literary fruit as an expression of the sentiments of an entire generation and its *Zeitgeist*. While Weininger, in contact with "ipsissimo Café Griensteidl," was formulating his critique of Mach in his dissertation in the spring of 1902, Hugo von Hofmannsthal was working on his "Lord Chandos" letter. The following famous passage from the letter is a poetic exaggeration of the central thoughts of Mach's "Introduction": "I have entirely lost the ability to think or speak coherently about anything. . . . I felt an inexplicable malaise when I even pronounced the words 'spirit,' 'soul,' or 'body'. . . . The abstract words, which the tongue must necessarily employ if it is to express an opinion about anything, disintegrated into dust in my mouth like mouldering mushrooms" (Hofmannsthal 1966, 341).

According to Hermann Broch, this lack of ability to make judgments, this "vacuum of values," was symptomatic of Hofmannsthal's era. Weininger recognized its dangers in his surroundings and in himself, and he named them "woman," "Jew," "Mach," and "Wundt." He sought escape from the void with a philosopher for whom the a priori existence and the freedom of the self were givens: "back to Kant!" (letter of March 2, 1902, Rodlauer 1990, 107–8).

How did Weininger arrive at this complete reversal? Among many possible causes that combined to produce Weininger's crisis in the winter of 1902–3, another factor has now come to light: the chairman of the Philosophical Society, Alois Höfler, was deeply involved in editing Kant's works. His edition of Kant's *Metaphysische Anfangsgründe der Naturwissenschaft* (Metaphysical Bases of the Natural Sciences) and Höfler's own *Studien zur gegenwärtigen Philosophie der Mechanik* (Studies on the Current Philosophy of Mechanics), conceived partially as an afterword to Kant's manuscript, appeared in Leipzig in 1900 as volumes IIIa and IIIb of the

Publications of the Philosophical Society at the University of Vienna. In the Society's 1901–2 annual, Höfler reported that he had been commissioned to edit Kant's *Metaphysical Bases of the Natural Sciences* for the Berlin edition of Kant's complete works as well (Kant 1903). He had been asked to undertake this task by the Prussian Academy of Sciences and had only been able to complete it with the help of several members of the Philosophical Society. He thanks by name those who participated in the "repeated reading and comparison of the texts," including the philosophy students Victor Kraft, Oskar Friedländer [Ewald],—and Otto Weininger.

It is likely that Weininger's deepened knowledge of the texts as well as Kant's compelling rigor showed Weininger the way to go when he turned his back on contemporary psychology.

In the introduction to his "Nature Theory," the Königsberg philosopher wrote:

> *True* science is only that whose certainties are apodictic; knowledge that contains only empirical certainty is not truthfully called *knowledge*. . . . True metaphysics comes from the essence of the ability to think itself, and is not to be disparaged as fantasy simply because it does not come from experience. Rather, it contains the *a priori* concepts and principles that are necessary in order to place the manifold *empirical ideas* in a regular relationship to one another, through which they first become *empirical knowledge [Erkenntnis]*, that is, experience (Kant 1900, 4, 8).

Looking back at his own education in his essay "Science and Culture," Weininger lampoons the "nonspirit" [*Ungeist*] of the science of his time. He wrote that science's understanding of itself "as comfort" had degraded "the human thirst for knowledge [*Erkenntnis*] to a monstrous degree unprecedented in all of human history" (Weininger 1904, 172). Weininger introduced this culture-critical treatise, which has been wrongly neglected by posterity in favor of *Sex and Character*, with a quotation from the Bible: "Woe to you lawyers! because you have taken away the key of *knowledge;* you have not entered yourselves, and those who were entering you have hindered" (Luke 11:52).

Looking at both texts together, one sees that Weininger chose to print the word "knowledge" in boldface. His quotation of these venerable sources betrays Weininger's effort to place his own writings in the line of a tradition that is above all criticism as well as to justify his own holy wrath. We should not be disrespectful when considering the evidence of his increasingly passionate, suffering-driven search for the true *ideas* behind phenomena; even his "strangest thoughts"[22] reveal a stance that the young Weininger had embraced in the prophecy of the condemned Socrates, the most impressive hero to Weininger in his Greek courses with Wilhelm Jerusalem. According to Plato's *Apology:*

You have done this to me because you hoped that you would be relieved from rendering an account of your lives, but I say that you will find the result far different. Those who will force you to give an account will be more numerous than heretofore; . . . and they will be harsher, inasmuch as they are younger, and you will be more annoyed. For it you think that by putting men to death you will prevent anyone from reproaching you because you do not act as you should, you are mistaken. That mode of escape is neither possible at all nor honourable, but the easiest and most honourable escape is not by suppressing others, but by making yourselves as good as possible (Plato [1914] 1966, 137–39).

Weininger's decided gift for languages[23] reveals its fateful drawback in the speed with which this voracious reader and avid debater went about absorbing disparate foreign ideas in an increasingly uncritical manner for his "work of clarification." Having decided to commit suicide, he wrote in his Notebook: "I believe that my intellectual powers are surely such that I would have become in a certain sense the resolver[24] of all problems. I do not believe that I could have gotten bogged down in error somewhere for very long. I believe that I would have earned the title of resolver, for that was my nature" (Weininger 1903, 603).

Fifteen years after the publication of *Sex and Character*—a symptomatic work for *fin-de-siècle* Vienna—the philosopher Ludwig Wittgenstein, who had grown up in upper middle-class Vienna, completed his enigmatic and highly influential first work, in spite of (and precisely because of) the "greatness" of Weininger's mistake in the eyes of his pronounced admirer and intellectual disciple.[25] His preface ends with the following words: "I am, therefore, of the opinion that the problems have in essentials been finally solved. And if I am not mistaken in this, then the value of this work secondly consists in the fact that it shows how little has been done when these problems have been solved" (Wittgenstein 1922, 29).

Proposition 6.43 of Wittgenstein's *Tractatus Logico-Philosophicus* states:

If good or bad willing changes the world, it can only change the limits of the
  world, not the facts; not the things that can be expressed in language.
In brief, the world must thereby become quite another. It must so to speak
  wax or wane as a whole.
The world of the happy is quite another than that of the unhappy.

II ✦
In Context

4 ✦

HOW DID WEININGER INFLUENCE WITTGENSTEIN?

Allan Janik

It is a distressing fact that we know precious little about the exact nature of Otto Weininger's influence upon Ludwig Wittgenstein (Wittgenstein 1977, 43). Thus at this time all answers to the question posed by the title of this article must be disarmingly conjectural. In various essays (Janik 1985) I have attempted to explore the ways in which Weininger's ideas might help bridge the gap between Wittgenstein's personal quest for integrity and his philosophical insistence that the most important questions in human life do not admit of answers. Till now I have preoccupied myself with Weininger's significance for understanding Wittengenstein's early work; here I want to extend that discussion to cover his lifelong quest for clarity. My assumption is that if Wittgenstein asserted that Weininger influenced him, that influence will refer to something absolutely central to Wittgenstein's philosophizing. So I shall be concerned here principally with the sort of influence that Weininger may have exerted upon Wittgenstein's *Philosophical Investigations* (1967) and *On Certainty* (1969). It will do well to preface the discussion with some observations on the meaning of "influence."

First of all, influence certainly does not mean that Wittgenstein endorsed or adopted any of the theses that Weininger advanced. The substance of Wittgenstein's philosophizing is radically different from Weininger's in every respect. Indeed, a philosopher of note is seldom "influenced" in the push-pull way that textbook histories suggest, such as Locke begat Berkeley who begat Hume, etc. That notion of influence, which construes the concept as the equivalent of causality in the history of ideas, would seem to be open to just the sort of difficulties that Hume found with causal arguments generally: the necessary connection cannot be inferred from mere conjunction. Moreover, in this case we have Wittgenstein's own statement that it is not anything positive in Weininger's work that is impressive but that Weininger's greatness lay in the monumentality of his very mistake (Wittgenstein 1974, 159). With a gesture in the direction of his early views about what the bivalence of the proposition that all propositions *must* be *either* true or false tells us about the world (i.e., how it is that we indirectly know how things are when we are sure of what is not the case), Wittgenstein suggests that by *negating* the whole of Weininger's *Sex and Character* you get an important truth. Unfortunately, the scope of Weininger's book is so wide-ranging and Wittgenstein's remark so isolated that this cryptic assertion alone is not sufficient to yield a clear meaning. Since we have virtually no other direct statements from Wittgenstein about the importance of Weininger for him, it is all but impossible to move from Weininger's work to Wittgenstein's in an informative and fruitful way. What we have to do in order to investigate the influence of Weininger upon Wittgenstein is to work backwards from central notions about Wittgenstein's conception of philosophy to see how they might be considered as emerging from a Weiningerian background.

If this seems strange, it should not, for it is altogether consonant with any robust understanding of the concept of influence as a matter of the *structuring of problems* rather than the details of their solutions (which, of course, can also be connected with the notion of influence but in a weaker and fundamentally less interesting way). But we are not yet finished with the concept of influence. The notion is interesting to the historian of ideas inasmuch as it refers to something *perspectival*. In the most significant sense it refers to a way of seeing problems such that certain of their aspects that were previously deeply puzzling are now accessible to explanation. Thus it is to learn, for example, the ways in which exposure to Haydn's string quartets affected Mozart's compositional strategy in approaching that genre. To understand Haydn's influence upon Mozart's string quartets is to learn how exposure to Haydn's work affected Mozart's understanding of just what sort of problems the string quartet actually presented. Thus construed, the concept of influence is intimately tied to understanding innovation and achievement in cultural history. It is much more a matter of explaining radical change in the history of ideas than it is of intellectual pushing and pulling. In short, influence, properly understood, refers to nothing less than the reconstruction of genesis of outstanding achievement. Thus, in the case of the question of Weininger's influence upon Wittgenstein it is a matter of asking: how is it at all possible that Wittgenstein attained the particular concept of philosophy that he did? And what role could Weininger have played in the development of that particular approach to philosophy that characterizes Wittgenstein's mature philosophy?

With that in mind let us look at Wittgenstein's mature view of philosophy. What is most striking at first glance is Wittgenstein's notion of philosophy as an activity directed against traditional philosophy in all its forms, not only its metaphysical (i.e., Scholastic or Cartesian) and transcendental (Hegelian or Kantian) forms, but also its traditional empiricist and analytic forms (Kenny 1982, 13). Wittgenstein is in this respect in line with the pragmatism of William James (and of his scientist-philosopher heroes Heinrich Hertz and Ludwig Boltzmann, whose proximity to pragmatism is all-too-seldom noticed) when he asks traditional philosophers whether their theories really make any difference to the practice of science or for that matter to art or religion or whatever. In this mood, Wittgenstein fully rejected the idea that philosophy could actually produce theories, not simply because he wanted to reform it such that it would conform to some ideal that *he* would impose upon it, but also on the good pragmatist ground that he shared, for all their differences, with someone like Otto Neurath, that *all* theories are as such on the same level: none are privileged. This means that where there is theory, there is science, regardless of what it calls itself. Try as we might, we can never succeed in producing a genuinely philosophical theory. But in rejecting the idea that philosophy could be a science, Wittgenstein, unlike Neurath and James, was not prepared to dismiss philosophical *problems* as *mere* pseudoproblems. On the contrary, for him the roots of the confusing pseudoproblems of philosophy are "deep disquietudes" rooted in our very language itself (Wittgenstein 1967, Part I, III).

For all that has been written about Wittgenstein, it is seldom noted how radically his later conception of language as a plurality of gamelike activities departs from the traditional accounts of philosophers and linguists (Janik 1989b, 5–7). For Wittgenstein, language is not merely a matter of words and sentences, but of their being *interwoven* with action. One of the most important aspects of the game analogy is to bring out how much more there is to language than semiotic units and syntax. Indeed, apart from linguistic behavior such as that of the baby who pulls its hand instinctively from the fire (Malcolm 1982), *all* human action is constituted through language inasmuch as nobody ever learns anything, including how to walk, in the absence of verbal encouragement in addition to instruction on what to do. This notion is thus a corollary to Wittgenstein's notion that we all learn through experience, but not our own experience. The point is that if we only look at words, sentences, and syntactical structures, the pragmatics of meaning through which the significance of those units is constituted will be wholly opaque to us. This is his point in wanting us to ponder the interactions of a group of builders who only use the words "block," "pillar," and "beam" as a *complete primitive language* (Wittgenstein 1967, Part I, 2); he wants to emphasize how much linguistic theorists from John Locke to Ferdinand de Saussure have left out of their accounts of language.

However important this conception of the constitutive role of language in human action may be, the story is only beginning to become interesting. No small part of Wittgenstein's well-deserved (if seldom well-understood) status in the pantheon of twentieth-century philosophers attaches to the fact that he was convinced that it was not mere superstition or ignorance (i.e., empirical factors) that had prevented philosophers from seeing this, but that this tendency was transcendental, to borrow a phrase from Immanuel Kant, in that it was rooted in a temptation presented by the very *forms* of words and sentences. Put differently, those very linguistic structures that make knowing and acting possible tend to deceive us when they themselves become the objects of inquiry.

Given the predominant role of representational expressions (i.e., nouns and verbs) in language as it is normally understood, we are tempted to forget that the representational function is but one of many linguistic acts and a highly developed one at that. So it is not that the forms of language themselves are not in order or that they are essentially deceptive, but that they tempt us to see language—and *a fortiori* ourselves—wrongly. This is where philosophical problems (which make up a wider class than merely the problems of philosophers) arise: words like "intention," "mind," and "thought" as well as "word" or "language" itself are as similar to words like "apple," "knife," or "shirt" that we are inclined to look for their meaning in the same ways. We are inclined to look for particular types of things that correspond to them rather than a loosely related set of actions. But this danger of "reification," as the Logical Empiricists were wont to call it, is only half of the problem for Wittgenstein, because what we in fact have to learn to grasp is that there is indeed something that corresponds to such words, but not *one* something. Instead, we must learn to see the plurality of loosely related referents as a family of concepts rather than members of a single species sharing fixed, common characteristics.

This position could be summarized in Wittgenstein's own favored expressions as follows. Typically metalworkers, actors, and concert pianists (to use examples that are not Wittgenstein's) are not particularly adept at articulating what they know qua metalworkers, actors, and concert pianists.[1] This should not be taken to mean that they do not really know anything, as Socrates wrongly inferred, but that their kind of knowledge does not lend itself to verbal expression. There are many things, as Saint Augustine pointed out with respect to the concept of time, that I fully well understand, but only as long as nobody asks me about them (Wittgenstein 1967, Part I, 89; cf. Augustine, 1963, 14). Wittgenstein's quasi-Platonic task is to assemble reminders of the multiplicity and nuances of those particular activities and, above all, to dissuade us from invidious comparisons; in this case from equating all knowledge with, say, physics. It is on his own account a literary effort to remind us of striking facts that the very nature of language tends to tempt us to pass over—e.g., the plurality of activities that correspond to the many modes of "thinking." Wittgenstein's uniqueness and standing in modern philosophy attach to his dual emphasis upon the facts that the human form of life is constituted by language and that there are quasitranscendental reasons why we are continually tempted to overlook or misinterpret ourselves when we theorize about language, knowledge, society, etc. So much for Wittgenstein's contributions to modern philosophy, but is this not a long way off from Weininger?

Certainly, at a cursory glance all of this would seem to have little indeed to do with the problems and views of the author of *Sex and Character*. However, this is only true to the extent that we confine ourselves to surface similarities. What Wittgenstein and Weininger share in their otherwise very different undertakings is the notion that there is a deep and ineliminable source of our tendency to self-deception in precisely those matters that are of greatest import to us. In Weininger this is connected with our sexuality in more subtle ways than are normally recognized in the literature; in Wittgenstein with our tendency to be dazzled by conventional grammar. By examining Weininger's way of articulating the problem of self-deception, we can come to see how he might have influenced Wittgenstein and what they do—and do not—have in common. However, a word of warning is necessary: in the absence of direct evidence from Wittgenstein himself as to exactly what he found so impressive in Weininger and in the face of the fact that similar ideas could be found in other authors Wittgenstein admired, to speak of Weininger in this context is conjectural and by no means excludes other parallel influences from philosophers from Plato and Augustine to Lichtenberg, Schopenhauer, and Kierkegaard. Nevertheless, there is one reason for asserting that his concern with a quasi-transcendental source of deception is connected with his admiration for Weininger: Wittgenstein is well known to have been taken by striking (i.e., puzzlingly startling) examples, and Weininger's work undoubtedly presented him with such striking examples in a way that the work of, say, Freud or Mach, with whom he has much more in common, did not. Moreover, Weininger alone of the figures that Wittgenstein claimed to have been influenced by strikingly emphasized this crucial point.

The fact that Weininger's work has itself come to be understood as forming a clichéd picture of the sexes should not obscure the fact that his work, no less than that of his admirer Karl Kraus, is fundamentally directed at exposing what Weininger took rightly to be the clichéd images of male and female that he found in his society. Weininger makes this clear on the very first page of his introduction to *Sex and Character*, where, following John Stuart Mill, he remarks that our conceptions as *partially* generalized abstractions stand between us and what they represent in two ways (Weininger 1980, 3). First, they oversimplify the multiplicity of the variations between individuals falling under the same concept. Second, they are as such imprecise.

Thus, in Weininger's view all of our concepts stand in need of a twofold clarification: an empirical and a conceptual one. (After the "linguistic turn" this would have to be, *pace* Weininger, nothing other than a critique of language.) We therefore find one of the many grounds for dividing his book into two parts in the way that he does. Empirically, his point of departure is that crude anatomy conceals the range of psychophysical sexual differences drastically and is itself one source of our tendency to produce a clichéd account of sexual differentiation. In line with the leading sexologists of the day, such as Havelock Ellis and Magnus Hirschfeld, he insists that, empirically considered, individuals are always sexually intermediate forms of which there is an infinite variety. Individuals are never absolutely male or female. However, as a gifted student of philosophy Weininger saw, as contemporary sexologists did not, that, if this were the case, then masculinity and femininity themselves needed scientific redefinition with respect to both the biochemical causes of sexual differences in individuals as well as the actual meaning of the terms "male" and "female." This eminently sensible undertaking is what Weininger's book vainly undertook to explore. An essential part of his investigation into the principles of sexual differentiation would have had to involve an account of the clichéd view of masculinity and femininity that corresponded to the sexual stereotypes he encountered in society. The resulting analysis is to be found in the last three chapters of *Sex and Character;* among other things, it bears essentially upon what Weininger terms "Judaism," but could have better been termed "conformism" to fit into his argument (Weininger 1903, 342–402, 403–41, 442–61).

From the start, in the face of incessant misunderstandings, it is necessary to emphasize that the second part of Weininger's book does not describe individuals but rather extremes along a spectrum between pure unbridled, unconscious instinct, the Female, and pure genius or rationality, the Male, neither of which do or can exist. Weininger's claim is that actual men and women will be more or less like these extremes in varying degrees and with all sorts of exceptions to the general truth. The Ideal Type Jew fits into Weininger's argument as the counterfeit (i.e., unreflective), pseudorationality of conventional mores. A discussion of the pseudomorality that is conformism is absolutely required by Weininger's general argument in the second part of his book (which we now know was always a part of his argument and not added after he wrote his dissertation).[2] Although Weininger insisted upon the identification of the Conformist Type, the Jew, with actual Jews as a matter of empirical fact (i.e., he basically claims something that assimilation wholly cancels) is incidental to his main argument. An analysis of conformism is required on Weininger's own view because real individuals, although always one or the other, male or female, are so in varying degrees, which is to say that they are intermediary forms. As the ideal type of psychophysical intermediacy, the Conformist must be absolutely mediocre. What is unusually clever (which is by no means the same as being true or correct) in Weininger is the way in which he characterizes how the conventional values of the conformist come into existence in all their bindingness; in its form (but not its substance), his argument anticipates such theories of the "social construction of reality" as those of Alfred Schutz, Jean-Paul Sartre, and Peter Berger.[3] At the middle of the spectrum the female's uninhibited sexuality and the male's unreflective demand for mechanical, external order meet in a drama that, Weininger thinks, is being played out in everyone's psyches. Actually, one of the problems with Weininger's book is that his views about actual moral relations between the sexes (i.e., male exploitation of female weakness) are not fully developed.

Conformism, then, involves corrupting reason into rationalization. The key to understanding it is the phenomenon of projection.[4] We project upon others what we find lacking in ourselves and thereby determine our conduct toward them as well as their conduct toward us. Our projections thus constitute actual social relations. To the extent that a person is male, he determines his own conduct according to Kant's Categorical Imperative, i.e., on the basis of a logical analysis of his projected course of action. To the extent that a person is female, she is passively receptive to her surroundings, i.e., indiscriminately seeking gratification from them. But these two types are never encountered in their absolute form but in varying degrees as conformism. To the extent that a person is conformist, he aggressively blends into his surroundings. Rather than assuming the role of legislator with respect to his own behavior, as Kant stipulates, he merely imitates what he finds before him. His attitude to everything in life is external, unreflective, and mechanical. The male has universal respect for personality and is consequently capable of renouncing sexuality rather than reducing a person to a mere means to his own pleasure. The female is entirely determined by her biochemistry to be wholly preoccupied with the gratification of her instinctual desires. The conformist's sexuality is rooted in the perversion of the former by the latter in a peculiar sort of conditioning. Thus, the conformist is a slave to a socially constructed *idea* of sexuality. What Weininger offers here is a not altogether uninteresting psychogenetic account of how the assumption of more or less typical females and conformist males condition one another into producing conformist behavior patterns.

As we have seen, the key to understanding society is the phenomenon of projection, according to which the female and the conformist male project onto one another what they find lacking in themselves. The male projects his desire to possess, i.e., the notion that happiness is a matter of what you have rather than what you are, upon the female's sexuality. In his desire to possess the female's sexuality, the conformist mythologizes himself as the deflowerer of virginity, which is the ultimate possession. In practice he requires the female to live in accord with his desire, i.e., virginally; for only then can he experience the consummate pleasure of possessing her. Thus, the very value that shapes the female's indiscriminate yearnings by demanding that they be held in control, precisely because it is wholly contrary to nature, becomes the cause of a deep inner division within her—hysteria. At the same time, from the proprietary sense that the conformist male projects upon her, the female comes to desire to have the same sort of social and political freedom that the male possesses, and the idea of woman's emancipation arises (presumably) as a reaction against being reduced to the status of a mere possession of the male. On the other hand, the shallowness of the conformist is such that he is prepared to do whatever is required to possess the female. So he acquiesces to become Don Giovanni actively as she projects her voracious but passive appetite upon him. The female in the woman is thus in a curious way the cause of her own frustration, which she seeks to eliminate politically, in a way that is wholly unnatural and can only lead to her yet higher degree of estrangement from Weininger's point of view. As things stand, the female both longs for and fears her seducer. Her fear is thus the source of her desire for emancipation, her longing of the modern cult of sexuality: "Thus one man is intent to show the other that he fulfills his sexual function with conscientious loyalty and delight. Today woman is determined such that she only appreciates what is 'manly' in men—the sexual side. Men receive the measure of their masculinity from her hands" (Weininger 1903, 444). In this way the pseudorationality of conventionalism arises. The female is wholly the slave of her passions and thus cannot be expected to do anything to change this situation. The male *is* able to do so, but given his commitment to the status quo, *will not*. Hope for human beings lies in the conformist's ability to grasp the error of his ways and, ultimately, to overcome the female in himself, even if this is not something that he can ever hope to achieve.

However fanciful this story may be—it is really a kind of Platonic myth—at its core lies the notion that, in social relationships as they stand, our very concepts of ourselves are subtly conditioned by what men and women expect of one another such that their actions are determined by something that is essentially foreign to their nature without ever being felt to be so. Moreover, in their unenlightened efforts to overcome their torments, males and females in fact intensify them. Furthermore, the female element in the human personality (remember, for Weininger this is something that ought to be biochemically determinable) moves us to act to gratify our desires immediately and unquestioningly at the cost (at least in his account) of abandoning all real chances for self-fulfillment. In short, our covert desire for autonomy is systematically undermined. Our psychic conditioning is such that we collectively condemn ourselves to collect water with a sieve, as Plato once put it. In seeking what we uninformedly (i.e., with respect to the stipulations of Kantian ethics) take to be self-fulfillment, we systematically frustrate and alienate ourselves, albeit in a way that we neither can nor will understand. In Weininger's view, the hope for real emancipation is that a study of sexuality that is at once moral and scientific, a kind of critical theory by today's standards, will show the way beyond self-centeredness. Interestingly, the sort of problem that preoccupied the Kierkegaard of *Either/Or* with respect to how the irrational person could ever be moved rationally to choose rationality does not seem to have occurred to Weininger (cf. Schrader 1972, 321–41). His hope seems to be that a truly moral science of sexuality will show us to ourselves in such a way that the rational demand to exercise self-discipline, to treat personality in ourselves or in others always as an end and never merely as a means, will become apparent to males who are capable of it.

Thus construed, the most important assumption in Weininger's work is that we cannot trust our own ideas. Like his admirer Sir Karl Popper,[5] Weininger insists that we must stand in a critical relation to our own ideas and beliefs—and in the end somewhat schizophrenically to ourselves. Here we can begin to glimpse what Wittgenstein probably meant by saying the book tells an important truth if only you put a "~" in front of it. The mature Wittgenstein, unlike Weininger, was convinced that philosophical problems about knowledge, thinking certainty, mind and body, and the like could only be "solved" to the extent that they were dissolved by coming to see the natural history of the human species rightly. This is principally a matter of closely looking at how human beings *learn* to perform the most fundamental tasks in life. Thus, the end to which he assembles reminders is to show us how our natural endowment—i.e., the natural rootedness of the social, or natural, character of language—so illuminates traditional philosophical problems as to eliminate them altogether from resting upon oversimplified questions, misleading examples, and misconceived comparisons.

For Wittgenstein, unlike Weininger, it is not a question of overcoming nature in us but of recognizing just what we have from nature. Interestingly, Rush Rhees comments upon the differences between Wittgenstein and Weininger with respect to their own Judaism in just these terms: for Weininger, it is a matter of identifying what is really Jewish in himself so that he can transcend it; for Wittgenstein, it is simply a matter of recognizing something that he may have no control over whatsoever (Rhees 1981, 197). Thus, Wittgenstein would seem to recognize, while Weininger would basically reject, our fundamental animality. Indeed, for Wittgenstein the idea that we can somehow transcend nature is all but incomprehensible: with a vengeance before which even an Aristotle would pale, Wittgenstein radically affirms our animality. Thus, in his last work he could insist upon considering man as an animal to the point of asserting that even logic had to be understood form this point of view (Wittgenstein 1969, 501).

Indeed, it is among Wittgenstein's most monumental achievements to have shown that the logic of life, that systemacity upon which human action is based, has precious little to do with formal logic. The uniqueness of Wittgenstein's position here is based upon his central insight into the nature of rule-following behavior, namely, that the sort of behavior through which human action is constituted is learned through practice alone, without recourse to any explicit rules (Wittgenstein 1969, 95). Thus, Wittgenstein describes the world-picture that is implicit in that system as a "kind of mythology" (Wittgenstein 1969, 475). The essential feature of this mythology is that our very participation in the myth prevents us from being able to give an account of the actual foundations of our knowledge and action in the form of a theory. Knowing and acting involve investigating reality (roughly: scientific activity), which itself is contingent upon our capacity to represent reality. However, even in everyday life this is a much more sophisticated procedure that we are inclined to think. Moreover, the capacity to represent reality is something we learn only after we have learned any number of other things, principally how to execute orders. So representation is an activity that already presupposes that we have learned a great deal. The kind of "knowing" that representation presupposes is principally a matter of drilling (*Abrichtung,* or "dressage," is Wittgenstein's word for it). It is a knowing with the body rather than with the mind, and for that very reason, like Augustine confronted with the question, "What is time?" we are entirely stumped when we are asked to give an account of what we know—again think of the metalworkers, actors, or concert pianists. The deeply puzzling character of the question tempts us to think that we need a theory to fathom the depths of its mystery; but in fact the solution lies so close as to be hidden on the surface (to borrow a phrase from Hugo von Hofmannsthal) of our conduct. For this reason Wittgenstein needs to assemble reminders for us, reminders that *strikingly* drive home how much we normally accept unquestioningly about the world and ourselves in the course of our normal routines.[6]

The point is that philosophers are continually tempted to overlook just those aspects of *learning* that contain the key to understanding why the *questions* that those philosophers raise are radically misconceived. The need for clarity about those misconceptions is connected to a basic misunderstanding of the logic of our language. This is why the clarity Wittgenstein seeks is very different from that of the formal logician. It dictates Wittgenstein's philosophical strategy and therefore explains why aphorisms, questions (often unanswered), and thought experiments play such a large role in this kind of philosophizing against the philosophers and against the philosopher in all of us. The actual dissolution of philosophical problems has to be a matter of seeing both how those problems arise out of a misunderstanding of the logic of language and how they disappear once we have grasped it correctly. All this turns upon something that cannot be represented: you have to look at the practice. Anthony Kenny has rightly argued that this notion of philosophizing ties it principally to the will rather than to the intellect (Kenny 1982, 26).

For reasons that are by no means arbitrary but lie deep within the nature of language, i.e., within human nature itself, the tendency to allow ourselves to be confused by the surface grammar of language must be combated by teaching us not something new and different to *believe* but to *do* something that traditional philosophical education rules out. This is why Wittgenstein's examples must be *striking* and why they frequently take the form of fictive natural histories.

Finally, Wittgenstein's point of contact with Weininger comes clearly into sight: for both Wittgenstein and Weininger, philosophical problems are problems that can only be solved by a change of heart. The desired transition from a theoretical to a practical perspective—for Weininger in ethics, for Wittgenstein in metaphysics and the theory of knowledge—is not a mere intellectual matter, because the temptation to confusion lies in our very ways of living rather than in the sphere of abstract thought. On the view that I have taken here, it was Weininger who first loudly and clearly raised the issue of just what it is about human knowledge and action itself that tempts us to misconstrue them as we seek to understand them. So it is not that Wittgenstein found something in Weininger that he could simply take over lock, stock, and barrel, but that he found a deep puzzle to ponder, which musings, *inter alia*, led him to the most radical critique of language—and philosophy—that our century has produced.

5 ✦

WEININGER AND LOMBROSO: A QUESTION OF INFLUENCE

Nancy A. Harrowitz

To better understand Otto Weininger and the influence of his *Sex and Character*, we need to better comprehend both the cultural context in which Weininger and his book appeared and other texts that may have influenced him. This may seem to be an obvious and clear task, but the issues surrounding Weininger's text are anything but obvious and clear, and so the task becomes fraught with difficulties. The concerns that a reading of Weininger raises—the dynamics of self-hatred, the question of the importance of milieu and historical context, the relations between different kinds of prejudice, for example—are not only polemical but diabolically complex.

A familiarity with the work of Cesare Lombroso is important to the project of comprehending Weininger for several reasons.[1] The first is a question of sources, since Weininger makes direct reference to Lombroso's work on women in the footnotes to *Sex and Character*. The others have to do with similarities between the two authors that go beyond Weininger's indebtedness to Lombroso for certain of his theories. These similarities paved the way for the warm welcome that a generation of Italian intellectuals gave Weininger's theories in the early part of this century. Finally, an examination of the relation of Lombroso to Weininger illustrates the problem of how to consider influence, whether it is the influence of intertextuality or that of historical context.

Cesare Lombroso was a well known and highly influential Italian criminologist who also considered himself a (pre-Freudian) psychiatrist. Lombroso's attempts to standardize an approach to the criminal resulted in his categories of the physical signs of a criminal body. Lombroso was born in Turin in 1835 and died in 1909. Educated as a doctor, his main interests included psychiatry and anthropometry, and he describes himself in his 1894 text *L'antisemitismo e le scienze moderne* (Antisemitism and Modern Science) as a practitioner of psychiatry and experimental anthropology. Lombroso was generally considered the greatest prison reformer since Cesare Beccaria. Some of his ideas, such as indeterminate sentencing, parole, and juvenile court, are still widely used in the United States. Along with Lombroso's innovative ideas regarding the criminal mind and body came a whole set of categories governing what might be called the "management of cultural difference." According to this approach, if society can understand the physical as well as the moral dimensions of crime, it can better contain its criminal elements.

During his time, and for at least thirty years after his death, Lombroso's theories were taken very seriously by scientists and the general public alike. Leon Radzinowicz writes that "virtually every element of value in contemporary criminological knowledge owes its formulation to that very remarkable school of Italian criminologists who took pride in describing themselves as the 'positivists' " (quoted in Lombroso-Ferrero 1972, IX). According to Leonard D. Savitz, who wrote the introduction to the most current edition in translation of Lombroso's *Criminal Man*, there is a general consensus that Lombroso and the school of positivist criminology that resulted from his theories had a tremendous impact on the development of criminology, and the country in which his theories had the most influence was the United States.[2]

In the later stage of his career, Lombroso turned his attention to two cultural targets that were much closer to him than the world of the criminal: woman and the Jew. The choice of subject is not surprising, since scientists since Darwin had been trying to understand the place of the female in evolution, and racialist science had been studying the Jew in relation to some of the same questions raised by studies of women and other groups. What perhaps is surprising is that Lombroso waited so long to study these two groups. In 1893 he published (with his son-in-law Guglielmo Ferrero) *La donna delinquente, la prostituta e la donna normale* (The Criminal Woman, the Prostitute, and the Normal Woman), thus turning his attention to the "fairer" sex. Fairer on the outside, perhaps, but with an atavistic viciousness lying just under the surface of calm, serene, and idealized nineteenth-century womanhood. We note a distinct difference between Lombroso's treatment of the male criminal, set forth in his 1879 text *L'uomo delinquente* (Criminal Man), and the female. Lombroso, in identifying the *"criminale nato"* (born criminal), does not attempt to define what is particularly "male" about these criminals. He does connect criminal behavior with atavistic signs that link the criminal with a primitive, savage world. When Lombroso concentrates on the female of the criminal species, as it were, the focus of analysis changes as he attempts to define what is female, as if the question "What is female?" were as important as "What is the female criminal?" In fact, he ultimately conflates these two questions, making his interpretation of the identity of the prostitute a middle ground to facilitate this move between the identity of woman and that of the female criminal. Just what *is* female for Lombroso, in the "normative" sense he sets out to establish, is laid forth in the last section of this long text.[3] For Lombroso, the three terms "woman criminal," "prostitute," and "woman," were inseparable, and he theorizes this inseparability over and over.

Criminality becomes the model by which to understand woman, because, as Lombroso repeats many times, the normal woman is but a criminal whose immoral, criminal tendencies are kept in abeyance by maternal instincts and by society. These points are made repeatedly in *La donna delinquente*, as he refers to "that latent base of immorality that is found in every woman" and "that latent base of evil that is found in every woman."[4] Woman's salvation—and, it would appear, also her damnation— is physiology: "maternity is, we would almost say, itself a moral vaccination against crime and evil."[5] It appears that not only maternity but also culture and bourgeois society help to keep the criminal tendencies in women at bay. Culture, for the male, is instead his product, and thus the male criminal, criminal behavior, immorality, and the like are atavistic throwbacks. The "normal" male hence has no connection to atavism. There is the sense here that the male criminal is in fact ultimately not responsible for his condition, because of the compelling force of atavism. Women on the other hand are all potential criminals, and only the soothing forces of culture and their maternal physiology may or may not keep this criminality suppressed.

Women are continually described by Lombroso as "closer to nature" than men: more atavistic, closer to her ancestor, the female savage. The sexual nature of primitive woman provides another link to modern woman, as Lombroso asserts that "if primitive woman was only rarely an assassin, she was, as we have proved above [. . .], always a prostitute, and remained thus almost until the semicivilized epoch; so even atavistically one can explain that the prostitute must have more regressive traits than the female criminal."[6]

Lombroso goes to great lengths to explain both his conception of the prostitute and the history of prostitution, since he believes that this history will shed light on modern woman. Another important aspect of prostitutes is their virility, precisely that which, according to Lombroso, makes them less female. Certain physical characteristics mark them as virile; for example, he describes the masculine larynx he claims is often found on prostitutes—"one would say the larynx of a man. And thus in the larynx, as well as the face and the cranium, the characteristics particular to them come out: virility"—and notes as well the "virile distribution of hair" found in many prostitutes.[7] He then offers a theory of the mutability of the characteristics of the young prostitute as she ages:

> Even in the most beautiful criminals, however, their virile aspect—the exaggeration of the jaw, the cheekbones—is never missing, just as it is never

missing in any of our great courtesans. Thus they all have a familial look which links the Russian sinners to those who pound the streets, whether they be gilded carriages or humble rags. When youth disappears, those jaws and plump rounded cheeks give way to prominent angles and makes the face completely virile, uglier than a man. Wrinkles deepen like a wound, and that once pleasing face shows the degenerate type which youth had hidden.[8]

We see in this description a discursive shifting from a scientific mode of observation ("the exaggeration of the jaw, the cheekbones") to a more poetic one ("wrinkles deepen like a wound"). This shifting ultimately ends in stereotyping: the image of the beautiful woman turns out to be but a façade, with an ugly wrinkled hag—a virile one in this case—lying just underneath the surface that youth provides. The underlying notion is of the woman as trickster and as falsification personified as she seduces her client through her youthful appearance, which hides the "man" underneath. The idea that a certain type of woman is really a man under the surface is compounded by what she does for a living, as it were. The fact that she sells sex, what is supposed to be specifically female sex, to her male clients, and that Lombroso is suggesting that she is not really female at all, casts an even more onerous light on the situation. What is being sold is pure artifice, then: not female, thus not female sex, but rather a kind of androgynous, falsified, and cheating substitution.

The contradiction in Lombroso's analysis of the prostitute is apparent: the "normal" woman is closer to nature, in other words more atavistic, than man. Primitive woman, as he states openly, equals prostitution. Yet the prostitute is figured as virile. So what is less female is at the same time more: more atavistic, i.e., more prostitute; more prostitute, less female. This confusion of categories is emblematic of Lombroso and provides a thematic link to the work of Weininger inasmuch as both attempt to theorize gender difference.

Lombroso, like some other nineteenth-century scientists, believed that women had much in common with children. They lie "naturally," he says, as if lying were part of their natures. At the beginning of the section of *La donna delinquente* entitled "Lie," Lombroso tells us that "to show that the lie is habitual and almost physiological to women would be superfluous because it is so widespread in popular legend." He then lists ten proverbs, such as "women always say the truth, but never in its entirety," and "women—says Dohm—use lies like the bull uses his horns."[9] He follows up the proverbs with citations from Flaubert, Schopenhauer, Zola, Molière, and Stendhal, all claiming the purported propensity of women to untruth.

Lombroso makes no distinction between quotations from the literary creations of these authors and direct statements from the authors themselves regarding the subject. In his analysis of what is female (and how male culture can manage to live with the female), Lombroso often uses proverbs to back up his conclusions. His adoption of cultural expressions such as proverbs and sayings to make a "scientific" point is the most audacious part of his argument, and shows the irrefutable link between the cultural prejudices he draws upon as evidence and his own bias toward the subject. No distance is thus taken between the proverbs Lombroso cites, the cultural voices he quotes, and the personal opinions and conclusions he expresses regarding women and lying.

According to Lombroso, women are morally deficient, vengeful, and jealous. In his discussion of women criminals, he points out their shortcomings and excesses in the area of language, saying that "one understands how the chattering about the crime is more frequent in the woman than in the man, because she must supplement all those means that the male has to relive the image of the crime, like drawings and writing, that we see lacking in the woman. The woman speaks often of her crimes, just as the man draws them, writes about them, or sculpts them in vases, etc."[10]

It would seem that women criminals, in Lombroso's appraisal, talk too much and write too little. Elsewhere he tells us that women are lacking skills and development in the graphic area of the brain, which would explain their reluctance or inability to write at a very sophisticated level. He tells us also that women criminals quite literally cannot keep their mouths shut about their crimes, that they are compelled to tell someone about them and to brag about them. At the same time, they will stick to the most audacious lies, even when confronted with absolute proof of their ridiculousness. Lombroso concludes from this that women have a poor sense of reality when it comes to truth, that reality is actually estranged from them in some way. His pinpointing of language as a locus of attack is significant in that language is very often, in the discourse of bigotry, exactly that part of the culture of difference that is singled out as particularly threatening. The charge that women lie, are unreliable linguistically, are underdeveloped in this area, and do not understand the difference between truth and lies thus fits into a more general attack. If the language of difference can be made out as entirely unreliable, then it proves in some way that the difference is unreliable, threatening, and unstable as well, not part of culture, unacceptable because of the threat of the unknown that it poses. Sander Gilman's landmark study of antisemitism and the role that language plays in the establishment of categories of intolerance demonstrates this point (Gilman 1986).

Lombroso's views of women discussed above proclaim a correlation to Weininger's text and show why Lombroso's theories would have appealed to Weininger. We can go beyond the question of directly cited textual influence and look at Lombroso's views on women and Jews together: a juxtapositioning that pulls Lombroso and Weininger even closer together than the citation of a few footnotes would suggest. As a major proponent of an important part of that new science, the originator of the atavistic theory of the criminal, Lombroso was thought to be the scientist who could challenge the theoreticians of antisemitism on their scientific methodologies and overall merit. Lombroso did just this with his text of 1894, a proported defense of the Jews from the biologically based racism developing at the time.

Lombroso begins his text by explaining its origin in the requests he received to write it and the investigative urge that spurred him on. As he says of antisemitism, "I felt that disgust that seizes even the least impatient scientist when he has to study the most revolting human secretions. Deciding whether hatred between peoples can be justified, in our times, is certainly a difficult and sad enterprise, and it is not easy to get comfortable with it."[11] Lombroso insists in this introduction that the new methods available to him from psychiatry and experimental anthropology, and his own new method of scientific inquiry, "safeguarded me against the perils of partiality, so great in matters like this."[12] Later in the preface, after listing some of the materials and authors he has consulted in his study, he says that "the help of such assorted experts from the nations richest with antisemites and with philosemites was a token to me of the rectitude and the impartiality of my judgment, for he who doubts the instrument that I have handled for a short period of time."[13] Clinging to his role as dispassionate objective scientist, Lombroso does not tell us that he himself is Jewish. We see nonetheless three points of anxiety thus far in this short preface that would seem to be related to this fact: his concern over justifying antisemitism, his worry about impartiality, and his justification of himself as a competent author of such a study. Similar claims are not made, for example, in his book on women, and yet that analysis would seem to warrant corresponding concerns. The emphasis on impartiality can be read as the prevailing ideology of scientific methods, and as a claim to authority and mastery over the material. It can also be read as an expression of Lombroso's anxiety that he is perhaps too close to the subject.

The text is divided into short chapters that discuss different aspects of antisemitism. The first, entitled "Cause," attempts to analyze the general phenomenon of racial intolerance. At the end of a short historical sketch of antisemitism, Lombroso tacks on some reasons for antisemitism that he directly attributes to the nature of the Jewish community itself: "Segregation of habitation, the dissonance of the customs, the food, the languages, and the competition in business that breeds jealousy, increases real and apparent disparities, making their vilification desirable and useful to individuals and even the state; finally the psychic epidemic that diffuses and multiples hates and legends."[14]

Religious and cultural difference itself is vilified in Lombroso's analysis, as he blames the victim and in so doing leads us into his next chapter, entitled "Difetti degli ebrei" (Defects of the Jews). Beginning this chapter with the statement that "the character of those persecuted certainly contributed to their persecution" allows Lombroso to continue on the path he initiated at the end of the last chapter, that of blaming the victim for the sins of the perpetrator.[15] He continues with an explanation of how certain traits and cultural customs of the Jews have contributed to their persecution and prejudice. Lying and cleverness are mentioned immediately as two of the defects; the lying brings to mind the critique Lombroso made of women. The figure of the Jew that Lombroso draws in this chapter is similar to the stereotypes used by many racist theorists: the cheating merchant, the dual personality, the person capable of chameleon-like rapid changes as the situation necessitates, etc.

The thrust of Lombroso's attack lies in his critique of what we might call the singularity of the Jews: those customary practices that constitute their difference from Christian society. Lombroso chooses three major points of attack: the use of Passover matzoh, the wearing of *tefillin* (phylacteries), and the practice of circumcision. Passover matzoh comes under fire precisely because it is a mark of difference: "the stupid ritual of Passover matzoh, which, since it differs from usage among the local people, naturally stirs up ridicule and revulsion, which grows due to the exaggerated importance that the Orthodox attach to it."[16]

What is particularly interesting about Lombroso's text is his logic of what constitutes difference and how he analyzes and interprets that difference. Elsewhere in his text Lombroso again points out *"gergo"* (jargon) as another difference that, along with strange customs, marginalizes the Jew (Lombroso 1894). Difference is perceived most dramatically when it is visual or aural. Another way in which cultural difference is figured as problematic in the history of antisemitic intolerance is through language. Language has been a crucial site of attention in the history of antisemitism. According to the theorists of antisemitism, language was the vilifying mark of difference that set the Jews apart. In *Jewish Self-Hatred: Anti-Semitism and the Hidden Language of the Jews*, Gilman maintains that language in the history of antisemitism, and especially during the Renaissance, was overdetermined as the most important demarcation of the radical split between Christianity and Judaism. The language of the Jews was seen as the location of fundamental theological differences. These differences were immediately translated into social sign through a displacement of theology onto language. Gilman analyzes the ways in which the language of the Jews often became a point of attack for their enemies. Hebrew and then Yiddish were perceived as secret or hidden languages, with magical properties. The hidden language was thought to conceal from the Christian world a number of religious and social differences that denied Christianity. The language of the Jews was thus perceived as both a foreign language and a discourse; as Gilman says, "it is evident that the myth-building that surrounds the concept of a 'hidden' language of the Jews links both language and discourse in the stereotype of the Jew" (Gilman 1986, ix). The differences between the Christian world and the world of Judaism were summed up in antisemitic theory under the rubric of language, and so the language of the Jews came under attack. Lombroso's choice of language as a point of attack thus fits into a long tradition of antisemitism: a disquisition on discourse as that which distinguishes, yet ultimately confuses, Jewish culture and the theology of Judaism.

Both too atavistic and too modern, the Jews become scapegoats for the modern age. The contradiction is obvious: Lombroso says repeatedly that the Jews do not sufficiently conform in either custom or dress to the country in which they live. How then could they bear the "wounds of modernity," as he claims elsewhere in his text (Lombroso 1894, p. 100), if in fact, as he suggests, they are living in a past age? The word that he uses for "wounds"—*piaga*—is a telling one, for it may also refer to stigmata.

Lombroso reads language and religious customs as primitive, yet the Jew is made to represent the worst of modernity. Finally he employs a Christian logic and vocabulary of relics, saints, and Jesus to analyze and then stigmatize difference. It is also revealing that Lombroso adopts the language of the scientists who had labeled the signs of hysteria "stigmata," a term that has a rich Christian significance. Not only do stigmata refer to the wounds of Jesus, but the verb "to stigmatize" has some interesting shades of significance. "To stigmatize" means to label in a negative way; the referent is both physical, as it refers to the wounds of Jesus left by the nails of the cross, and cultural, as it refers to that which is different and undesirable. A great irony is created by Lombroso's choice of the term "stigmata" in the particular context in which he uses it: Lombroso the Jewish scientist uses the word to refer to the marks of difference apparent on the bodies of criminals. In *La donna delinquente*, he also uses it metaphorically: "an important stigmata of degeneration is the lack of maternal affection in many female born criminals."[17] His own stigmatization as a Jew can thus be seen as displaced onto the even more unfortunate and stigmatized body of the criminal, the woman, and the all-so-distant figure of the Orthodox Jew.

The logic of cultural difference becomes a pretext for derision as Lombroso attempts to assign a logic to, and then make absurd, the practice of religious ritual. In this text, on the surface an objective scientific defense of the Jews, Lombroso adopts the logic of antisemitism in order to analyze the practice of cultural difference. He attacks the Jews for their cultural difference, for those practices that in fact make them Jewish, and he singles out their alleged attitudes toward language as the basis of this critique of difference. Purportedly an examination of the relationship between antisemitism and modern science, the text quickly changes direction. It soon becomes clear that it is not really a book on this topic at all, but rather one on two related subjects: who the Jews are and how Lombroso feels about that. The text would have been more accurately entitled "Antisemitism and the Modern Scientist"—the scientist, of course, being a Jewish one, represented by Lombroso himself.

Lombroso's conclusion is that assimilation is the answer to the problem of antisemitism; in other words, the solution is the total obliteration of difference. Lombroso employs a different kind of logic in his last assessment of cultural practices, as he explains the need for assimilation:

> It is time for the Jews to persuade themselves that many of their rituals belong to other epochs and that their useless strangeness (matzoh and circumcision, for example) make one suspect profane customs for which they themselves feel a maximum disgust. If all other religions have modified their essence, not only their dress, according to the times, why can't they [the Jews] modify at least a smattering? Why not renounce that savage wounding that is circumcision, those many fetishes of sacred writing or of some of their sentences, that they place around the house and even bind onto their bodies, just like amulets, thus conserving without knowing it that adoration of letters that the first discoverers had and that savages still have?[18]

Lombroso lists here just exactly what it is that bothers and frustrates him about the Jews: the dress, customs, and religious habits that separate them from other people. He goes further in his assessment of *tefillin* and *mezuzot*, calling them fetishes.[19] Lombroso's desire for Jews to give up their religious practices because they are outmoded, not reasonable, and the like is based on a logic of culture that becomes meaningless if applied to religion. The equivalent might be telling Catholics to give up the concept of the Virgin Mary because such a story is impossible medically or scientifically, and is based on a primitive story that modern science has proved untenable. Seen in this light, applying what Lombroso would call scientific logic to religion is nothing short of absurd. Once again, however, it must be noted that what Lombroso is attacking are differences that are strongly visual.

Unlike Weininger, Lombroso is attempting to save the Jews from something: the racist rhetoric of biologically based antisemitism. In so doing, Lombroso has adopted, wittingly or not, the racist logic of the erasure of difference. The topic of assimilation for the Jews in the late nineteenth century is a difficult and complicated one. The assimilationist movement was not always an attempt to leave Judaism behind and convert to Christianity, but rather in part an attempt to move away from Orthodoxy, although the ramifications of assimilation are every bit as serious as outright conversion.[20] Assimilation and a physical exodus to another place were both seen as potential ways to eliminate the uncomfortable status of marginality, two sides of the same coin. Theodor Herzl's solution was Zionism: a land where Jews would not be outsiders. Lombroso's solution was the obliteration of difference.[21]

Lombroso's defense of the Jews lies almost entirely in his criticism of the sense of proportion involved. To his credit, he does take on the most ferocious theorists of antisemitism, destroying their arguments in his discussion of the problem of biologically based racism. He does not believe that cultural differences, although they make for divisiveness and derision, are reason enough for the viciousness of antisemitism, and he posits extreme antisemitism as a disease in itself. He discusses the political scope of antisemitism, and how it has been used by political factions for their own ends. "Another epidemic bacillus" is how he describes that which propagates antisemitism, which he calls elsewhere "the germs of the illness."[22] Lombroso is using terms he can understand in a scientific framework of illness—an illness that then has a potential cure. However, his cure for the illness is the demise of the patient—no more germs, so no more epidemic. This is a haunting precursor of Weininger's solution of the extinction of the human race that he posits at the end of *Sex and Character*.

LOMBROSO, WOMEN, AND JEWS

Like Weininger, Lombroso ends up joining his analyses of women and Jews. Unlike Weininger, Lombroso's way of doing this is not overt. The intersection of women and Jews comes about almost, it would seem, by accident, when Lombroso is busy determining the "real" nature of woman. In *La donna delinquente*, Lombroso provides a short history of prostitution that is divided into sections, one of which is entitled "Sacred Prostitution" and deals with the history of prostitution within religious sects. It is here that Lombroso's prejudicial opinions regarding Jews and women are most clear: namely, when the two categories collide and the topic becomes Jewish women, which in turn becomes, in Lombroso's perspective, Jewish prostitutes. This collision—or collusion—creates a very great moment of tension in the text, as we will see presently.

At the beginning of the section dealing with religious prostitution, Lombroso states, "Among the Jews, before the definitive version of the Tablets of Law, the father had the right to sell the daughter to a man who would make her his concubine for a period of time established by the sales contract. The daughter sold in this way for the profit of her father did not gain anything from the forced abandonment of her body, except in the case where the man would engage her to his son and so would substitute her with another concubine. The Jews trafficked thus in the prostitution of their own daughters."[23] This shocking passage brings up not a few questions pertaining to its interpretation. Could this terrible accusation possibly have been true in any way? Could Lombroso have had some kind of source for this statement, even an untrue one? The answer to the first question is probably no, to the second probably yes.[24] The kinds of questions generated by this passage go well beyond any that are localized in the sense of looking at biblical history and its interpreters through the centuries to determine if Lombroso was right or wrong. What is important here is not so much proving that Lombroso either had a source or even made this up entirely out of his own prejudices to serve his own agenda, but rather that he gives the episode so much emphasis and that he frames certain questions within the context of this passage. Other forms of religious prostitution merit a paragraph here, a sentence there in this chapter. Three full pages are devoted to the role of the Jews in prostitution, and other references appear elsewhere in the text. In fact, it is clear from this section that Lombroso makes the connection between Jews and prostitutes just as often as he is able.

The question of the interpretation of the passage itself and the images that are embedded within looms large in this scenario. The first image is the stereotype of the greedy Jew who capitalizes on the body of his female child. This image is emphasized with the words "for the profit of her father." Even more insidious is the notion that somehow the daughter is being deprived of the profit she herself could have made! Lombroso is careful to point this out, as he says that "the daughter sold in this way . . . did not gain anything"—as if her profit from prostitution would have made the outcome positive and therefore fully acceptable. The second image is that of the Jewish woman as prostitute. Here the daughter is figured as a potential prostitute who is stymied by her father's insistence on making the profit himself. This last point is emphasized once again by the statement that "the Jews trafficked thus in the prostitution of their own daughters." The connection between Jews and prostitutes made in early modern culture has been analyzed by Sander Gilman in " 'I'm Down on Whores': Race and Gender in Victorian London," as he says, "The relationship between the Jew and the prostitute also has a social dimension. For both Jew and prostitute have but one interest, the conversion of sex into money or money into sex" (Gilman 1990b, 161). This is an apt description of Lombroso's passage, as the two parties—father and daughter—are literally competing for the right to profit from her body.

There is something so intense about the intersection of women and Jews in Lombroso's text that it causes an outright derailing of his scientific methodology. This is even more noticeable in a text that obsessively cites its sources, whether they be physical measurements from studies or proverbs. Here instead Lombroso does not cite other scholars at all. There is a self-confidence about the material presented in this section that creates a different tone than found elsewhere in Lombroso's work. Usually in his texts there seems to be the assumption that citations from other experts, numbers from studies, measurements, and so on are required to support his statements, even if these "proofs" are specious. In this section, however, there is the sense that because he is dealing with a biblical text—in other words, with common cultural knowledge—and perhaps also because he himself is Jewish and these are his forebears whose behavior he is analyzing—he does not need to cite anyone else and is free to come up with these outrageous interpretations.

Already in this text we have seen Lombroso mingling the terms for the "normal" woman, the prostitute, and the criminal. When the figure of the Jewish father is introduced as another player in Lombroso's drama of cultural difference, the confusion level becomes so high that the potential for overt fictionalization is created. At best, we can view this as a confusion between different biblical laws regarding the legislation of slaves and marriage contracts. At worst, it is a deliberate misreading and misinterpretation of the story of the biblical Jews, designed to link them to cults of prostitution and to infer a connection between pernicious antisemitic stereotypes and biblical paradigms, as if the stereotype of Jew-as-profiteer is already imbedded in these first biblical Jews and thus is an inseparable part of what is Jewish. The identity of these biblical Jews would seem to furnish a key for Lombroso so that he may understand the identity of modern Jews. It is also noteworthy that he uses the term *"Gesù Cristo"* to refer to Jesus. The title "Christ," or Savior, implies belief in the tenets of Christianity.

What is at stake for an author like Lombroso, Jewish himself but first and foremost a scientist, when he confronts the issue of the identity of the Jews, both modern and biblical? Similar questions have been asked of Weininger, the converted Jew. Robert Oden, in "Religious Identity and the Sacred Prostitution Accusation," formulates related questions that are raised by what he calls the "accusations of sacred prostitution":

> Perhaps sacred prostitution ought to be investigated as an accusation rather than as a reality. Perhaps, then, this alleged practice belongs in the same category with cannibalism, sodomy, and abhorrent dietary and sexual practices generally—that is to say, in the category of charges that one society levels against others as part of that society's process of self-definition. . . . Viewed in this way, the accusation that other societies utilize religious personnel as part of sacred sexual rites surely tells us something about those who formulate and repeat the accusation. . . . The accusation may tell us little or nothing about those religions against which the charge is leveled (Oden 1987, 132–33).

Oden's double charge is well taken in the consideration of Lombroso's versions of biblical episodes and is pertinent to our comprehension of Weininger as well. The accusatory nature of Lombroso's agenda regarding Jewish women is better understood in the light of Oden's theory regarding the identity of the accuser in relation to the accusations that are made.

In his meditations on women, Lombroso sets up a misogynist model for the interpretation of female behavior that reinforces negative stereotypes about women and posits the female criminal as the woman who exemplifies the worst traits of his stereotypes, but who is typical of "normal" women in many ways. Fear of what is female is categorically structured in his text as we learn that the average woman is but a criminal waiting to strike and a prostitute waiting to be unleashed. Here and in his other works Lombroso marginalizes the notion of criminal through his attempts to measure and categorize the correlations between physical difference and behavior. He attempts to quantify difference as he reads physical signs of difference and links them to types. Lombroso finds himself concluding, as we have seen, that the female criminal quite often demonstrates male characteristics. He thus blurs the distinctions between men and women in his discussions of both the criminal and women.

This confusion is apparent as well in Lombroso's study of the Jews, who are at once too primitive and too modern. Another kind of distinction is also challenged as Lombroso mixes cultural categories through which he reads Jewish religious practice. His emphasis on the physical quantification of difference underscored the acceptability of biologically based theories of the inferiority of certain groups popular at the time, even though in his book on Jews he denied the racist theorists any validity as he maintained that the Jews were not a single race.

LOMBROSO AND WEININGER

These two theorists of difference, Lombroso and Weininger, share some distinct attributes. First, a theoretical similarity is found in their tendency to blur the very differences that they seek to stigmatize. Just as striking, however, is a dissimilarity in the reception of certain of their texts: Lombroso was a world-renowned criminologist, yet there are literally only a few lines in print about his text on antisemitism, while Weininger, a young student of philosophy and characterology, was hailed by many important figures of his day as a genius who understood both the nature of sexual difference and the nature of the Jews.

Both Weininger and Lombroso were Jewish, although Weininger converted to Christianity. Lombroso does not as easily fit the portrait of the antisemitic Jew: his Jewish background shows no sign of restlessness, no conversion, no abandonment of the faith. He did, however, write the very problematic text on Jews discussed here and an equally problematic one on women. Important for the study of Weininger reception in Italy, Lombroso's theories about women in part paved the way for the warm welcome that Weininger's text was later given. Through his influential theories and his attitude toward difference, Lombroso helped create an intellectual atmosphere in Italy that at the beginning of this century was receptive to Weininger and hostile to Freud.[25] In addition to the direct influence on Weininger that Allan Janik has demonstrated (Janik 1986), Lombroso's reading of the motives for antisemitism and the place of the Jews in culture provides a link to Weiningerian theories of cultural and sexual difference and ways in which those theories are interpreted. It is in part the confusion of category in Lombroso's work that would allow a future generation of Italian intellectuals such easy access to Weininger's blending of categories of difference. Lombroso's particular brand of cultural intolerance and its connections to Weininger reception in Italy furnish a link to the theories that informed the web of political and social distortions of the Holocaust; and Lombroso's theories were made to fit a later brand of racism and intolerance that provided the theoretical base for the Holocaust. Lombroso is the figure of the dispassionate scientist who banks on the impartiality of scientific method, who flinches in the face of difference, particularly his own, and then pulls out the measuring devices to show positively that difference does exist physically, even to the naked eye.[26]

Weininger's text is much more complicated than a simple diatribe against two groups, women and Jews, who at the time were often the target of abuse and attack. Weininger, in his insistence that he is talking about "qualities" or "tendencies" rather than "people," intrigued his intellectual generation and one or two subsequent generations by his formulation of women and Jews into recognizable groups of traits that are, however, largely disembodied. His description of Judaism and antisemitism provides a kind of road map for self-hatred: "I must however, make clear what I mean by Judaism; I mean neither a race nor a people nor a recognised creed. I think of it as a tendency of the mind, as a psychological constitution which is a possibility for all mankind, but which has become actual in the most conspicuous fashion only amongst the Jews. Antisemitism itself will confirm my point of view" (Weininger 1906, 303).

This is a circular argument, and it sets the stage for Weininger's description of antisemitism. If Judaism is a tendency of the mind and Jews are the only ones who have this tendency in a conspicuous fashion, then Jews are the only ones who are Jews, according to Weiningerian logic. There are also the "near-Jews," the only ones who are capable of hating the Jews:

The purest Aryans by descent and disposition are seldom Antisemites, although they are often unpleasantly moved by some of the peculiar Jewish traits; they cannot in the least understand the Antisemite movement.... The aggressive Antisemites, on the other hand, nearly always display certain Jewish characters, sometimes apparent in their faces, although they may have no real admixture of Jewish blood. The explanation is simple. People love in others the qualities they would like to have but do not actually have in any great degree; so also we hate in others only what we do not wish to be, and what notwithstanding we are partly (Weininger 1906, 304).

The connection between this statement and Weininger's own life is unmistakable, as Weininger the convert speaks about the dynamics of self-hatred as he sees them. The failure for Weininger of conversion from Judaism to anything else is made clear in his articulation of what is and what is not Jewish as simultaneously a racial issue, as he discusses elsewhere physical traits of Jews, and a psychic issue, as he defines Judaism as "tendencies"; Weininger has thus set up a paradox from which no conversion is possible. Judaism both is and is not racial, and is and is not a set of "tendencies" synonymous with "being" Jewish (i.e., found only among Jews). And antisemites (like Weininger) find themselves trapped within the same paradox. If they hate Jews, they must be to some degree Jewish in their psychic make-up; therefore, if they are self-hating Jews, there is absolutely no escape from this condition, whatever their new religious status.

Weininger also confuses other categories in his analysis of Jews and woman. Like the Jew, "woman" does not always refer to a human being but often to the quality of the female element: the abstract idea, as he calls it. To make direct comparisons between the Jew and woman, Weininger labels the Jew as womanly: "some reflection will lead to the surprising result that Judaism is saturated with femininity, with precisely those qualities the essence of which I have shown to be in the strongest opposition to the male nature." He takes us through this argument of comparison between the Jew and woman: they both lack a "real sense of landed property"; they both are "wanting in personality," which means they cannot grasp the "conception of a State"; they both lack dignity; they both are "non-moral" and more involved in "sexual matters" than are Aryan men (Weininger 1906, 306, 307, 309, 311). This last idea bears a strong resemblance to the way in which Lombroso assesses Jewish women as bearers of syphilis and as prostitutes sold by their greedy fathers.

At the end of the chapter on Judaism, Weininger lines up the opposing camps: Jewish and Christian, business and culture, female and male, race and individual. He states very emphatically that there are only two poles, no middle way, and that a decision must be made. Here he clearly departs from his stated intent of examining qualities, abstract ideas of Jewish and female, as he is now addressing real groups in what is a political as well as cultural agenda. In his last chapter he proposes that the only solution to the problem of woman is for woman to overcome her femaleness through an abandonment of her sexuality. Weininger views undesirable sexuality or religion as a state to be conquered. His "solution" calls for, quite simply, the end of the human race. The erasure of cultural, sexual, or religious difference Weininger advocates is a kind of total assimilation, not dissimilar to Lombroso's solution to antisemitism. Weininger's assimilation is, of course, much more radical.

In sum, it is clear that Weininger's theories about Jews and women have several major points of comparison to Lombroso's theories that cannot be ignored and that go far beyond some borrowing of Lombroso's theories regarding women. Both authors end up problematizing the relationship of the terms "Jew" and "woman." Their versions of this differ considerably: Weininger creates the womanly Jew; Lombroso, rather than overtly feminizing the male Jew, puts the terms "Jew" and "woman" together in an explosive combination resulting in the figure of the prostitute. His feminization of the Jew is limited to deprecatory remarks regarding the inability of the Jews to withstand the physical rigors of living in Palestine. Both authors clearly advocate assimilation as a solution to cultural or sexual difference, and both authors confuse definitions of woman and Jew to arrive at their solutions to difference.

The history of Weininger criticism is fraught with disagreements on how literally his text can or should be read, and how it should be contextualized. The disagreements themselves signal some evident dangers in interpreting a text like that of Weininger. First and foremost is the risk of creating a critical atmosphere that can function as a kind of apology. It is important to avoid the pitfall of reading writings like those of Lombroso or Weininger through a modern perspective that ignores contextualization and an understanding of the historical period that produced them, but it is equally important not to be blinded by the god of contextualization to the point where the pernicious content and influence of such texts are ignored or made less significant. There is a delicate middle ground between an overly apologetic stance toward the text, generated by perhaps too much sympathy for the historical conditions in which the author found himself and fostered as well by a certain blindness to the overt perniciousness of the text, and a naive horror that does not take into account at all the conditions that produced the writing.

As examination of Lombroso's work as a source for Weininger is, I believe, illustrative of the pitfalls involved in interpreting Weininger. Looking at Janik's useful assessment of Lombroso as a direct source for Weininger on the subject of women provides a key to a reading model I am proposing for both Lombroso and Weininger. Janik, in *How Not to Interpret a Culture: Essays on the Problem of Method in the* "Geisteswissenschaften," asserts the following:

> Even a cursory glance at Weininger's notes and references indicates that he was heavily indebted for his data about women to a work called *La Donna Delinquente e La Prostituta [sic]* by Cesare Lombroso, Professor of Forensic Medicine and father of modern criminology. . . . Not a little of the "empirical data" upon which Weininger based his reasoning is to be found in Lombroso's study of the female offender. For example two ideas which were to recur as central themes in *Geschlecht und Charakter*, namely that women are generally less sensitive to perceptual stimuli and the notion that women are more prone to lying than men (for which he advances eight causes) are already central themes in Lombroso's work. In fact most of the things that we find obnoxious and repugnant in *Geschlecht und Charakter* today, can be found in *La Donna Delinquente* (Janik 1986, 40–41).

Janik's evidence for supposing that Lombroso had a major effect on Weininger's theories regarding women is indisputable. His and other scholars' emphasis on contextualizing Weininger within the cultural milieu of turn-of-the-century Vienna, including within the painful debates regarding assimilation that were taking place in the Jewish community, is crucial. What is much more arguable and pertinent to a meaningful discussion of influence is the tone and meaning of Janik's statement that "in fact most of the things that we find obnoxious and repugnant in *Geschlecht und Charakter* today, can be found in *La Donna Delinquente*." An examination of Lombroso's work discloses, I believe, striking similarities between the two authors that go beyond the footnotes that Weininger allocates to Lombroso in his text. The question of influence, however, is not easily shunted off to a question of footnotes, nor is the perniciousness of Weininger's text explained or excused by its indebtedness to Lombroso. Reading Lombroso will provide some direction for reading Weininger, but not just in the interest of assigning blame. Is the purpose of tracking down sources and demonstrating that ideas have come from other thinkers to exculpate the one who has borrowed, on the excuse that those ideas were not original to that person anyway? Is there a notion of original sin floating around here? Is Weininger any less responsible for his text if he was not the author of all of its ideas? Does the demonstration of influence mean "not guilty"? To state that what we find obnoxious in Weininger is already in Lombroso, as if that were any kind of answer, is to displace a very important question. If what is implied in Janik's statement is that if these sentiments are already in Lombroso, then Weininger isn't such a "bad guy" after all, the essential question is still being ignored: why did Lombroso write these theories about Jews and women? A more detailed look at Lombroso within the context of the science practiced in his day demonstrates that his theories regarding women are not all original either, that they are a composite of misogynist proverbs, the theories of other scientific experts, and his own opinions.

A look at a model of analysis proposed by Saul Friedlander in his assessment of historical narratives regarding the Holocaust is useful here. Friedlander, in discussing what he calls "the basic narratives underlying the historical representations" of the Holocaust, specifies the differences between the "structuralist" approach to understanding the Holocaust, which is to cast it in terms of nineteenth-century development of racialist ideas, and the "liberal" approach, which attempts to assign responsibility through an analysis of German politics and policies in the Nazi era (Friedlander 1988, 67). Friedlander points out that the structuralist approach has the tendency to place responsibility for the event on so many sources that the notion of guilt itself can be dispersed: "in the structuralist view, there are many active and almost independent subgroups within the wide category of perpetrators; these subgroups interact with one another in such a way that it becomes extremely difficult to pinpoint where the responsibility lies (Friedlander 1988, 70). The model that is thus created would appear to be a binary one, either "many sources = displaced responsibility" or "single source = specific responsibility." Friedlander points out, however, that "both the liberal and the structuralist approach belong to a common consensus about basic responsibilities and basic victimization, notwithstanding the divergences just described" (Friedlander 1988, 71). We can use this useful model of divergencies sharing a common basis about what constitutes responsibility that Friedlander proposes to ponder both the question of influence regarding Lombroso and Weininger, and, as the essays that follow will discuss, the influence of Weininger on many other thinkers and writers. Considering the problem in this way, it becomes clear that we may fully appreciate the depth to which Weininger owed some of his beliefs about women to Lombroso without lessening the impact of those theories reformulated and re-presented a generation later. To acknowledge sources should not mean an automatic exculpation of the borrower.

Perhaps the notion of originality, when it comes to the expression of prejudice, is really not relevant at all. Plagiarism is, after all, the *modus operandi* of the dissemination of bigotry.

6 ✦

OTTO WEININGER AS LIBERAL?

Steven Beller

Otto Weininger has been one of the great *bêtes noires* in the cultural history of turn-of-the-century Austria. In almost all accounts of his life and work in current studies on Viennese culture, Weininger appears as one of the main proponents of antifeminism and anti-Semitism. As such he is seen as one of the classic examples of the Jewish self-hater.[1] Recently, however, it has become apparent just how influential Weininger was for a great number of people at the core of Vienna's cultural elite. This has brought about a reevaluation of his work. Allan Janik has been especially active in this respect, showing how misleading it is to dismiss Weininger as a misogynist and Jewish self-hater, or as a "therapeutic nihilist" (Janik 1986, 35–46). Here I would like to contribute to this reevaluation by approaching Weininger from a perspective that was central to his concerns: the problem of the rational individual faced with the twin threats of irrationalism and collectivist thought.

If one looks at Weininger from the perspective of the *fin-de-siècle* crisis of a liberalism besieged by collectivist and irrationalist forces on all sides, then he appears in the liberal camp, broadly defined. This is so because Weininger is in agreement with two central tenets of liberalism: the ultimate rationality of human beings and the right of individuals to decide their own fate. He also shares liberalism's aversion to and fear of irrationalism, which, especially in the form of anti-Semitism, he saw as a product of the defeat of the rational person. Irrationalism, for Weininger, is rooted in humanity's lesser being, and is external and inferior to the real inner person, who is ethical and logical. While Weininger veers off into a misguided argument based on false premises, the intention and the main thrust of his message are, I would claim, liberal. The very problems with Weininger's approach are indeed symptomatic of liberalism on the run.

This can be well illustrated by looking at Weininger in the context of his views on Jews and Jewishness. On these issues he can be seen as an extreme case of a particular form of liberal theory, what one might term "intolerant liberalism." American liberalism has tended, at least in recent years, to a pluralistic approach whereby different philosophies of life, different religions, and different ethnic and cultural identities are allowed to exist side by side, albeit under an American umbrella. This might be called "tolerant liberalism," according to which individuals are free to be themselves. The nineteenth-century model of liberalism, which to a great extent still exists in European countries such as France and England, tended not to allow such diversity, but rather exerted immense pressure for the "stranger" to conform not only to a lowest common denominator of social norms, but also to the whole set of social and cultural-national values and standards of the community concerned.[2] In other words, "strangers" were free not to remain as they were but rather to change, to become the same as those in the host community, to adopt their mores and value system. This tradition of "intolerant liberalism" was the one in which Weininger grew up and operated.

According to such thinking, the emancipation of the Jewish individual was equated with complete assimilation into Western (in Weininger's case, German) society. This was the dominant assumption in the Enlightenment rationale of Jewish emancipation in the eighteenth century and continued as German liberal orthodoxy throughout the nineteenth century. In this schema there was the "bad" Jew and the "good" Jew. The "bad" Jew was what opponents of Jewish emancipation claimed all Jews to be: dishonest, uncivilized, money grubbing, and under the thrall of a superstitious (and implicitly irrational) religion. Where proponents of emancipation differed with opponents was often not so much in thinking that this image of the unemancipated Jew was false, but rather in believing that the "bad" Jew could be transformed into the "good" Jew. That is to say that the Jewish individual could be regenerated into becoming "good," in other words German. From Dohm to Freytag, the emancipationists' main rationale was: "Let them cease to be Jews!" (Sorkin 1988; Mosse 1971, 37–41, 63–72; Arendt 1946; Mayer 1918, 386–91).

This argument for emancipation thus assumed a quid pro quo that Jewish individuals would be given the rights of citizens in order for them to free themselves from their "bad" Jewish past. It was hoped that through a program of education in secular culture and occupational restructuring Jews would leave their former identity behind and, in the "second emancipation" (i.e., assimilation), complete the integration necessary to make the emancipation worthwhile.[3]

Numerous liberal Jews thought the same way. In the long struggle for emancipation, many Jewish leaders had come to the conclusion that in order to *deserve* emancipation, Jews had to reform themselves, show themselves worthy of their release from oppression. Therefore on the one hand much emphasis was put on Jews acquiring the new secular culture at the expense of the old monopoly of religious learning that had long been given priority. Societies were also set up to attempt to restructure Jewish occupations away from the "nonproductive" fields of finance and trade and toward farming and the crafts (Sorkin 1988, 26–40, 118–123; Stölzl 1975,

126–129; Katz 1973).[4] Although the latter strategy met with far less success than the former, Jews adopted both in direct response to the critics of emancipation and to their own perception of failings in the Jewish community.

Heinrich Jaques's *Denkschrift über die Stellung der Juden in Österreich* of 1859 is a good example of this view as expressed by a Jewish liberal in Austria. This is an emancipatory piece, arguing for granting the right to own property and to enter the civil service. Jaques started by accepting the stereotypes of "Jewish money" and Jewish revolutionaries, but claimed that if Jewish youth had an alternative to making money—namely entry to the bureaucracy—and if Jews generally could have the conservative experience of owning property, both of these specters would cease to haunt the Austrian monarchy (Jaques 1859, 26, 37, 47).

As for the bogey figure of the Polish Jew, which was used as evidence of the Jews' unfittedness for full rights, Jaques retorted that it was wrong to lump civilized Western Jews with their Galician coreligionists and that it was not only the Jews in Poland who were uneducated. Virtually everyone in that country, he argued, including the Polish nobility, was culturally backward and in need of some German culture "um erst recht Menschen zu werden" ("to become truly human beings") (Jaques 1859, 46–47). Jaques's final plea was that Austria needed to utilize all its talent to compete in the modern world, whether that talent came from a noble palace in Vienna or a Jewish shtetl in Galicia. Thus at its base his work was an argument for the right of the talented individual to act free of the restraints of creed or caste (Jaques 1859, 50).

The period that followed the publication of Jaques's pamphlet saw the Jewish question approached mainly in the spirit he typified. In the liberal era in Austria Jews were granted full rights, and many Jews did their best to regenerate themselves in the image of the German liberal ruling class. For a time it appeared that they were integrating well into that society, yet the assimilation brought its own problems. Jews now found themselves in a double bind. Whereas before they had been mainly criticized for being too otherworldly and uncivilized, now they were seen as the symbol of an unwanted modernity, as materialistic, superficial, and too abstract in their thinking, lacking the depths of Germans (Mosse 1971, 81; Stölzl 1975, 110–12; Lessing 1930, 83–84; Bahr 1906, 69; Chamberlain 1899 vol. I, 450–51). While in some respects this new image was the same as the previous one—in the identification of Jews with money, for instance—in others it was the reverse, with writers unfavorably contrasting the "fake" modern Jew with the good "real" Jew who followed tradition.[5]

Furthermore, Jews themselves criticized the results of assimilation on the same lines as this new anti-Jewish critique. In 1884 Joseph Bloch, in the first issue of the *Österreichische Wochenschrift*, described the new generation of Jews growing up in Vienna as one filled with the spirit of "religious nihilism" and therefore infected with Jewish anti-Semitism (Bloch 1884). Articles in the Jewish weekly *Die Neuzeit* in the late 1890s frequently criticized Jews in Vienna for being corrupted by the materialist age. One article called modern Jews "Formjuden mit Culturstaub bedeckt" ("from Jews covered with cultural dust") who had lost the "idealist trait" of Judaism (Walden 1896, 139). Another complained that Jews had lost their inner base of values and hence any way of measuring the outside world (*Die Neuzeit*, January 6, 1899, 5). The new, American style of education was blamed for destroying any higher ideals among Viennese Jewish youth; having been processed by the Franco-American "moral factory," they were criticized for being ignorant of Judaism, and neglectful of the past, and lacking in idealism, caring instead *only* about being good citizens (Marsky 1900).

The views of Theodor Gomperz, a friend of Jaques and one of the more prominent Jews in Viennese liberal culture, illustrate the ambivalences to which a Jewish liberal was prone by the late nineteenth century. On the one hand, Gomperz opposed any obstacle to assimilation. He thus despised Herzl's Zionism and saw efforts to form a Jewish Nationalist party as a tragic, retrograde mistake (Gomperz 1905, 196–99; Gomperz and Kann 1974, 445–49). In addition, he hated anti-Semitism for precluding the existence of any truly liberal state (Gomperz and Kann 1974, 67–68, 123–24, 133, 154, 305–9, 351). In all this Gomperz was a typical liberal of his time, rejecting any unnecessary differentiation within society. His frequent criticisms of Jewish behavior were made out of a sense of frustration that Jews were defeating their own arguments for being treated as responsible citizens (Gomperz and Kann 1974, 104–5, 154, 168, 263, 382). Indeed at one point he was so overcome by shame at the antics of a group of *nouveau riche* Jews that he wrote, "Tout entendre c'est comprendre Lueger!" (To hear all of this is to understand Lueger) (Gomperz and Kann 1974, 263).

On the other hand, when it came to defining the Jewish character, Gomperz adopted a mild form of what one might term the "modern" critique. He made two attempts to formulate his approach to the Jewish question, with the latter being the more comprehensive. His first effort, written in 1881, arose as a response to the emergence of anti-Semitism in Germany and especially to the role played by Heinrich von Treitschke, the German historian. In Gomperz's view the whole Jewish question was a result of German impatience with the Jews for not becoming completely German quickly enough. Yet for him, "The Jews provide a powerful proof not so much for the absolute permanence of racial characteristics, as for the opposite" (Gomperz and Kann 1974). He saw Jewish history as one of change. In antiquity they had been a people steeped in religion. This, he thought, might account for the fact that the Jews had not made a major contribution to the culture of the ancient world. They had been artisans, thinkers, and merchants, but in none of these fields had they reached the heights. In the Middle Ages they had become a "merchant people" (Gomperz and Kann 1974) who had developed its "sharpness of intellect" through Talmudic study and the exigencies of survival in a hostile world. At the same time, however, their commercial character had led to a decline of morality, to greed, and to vanity. Yet wherever they now were, Gomperz mused, Jews had taken on the characteristics of the "medium" in which they lived.

Jews, according to Gomperz, could be changed, and if there were such things as ineradicable racial characteristics, then he consoled himself with the thought that these "lie at a depth to which the categories of bad and good never reach" (Gomperz and Kann 1974). At this level, perhaps Scherer was right in seeing the Germans as being passionate, the Greeks and Italians as having a sense of form, and the Jews as being pliable (and, like their cousins the Arabs, sober, moderate, and free from wants). At this point, however, Gomperz, a famed positivist, reminded himself that "one is always running the risk here of mistaking the fleeing for the permanent, and the acquired for what is original" (Gomperz and Kann 1974, 121–24). Commenting on the new anti-Semitism, he wrote that "the mistakes that cause our outrage are travesties and misunderstandings based on scientific truths" (Gomperz and Kann 1974, 121–24). He ended his thoughts on the subject by quoting Renan: "Race, as we understand it, . . . is something that makes and unmakes itself."

In this early essay Gomperz already showed a certain ambivalence about the racial characteristics of Jews, and he preserved his liberal position by casting doubt on the whole issue, despite his suspicions that there was in fact a Jewish race. Further, he displaced this racial question to a realm beyond good and evil, that is, beyond any social relevance, and he chose a possible racial characteristic—pliability—that, if anything, shows how adaptable Jews are. If Jews are a race, Gomperz argued, their special quality is their ability to assimilate (Gomperz and Kann 1974, 121–24).

In his 1904 essay Gomperz developed some of his earlier ideas and added others (Gomperz and Kann 1974, 384–89). This time his main concern was the nature of Jewish intellect. Gomperz started from the, for him, empirical fact that, despite the obvious intellectuality of the Jews, there were very few Jews in the first rank of culture and no Jewish poet-philosopher. This was because, thought Gomperz, Jews lacked "the unconscious, dusky, dreamy, intuitive quality." He continued: "I would almost say that for certain forms of creativity it is too bright in Jewish heads."[6] Gomperz explained this by appealing to the Lamarckian idea of inherited characteristics, blaming this Jewish deficiency on history in a way similar to the argument he had made in 1881. Geniuses, he reasoned, could only be produced on native soil, so when the Jews had been in Palestine they had produced religious geniuses of the first order. Now, however, they had no native soil, and so their spirit had "something insufficient, something brittle and ambivalent" (Gomperz and Kann 1974, 384–89) about it. And, Gomperz suspected, this could not be explained solely in terms of the Jews being a "merchant people," but probably had something to do with racial traits.

Ironically, what Gomperz was in effect describing was a problem of assimilated Western Jews such as himself. As his son Heinrich later noted, Polish Jews could be seen to have precisely the "popular twilight-nature" that Gomperz denied the Jews as a whole. All this talk of racial traits seems a bit odd coming from someone as reputedly liberal and positivist as Gomperz, but it is important to note that, while Gomperz remained ambivalent and confused on the issue, he still remained true to the liberal concept of the individual. Citing Spinoza's pantheism as evidence against the idea that Jews are racially amythological, he stated; "One should never forget that no definition of national or racial character can claim absolute validity. One is always talking about more or less. Human beings are, after all, human beings, and in any individual an element that is foreign to most of his people can be mightly developed." He concluded, "There are no limits to the potential of genius!" (Gomperz and Kann 1974, 389). In his belief that individuals could overcome even their racial heritage and that political liberalism should defend their right to do so, Gomperz was typical of liberal thought in the Vienna of 1900.

The greatest threat to this way of thinking in Austria was the organized social and economic anti-Semitism of Karl Lueger's Christian Socials and of the various extreme nationalist movements in the Austrian part of the Habsburg Monarchy. The concept of Jewish assimilation, based on the idea of an autonomous, rational individual, foundered on a rock of corporatist and collectivist thinking that rejected Western liberalism and adapted the traditions of an irrationalist and superstitious past to suit its own ends: exclusion of the Jews and/or other nationalities to the advantage of the "People" (Pulzer 1964, 33–37, 42, 60, 66, 128–85). There is no better example of this tactic than that provided by the Hilsner Affair of 1899–1900, when liberals saw the Czech nation being corrupted by the unscrupulous exploitation of the myth of ritual murder, by the Christian Socials in Vienna, and by Czech nationalists in Prague. The attacks on Thomas Masaryk for pointing to the absurdity of the accusation were seen as exemplary proof of the dire threat that anti-Semitism and extreme nationalism, in their appeal to the masses, posed to the freedom of the individual to speak the truth (*Neue Freie Presse*, November 28, 1899, 1–2; November 15, 1900, 1–2; Beller 1989a). It was little comfort to liberals that Lueger left it to himself to decide who was a Jew and who was not, for this famous tactic, so often quoted by defenders of Lueger and his Christian Social party to make their brand of anti-Semitism appear nonracial and thus relatively harmless, still left it to others to decide an individual's fate. Indeed the Christian Socials' anti-Semitism was an extreme threat to the liberal ideal precisely because it could seem "harmless" and yet at the same time sacrifice the autonomy of the individual to the whim of others. Furthermore, Lueger's interpretation of his movement's anti-Semitism was not uniformly found in the Christian Social ranks; many of his supporters held to a racial anti-Semitism that allowed no "exceptions" (Beller 1989b, 193–97).

It is against this background that we should view Otto Weininger's work. Such an examination will reveal that what Weininger has to say about Jews, pathological and wrong-headed as it may appear, is essentially a compendium of what others, including many Jews—and Zionists—were saying about modern Jews. Much of this common wisdom was of course prejudiced, but a significant proportion of it was a mirror of social and psychological realities. Furthermore, in his belief in the individual's ability and right to overcome one's lesser self, Weininger is politically very firmly in the liberal tradition. If he attacks positivist liberals, it is not because he has taken an irrationalist viewpoint, but rather because he thinks they are undermining the very fabric of liberal society and thought by questioning the autonomy, indeed the very existence, of the self and thereby doing away with the rational, responsible individual.

Weininger's main work, *Sex and Character*, starts out as an attempt to define the sexual characteristics of man and woman. The crux of the argument is that every individual, male or female, is to some degree bisexual. This assumption, based on Weininger's own interpretation of theories that seemed to be the most up-to-date in biological science (but that soon proved to be erroneous), allows Weininger to construct two ideal types, Man and Woman, which, as he often stresses, are not empirically to be found in any one person, but are the abstract male and female principles (Weininger 1906, 79–84).[7] What Weininger is essentially doing is using sexual types to describe psychological states, a procedure that was deeply embedded in Western culture and especially a German culture indebted to Goethe. Weininger was part of a tradition that was to reach its apogee in Jungian psychology.

Studies of Weininger usually focus on his devastating attack on Woman. Certainly what he says about Woman causes understandable outrage in the context of modern thought on the sexes. This concentration on his "antifeminism," however, has led to a relative and unfortunate neglect of the central character of the book, which is Man, Weininger's ideal.

Weininger's Man is ideally the Genius. In adopting this ideal, Weininger is putting himself at odds with positivist science, for it is his claim that science is not enough: men cannot rest content with knowing how; they must also seek to know *why*. Man's purpose (that is, the goal of that part of each of us that is "Man"), his ideal, must therefore be to give meaning to the world (Weininger 1906, 153–85, 209–11). Similarly, Weininger rejects any doubt about the existence of the self, for he argues that the self is a self-evident assumption of logic and ethics, which is necessary for an understanding of the world. The Genius believes in himself precisely because he knows that his self is the basis of all logic and ethics, and, as a reflection of the ethical self, aesthetics as well. Indeed logic and ethics are the same, for the highest goal of Man is to give logical meaning to the world, is the will to value. In other words, Weininger's human ideal is a warmed-up version of Kant's intelligible self (Weininger 1906, 159–68, 242–44, 321).

Man's mortal enemy is Woman, that is, the animal, the material, the earthly in each individual. What Woman really represents is Weininger's fear that Man's higher self will be distracted from the pursuit of knowledge and meaning by the allures of hedonistic pleasure and the irrational realm of feelings. This is what Weininger sees going on around him, culture becoming effeminate, given over to pleasure-seeking instead of higher ethical and idealistic pursuits (Weininger 1906, 282–85, 329–30, 332–37). Everyone, in Weininger's view, must battle against this in their own person and actions. He is doubtful whether any woman will be able to overcome her female self, but his message to men is that they must help women to do this, for it is ultimately their responsibility. They are the ones who, having more Man than Woman in them, should know better, yet they persist in treating women as means to an end (pleasure) rather than ends in themselves (moral beings).

Therefore, Weininger argues, while it is too dangerous to give women the vote (a position held by many political liberals of the time) or to allow them an active role in politics, they must in all other respects, especially in the law, be treated as equals, as proper human beings, for only then will there ever be a chance of the miracle happening: the real emancipation of women *from Woman* (Weininger 1906, 305–6, 312).[8] What he wants, in other words—and this closely parallels the emancipationists' goal for the Jews— is for women to be free to develop the Man in them, to become rational, moral beings, and to shake off their lesser selves. In proposing such a legal equality for women, it should be noted, Weininger was being fairly progressive for his time (Kolleth 1986).

This is not to say that Weininger's theory of sexual politics "works." From our contemporary perspective it is plainly unbearably condescending in its idea of men treating women *as if* they are equal. Moreover, the whole of Weininger's argument, despite this egalitarian gloss, is still based on his acceptance of the positive male and the negative female stereotypes so typical of his age. His obsessive identification of all that he fears with the feminine severely compromises whatever else he might have to say of value about the relationship of the sexes or the dangers of irrationalism, and understandably makes his work deeply alienating to the present-day reader. On the other hand such gender-stereotyping attitudes as Weininger held were very common among other political liberals of his time and place. What is more interesting than his faulty stereotyping is the fact that Weininger does, *despite his prejudices*, propose women's legal equality.

Furthermore, to understand Weininger one must understand his labeling. This point is not always easy to see, for Weininger's approach is not without confusion, as evidenced by his use, in unguarded moments, of the term "women" where, according to his own theory, "Woman" should have been used.[9] These lapses were undoubtedly due to his own lack of clarity about what he wanted to say. If one looks beyond these inconsistencies, however, the main thrust of Weininger's argument reveals itself not to be against women as such, but against the apparent surrender of the "masculine" bastions of logic and ethics to the "feminine" realm of feelings and sexual desire, which he saw occurring all around him in turn-of-the-century, "modernist" Europe. Thus Weininger's tirade against Woman is in effect an attack on modern aestheticist culture, on the hedonism of the demimonde, in which the sexual and the "feminine"— Weininger's Woman—were exalted, while women, as human as opposed to sexual beings, were denied equality with men.[10] One might say that the label he chose was "Woman" but that what he meant by this was "modern aestheticism."

In the same way, Weininger's attack on the Jews is essentially an attack not on empirical Jews but rather on nihilism, the consequence of secularization, and, ironically, assimilation. If Weininger is keen to stress that he is not talking about individual men and women, he is doubly keen to assure the reader that what he means by the Jew is not exclusively the Jewish race, people, or set of individuals. Instead he is talking about the "Platonic idea" of Judaism, which is Jewish solely because, he claims, Jews over the ages have provided most of the evidence for this state of mind, this "psychological constitution which is a possibility for all mankind." He states this at least three times in his chapter on Judaism, even claiming that some Aryans are more Jewish than Jews and that there are "real Jews" who are more Aryan than certain Aryans. Nor does he neglect to mention that he himself is of Jewish descent (Weininger 1906, 303–6, 311–12).

Given these caveats, what does Weininger define as Jewish? His catalog of Jewish faults is fairly hideous and reveals, to say the least, Weininger's troubled relationship with his Jewishness. Yet most of his main accusations are ones we have heard already in various forms, such as

Jews have no sense of property and are attracted to anarchic communism; Jews lack depth, firm identity, sense of higher ideals, and an awareness of the transcendental plane (Weininger 1906, 306–7, 313–16). The core of all these faults is that "the Jew" is the unbeliever, or in Joseph Bloch's language, the "religious nihilist." The Jew does not believe in God and so does not believe in himself, let alone anything else. Therefore he has no sense of identity and drifts from one disguise to another. (Weininger 1906, 321–25). As we have seen, these views were shared by at least some of Weininger's Jewish contemporaries. It is perhaps revealing to consider that Herzl's Zionist critique of Viennese Jewry is really very similar to Weininger's image of the Jews, in that it also stresses their lack of inner substance and their combination of vanity with lack of self-respect (Herzl 1983, vol. 2, 125–28, 140–41, vol. 3, 455; 1902, 1–20). Indeed, while neither Weininger nor Herzl is completely objective in their assessments, they both are, in their own ways, describing the predicament faced by many assimilated Jews who had lost contact with "real" Judaism and felt the need for a value system in which they could believe (Klaren 1924, 202–3).

Weininger's solution to this problem is radical, but radically individualistic, even more so than his solution for Woman. He argues that anti-Semitism is totally wrong-headed and is indeed a symptom of the Jewishness of modern times, for not only is it a projection of the Jewish part of the anti-Semite's self, but the whole approach of treating people in terms of groups betrays a Jewish taint, as opposed to the individualism of Aryan Man (Weininger 1906, 305–6, 312). He believes that Zionism is a morally commendable idea but can only work if each Jew has already solved the problem of overcoming the Jew in oneself, the self-emancipation of Jews from Judaism (Weininger 1906, 312).

The irony of Weininger's theory is that the reward for shaking off the Jewish self is to rise above the Aryan and become the greatest of all geniuses, the religious genius, the founder of religion. Judaism thus ends up becoming the necessary prerequisite in the dialectical emergence of Christianity. Judaism is also given the rather questionable honor of existing in order to be overcome. Nevertheless it is the spiritual crisis of the Jew that is seen as the fount of ultimate knowledge. The Jew's struggle against himself, for true faith, makes the Jew, in Weininger's roundabout logic, the hope of the world (Weininger 1906, 325–29).

It is clear from this that individual Jews—and it should be reiterated that Weininger is not necessarily talking about Jewish individuals but rather anyone with "Jewish" attitudes—must be given the right to try to be full human beings, for it is in their self-overcoming that spiritual progress will truly occur. This is indeed what Weininger demands for Jews as well as women and blacks. Although such groups face numerous difficulties in realizing their humanity, they must be treated as equals, for as Weininger writes, "We must try to respect mankind, and to venerate the idea of humanity (by which I do not mean the human community but the being, man, the soul part of the spiritual world)" (Weininger 1906, 338). In this assertion Weininger is really only following the logic of "intolerant liberalism" in its arguments for emancipation, albeit in an extreme form. Above all, he shows how far he is from the irrationalist and antiliberal politics of contemporary anti-Semitism. If his views betray a panoply of prejudice, the political structure in which he places them is classically liberal.

Furthermore, the ideal to which he appeals, although tempered by Weininger's perceived necessity for belief, is essentially an appeal to a higher, inner form of reason, to the "God in Man" rather than to lower considerations of race or nation (Weininger 1906, 313). In a world increasingly under the sway of the mass, irrationalist politics of anti-Semitism and nationalism, Weininger's voice was one attempting to save the rational individual from the materialism of race and the destruction of moral values. The context in which he lived, and his own perception of that environment, led him to a world view encrusted with some of the more virulent prejudices of his age. Yet this should not obscure the fact that in his rationalism, and in his faith in and defence of the individual, Weininger remained very much within a liberal tradition that stretched back to the beginnings of Jewish emancipation and assimilation, of which he was so much a product.

7 ✦

OTTO WEININGER AND SIGMUND FREUD: RACE AND GENDER IN THE SHAPING OF PSYCHOANALYSIS

Sander L. Gilman

THE BODY OF THE JEW

In the summer of 1904 the Berlin ear, nose, and throat specialist Wilhelm Fliess wrote a sharp note to his friend and colleague Sigmund Freud, accusing him of having leaked Fliess's concept of bisexuality to Otto Weininger, either directly or through Freud's patient the psychologist Hermann Swoboda (Freud 1955, 463–68). Freud replied that he had totally repressed the memory of Weininger's visit. In a later letter to David Abrahamsen concerning Weininger, Freud noted that he had seen Weininger's *Geschlecht und Charakter* only in manuscript, as a draft of his dissertation, which totally avoided discussion of the "Jewish question" (Rodlauer 1987; Le Rider 1985, 96). While for Freud Fliess's accusation concerning Weininger marked the end of his "homosexual cathexis" with Fliess, his memory of the matter repressed the intense anti-Semitism of Weininger's text.[1] Weininger's juxtaposition of the sexual and the racial linked two aspects of the Jew long related within medical science in the popular culture of *fin-de-siècle* Vienna. In 1904 Otto Weininger and his views came to have a role in Freud's discovery of his own identity as a Jewish male.

Otto Weininger had published his revised dissertation as *Geschlecht und Charakter* (Sex and Character) in 1903 and killed himself shortly thereafter in the house of Vienna in which Beethoven had died (Gilman 1986, 244–51; Le Rider and Leser 1984; Heller 1978; Gay 1988, 154–55; Arens 1989a, 1989b; Nicolino no date, 103–10). His book which is a work of intensive, undisguised self-hatred, became an immediate bestseller that had unprecedented influence on the scientific discourse about Jews and women at the turn of the century (Dallago 1912; Lucka 1921). This book was fundamental in shaping at least some of Freud's attitudes toward the nature of the body, especially regarding bisexuality and its relationship to the concept of polymorphous perversity. More specifically, it also helped shape his views on the complex relationship between his racial identity as a Jew and his sexual identity as a male. It is in Weininger's image of the Jewish body that these two definitions meet. Freud's incorporation of this image into his work is paralleled in the theories of a number of other *fin-de-siècle* thinkers whose reading of Weininger also repressed the question of the relationship of sexual identity to sexual anatomy. For example, the lesbian feminist Charlotte Perkins Gilman saw Weininger's work as a major contribution to the science of gender (Gilman 1906). And Ludwig Wittgenstein, the homosexual, partially "Jewish," Catholic philosopher, incorporated aspects of Weininger's philosophy into his world view (Le Rider 1990c).

Central to Weininger's study of the relationship between the masculine and the feminine is the dichotomy between the Jew and the Aryan (Weininger 1906). What contemporary science saw in the form of the body, Weininger saw in the structure of the psyche. Weininger's work, while in no way innovative, summarized a psychological spectrum that runs from Jewishness at one pole to the Aryan mind at the other. His polemical restatement of Arthur Schopenhauer's views on women simply extended the category of the feminine to the Jew. This scale mirrored that on which the masculine and the feminine served as the antithetical points. For Jews and women, such a view of bisexuality or "biracialism" meant that the biological antithesis between the self and the other should have vanished. For Weininger, the Jew who converted to Christianity, it meant that he saw himself as less "Jewish" on such a scale than the arch-anti-Semite Richard Wagner, whom he labels as "having an accretion of Jewishness in his art" (Weininger 1906, 305). For Weininger, Jewishness is a mind-set that does "not refer to a nation or to a race, to a creed or to a scripture. When I speak of the Jew I mean neither an individual nor the whole body, but mankind in general, in so far it has a share in the platonic idea of Judaism" (Weininger 1906, 306). He constructs the image of the Jew, like that of the woman, as an inherently negative quality of the psyche that must be transcended. It is this link between the Jew and the woman that is reflected in Freud's work.

Weininger serves Freud as a touchstone for the definition of the diseased Jew, the antithesis of the Jewish physician, whose role is to heal. For Freud, Weininger's disease is his self-hate, both as a Jew and as a homosexual; the proof of his disease is his suicide. It is of little surprise that Weininger appears in Freud's work in the context of the debates about sexual identity; what is less evident is that one further response is to be found within Freud's internalization of the meaning of the Jew within aspects of his psychoanalytic work.

It is in a footnote to his argument about castration anxiety in his account of the 1909 case of Little Hans that Freud cites Weininger's text and his life as exemplary cases of the internalization of self-hatred. Here the question of the nature and form of the male body stands at the center of Freud's concern, to quote his paraphrase of Little Hans's argument: "Could it be that living beings really exist which did not possess widdlers? If so, it would no longer be so incredible that they could take his own widdler away, and, as it were, make him into a woman!" (Freud 1955–74, vol. 10, 36). To this statement Freud appends a long footnote that relates the child's anxiety about castration to the nature of anti-Semitism.

It is important to follow Freud's unstated pattern of thought: if—asks the child—I can be circumcised and my Jewishness revealed, that is, if I can be made into a Jew, cannot I also be castrated and my hidden femininity is revealed, that is, cannot I be made into a woman? Freud's note attempts to "demonstrate the typical character of the train of thought" of the five-year-old child:

> The castration complex is the deepest root of anti-Semitism; for even in the nursery little boys hear that a Jew has something cut off his penis—a piece of his penis, they think—and this gives them a right to despise Jews. And there is no stronger unconscious root for the sense of superiority over women. Weininger (the young philosopher who, highly gifted but sexually deranged, committed suicide after producing his remarkable book, *Geschlecht und Charakter* [*Sex and Character*, 1903]), in a chapter that attracted much attention, treated Jews and women with equal hostility and overwhelmed them with the same insults. Being neurotic, Weininger was completely under the sway of his infantile complexes; and from that standpoint what is common to Jews and women is their relation to the castration complex (Freud 1955–74, vol. 10, 36).

Freud's example for the problematic relationship of the Jew to his circumcised penis is Weininger, whose views on the nature of bisexuality draw on the model that had been explored by ethnopsychologists who argued that qualities of the body are (usually incompletely) transferred to the psyche.

The roots of this view lie deep in the theories of ethnopsychology as formulated in the 1860s by two Jews, the psychologist Moritz Lazarus and his brother-in-law, the philologist Heymann Steinthal. In the first issue of their journal of ethnopsychology and linguistics, *Zeitschrift für Völkerpsychologie und Sprachwissenschaft*, they outlined their assumptions about the knowability of the mind (Lazarus and Steinthal 1860; see also Belke 1971–86; Schmiedebach 1988). Lazarus and Steinthal studied the psychology of human beings in groups (*Gemeinschaft*). Unlike other fields of psychology of the time, where laboratory and clinical work was demanded to define the arena of study, ethnopsychology depended on historical and cultural/ethnological data. The work of the ethnopsychologists was highly medicalized: Lazarus studied physiology with the materialist Johannes Müller and co-founded the Medical-Psychological Society with the Berlin neurologist Wilhelm Griesinger in 1867. While Lazarus and Steinthal wished to separate their psychology from materialistic physiology, they were bound by the scientific rhetoric of the materialistic arguments about inheritance. The great laboratory psychologist Wilhelm Wundt remained the leading proponent of their views of "universal mental creations" well into the twentieth century (Wundt 1916, 2). Freud made extensive use of Wundt's explication of these theories in his *Psychopathology of Everyday Life* (1901) and *Totem and Taboo* (1913) (Tögel 1989).

Freud, like the ethnopsychologists, needed to separate the idea of the psyche from the body and to eliminate the image of the fixed, immutable racial composition that determines all thoughts and actions. Weininger undertook quite the opposite, for he saw race as one of the two constituent factors of the psyche, along with gender. But all of these thinkers viewed the psyche as separate from yet still part of the body. It seemed to be impossible, despite the needs of such ethnopsychologists to avoid the pitfalls of race, of ever truly separating the mind from the body.

Lazarus and Steinthal construct the concept of peoples (*Völker*), but they stress that these groups are defined by the individuals within them and are not fixed biological races (Lazarus and Steinthal 1860, 5). "Human beings," Lazarus observes, "are the creation of history; everything in us, about us, is the result of history; we do not speak a word, we do not think an idea, there is neither feeling nor emotion, which is not in a complicated manner dependent on historical determinants" (Lazarus 1862, 35). The standards for definition of a people are fluid and change from group to group; thus the standards for being French are different than those for being German. Even though a "people is a purely subjective construction," it is reflected in "a common consciousness of many with the consciousness of the group" (Lazarus 1862, 35–36). This "common consciousness" exists initially because of the "same origin" and the "proximity of the dwellings" of the members of the group, and "with the relationship through birth, the similarity of physiognomy, especially the form of the body, is present" (Lazarus 1862, 37). For Lazarus and Steinthal this "objective" fact of biological similarity lays the groundwork for the "subjective" nature of the mental construction of a people (Lazarus 1862, 38). But the biological underpinnings of this argument are clear: the Irish eat potatoes as a reflex of being in Ireland, which makes them Irish, and they are Irish because they eat potatoes (Lazarus and Steinthal 1860, 39). Could one not argue that Jews are Jews because they circumcise their male infants and that they circumcise their male infants because they are Jews? These acquired characteristics are localized not within the body but within the language of the *Volk*. Lazarus and Steinthal are developing a definition of group identification that is rooted in a biological (and therefore for them observable and demonstrable) relationship but that self-consciously builds a sense of group cohesion upon this basic identity. This is an answer to the argument about "race" constructing the mentality of the group, for here it is the group that is constituted based on the biological accidents of birth and dwelling, not the inborn identity of blood. And yet it is the observable, biological relationship that structures their argument.

The relationship between mind-set and race reappears within *Sex and Character*, but with quite a different focus. Weininger's work on the sexual is important in understanding Freud's response to Weininger's equation of the Jewish male with the Aryan female as well as in seeing how Freud can avoid a claim for the visualization of science. Weininger's "laws of sexual attraction" postulate the existence of a biological (i.e., real) explanation for sexual attraction. This is much the same ground that most of the post-Darwin biologists plowed. For Weininger the basis of attraction is the existence of both male and female qualities of mind in every individual. Just as the Jew, for Weininger, is a quality of mind that can be expunged, so is the feminine. Because to him masculinity and femininity are abstractions, the possibility for bisexuality arises. Weininger states this literally in the form of mock-formulas, with *"M"* and *"W"* representing the male and female mentalities, and other such pseudomathematical parallels. This model of the "mixed" race is carried over into his representation of the relationship between Jew and Aryan.

When Weininger wrote, there was a set model for the relationship between models of sexuality and models of race. The model of racial attraction is more directly stated by the nineteenth-century French writer Abel Hermant: "Differences of race are irreducible and between two beings who love each other they cannot fail to produce exceptional and instructive reactions. In the first superficial ebullition of love, indeed, nothing notable may be manifested, but in a fairly short time the two lovers, innately hostile, in striving to approach each other strike against an invisible partition which separates them. Their sensibilities are divergent; everything in each shocks the other; even their anatomical conformation, even the language of their gestures; all is foreign" (Ellis 1920, 176).

Weininger's first law of sexual attraction is a response to this view. Sexual attraction, he argues, is based on wholeness and complementarity. One strives to have a complete male and complete female by combining the masculine and feminine natures of two individuals, each of which has both masculine and feminine qualities. Weininger's second law attempts to explain the strength of sexual affinity in any conceivable case. For this he adds in the "race factor" as well as "the health and absence of deformity in the two individuals" (Weininger 1906, 38). Weininger accepts the premise that Jews look different, that there is a "universally acquired correspondence between mind and body," and that, "the science of character can be linked with morphology, [which] will be valuable not only to these sciences but to physiognomy" (Weininger 1906, 60).

It is the form of the Jewish body that evokes Freud's interest in

Weininger, for to Freud it is the form of the body that determines the state of the psyche. The "diseased" body gives rise to the "diseased" mind, or at least the discordance between the image of the body and that of the mind leads to psychosis. It is the homology between the body of the Jew and the body of the woman that for Weininger provides the antithetical image of the Aryan male, which to him, the self-hating convert, was the ultimate Aryan. His body is intact, not diseased, and his soul reflects the natural balance between the masculine and the feminine within the bisexual model.

The intact penis, Freud argues, despises the circumcised penis, which is seen as analogous to but not the same as the castrated woman. But in the child—the non-Jewish child—circumcision's absence leads to the neurosis of anti-Semitism. Here is Freud's first attempt—much more detailed in his later works such as *Totem and Taboo* and *Moses and Monotheism*—to deal with anti-Semitism as a disease of the uncircumcised. Cesare Lombroso had stated this quite clearly in a review of Max Nordau's polemic against modernism entitled *Degeneration*, calling anti-Semitism a sort of "disease" that afflicts people like "madness." According to Lombroso, Richard Wagner is in many of his works "not only mad but imbecile. . . . When he wrote 'Judaism in Music' [his polemic against the Jews], he had a sort of delirium of persecution against the Jews" (Lombroso, 60).

As early as 1907 Freud had seen anti-Semitism as a neurotic symptom (Nunberg and Federn 1975–76, vol. 1, 134–37). Theodor Adorno's work on the authoritarian personality in the 1940s evoked this view of "anti-Semitism as 'symptom' which fulfills an 'economic' function within the subject's psychology" (Adorno et al. 1950, 627). Even in contemporary discussions of hatred of Jews, psychoanalytic models have been used to explain the universal underpinnings of the phenomenon (Kuttner 1930; Bohm 1930; Feller 1931; Ostow 1983). In 1919 Freud again states that in the practice of circumcision "we may also trace one of the roots of the anti-Semitism which appears with such elemental force and finds such irrational expression among the nations of the West. Circumcision is unconsciously equated with castration. If we venture to carry our conjectures back to the primeval days of the human race we can surmise that originally circumcision must have been a milder substitute, designed to take the place of castration" (Freud 1955–74, vol. 11, 95–96).

Freud also sees circumcision as a sign of "primitive peoples," and he, like most of his contemporaries, cites parallel cases from Australia (Freud 1955–74, vol. 22, 86). In 1893 Arthur H. Daniels introduces his discussion of the meaning of circumcision by noting that "it is by no means a distinctively Jewish rite" (Freud 1955–74, vol. 22, 86). However, although the rite may be "primitive," it is also assumed to be a primary sign of Jewishness.

The scientific debate about circumcision not only affects the way the male Jew understands a central part of his anatomy, his penis, but also forms his understanding of his place in the social fabric. For Weininger the debate about the Jewish body is distanced once he reduces the nature of the masculine and feminine to psychological constructs (like the Jew and the Aryan). The "real" nature of his own circumcised, homosexual body is thus subsumed to the abstractions lodged in the psyche.

The meaning of the genitalia remains central for Freud. He can, in *Civilization and Its Discontents* (1930), without hesitation paraphrase Havelock Ellis's view that "the genitals themselves, the sight of which is always exciting, are nevertheless hardly ever judged to be beautiful; the quality of beauty seems, instead, to attach to certain secondary sexual characteristics" (Freud 1955–74, vol. 21, 83). Here Freud's comments ring with a claim for universality, but he also notes that "the pride taken by women in the appearance of their genitals is quite a special feature of their vanity; and disorders of the genitals which they think calculated to inspire feelings of repugnance or even disgust have an incredible power of humiliating them, of lowering their self-esteem, and of making them irritable, sensitive, and distrustful" (Freud 1955–74, vol 7, 84). Clearly, then, it is the male who thinks his genitalia are ugly (the traditional antithesis of beautiful).

But is it every male who sees his penis as unaesthetic? Or do only those males who see their genitalia as "disordered" feel this sense of "repugnance or even disgust"? It is possible that it is the debate about the diseased or disordered nature of the circumcised penis that places these remarks into a meaningful context. Freud's argument in *Civilization and Its Discontents* that the genitalia are ugly comes in a rather odd context, for he goes on to conclude that "happiness, in the reduced sense in which we recognize it as possible, is a problem of the economics of the individual's libido. There is no golden rule which applies to everyone: every man must find out for himself in what particular fashion he can be saved" (Freud 1955–74, vol. 21, 83). This quotation, known to every school child in Germany, had been scribbled by Friedrich the Great on the margin of a report opposing the establishment of Roman Catholic schools in Prussia in 1740. By the *fin-de-siècle* this phrase had become standard in the political rhetoric of Jewish emancipation, a fact that would have shocked Frederick, who shared his idol Voltaire's negative attitude toward the Jews (Gilman 1969, 69; see also Freud 1955–74, vol. 20, 236). Freud contextualizes his understanding of the meaning of the genitalia in the terms of the meaning attributed to his body in the scientific literature of his own time.

It is not only in Freud's works that the debate about the nature of the Jewish body appears within the parameters employed by Otto Weininger. The sexual identity of the Jews becomes a theme in the early psychoanalytic literature, which is of little surprise, as most of the early psychoanalysts were Jews who were forced to deal with the question of the meaning of their own bodies within the medical and psychological literature of the day. All of the charges about the diseased, pathological, ugly nature of the male Jew's body are those leveled at Jews in general, and all are reversed by the Viennese-Jewish literary critic and psychoanalyst Otto Rank. In his essay "The Essence of Judaism" of 1905, he unites a number of issues from the medical and forensic literature and reverses their implications (Klein 1981, 170–72). Society, Rank argues, moves toward ever greater sexual repression until it "reaches the neurotic stage of anti-sexuality, a disturbance of consciousness." This disease state has yet been reached by the Jews, as they have preserved themselves at a more "primitive" yet "relatively favorable stage of the repression process" through their closer ties to nature. Echoing Weininger's parallel, Rank sees the now positive, primitive sexuality of the Jew to be "like [that of a] woman, they have remained 'unchanged.' " The "essence of Judaism is its stress on primitive sexuality," which is similar to the wellspring of artistic creativity, for the individual artist exists because of a repression of sexuality. Jewish sexuality, unlike that of the artist, provided the impetus for the selection of "specifically Jewish professions, which are simple, sensible attempts at preventing nervous illness." As a result Jews "became physicians. For, the Jews thoroughly understand the radical cure of neurosis better than any other people. . . . They brought matters to such a point that they could help others, since they have sought to preserve themselves from illness." Here we have the entire repertoire of charges: Jews have perverse, atavistic sexual practices; they sexually resemble women; they have a special relationship to mental illness and its cure. Rank's answer to Weininger is much more direct than Freud's, yet all three remain within the realm of debate outlined by the medical literature of the *fin-de-siècle*. Weininger abandons the Jewish body, Freud reconstitutes its meaning, and Rank glorifies it.

THE MIND OF THE JEW

If Freud's overt reading of the "highly gifted but sexually deranged" Weininger was in the context of the meaning of the Jewish body, his subliminal reading was in the context of the meaning of madness in terms of being able to write such a book as *Sex and Character*. The question of the relationship between the idea of madness and the meaning of creativity was much discussed at the turn of the century, especially within the reception of the work of Cesare Lombroso. The question of race (which Lombroso addresses) became a central factor in these debates. That Jews were active within the spheres of culture and science could not be contradicted, but was their activity to be understood as "creative"? Thus an acknowledgment of the seemingly central role of Jews in culture could be countered by arguing that this type of culture was superficial or perhaps even corrupting. Indeed, it could even be argued that the "creativity" of the Jews was really a sign of their diseased, "mad" state. Lombroso cites the key example of this relationship for the *fin-de-siècle* scientist: Heinrich Heine. Heine's illness, according to Lombroso, was not madness but a disease of the spinal cord that "may have given a morbid character" to his writing (Lombroso 1895, 152).

The debate about the nature of the Jew's creativity ran through the medical as well as the popular literature of the *fin de siècle*. It is in Weininger's *Sex and Character* that this view (espoused by German writers such as F. M. Klinger in the early nineteenth century) enters into the discourse of medicine. For Weininger Jews and women have "no genius." He attacks Spinoza and Heinrich Heine as the representative Jewish thinkers who are viewed by his contemporaries as "creative" geniuses. But they are for him incapable of true genius: "The philosopher Spinoza, about whose purely Jewish descent there can be no doubt, is incomparably the greatest Jew of the last nine hundred years, much greater than the poet Heine (who indeed was destitute of any quality of true greatness) (Weininger 1906, 216). What passes for genius in the Jew and the woman, he says, is but "exaggerated egotism" (Weininger 1906, 317). Jewish creativity is inherently superficial.

What characterizes the woman is her language: "The impulse to lie is stronger in woman, because, unlike that of man, her memory is not continuous, whilst her life is discrete, unconnected, discontinuous, swayed by the sensations and perceptions of the moment instead of dominating them" (Weininger 1906, 146). Women's language is lies: Jews' language is speaking so (racially) distinctively that it marks the speaker as a Jew: "Just as the acuteness of Jews has nothing to do with true power of differentiating, so his shyness about singing or even about speaking in clear positive tones has nothing to do with real reserve. It is a kind of inverted pride; having no true sense of his own worth, he fears being made ridiculous by his singing or his speech" (Weininger 1906, 324).

Jews and women, for example, have no "true humor," for true humor must be transcendent; Jews "are witty only at [their] own expense and on sexual things" (Weininger 1906, 318). Jews are inherently more preoccupied by the sexual but less potent than Aryans (Weininger 1906, 311). Their obsession is rooted in the fact that sex breaks down boundaries between individuals. Jews, like women, are also "devoid of humor and addicted to mockery"; "the Jew who does not set out, like the humorist, from the transcendental, and does not move towards it, like the erotic, has no interest in depreciating what is called the actual world, and that never becomes for him the paraphernalia of a juggler or the nightmare of a mad-house" (Weininger 1906, 319).

It is this view that is reversed by Otto Rank in "The Essence of Judaism" (1905), when he notes that "where the religion [of the Jews] is insufficient [to maintain psychic balance], Jews resort to wit; for they do not have their own "culture' " (Klein 1981, 171). By "culture" Rank is adapting and reversing Weininger's view of the centeredness of the Christian. "Culture," for Rank, is an advanced state of sexual repression. The Jews exist in a much more "primitive" and "natural" state in which this level of repression has not yet taken place. Humor becomes an atavistic sign of their sexuality.

Weininger continues his argument by declaring that Jews are histori-cally extremely adaptable, as can be shown by their talent for the superficial areas of "creativity" such as journalism, but that in their essence they are truly unchangeable. They lack deep-rooted and original ideas and are the essential unbelievers, not even believing in themselves (Weininger 1906, 320, 321). The Jews have no center. They are critical, not critics. They are not merely materialists, but rather doubt all and any truths. They are irreligious; indeed, their religion is not even a real religion but a reflection of the Jewish mind, which always demands multiple choices. It is not the historical treatment of the Jews that has made them what they are for "outward circumstances do not mould a race in one direction, unless there is in the race the innate tendency to respond" (Weininger 1906, 308). And the Jewishness of the Jew is immutable. The Jew is a "parasite" who is "a different creature in every host and yet remains himself" (Weininger 1906, 320). The Jew is the disease in the body politic.

It is within science, most specifically within medicine, that this immutability of mind and spirit, this moral "madness," most clearly manifests itself. For the Jews there is no transcendentalism; everything is as flat and commonplace as possible. Their effort to understand everything robs the world of its mystery. Evolutionary theory ("the ridiculous notion that men are derived from monkeys" (Weininger 1906, 314–51), for exam-ple, is mere materialism. And materialism is the essence of the Jews.

The change in nineteenth-century medicine from its focus on bacteri-ology in the 1880s to its focus on biochemistry at the turn of the century meant a real shift of the medical scientist's interest from the organic to the inert, a phenomenon that was the subject of medical debates of the period. Emil Dubois-Reymond, for example, excoriates the direction in which modern medicine is moving as being "too utilitarian, too materialistic, and . . . in the process of being destroyed by the very industries to which it gives rise." This he labels as the "Americanization" of medicine. John S.

Billings, the founder of the Johns Hopkins University Hospital in Baltimore, defends this "dreadful permeation of European civilization by realism" as merely the natural progress of science (Garrison 1915, 234–35). For Weininger, this "Americanization" is the result of the "Jewification" of modern medicine. Jews are natural chemists, he argues, which explains why medicine has become biochemistry: "The present turn of medical science is largely due to the influence of the Jews, who in such numbers have embraced the medical profession. From the earliest times, until the dominance of the Jews, medicine was closely allied with religion. But now they make it a matter of drugs, a mere administration of chemicals.... The chemical interpretation of organisms sets these on a level with their own dead ashes," for the Jews focus on the dead, the inert (Weininger 1906, 315).

Weininger views the turn of the century as the age of feminization, another corruption of society caused by the Jews: "This is the age which is most Jewish and most feminine. . . . It is a time when art is content with daubs and seeks its inspiration in the sports of animals; . . . a time for originality and yet with the most foolish craving for originality. The choice must be made between Judaism and Christianity, between business and culture, between male and female, between the race and the individual, between unworthiness and worth. . . . Mankind has the choice to make. There are only two poles, and there is no middle way" (Weininger 1906, 329–30). Jewishness, like the feminine, is a state condemned to be uncreative. This litany of hate places the Jew in an antithetical relationship to true creativity, which bears a great risk for madness. Weininger's position is hardly unique. It reflects the general view of anti-Semitic racial science about the special nature of the Jew, which linked creativity to Jews, their "madness," and the ultimate source of their madness, their sexuality.

Now we must imagine Freud confronting this view. Of all of the topics about the nature of the psyche he could have addressed, why did creativity so capture him? This is indeed as idiosyncratic as his choice of dreams or jokes or slips of the tongue as means of discussing the normal structure of the psyche, each of which can be linked to debates within the racial science of the late nineteenth century (Gilman 1985, 175–91).

On the surface Freud's view of creativity is quite different. In his writings from the close of the nineteenth century through the onset of World War I, he sees creativity, as he does dreams or slips of the tongue or neurotic symptoms, not as a set of formal processes or disease mechanisms in a subset of the population but as clues to the normal functioning of the unconscious in everyone. Where Lombroso saw the mad and their aesthetic productions as throwbacks to an earlier, more primitive state of development or as a sign of the diseased nature of the Jew, Freud sees all creativity as a sign of the universal, underlying forces that make all human beings human. He also sees it as pathological in that it is the result of deviation from "normal" psychological development. But such pathologies can occur in *all* human beings, not merely a predestined subset. He studied the creative to understand the centrality of unconscious processes, especially the role of unconscious motivation in human action.

Freud, in his case studies of Leonardo (1910) and Michelangelo (1914) as well as in his critical readings of the creative works of Wilhelm Jensen (1907) and the autobiography of Dr. Daniel Schreber (1911), looks at the creative work as a sign of the displacement of psychic (which for Freud means sexual) energy into a different, seemingly unrelated undertaking (Gedo 1983; Hare 1987; Mason 1988). The creative impulse is a form of displacement or repression analogous to the symptoms of the neurotic, which parallel the experiences or fantasies that underlie them but do not directly represent the underlying conflict that gives rise to them. For Freud it is in the sphere of the sexual that these products (whether neurotic symptoms or works of art) always arise. By Freud's definition, the creative individual is one who *must* sublimate sexual drive into the realm of fantasy. Thus Weininger, whom Freud sees as being "completely under the sway of his infantile complexes," would be creative through his "relation to the castration complex" (Freud 1955–74, vol. 10, 36n) that underlies his own sexuality. The creative individual, such as Weininger, sublimates urges and anxieties into the work of art.

The reason for this sublimation, as in the case of the creative personalities Freud studied, is the socially unacceptable direction of the expression of their sexuality, such as the homosexuality of Leonardo and the incestuous leanings of Jensen. The active, social repression of these drives in a few individuals leads to the total sublimation of sexual curiosity into the creative process and the true work of art (Freud 1955–74, vol. 9, 167–76). The creative object thus represents the fixed fantasies of the individual. The essential nature of the process of creativity is to mask the inherently socially objectionable nature of its origin. Works of art "conceal their personal origin and, by obeying the laws of beauty, bribe other people with a bonus of pleasure" (Freud 1955–74, vol. 23, 187; see also Hanly 1986; Kaplan 1988) The overarching "laws of beauty" and the technique of the aesthetic are the means by which the creative works. It is the universal mask that hides and manipulates. It is separate from the creative impulse and shapes how the observer sees the work of art. Creativity is thus viewed in terms of the creator who produces a product, which is implicitly a commodity inherently attached with value. This product is cast in a form that is universal, and it manipulates the reader or viewer through its evocation of some universal law (the aesthetic). The creativity of the artist is the placing of a repressed aspect of the artist's psyche into the realm of the aesthetic. As Joseph Breuer writes, commenting on the ultimate creative figure for nineteenth-century German culture in the *Studies in Hysteria* (jointly authored with Freud in 1895), "Goethe did not feel he had dealt with an experience till he had discharged it in a creative artistic activity" (Freud 1955–74, vol. 2, 207).

But it is the act of seeing—the observer's act of seeing and responding to the creative product of the artist—that defines creativity for Freud. To use one of his examples, we—the naive viewer—look at Leonardo's *Holy Family* and "see" its perfection and beauty, but also are instructed in its "meaning" by the psychoanalyst, who is able to see beneath the initial evocation of the aesthetic (which disguises the artist's motivation) and interpret the work of art and the psyche of the artist. The uninformed viewer's response is aesthetic; it is with the aid of the interpreter (Freud) that one can understand the source of the artist's creativity and thus truly appreciate the unseen aspect of the work of art. It is here that we learn to distrust the initial act of seeing and to link that act not with a visceral response but with the act of knowing. Freud's focus seems to be solely on the motivation that underlies creativity. It is the discovery that the creative individual is "subject to the laws which govern both normal and patholog-ical activity with equal cogency" that Freud illustrates (Freud 1955–74, vol. 11, 63), but his hidden agenda is to undermine our sense that we can see the world directly.

This is clearest in Freud's popular essay on "Creative Writers and Day-Dreaming," which was presented as a lecture to a lay (i.e., nonmedi-cal) audience in Vienna in 1907 (Freud 1955–74, vol. 9, 143–53). Freud's overt intention is to present the parallels between creativity and childhood play. He defines creativity and the special status of the creative artist as follows: "We laymen have always been intensely curious to know—like the Cardinal who put a similar question to Ariosto—from what sources that strange being, the creative writer, draws his material, and how he manages to make such an impression on us with it and to arouse in us emotions which, perhaps, we had not thought ourselves capable" (Freud 1955–74, vol. 9, 143). Freud places himself as a "layman" in opposition to the "creative" individual who makes a world that seems complete and who uses that world to manipulate our ("lay," or "noncreative") emotions. But it is a very special "lay" observer, one who has the insight into the underlying meaning as well as the immediate effect of the creative. Freud's initial analogy is to the play of the child. Play is rooted in childhood fantasies of being able to control at least the immediate world of toys rather than the real world, which is beyond the manipulation of the child (Kofman 1988). It is in this universe in which uncontrollable realities are transmuted into manipulable fantasies into which the child escapes, "for many things which, if they were real, could give no enjoyment, can do so in the play of fantasy" (Freud 1955–74, vol. 9, 144). But it is strangely humor that is for Freud the ultimate example of how the healthy adult can escape back into this world of playfulness, for "by equating his ostensibly serious occupations of to-day with his childhood games, he can throw off the too heavy burden imposed on him by life and win the high yield of pleasure afforded by *humor*" (Freud 1955–74, vol. 9, 145 [Freud's emphasis]).

Fantasy is like dreaming. It uses everyday impressions that are related to earlier (infantile) experience and "creates a situation relating to the future." Thus in addition to being like the playful child, the creative individual is also like the neurotic in another central aspect, for both have the compulsion to tell (represent) their fantasies (Chasseguet-Smirgel 1984): "there is a class of human beings upon whom, not a god, indeed, but a stern goddess—Necessity—has allotted the task of telling what they suffer and what things give them happiness. These are the victims of nervous illness, who are obliged to tell their fantasies." (Freud 1955–74, vol. 9, 146). In paraphrasing Goethe's *Torquato Tasso* in this passage ("and when a man falls silent in his torment/A god granted me to tell how I suffer"), Freud elides the artist as figure (Tasso) and the artist as author (Goethe, the ultimate example of the creative individual in German culture) with the mad person as figure (Tasso) and the healer of the mad (Freud). The artificial line that Freud had drawn between the creative individual as neurotic on the one side and himself (and his listeners) on the other is shown to be a false dichotomy. The informed, psychoanalytically instructed observer "sees" below the surface. Freud joins the world of art as artifact and inspiration in his creative role as the psychoanalyst, but only in the most hidden and covert way.

In Freud's essay of 1907 the creative individual is also not gender-neutral. Young women have more erotic fantasies than do young men, he argues, who have in turn more fantasies of ambition. Both must learn to conceal and repress these drives, as they are unacceptable in polite society: "the well-brought-up young woman is only allowed a minimum of erotic desire, and the young man has to learn to suppress the excess of self-regard which he brings with him from the spoilt days of his childhood, so that he may find his place in a society which is full of other individuals making equally strong demands" (Freud 1955–74, vol. 9, 147). Human sexuality, the wellspring of creativity, is initially and more strongly present in the phantasm world of the female. Although these trends concerning the nature of the creative impulse merge at some point early in the life cycle, it is the female whose fantasies are the more sexualized in their most primitive (i.e., earliest) form.

Thus in this text Freud provides a set of working hypotheses about creativity: first, that creativity has to do with the representation of internal stories in a highly affective and effective manner; second, that creativity is parallel to the states of childhood and neurosis in that it is an attempt to gain control over the world by creating a world over which one can have control (humor being the prime example of this control); third, that there is a difference but also a similarity between the fantasy life (and therefore the creativity) of men and women. All of this is framed by a most ambiguous narrative voice that claims that the creative artist is different from the author of the text that we are reading (this is made evident in the banality of the hypothetical novel that Freud outlines in his essay), yet that parallels his experience with that of both the artist in reality and in the work of art.

Freud is, however, not interested in the problem of creativity for its own sake. He sees his explanation of the nature of creativity as one of the central proofs for the validity of his science, psychoanalysis. In his programmatic text of 1913, "The Claims of Psycho-Analysis to Scientific Interest," Freud outlines the theory of repression as not only the key to an understanding of the production of the beautiful but also one of the substantial pieces of evidence of the explanatory power (i.e., scientific validity) of his views. He stresses the power of the aesthetic on the viewer, but leaves the door open to yet further meaningful contributions to the understanding of the aesthetic through the science of psychoanalysis: "most of the problems of artistic creation and appreciation await further study, which will throw the light of analytic knowledge on them and assign them their place in the complex structure presented by the compensation for human wishes. Art is a conventionally accepted reality in which, thanks to artistic illusion, symbols and substitutes are able to provoke real emotions. Thus art constitutes a region half-way between a reality which frustrates wishes and the wish-fulfilling world of the imagination—a region in which, as it were, primitive man's strivings for omnipotence are still in force" (Freud 1955–74, vol. 23, 187–88).

Freud's reading of the work of art is clearly both within the paradigm of late nineteenth-century visual and literary art, and, more importantly, still bound by Lombroso's association of the creative with the primitive. But it is not the "primitive" localized in the inhabitants of the asylum or the prison, the throwback, but the "primitive" within each and every human being. Freud seems to need to associate the creative with the universal and with a universal science, psychoanalysis.

What is clear is the basic difficulty of Freud's argument: if sexual repression is the key to creativity, why are not all sexually repressed individuals creative? After World War I Freud himself became quite aware of this objection, as he later noted in his study "Dostoevski and Parricide" (1928): "before the problem of the creative artist analysis must, alas, lay down its arms" (Freud 1955–74, vol. 21, 177). Or, as he states in his "Autobiographical Study" (1925), psychoanalysis "can do nothing towards elucidating the nature of the artistic gift, nor can it explain the means by which the artist works—artistic technique" (Freud 1955–74, vol. 20, 70). But the question should better be asked in reverse: why are Freud's early categories of creativity so constructed as to make all human beings potentially creative? Why does he need to universalize the question of the creative? Why does he need to place creativity within those sexual drives and psychic phenomena that are, according to Freud, present in all human beings, not merely in the insane? Why does the feminine seem to have the closest relationship to the wellspring of the creative? What do sexuality, creativity, and madness have to do with one another at the turn of the century? Why must Freud maintain that creativity is like neurosis in its inherent characteristic of repression?

The meaning of Freud's representation of the creative, seen not as Lombroso's "throwback" or deviant but as a reflection of universal processes, can be understood in the context of Freud's role as a scientist and a Jew in *fin-de-siècle* Vienna. One can assume that the question of creativity had a special significance for Freud, especially from 1903 to 1910, the period in which Weininger's views were most widely circulated and discussed in Vienna. These views were read against the more general debates within psychiatry about the special status of Jewish genius (Hirsch 1894). Freud needed to move the question of the Jew's madness and creativity onto another level of debate. For Freud the special definition of these concepts and their relationship becomes part of his proof for the universality of the human psyche. His stress on the sexual etiology of all neurosis leads to his view that creativity is analogous to neurosis in its repression of conflicted sexual identity. The subtext that links the creative, the psychopathological, and the sexual is, as we have seen, linked in the portrait of the psyche of the Jew, which existed at precisely the point at which Freud's interest turns to the question of the creative.

Freud's response is to separate the question of Jewish madness and creativity from the universal laws that he sees as causing psychopathology. These laws are parallel to the laws that determine the creative. Freud begins, in the first decade of the twentieth century, to refashion Lombroso's separate categories of the normal and the abnormal. He is forced to do so because, unlike the Italian Jew Lombroso, he first senses (according to his own active memory) his difference from everyone else when he begins to study medicine and is confronted with the image of his own "racial" difference. For Freud science and race are linked experiences (Olender 1989). Weininger sees as the salient example of this association the nature of "Jewish" medicine—a purely mechanistic, materialistic medicine, more chemistry than the art of healing. Jews are not creative, especially in this realm of science, but rather destructive.

Freud first struggles to show how everyone who is creative or dreams or is mad responds to the same, universal rules of psychic organization. His science, the science of psychoanalysis—which evolves in the closing decade of the nineteenth century, while rooted in a materialistic paradigm—self-consciously attempts to move medicine toward an understanding of the dynamic processes of the psyche, the immaterial aspect of the human being. Freud thus abandons chemistry for metapsychology. This he is constrained to do because of his certainty than human sexuality—associated with the obsessive hypersexuality of the Jews, the very source of their perverse "madness"—lies at the center of human experience. Freud positions himself (more and more successfully as his thought develops after World War I) in opposition to the positivistic clinical gaze of Jean-Martin Charcot and the materialistic brain mythology of Moriz Benedikt. His is not the medicine sketched by Weininger and has, therefore, at least the potential to claim a position as creative. But Freud does not do this unambiguously, as seen in his 1907 essay, for in openly labeling himself as "creative" he would be labeling himself as a Jew. He would thus be setting himself off from the universal role of the "layman" (to use his word) as the observer. But he is not the "layman," he is the scientist-physician. And his science must be universal, not particular, in its claims for creativity. The scientist-physician lays claim to the universal gaze, unencumbered by national or racial perspective, especially in the arena of sexology, where the accusation is that Jews, by their very nature, are predisposed to seeing the sexual everywhere.

Freud thus has the creative operate as a reflex of that force that is present in all human beings—sexuality. It is this force that has been used to label the Jew as different. It now becomes the source of all human endeavors, including the truly creative. But this is present more in the feminine fantasy than in the masculine, a view that certainly mirrors Weininger's dismissal of the sexual contamination of Jewish (not feminine) creativity. Freud reverses all of the poles of the anti-Semitic discourse on creativity that framed Weininger's view. Weininger's link between madness and creativity is maintained, but these tendencies are now seen as a product of universal rather than racial psychology. What is striking in all of Freud's discussions of creativity between 1900 and 1919 is that he never evokes any Jewish writer or painter—neither his contemporary and neighbor, the playwright Arthur Schnitzler, nor the best known German artist of his day, the Impressionist Max Liebermann, nor the classic examples of Jewish creativity, Spinoza and Heine—in his discussions of creativity and the nature of the creative (Gilman 1990a). Creativity is universal; Freud's examples are not. They self-consciously eliminate the Jewish component in European culture (Homans 1989, 88–95).

Freud is still limited by the context of his struggle with the anti-Semitic implications of madness and creativity in his age. It is only with the triumph of the Nazis, in 1938, that he finally confronts this question in a German émigré magazine. His answer to the rise of anti-Semitism is a paraphrase of a lost or invented essay reputedly by a non-Jew, in which the contributions of the Jews to the Diaspora are evaluated: "Nor can we call them [the Jews] in any sense inferior. Since we have allowed them to co-operate in our cultural tasks, they have acquired merit by valuable contributions in all the spheres of science, art, and technology, and they have richly repaid our tolerance" (Freud 1955–74, vol. 23, 292). "Science," such as psychoanalysis, and then "art" represent the Jews' creative contributions to German culture. But each are creative, and each marks the positive presence of the Jew in European society. The ambiguity of creativity in the *fin de siècle* vanishes in the harsh light of the Nazi realization of the view of Jews in German culture as represented by Weininger. It is against this that Freud reacts.[2]

8 ✦

CHARACTEROLOGY: WEININGER AND AUSTRIAN POPULAR SCIENCE

Katherine Arens

In turn-of-the-century Austria, a branch of popular psychology known as characterology arose, falling somewhere between the medical community and a more popular audience (Arens 1986), and questioned whether an individual is a product of biological inheritance (a conservative variant of Darwinism) or environmental influences (a late, more liberal permutation of Lamarckianism stressing cultural improvement [cf. Boyer 1981; Rabinbach 1983; Bottomore and Goode 1978]). Despite the scientific origins of this debate (cf. Lesky 1976), the paradigm of characterology particularly affected the general public, as various popular texts attest, even if this public may not have been educated into all its ramifications. Notable cases, such as that of Sigmund Freud's and Josef Breuer's Anna O., reflect these widely accepted assumptions about the mental constitution of individuals.

To investigate this popular science, the familiar nineteenth-century philosophical-medical definitions of character will first be presented as keys to the norm for discussions of the mind and personal development. Then, Otto Weininger's *Geschlecht und Charakter* (Sex and Character) (1927 [1903]), a work with little theoretical adequacy but great persuasive power for its intended audience, will serve as a model of the popular debate based loosely on the dominant biological-psychological issues of the day. Finally, the cases of Arthur Schnitzler and Karen Horney will demonstrate the importance of considering both the scientific paradigm and its popular environment when evaluating the reception of bodies of work, either popular or scientific.

THE BACKGROUND: MIND MODELS IN PHILOSOPHY AND MEDICINE

Characterology is today identified as a branch of popular psychology, but psychology did not exist as an independent discipline at the start of the nineteenth century in Germany; there was no separate discipline with the purview of studying mind in the world (cf. Arens 1989b). However, starting in the eighteenth century, particularly those philosophers interested in education, conceptualization, and moral development had devoted their time to a part of the field of practical philosophy known as "faculty psychology" (cf. Zilboorg and Henry 1941; Young 1970; Wyss 1973; Ellenberger 1970). In this model, the "faculties of the mind," which are posited mental entities controlling facts of the human mind such as reasoning, emotions, and even language, perform individual tasks within the total personality. Since these faculties are innate, the human organism was believed to be predisposed to certain functions that were designed by the deity to facilitate life on earth. For example, the faculty of reason prolonged survival, and the faculty of speech developed communities. More importantly for the scientific debate, these ideas created a model of the normal biological and cognitive human, the morally and physically healthy mind and spirit.

Nonetheless, by the end of the eighteenth century, the discussion of faculties was changing terms: faculties were no longer really structural units of the organism, but rather arbitrary names for typical habits of mental activity. At the same time, the practical philosophy to which this new concept of faculties was tied became linked to various historical and practical disciplines in the humanities and social sciences. The result was a series of investigations stressing the historical and cultural variability of mental processing habits. For instance, Immanuel Kant, in his work on anthropology in the 1780s, started to correlate mental types with character, national type, and morality; mental activity was thus considered to be under the auspices of historical or geographical influences. After 1800, his disciple Johann Friedrich Herbart expanded notions of conceptual threshold and learning abilities into the distinct field of educational psychology; he demonstrated the adaptability of conceptual patterns through structured habituation of the individual mind.

Shortly after 1800, the mind model used in practical philosophy was also adopted by the emerging professional medical community, where it received a small but crucial twist of focus. The resultant model for healthy mental function presupposed a correlation between inborn mental activity and individual experience or learning; in consequence, a classification of deviant behaviors and physical formations should correlate with the mind's malfunctions or illnesses. The philosophers had stressed interaction between mental activity and environment mediated by the body in typical patterns; in adopting their model, physicians and early medical psychologists sought the abnormal. Mental malfunctions were thought to be predicated on abnormal interactions between the body and the environment, which would ultimately yield sick, bent, or malformed individuals, victims of stunted development who could not participate in their cultural group. The philosophers' focus on the learning process of the normal human thus receded in importance as the physicians focused on the finished human with symptoms or illness caused by misguided mental activities.

Several notable medical texts document this shift. Perhaps the most notable was a textbook first published in 1845 by the psychiatrist Wilhelm Griesinger that was to be a standard for several decades: *Pathology and Therapy of Psychic Illnesses* (Griesinger 1882). In it, Griesinger fused psychology with neurology and anatomy, systematically cataloging mental illness by correlating behavioral symptoms with physical causes. His catalog stressed the reciprocity of physical experience and mental functioning, emphasizing an individual's learning from the environment to explain how physical symptoms can be correlated to weaknesses in mental process. This furthered the move to systematize physical symptoms as keys to mental illness. The patterns of patients' thoughts (stressing *how*, not *what*, they thought) were described as distinguishing symptoms of mental illness, rooted in patterns of mental activity aggravated by weak organisms and improperly formed in a developmental interface. The diagnosing physician was to use the predominance of the physical symptom to uncover the interaction between mind and body.

The philosophers' focus on normal function was thus not totally lost in the medical community: physiologists and physicists joined with psychologists to determine normal thresholds for sense organs. Wilhelm Wundt and Hermann Helmholtz, whose laboratories in Leipzig and Berlin lasted well into this century, continued this line of pure research by determining limits on the perception of stimuli, such as variations in lights and tones. In Prague and later in Vienna, Ernst Mach expanded this idea to limit the validity of results in scientific experiments. He believed the physical world, and thus all science, is limited by our senses, inherited language, and conceptual tools. These projects were paralleled by the expositions of William James in the English-speaking world. Together, they elaborated a psychology that focused on development—on the interactions between mind, body, and physical environment, and thus on wellness and normal function.

In the nineteenth century, then, two parallel models of the mind pervaded Germany and Austria, both positing that an organism sponsors mental activities to foster its survival and development. One was institutionalized in the medical schools, particularly at Vienna, with its stress on therapeutic nihilism and physical self-healing; it focused on illness and physical symptoms. The other was institutionalized in physiology, physics, and educational psychology; it focused on wellness and normal function. Despite their common stresses on the interactions between mind, body, and environment, these two models were not resolved institutionally; psychology still did not exist as an independent academic department at the end of the century, except in unusual circumstances. A disjunction began to separate cognitive theory, laboratory research, and practical diagnostics and therapy, as theory on the mind in itself was gradually relegated to philosophy, while the mind-body link tended to be turned over to medicine.

The debate about characterology took place in the void between these fields, playing out an ideological battle and ultimately fighting for institutional confirmation. Despite its weaknesses, Weininger's work typifies this struggle, since he was trained in physiology and philosophy, and wrote a dissertation acceptable to and debated in both communities. His work assumed the texture of both scientific discourses—their acceptable terminological and methodological premises—while reordering their priorities to appeal to the community of popular readers.

WEININGER'S *SEX AND CHARACTER*

Otto Weininger was in a position to capitalize on the intellectual and scientific conflicts in turn-of-the-century Vienna. His infamous *Sex and Character* was originally written as a dissertation and then expanded in 1903 to become a popular success, appearing in almost thirty editions by 1940. The basic material may have been stolen from Freud (some contend that Freud's patient Hermann Swoboda showed one of Freud's unpublished manuscripts to Weininger or discussed it with him) (cf. Johnston 1972; Le Rider 1985). Yet Weininger's life history enhanced the public legend he would become: in several quarters, he was declared a lost genius of the age when he committed suicide at age twenty-three. Like the many other suicides of his days, he became identified with the spirit of a generation whose aims were not fulfilled, nor even fulfillable within the context of their restrictive society. More importantly, he brought a version of a technical debate to a popular audience through his high-flown rhetorical buttressing an overly simplified logic drawn from the prevailing scientific paradigm: all human types are composed of male and female sides that influence their characters and behaviors.

Weininger probably distorted his sources; the material itself is not credible in modern scientific terms. Nonetheless, this does not detract from the significance of his book as an index for the interface between the medical and popular communities. It became the Viennese populace's introduction to scientific racism, seemingly supported by the major intellectual trends of the day. Weininger drew "proofs" from his dissertation adviser (Friedrich Jodl, a respected member of the University of Vienna's philosophy section); from current medical research (without explicitly mentioning Freud, which lends support to the assumption that he stole material, since Freud had been publishing for ten years); from other popular characterology texts (for example, Paul Möbius's *Über den physiologischen Schwachsinn des Weibes* [Leipzig, 1901]); and from a physiology resembling that of Wilhelm Wundt's famous Leipzig laboratory (Boring 1950–57).

A book that looked like a synthesis of the expanding science of the day therefore could appear credible to an uncritical public. Moreover, it articulated one of the prevailing stereotypes of the *fin de siècle:* the doctrine of the active masculine principle and the passive feminine principle. Those persons or races with a preponderance of either principle, or "protoplasm" (Weininger's term), in their make-up were classified as innately passive or active. The active were innovative and strong; the passive, receptive and weak.

Sociologically, these doctrines answered other popular needs. Anchoring mental activity to an organism removes morality from the arena of conscious choice; sexual deviance, for example, could be reclassified from a crime into an organic imbalance (a popular choice, since homosexuality was an arrestable offense in Austria, but not in France, at the turn of the century) (Markus 1984, 90ff.). This sort of thinking could seem plausible at the end of a century that had set up ethnographic museums with models of physiological types and that enumerated the physical characteristics of the "criminal type"—identifying innocent minds as well as guilty ones through physical characteristics. Only the twentieth century, familiar with Nazi eugenics and racial programs, would deem this particularly spurious (Cocks 1985).

These stereotypes about the mind-body link, based on the scientific theory of the nineteenth century, structure Weininger's argument about the individual and culture in *Sex and Character*. Since his definitions of character retain the scientific flavor of his argumentation and part of its speculative flash, they serve as a model for his interweaving of scientific paradigm and popular prejudice.

Weininger's first approach to character proper occurs in the fifth chapter of his volume, "Characterologie und Morphologie" (Weininger 1927, 60). Following the pattern of nineteenth-century experimental psychologists (particularly Gustav Wundt and Theodor Fechner), Weininger begins by asserting a correspondence between the physical and psychic characteristics of an individual, saying that "psychic types of the female and of the male . . . are mediated in spiritual terms, as well as in physical ones" (Weininger 1927, 60). Just as his contemporaries assume that different geographical and cultural experiences differentiate peoples, Weininger relies on a nonsymmetrical development of mental activity conditioned by sexual difference.

Approaching character through sexual types will create a "psychology of individual differences" (Weininger 1927, 61) in which psychological reactions are analyzed as organically conditioned. In physiology and thus in psychology, every individual oscillates between masculine and feminine poles due to periodic functions in their sexuality (here Weininger is echoing the work of Freud's friend Wilhelm Fliess without attribution [Weininger 1927, 61]). The degree to which an individual has specific characteristics of either sex will determine the degree to which he or she will be drawn to the opposite type (Weininger 1927, 65). Many intermediate stages exist, for the pure man and the pure woman are fictions. But the degree of mixing is partly determinable through morphological characteristics (he later equates female with passive and ultimately with Jewish [Weininger 1927, 89ff.]).

With these definitions, Weininger moves characterology away from the prevailing paradigm about the mind while using a number of its assumptions. He cites the interface between individuals and their environments as determining character, yet throws out the study of sense impressions or feelings that would account for true individuation found in the work of Helmholtz and Fechner, James and Richard Avenarius. Weininger's science is thus more than the study of individual differences, more than psychology in any narrow sense (Weininger 1927, 96). His characterology uses "the concept of a constant, unified essential being," which no longer considers the individual to be a product of his experiences: "the character is not something poised behind the thinking and feeling of an individual, but rather something that reveals itself in *every* thought and every feeling of that individual" (Weininger 1927, 98). Weininger's contemporaries deal in the norm and deviance of experience conditioned by or conditioning mental activity, and try to explain the relationship between individuals and their cultural norms. In contrast, Weininger turns back to a study of the permanent patterns of this mental activity—the permanent biological underpinning of the temporary states of each individual. Individuation may have to do with cultural experience, but character, rooted in biology, takes utter precedence in humans.

Weininger thus studies essences of human beings, not the differences between individuals. He does not study the metaphysical essence that might be called the soul—he is not norming behavior to the degree that eighteenth-century faculty psychology could. Instead, he defines a new, unchanging foundation within an individual that conditions differences in behavior and cognition. Here he diverges significantly from his eighteenth-century sources, arguing that neither perceptions nor a predisposition of the mental character will explain character. Weininger knows the philosophical model of the faculties, as well as the restrictions that the organism will impose on it (the medical or Empiricist restrictions), but he wishes to posit an organic transcendental ground for perception in *gendered* terms instead of purely biological ones. Both Idealists and Empiricists spoke of typical bodies functioning properly; physicians discussed disease as originating in weaknesses in psychophysical interactions between mind and body. Only Weininger posits physical types with innate strengths and weaknesses that predetermine psychical types—a structural or biological *a priori* of the body instead of the mind.

Weininger does not refute his sources in philosophy and medicine; instead, he muddles their distinct priorities. For him, the *a priori* difference between men and women lies in their different experience of sexuality (Part II, Chapter 2). This difference ultimately distinguishes male and female consciousness, a gendered perception that will affect all development through the stimulus of culture and environment (Part II, Chapter 3). Despite their shared experience in culture, the male thinks in more clearly articulated units than does the female (Weininger 1927, 120–21). The woman must therefore rely on the man to clarify the "Henides" ("raw idea units") into discrete, usable concepts. Again, Weininger describes only a typical, predetermined woman, and not an individual experiencing growth through mental activity and the common experiences of culture and history.

At this point in his text, the question of "Giftedness and Genius" arises (Chapter 4), since genius correlates with an individual's clarity in thoughts. This chapter elaborates Weininger's ideas about what is inherited in mental activity and what is learned. Talents may be inborn and are thus inheritable. Genius is, however, a mark of scope and intensity of character—a scale factor that is not necessarily inborn, but that may accompany talent. Genius is characterized by intense cycles in a person's basic constitution and by an ability to communicate them to others. Genius is thus inherently incompatible with the passive female (Weininger 1927, 139). The genius also possesses an almost universal ability to remember experiential, but not necessarily learned, data (Weininger 1927, 140–41). This claims that genius is in fact inborn to the male or is more likely to be. As a "consequence" of this fact, men possess a memory for universal categories of information, while women only remember their drive for procreation and the moments in society that aid it (Weininger 1927, 153). Nonetheless, memories are the key to the individual of either sex: "what a person never forgets, and what he cannot remember—these make most possible the uncovering of his essential being, his character" (Weininger 1927, 153). These disclaimers on talent and genius play both ends of the nineteenth-century mind model to the middle: without cultural experience, one cannot ascertain what one is born as, yet that experience will not influence the inherited constitution. Weininger needs to consider both mind and world experience as documentation, as his contemporaries assume, yet refuses to acknowledge development or the history of an individual's experience of the world. Thus for him, biology and biography belong to psychology; still, these are only diagnostic tools and have nothing to do with development, as Freud had assumed.

Freud concurs that consciousness documents both subjectivity and objective experience, a "will to value" (Weininger 1927, 167). However, Weininger finds genius in the man whose consciousness transcends time (Weininger 1927, 168), whereas in Freud's model, only the substrate of consciousness, mainly biological inheritance, is timeless, while con- sciouness is built through individual experience. Freud's individuals are caught in social time and must work to survive; Weininger's genius clarifies the past and gives it a form for others to receive. Weininger thus evaluates successful personalities against much stricter norms than Freud does, since not only the quality and scope of mental function but also its essential states are inborn. Weininger's significant person (usually male), such as the creative scientist, makes history (Weininger 1927, 172). The woman, in contrast, does not even have her own psychology, because she is not interested in herself and so has not generated any women's psycholo- gists (Weininger 1927, 182); she therefore lacks a causal, continuous picture of history. Weininger comes very close to stating that there is no true reciprocity between the woman and the environment, since commu- nication of such experience requires an active or self-reflexive character, which the woman by definition lacks. Because of their innate constitu- tions, Weininger's people are largely immune to the environmental conditioning stressed by Freud and the contemporary scientific commu- nity (of note is Ernst Mach's position [cf. Arens 1985]).

Yet whereas the woman may not be able to influence the environ- ment, Weininger's (male) genius may influence the outside world to an inordinate degree. The genius is the strongest possible personality, characterized by a sense of the whole that enables him to filter experiential data on a large scale into a coherent world view (Weininger 1927, 213). While the normal individual has a restricted world within him, the genius has the "living macrocosm in himself" (Weininger 1927, 212). No matter the scope of his personality, all that the person feels of the world or of himself stems from his constitution (Weininger 1927, 226). Each individual is the center of a united picture of the way in which the sensible world relates to itself—an anchor for communication and coherency (Weininger 1927, 190ff.). Within Weininger's framework, then, personality or character is the central event of consciousness, not any historically developing constellation of mental activity and experience: consciousness is not a product, since a person is constituted biologically, not historically. Time and the world exist within the self, as the core of our *Weltanschauung* influenced by this "ego-event" (Weininger 1927, 211).

Weininger is in this respect a modified solipsist stressing the filtering mechanisms and primacy of the ego over environment; he undoes the conclusions of historicism while purportedly relying on culture for evidence. For Weininger, the first thing one knows is the fact of existence, a sense of self or of the soul preceding all world experience (Weininger 1927, 209–11). The passive or active character of this experience—that is, its femaleness or maleness, respectively—will determine the nature of the world. The male will build a universe; the woman (or the female type, such as the Jew or homosexual) forms only an aggregate of impressions, not a coherent world view (Weininger 1927, 269). The book finishes by equating the woman and the Jew in a culture of narrow bestial consciousness. The ultimate program of this purportedly scientific discussion is clearly a justification of racism and sexism, a reduction of cultural influences to cultural products of weak constitution types. Where Weininger's medical contemporaries explored individual illness on the basis of normative biological potential, he explored typologies of illness that constitute culture. Where philosophers stressed that mind made the world, Weininger demonstrated that the body made the mind in order to fabricate a world (accordingly the mind is not a product of world, as David Hume and John Locke had posited).

This is as far as Weininger stretches the discourses of the medicine and philosophy he had inherited, but not the end of his expositions. Weininger realized that his philosophy of individual character would affect not only theory but the practical institutionalization of the sciences as well. Freud, Mach, and the medical community believed that psychology would necessarily stand next to medicine and the humanities or sciences. In a ploy for distinction or originality, Weininger believes that he has stretched psychology into two sciences. The world view of the individual (in terms of personality, not only character) will be influenced by innate constitution as well as experience. Therefore, Weininger's characterology supplements psychology proper while remaining differentiated from it; characterology is the science of innate constitution, while psychology is the science of experience (Weininger 1927, 205). With this observation, Weininger also asserts the priority of characterology over psychology. Psychology is colored by the values that the individual's mind embraces, and thus it depends on the results of characterology before it can exist itself (Weininger 1927, 262–63). Characterology will describe the constitution of the individual; psychology, what this individual experiences (not necessarily how the individual changes, as his contemporaries did).

Weininger's *Sex and Character* is not exhausted by this exposition, but it clearly rests on a modified Darwinian point of view, assuming that inheritance determines the individual. Weininger intends to produce an encompassing theory supported by vague references to acknowledged experts in philosophy, physiology, and psychology. The discourse he adapts reimposes on a model for mental activity the strict biological hierarchy that had been rejected almost a century earlier. Like the earliest faculty psychologists (practical philosophers), Weininger presupposes a fixed, deepest level to the human spirit. Yet whereas the philosophers had specified this level as "mental activity," a potential for development, he designates it as "character," a pregiven mixture of male and female cellular matter that predisposes all other facets of personality—a pattern of how one acts, speaks, or otherwise deals with experience that does not develop through culture (it may be "refined"). The scope of this character and its talents may vary, according to the genius or giftedness of the innate constitution, which serves as an intermediate scale factor. The most superficial layer of the individual is the personality—the historical experience of the individual filtered through character. Only personality and fleeting moods are conditioned by the environment, not the essential scope and quality of a person's mental activity.

In general, then, Weininger's expositions about character correspond with his sources: he acknowledges the reciprocity of mental activity and physiology in the formation of the personality. His valorization of a mental biologism, however, places him apart from his contemporaries, for he posits a mental *a priori* that consists of a gendered activity or passivity, not merely a set of mental activities or strategies that evolve through contact with culture. Therefore, Weininger has introduced a turn to the model that we identify today as conservative, virtually proto-Fascist: where his contemporaries clearly believed in the evolution of the individual ego (both mind and personality), he believes in a fixed character and a changing (not necessarily evolving) personality; in other words, people don't change, their situations and thus their momentary reactions do.

With Weininger's work, a version of a scientific paradigm has entered the public sphere in two ways. First, it originated as a dissertation acceptable to institutionalized science and philosophy, not only to the theory community. This means that his work represented a facet of the discussion that *was acceptable to the public curators of science*, not just an isolated stab into the realm of theory; Weininger was not alone, or if his version of the paradigm was deviant, it was at least on the fringe of the public debate in the scientific community. The second way in which Weininger's work entered the public sphere was a popular science bestseller, suiting the general reader so well that it stayed in print into the Nazi era; it touched a public chord. Weininger's work and his sources thus span the paradigm: they represent the range of possible weightings of the factors involved in this type of scientific discussion. That is, both variants recognize the importance of the mind-body link in the question of individual development and adaptation. However, philosophers tend to stress or valorize adaptability, while physicians tend to make the mind the victim of the body. In the most extreme variant, Weininger stresses that something like hormones (his gendered plasmas of maleness and female-ness) limit both mind and body; he has become the most deterministic of the camps.

Why is this range important? A scientific paradigm is broader than any individual experimental model. Therefore the development of the para-digm cannot be traced by following any single science. The public face of the paradigm is also constituted by factors such as its institutionalization, its distinctive discourse (its habits of language and metaphor), and its public reputation. Weininger's Vienna provides documentation of the effects of the paradigm in institutional contexts. To judge the status of his version of the paradigm in its historical context, we must turn to other confrontations of this paradigm with the public sphere—to the cases of a writer, Arthur Schnitzler, and a physician and psychoanalyst, Karen Hor-ney.[1]

POPULAR CONSEQUENCES: RHETORIC FOR THE PUBLIC

Late nineteenth- and early twentieth-century biological thought played out the issue of individual adaptation with its own distinctive vocabulary, stressing not mind and body individually, but the organism surviving in the environment. In Vienna at this time, the terms of the discussion were only the most simplistic variants of the richness of either Darwin's or Lamarck's full theories: they remained a question of "hered-ity" or "environmental adaptation."

These are the terms that underlie a character study written by a member of the turn-of-the century medical establishment for a popular audience. This physician-turned-popular-author, Arthur Schnitzler (1862–1931), was a member of the Jewish upper-middle class and the intellectual circles so prominent in Viennese culture under the Hapsburg Empire. Through the coffeehouse society of the city, Schnitzler remained in almost daily commerce with scientists such as Otto Brahm (whose *Tierleben* remained a standard in zoology) and Freud, financiers such as the Wittgenstein family, musicians, and publicists. His position and contacts make his work a plausible norm for the continuing intellectual discourse of the first quarter of this century (Johnston 1972). Nonetheless, as a physi-cian, his views are strongly influenced by the paradigm on the mind under discussion, representing the camp in which inheritance primarily deter-mines the individual. Schnitzler's works stress personality and character, presenting stories as case studies to be diagnosed by the audiences.

Schnitzler's slim volume, *Der Geist in Wort und der Geist in der Tat* (The Mind in Words and Actions), is his work on characterology, intended for a popular audience (see Arens 1986 on Schnitzler 1927). The book is divided into an unmarked preface, a chapter on each of the two major topics—words and actions, and "An Intermediary Chapter on Aptitudes [Giftedness] and States of the Soul" (see Arens 1986). The preface explains the subject as a question of innate character types as revealed in an individual's words and deeds, "insofar as mind can manifest itself, primarily by means of actions" (Schnitzler 1927, 5). Schnitzler intended this book to be a study of the human spirit types observable in the world, based on a picture of the total person in culture, not only in psychology or anthropology. He stresses the three-layered Darwinist model familiar from Weininger: the constitutional predispositions of humans, their specific gifts or aptitudes, and their moods, or "states of the soul."

Schnitzler defines the individual as an interplay between permanent and mutable forces that is determined by mutable, acquired characteristics as well as immutable, inherited ones. Schnitzler is, to be sure, not interested in inheritance *per se*, but his sketches about the character stress human motivation and responsibility with respect to social and ethical environments; he seems to advocate a type of social Darwinism. Schnitzler does not assume that essential changes can take place in individuals, for their predispositions render only their moods and fluid states correctible. One's fundamental constitution (*Geistesverfassung*) does not change. Moreover, the constitution will predetermine one's inclinations for particular careers, since it conditions an individual's interactions with the environment—for instance, whether one is more interested in the present or the past (as a journalist or historian, respectively), or in spiritual growth or in appearances (as a poet or a mere literature critic, respectively). This constitution is attenuated through the particular gifts given to that individual: the free movement and strength of purpose that determine the effectiveness or creative scope of that individual's actions. A genius is, for instance, characterized by great gifts—flexibility and strength of purpose. He (never she, as for Weininger) may, however, be a genius in any of the innate types described by Schnitzler: a genial historian or priest. But even a genius may be subject to moods and other transitory fluctuations of state that may render him ineffectual for a time. That is, in Schnitzler's conception, individuals can only become better, but not different, variants of what they already inherently are. The psychobiological constitution set at birth will limit an individual throughout a lifetime. Schnitzler thus begs the question of nature versus nurture by amalgamating mind into the substrate of individual body; he thus stresses individuality at the expense of change.

These characterological distinctions carry over into Schnitzler's literary production, if they are not read with the eye of modern prejudice. His short story "Leutnant Gustl" (1900) presents the inner life of a middle-class army officer in perpetual fear of losing his "honor" as an officer, who is living on promises of a never-to-be realized allowance from a rich uncle (Schnitzler 1982). Gustl's hypertrophied sense of honor leads him to assume insults at a concert when a baker of a class that is "*nicht satisfaktionsfähig*" (not capable of satisfying honor in duels) bumps into him. This puts him in a dilemma: he already has a duel the next day. Puzzling all night, he is saved by an act of God: the baker died of natural causes during the night, and therefore no one in military society will ever learn of his shame.

The modern reader may assume that this piece exemplifies the psychological stress placed on the individual by a restrictive society, and adds a critique of its social and political institutions. Schnitzler's contemporaneous readers, however, would provide a different diagnosis. They would consider the innate disposition of Gustl in characterological terms. Gustl has a rich uncle whom he expects to support him (but who will probably not)—an uncle with an estate (probably in Hungary, since the servants did not speak German); his mother is the mainstay of the family, while his father disapproves of him; his sister is in the Sängerverein, the citywide public choir, while he himself has never been to the opera; he has a twenty-eight-year-old unmarried sister; he himself is twenty-three or twenty-four, and was scared of the dark in the woods as a child. The audience of 1900, believers in the power of inheritance, would interpret Schnitzler's story very differently: not as a criticism of the honor code of the army, (a given for the nonmilitary), but rather as a portrait of a lower-middle-class person who cannot cope with his position and its attendant responsibilities. Moreover, for the Viennese, the fact that he is from the provinces, from Graz, where old army officers go to retire on meager pensions, he is of suspect lineage, possibly even partially non-Germanic—a member of a questionable element in the empire's structure.

The diagnosis of "Leutnant Gustl" by its original audience would thus differ considerably from that of the modern audience. It would have been seen as a confirmation of class prejudices instead of a castigation of its moral system. When the office corps mustered Schnitzler out as its reaction to this piece, it purportedly was reacting to slander by a "Jewish doctor." The actual situation may have been much more serious than retribution against an individual, possibly even reaching the heart of the military structure of the period. The military establishment may have been exercising an early form of "damage control" vis-à-vis racial prejudice within the monarchy; it was not so much censoring Schnitzler as affirming the solidarity of the corps and its selection criteria (based on ethnic and a certain degree of class diversity). By officers' standards, this "Gustl" of questionable lineage is not a victim of society but instead has risen to his position on the strength of his personality, as demonstrated by his assumption of the officers' code. However, if the German-Austrian public were to stress his innate characterological deficiencies, such visibility might damage the corps and its purported ethnic diversity in the long run. Today, we are tempted to see Gustl as a case of burn-out; then, he was seen as someone who had overreached his innate abilities and reached a well-deserved end, thus showing the limitations of the military selection system of the day. The Viennese audience would all too easily generalize Gustl's individual case into a statement against nondominant classes in the empire, no matter that Schnitzler probably considered him only an interesting and utterly discrete individual.

In its original context, then, the scientific paradigm of characterology would have lead Schnitzler's audiences to very different judgments about the psyches of particular individuals than we would reach today. Life histories and psychological stresses would receive vastly different weightings, since Schnitzler's novellas and plays were written to conform to 1900's standard, middle-class expectations and prohibitions, as were Weininger's text and many of Freud's works. For instance, Freud changed the identification of the seducer in the Katharina case from the father to the uncle. Why? The answer lies in the conservative view of human potential held by his audiences. An uncle-seducer would have sounded less offensive, less disruptive of the harmless image of the family that that audience had; Freud's case histories were written for a Darwin-conditioned audience who would assume that the female was indeed innately different than the male and so would tend to be "hysterical" for no seemingly serious cause. Only in later editions of his *Studies on Hysteria* did Freud add a footnote explaining that discretion had caused him to alter his evidence and blame the uncle instead of the father (cf. Thornton 1984, esp. 155ff.).

The character values that Schnitzler's audiences accepted are easily documented by sales figures—his values matched those of his audience, no matter if he was trying to discuss individuals or social or racial types. However, the issue of cultural communication is not confined to literature nor to the question of Schnitzler's commitment to Darwinism, for it can also be found in the discourse between noninstitutionalized science and culture. The early history of the Freudian movement provides cases of a mismatch between scientific paradigm and discourses, particularly since cases were played out on the margins of the debate between science and social science.

The case of Karen Horney is one of several major institutional and personal break-ups in the early development of analysis, one that culminated with her exclusion from the New York Psychoanalytic Society and Institute in 1941 (see Quinn 1987). While personal quarrels and allegations of heresy contributed to this exclusion, the mismatch between the paradigm underlying Freudian theory and the discourse used to popularize this theory may also have played a significant role.

Karen Horney was a medical doctor trained outside the Freudian establishment proper, in contact with the medical paradigm asserted here. She studied at Freiburg and Göttingen between 1906 and 1909, submitting a thesis on psychiatry in the Kraepelinian mode (the prevailing style in Berlin at the time, stressing innate psychological types). Moving to Berlin, she met Karl Abraham in 1910 and underwent analysis for two and one-half years. Their institutional situation was atypical for the first-generation Freudians, since they were not in personal contact with the Freudian establishment in Vienna, although they were "certified by letter" (i.e., by Freud's approval given in writing) as the most famous exogenous Freudian group before the World War II era emigration out of Vienna. They had a clinic at their disposal, and conducted seminars and discussions on the Viennese pattern. The Berlin theorists were largely medical doctors, enjoying enormous latitude in their experimentation with the Freudian material. They also had access to "modern" trends in medicine, particularly the German model for psychiatry set up in clinics (most notably by Wilhelm Griesinger) in the last part of the last century.

Rhetorically, Horney was a powerful and popular advocate of the structure of neuroses as a key to individual wellness (Quinn 1987, 148). Her wide theoretical basis included not only the Freudian material but also ego psychology; even Weininger was in her reading canon when she was a medical student, in early 1907. Although she clearly considered his work valid, his statements about the dangers of feminity disturbed her: "The man impresses me frightfully in part and I am looking for points of attack. He confuses me at the moment because he brings forward so many really plausible observations in support of his thesis. But it cannot, must not, may not be like that" (Quinn 1987, 102–3).

As one of the earliest analysts to leave Europe, coming first to Chicago in 1932, Horney turned her hand to what would become her most familiar métier, organizing a training program for analysts. She integrated into the American scene more willingly than many émigré analysts, turning her hand very quickly to presentations, lectures, and papers in English. Through this, she found new audiences in the Midwest, especially among medical doctors (Quinn 1987, 255), who were being asked to consider psychoanalysis as an ancillary tool, particularly with respect to "women's issues." Additionally, she requalified for medical boards on the first try, which some of her fellow émigrés never managed (in part because board requirements were tightened to exclude emigrants). As a result, several colleagues thought she had let pragmatics triumph over piety to the cause—that she was moving away from the Freudian establishment.

While the Freudians were stressing sexuality, Horney, in her mature work, found a link to the Lamarckian variant of the paradigm discussed here; she began to stress social factors in analysis under the influence of Henry Stack Sullivan and Erich Fromm (Quinn 1987, 269). This raised professional disagreements with Sandor Rado and Helene Deutsch in Washington in 1933, causing Horney to leave Chicago. The "official" version, according to Franz Alexander, is that she was hostile to Freud (Quinn 1987, 273). It is more likely that she ran afoul of bureaucracy when she sided with a secular leader of the institute (Lionel Blitzsten) about how the institute was to be run. In any case, Horney clearly lost round one of "paradigm versus institution." She was in fact rejecting the biology/social science link that the first-generation Freudians were stressing.

Round two of the "theory versus interpretation" war was played out in New York after 1934. Horney's work pulled her farther and farther from orthodoxy: the New York Institute interfaced with the New School for Social Research, putting her into contact with the Gestalt psychologists Max Wertheimer and Erich Fromm, among others. As her theory grew, she maintained clinical research, keeping case histories when many emigrants were theorizing without data.

Her new work found acclaim (notably by Margaret Mead and Fromm [Quinn 1987, 310]), particularly for the historical-social dimension that Weininger's audience had rejected. Her *The Neurotic Personality of Our Time*, together with its companion volume, *New Ways in Psychoanalysis*, socialized the libido theory, purportedly while attacking Freud (Quinn 1987, 314, 316). Yet it was classic bad timing for publishing on the social nature of Freudian theory instead of its biological inheritance: it was 1937, Freud was near death and being harassed by the Nazis, and he was forced to move to London (Quinn 1987, 322ff.). The New York Institute would have none of it, for they were gradually but systematically excluding social thought from the purview of an analytic institution as more and more analysts arrived from Europe. It took three years for the Institute to arrange it, but they slowly edged her out. On March 28, 1941, the New York Psychoanalytic Society voted to remove Horney from her teaching role (she could be a "Lecturer" but not an "Instructor").

How far did Horney's work actually diverge from the Freudian paradigm? One of her most famous essays, "The Flight from Womanhood: The Masculinity Complex in Women as Viewed by Men and by Women" of 1926, demonstrates her variant of analytic theory (Horney 1967). Here she explicitly contrasts her position with that of Freud and Helene Deutsch (an orthodox Freudian who bought into the woman's "castration complex"), putting sociology on an equal footing with biology. First, Horney offers a survey of analytic work on the feminine, praising the contributions of Freud, Abraham, and Deutsch. Yet she asks: what can we do to specify further the nature of the feminine, work that Freud himself admits is still outstanding and needed?

Her "transgression" begins early: her inspiration comes from Georg Simmel and philosophy, who suggest that civilization tends to obscure facts of nature because the "human" has virtually always been defined synonymously with "male": "The question then is how far analytical psychology also, when its researches have women for their objects, is under the spell of this way of thinking, insofar as it has not wholly left behind the stage in which frankly and as a matter of course masculine development only was considered" (Horney 1967, 57). Horney then rereads the stages in the Oedipus complex, moving from Freud's genital model into a social model. What about motherhood as a sublimation for loss, for instance? Deutsch had defined a woman's masculinity complex as a way to compensate for a lost penis, a way of "taking the male's part" in order to avoid the fear of castration or the sense of being inadequate in sexual identity. Horney broadens the woman's sense of loss beyond this primary penis envy to include cultural loss in terms of status and the guilt associated with femaleness in a male-oriented society. In this, she systematically takes apart Freud's model as unfair and purely inadequate to "the actual disadvantage under which women labor in social life" (Horney 1967, 69). Horney admits that this is a one-sided reading from the social viewpoint, but posits it as a necessary corrective.

This approach is very typical of Horney's discourse: "this is what was done; this is what is wrong; here is an opposite reading." But what has she actually accomplished with this rereading, since Freud's own work accounts for acculturation (for instance, when he identifies servants as less prone to sexual neurosis)? Horney was right that her work was an extension of Freudian theory, but it was not a refutation. At the worst reading, she stressed ego psychology instead of sexual models, which Freud's own daughter did!

Why, then, was the rejection of Horney so vehement? My suggestion is that she was caught in the Freudian establishment's ongoing attempts to exclude social psychology from the Freudian models. Like Weininger, she did not move beyond the boundaries of the scientific paradigm. Where Horney did transgress, however, was in discourse: she drew communicative and evaluative strategies from the sociologists and anthropologists who were characteristically popular in the United States in the late 1930s and 1940s, and not from the physicians and biologists who had provided Weininger and Schnitzler with an image of biological humanity. Anna Freud's ego psychology was weighted differently than that of her father, but her diction and argumentation sounded much like his (the same holds true of Helene Deutsch's definitions of the castration theory and the like).

The evolving shape of the Freudian institute supported the familiar paradigm, but it chose to express itself in the popular terms of Weininger's Vienna of 1900 by stressing biological continuity instead of cultural mutability, and innately rejecting "new" approaches like Horney's.

As current receptions of Freud suggest, this break between the paradigm and the discourse may not have been resolved yet today (were it to be, a uniform institutional configuration for psychology and psychoanalysis might exist). In America, the analytic concepts represented by common Freudian terminology are rejected by anti-Freudians in part because they represent an unnecessarily antifemale or Victorian bias based on an innate biological inferiority of women. These objections ignore the protocol of the turn of the century outlined above. It may not be that Freud's theory is biologically conservative in all aspects. Instead, cases may have been *reported* to reflect a conservatism about issues that were distasteful to the society of the time, such as child abuse (see Masson 1985). The question of the adaptation or inheritance of the individual has not been resolved by current Freudian theorists in a decisive twist of the inherited paradigm. Instead, it seems again that reception is tied to the discourse used to express the paradigm and that strategies of expression override the integrity of the scientific paradigm.

As in the case of Schnitzler's story, the unarticulated tensions underlying a conflict in scientific paradigms may again be the underlying cause of this prevailing ambivalence about Freud's work. The examples in Freud were written to conform to the standard, middle-class expectations and prohibitions of a 1900 audience, which explains, for instance, why Freud would have changed the seducer in the Katharina case from the father to the uncle—that would have sounded less offensive, less disruptive of the harmless image of the family which that audience had). But to the modern ear of American critics of Freud, as Horney concurred, Freud seems to describe symptoms as if they were innate psychological weaknesses of individuals.

That Freud did not resolve this ambivalence may not have been an accident but rather a marketing ploy. He was a skilled writer whose model rested on the assumption that experiences uniquely condition individual egos. Nonetheless, he was able to write for a Darwin-conditioned audience who would assume that the female was indeed innately different from the male. Thus Freud could portray females as "hysterical" without having to specify completely if he believed that they were born predisposed to this illness, as he outlined the aetiology of such innate pathology. As we have seen, this is what the audiences of Schnitzler and Weininger did actually expect; they did not actively consider individual change, except in terms of "fluid states."

CONSEQUENCES OF THE CONFLICT

Otto Weininger's work has long been considered one of the most infamous products of the Hapsburg Empire's intellectual community. While one cannot deny that his text has not held up as science, the present discussion suggests that one should not assume that its claim to be science has always been as it is seen today. We have shown that Weininger's work was conceived in terms of the dominant philosophical and medical paradigms of his age, albeit with emphases that place him at the edge of that paradigm. Nonetheless, he *sounded* credible to the scientific ears of the day, at least on a first reading.

When one realizes this, Weininger's work can be taken as a norm for popular science in turn-of-the-century Vienna, for a discourse that could be used to spread the scientific paradigm to the public. Paradoxically, his importance is greater than he might deserve in the scientific sense; his was one of the first modern scientific best sellers in the German-speaking popular world, and so serves not only as a reference point against which to estimate public knowledge of science vis-à-vis the vanguard of research, but also as a norm for the discourse criteria that could cause the success or failure in the reception of a work in the prevailing scientific paradigm. The cases of Schnitzler and Horney confirm that Weininger was indeed working in the prevailing paradigm and writing in the discourse that the public expected. When Schnitzler's work was read by different audiences, its messages changed; when Horney tried another discourse and stepped into an alternate institutional locus, she was ejected from the othodox Freudian community.

The case of Weininger thus confirms the importance of considering a scientific paradigm apart from its discourse. Moreover, it suggests that the public in the Hapsburg Empire enforced a conservatism about individual adaptation that could even go beyond accepted institutional norms, and that applied crucial pressure in the public sphere in political and scientific battles of the twentieth century.

9 ✦

OTTO WEININGER AND THE
CRITIQUE OF JEWISH MASCULINITY

John M. Hoberman

Although Otto Weininger's *Geschlecht und Charakter* (Sex and Character) (1903) is generally acknowledged to be an expression of Jewish
self-hatred, it is seldom read as a product of Jewish experience. For
whatever reasons, the origins of Weininger's self-hatred are little examined. This lack of interest in the Jewish circumstances from which the
book developed represents one aspect of Weininger's posthumous success, in that he has succeeded in diverting his readers' attention from the
fact that he was a Jew who shared a set of difficult social circumstances and
imposed stereotypes with many other European Jews. Even the bombastic
anti-Semitism of Weininger's chapter entitled "Jewry" has not been
enough to stimulate much interest in what his experience as a Jew must
have been like. On the contrary, until recent Weininger scholarship, the
"Jewry" chapter was frequently overlooked altogether. A review of *Sex and
Character* published in 1905, while noting the author's "philosophy of
coitus" and his methodological errors as a psychologist, does not even
mention Jews (Hensel 1905). Writing in 1931, Egon Friedell notes in the
masterwork of "this tragic thinker" the ethos of Immanuel Kant, the
empyrean heights of Henrik Ibsen, and a Nietzschean knowledge of the
soul, but nothing having to do with the Jews (Friedell 1931). Even today it
is clear that Weininger's role as an *agent provocateur* in the war between the
sexes continues to dominate the discussion, while his Jewishness is
accorded secondary status. In this sense, the author continues to dictate
the form of his own reception, even if he has not entirely succeeded in
removing the label of "Jew" from himself.

An examination of Weininger's Jewishness is still not enough, however, if it perpetuates his failure (or refusal) to distinguish between the
Jewish males and Jewish females of this period.[1] Indeed, anyone familiar
with the Jewish stereotypes of the *fin de siècle* will understand why
Weininger would have wanted to suppress this distinction. The contrasting portraits of "ugly" Jew and "beautiful" Jewess were standard images
in the racial folklore of this era,[2] and it is even possible that the passion of
Weininger's misogyny was fueled in part by an unacknowledged resent-

ment of this popular invidious comparison.[3] What is certain is that
Weininger's ostensibly ungendered defamation of the Jews as a type is in
fact an unerringly precise defamation of the Jewish male as he was
commonly portrayed at this time by Jews and Gentiles alike.[4] In classic
projective fashion, Weininger unloaded a set of anxieties about being
Jewish and male onto an abstraction he calls "Jewry" or "the Jew."[5] These
anxieties cohere to form the syndrome I will call the "Jewish male
predicament." The fact that Weininger's scathing portrait of the Jewish
male did not even arouse controversy suggests that this predicament was a
real factor in the lives of European Jews at this time.

Weininger's conceptual strategy in the "Jewry" chapter of *Sex and
Character* obscures his fixation on the Jewish male predicament in two
ways. First, he offers an abstract, almost otherworldly definition of Jewry: it
is "a mind-set" (*Geistesrichtung*), a "psychic constitution" (*psychische Konsti-
tution*), that has achieved its most notable historical realization in the Jews
while remaining a possibility for the rest of mankind as well. In short, he
gives a conspicuously antibiological image of the Jew at a time when Jews
were discussing their own "racial" biology often and with less embarrass-
ment than we might think (Weininger 1922, 402). Weininger's insistence
on the abstract essence of Jewishness is contradicted, however, by his
all-too-specific and unflattering reference to the Jewish matchmaker
[*Kuppler*] as well as his inventory of "Jewish" character defects examined
below. These alleged deficiencies must be interpreted in the context of
the social world in which many Jewish men struggled to achieve a viable
male identity in the face of anti-Semitic folklore and discriminatory
practices that limited Jewish access to privileged male venues such as the
officer corps, university fraternities, and gymnastics clubs.[6]

In a similar fashion, Weininger subsumed men and women into the
grand sexual bipolarity of Man and Woman that has done so much to give
this long and unwieldy dissertation its enduring popularity. Some real
alternatives to these abstract creatures were the "alien" Jewish men who
longed for "Germanic" women, and the Jewish "beauties" who married in
upwardly mobile fashion into the gentile nobility. Because such scenarios
represented precisely that complex of problems Weininger was fleeing
from, the purpose of this essay is to reconstruct in some detail the
emotional predicament he was unable to deal with in a more direct
manner.

Weininger's most obvious acknowledgment of this "predicament" is
his equating of Jews and women. Yet even here, as he aims most directly
and insultingly at the Jewish male deficit that terrified him, the abstract
approach is evident. Jews and women lack "personality," they "stick
together," they are drawn to art galleries and the theater, they share a lack
of stature [*Größe*] and capacity for genius, they possess a chameleonlike

quality, they lack a sense of humor, and they are unable to grasp Kantian reason. Jewry is "soaked" in femaleness, Weininger says, yet his arguments have a curiously oblique quality (Weininger 1922, 408, 410, 420, 425, 406, 407). In fact, he was well aware of more straightforward ways to impugn the masculinity of the Jew.

The real leitmotif of Weininger's argument is the Aryan/Jew dichotomy made notorious by the Nazis; it is frequently forgotten that this typology, like the term "race" in German, French, English, and other languages, was a *fin-de-siècle* convention employed by Jewish as well as gentile commentators. Thus Richard Wagner's Siegfried—the male ideal created by "the most profound anti-Semite"—is for Weininger nothing less than "the most un-Jewish [type] that be conceived," and he makes a point of reiterating this characterological polarity (Weininger 1922, 404, 434). His dichotomizing procedure presents these opposed types in terms of their bipolar features. But Weininger's procedure must not determine our own, since its purpose was to create the stereotypical Jewish male whose real experience was both more complicated and more dignified than Weininger could allow. Indeed, for the modern reader of *Sex and Character*, Weininger's identification of Jewish traits—for all of his bipolar rigor— may often seem arbitrary or incomprehensible, since the cultural context for his remarks is not always evident from the text. Why, for example, should the Jews' abstention from violent crime be a liability? How could their devotion to family life be a defect of character? What is implied in the claim that the Jews are estranged from nature? Why does Weininger allege that the Jews lack "vibrancy" [*schwungvoll*]? The remainder of this essay attempts to reconstruct this context both in its major themes and in some of its significant details.

Weininger's disparaging portrait of the Jew grew out of his sense that Jews were both unworthy of exercising an entire range of masculine roles and privileges and unable to experience masculinity in its most genuine (i.e., Germanic) sense. By the time Weininger absorbed it, this intuitive sense of the Jew's deficient masculinity had been germinating for centuries, dating from the Middle Ages. This image of the Jewish male has always combined interrelated physical and characterological critiques of its subject. Thus the medieval association of Jews with the devil gave rise to a set of popular beliefs bearing on the bodily peculiarities of the Jews, ascribing to them horns, a tail, an odor (*fœtor judaicus*], mysterious skin diseases, and even male menstruation (Trachtenberg 1983, 44–52). Later versions of these traditional ideas about the physical anomalies of the Jews acquired new importance as "scientific" racism developed during the nineteenth century, and a few variations on this folkloric material appear in *Sex and Character*. In this vein, Weininger refers to "the diminished sexual potency of the Jew and the greater weakness of the muscles and body," leaving the rest of the contemporary physical critique of the Jew unspoken.[7] In this sense it is true that Weininger is less interested in racial biology than many of his contemporaries, including any number of racially self-conscious and sometimes racially chauvinistic Zionists (Waldenburg 1911).[8]

Like Max Nordau and Jewish physical culturists all over Europe, Weininger understood that the "physical rehabilitation" of the Jews was closely bound with the issue of masculine self-respect. The fundamental point of Nordau's famous call in 1898 for a "muscular Jewry" (*Muskeljudentum*) was not physical achievement per se but rather the Jew's struggle to achieve a full-fledged masculine identity in Europe. Terms like "self-respect" (*Selbstgefühl*), the "cultivation of men" (*Manneszucht*), "dignity" (*Stattlichkeit*), or "men with a bold look" (*kühnblickende Männer*) illustrate Nordau's instrumental approach to physical culture (in this case, German gymnastics, or *Turnen*). Oppression, he says, has reduced even "the strength of our voice to a whisper," but physical self-confidence can restore its resonance. And Nordau even challenges the traditional Jewish adage that "knowledge is strength." "Is that always true?" he asks. "I'm afraid that sometimes it is weakness, because it demoralizes." He describes in painful detail an image of the contemporary male Jew as one who is physically out of control—pathetically clumsy, tripping over his own feet, unable to stand erect.[9] The caricatures of "Jewish soldiers as ridiculous scarecrows" that appear in boulevard magazines provide amusement, he says, to Jewish and Christian anti-Semites alike (Nordau 1902b, 2; 1900, 2; 1902a, 4, 2).

For Weininger and Walther Rathenau, among others, this climate of ridicule was unbearable,[10] and the Jewish self-hatred these men cultivated has become a familiar category for analyzing identity problems associated with modern Jewish experience.[11] At the same time, however, the historical development of this male identity problem has received little attention. Weininger's correct intuitive sense that Jews had somehow been excluded from the aura of Aryan manhood or our own retrospective confirmation of this exclusion does not address the origins of these masculine norms or why they could not accommodate the Jewish experience.

The Jewish male predicament grew out of a long and ambivalent involvement with the masculine norms of nineteenth-century Europe. These standards of behavior and feeling brought the "racial" dichotomy of German and Jew into every sphere of life, confirming the deficient character of Jewish experience. A case in point is the Jew's alleged estrangement from the world of agriculture and its cultural symbolism: rootedness in the soil, the timeless rhythm of the seasons, the sheer vitality of nature, the endless struggles against wind and weather—the blows of Fate that forge the quiet heroism of the peasant soul in the face of the elements. Racial folklore denied all of this to the Jew, and this exclusion meant in turn estrangement from the basic human drama of the soil. Similarly, the Jew who was denied admission to the officer corps or declared ineligible to pursue satisfaction in a duel was exiled from an entire world of male drama—the stage upon which a man could demonstrate a spectrum of masculine qualities: loyalty, self-control, chivalric feeling, and that capacity for spontaneous exuberance that enabled a man to be a courageous soldier, a boon companion, a passionate lover.

In short, the exceptional status of the Jewish male has been his exclusion from a European ideology of adventure. Michael Nerlich has described this doctrine as "the systematic glorification of the (knightly, then bourgeois) adventurer as the most developed and important human being." For the adventurer the world is a field of action on which he explores his own capacities, and the role of other people is to serve the ends of an essentially aesthetic project whose perfect result is a kind of male *grandeur:* "It is a world specifically created and designed to give the knight an opportunity to prove himself." This doctrine, and the military culture from which it derives, have shaped the predominant image of masculinity in the West. It is important to keep in mind that this ethos of self-assertion prescribes not merely action but a style of action: risk-taking as an end in itself, a contempt for those outside this male caste, and a martial athleticism. The supreme claim inherent in this doctrine is the idea that military adventure itself represents the highest ethical value (Nerlich 1987, xx, 14, 11).

The cultural legacy of the ideology of adventure is complex beyond calculation, in part because adventure has assumed other than military forms. The Crusades, for example, combined military activity with geographical exploration and a religious mission, not to mention the righteous slaughters of Jewish communities along the Rhine. Conquest can thus take various forms, from achieving dominion over territory to the extermination of the alien or even the domination of a market. And all of these forms of adventure have accommodated the figure of the Jew as antitype. "Evidence is indeed accumulating," a Jewish historian wrote in 1898, "to prove that the Jews were personally concerned in most of the great exploring enterprises in the middle ages"—a repartee to those who had asserted otherwise (Abrahams 1898, 232). Here is one source of centuries of interest in whether Columbus was a Jew.[12] Nineteenth-century ideas about the inability of Jews to sail or swim are in all likelihood thematic offshoots of the same legacy. Werner Sombart's notion of the "superentrepreneur" (*Überunternehmer*) is yet another variation on the theme of the adventurer, the point of which is to rescue the heroic ethos of capitalism from the Jews. Sombart's anti-Semitic distinction between the entrepreneur (*Unternehmer*) and the trader (*Händler*) exploits in the most straightforward

manner the dramatic potential of the ideology of adventure. The noncapi-
talist entrepreneur, he says, might be "an African or a North Pole
explorer," while a capitalist entrepreneur "of the right kind is always a
conqueror, with the determination and will-power to overcome all the
difficulties that beset his path." The trader, in contrast, is the Jewish
antitype who lacks a "definite calling," and is mesmerized by speculation
and profit (Sombart 1962, 164, 165). Having rewritten the role of the
Crusader for the creative titan of the industrial epoch, Sombart preserved
the medieval distinction between the knight and his submasculine inferiors by excluding the Jew from the drama (and thus the virility) of the
entrepreneur's modern role. It is no accident that Sombart's famous book
on *The Jews and Modern Capitalism* (1911) includes an intimate "anthropology" of Jewish experience comparable in both tone and content to that of
Otto Weininger.

Medieval Jews could not participate in the ideology of adventure. By
the thirteenth century they were losing their previous right to bear arms
(Biale 1986, 74), sealing a vulnerability that was wholly antithetical to the
empowered status of the knightly caste. It is also clear that many Jews
rejected the ethos of the *miles christianus* (Christian soldier)—the weapons,
the horses, the hunting—on ethical grounds (Abrahams 1898, 376; Biale
1986, 73). Both the "instinctive" antipathy of the Jews toward violence and
the predatory instinct, and the image of the weak Jew were in the process
of being born.

The image of the unmasculine Jew is thus of medieval rather than
ancient origin. As Maurice Keen has pointed out, "For the perfect model
of knighthood one should look to Judas Maccabeus, the Old Testament
Jewish hero, who was *preux* and *hardi* (gallant and bold), handsome but
without pride, ever honourable, a great fighter who died armed in God's
causes." As strange as it may appear to modern eyes, the liturgical use
during the medieval period of Old Testament heroes like Abraham,
Gideon, and David makes it clear that the Jew could serve as a male role
model during the Christian Germanic age of *êre* (honor) and *rîterschaft*
(knighthood) (Keen 1984, 14, 53).

This ostensible paradox is easily resolved by recognizing that the
poisoned image of the Jewish male is a postmedieval construct that
assumed its modern form and special virulence only toward the end of the
nineteenth century. The military unfitness of the Jew, derived from both
physical and characterological defects, was now one element of a highly
elaborated racial folklore concerning the purported deficiencies of the
Jewish male. By the age of German Romanticism, "the stereotype of an
alleged Jewish cowardice was so deeply anchored in the collective unconscious [of German society] that putting one's life on the line for the
Fatherland was the only way to break out of the 'magic Jewish circle' "

(Frühwald 1989, 75). By the end of the century, caricaturists had recorded every nuance of the Jew's ignominious failures to achieve equal status with the gentile male (Fuchs 1921). This is the world into which Otto Weininger was born in 1880, and his reaction to it was a paroxysm of self-rejection and Jewish self-hatred.

Weininger understood that the Jew was an antichivalric type, and described his "incommensurability with everything aristocratic" and the impossibility of the concept of a Jewish "gentleman" (Weininger 1922, 408)—a term that was being used in Germany by Wehrmacht psychologists during the Nazi period (Geuter 1984, 209). Sombart even more explicitly preserved the characterological distinction between male types: "The Jews' whole being is opposed to all that is usually understood by chivalry, to all sentimentality, knight-errantry, feudalism, patriarchalism" (Sombart 1962, 247). The anti-Semitism that inspired these remarks does not make them any less true as useful cultural observations. For while both men employed an ahistorical, and therefore untenable, notion of a Jewish essence, the more important point is that both recognized a conflict between opposed sensibilities that was experienced as such on both sides of the "racial" divide. This mutually critical dialogue between male groups would be better known if the traditional historiographical emphasis on German and Austrian opinions about Jewish deficiencies had not obscured contemporary Jewish critiques of the Germanic male type.

The Germanic critique of the male Jew as an antigentleman—a critique also accepted at least in part by many Jews at the time—focused on his lack of personal dignity in terms of his appearance, his demeanor, the many nuances of bearing and sense of one's worth that were expressed in the German words *Haltung* (bearing) and *Habitus* (personal appearance). One of Weininger's contemporaries, a contributor to the Viennese Zionist newspaper *Die Welt*, wrote of a hidden dimension of Jewish male humiliation that played itself out "under the surface" of daily life: "the countless insults, threats, impediments" that never reached the eyes of the public (Groller 1900, 4). To some extent such experiences, and thus one's sense of oneself as a man, were a function of class. It was the rich, *die Cavaliere*, this author resentfully notes, who could afford to live out the imperatives of the important dueling subculture of this era (Frevert 1991). The memoirs of Willy Ritter Liebermann von Wahlendorf (born 1863), the dashing scion of a wealthy Berlin Jewish family, make it clear that a well-born Jew with the right connections and sufficient panache could cut a respectable figure in the Teutonic world of student fraternities and the officer corps, and feel profoundly at home in this brotherhood of "honor" and camaraderie (Liebermann von Wahlendorf 1988, 40ff.). There was, then, a spectrum of Jewish experiences involving masculine identity that extended from total exclusion to an almost total integration. For most Jews, however, including

Otto Weininger, the issue of male identity was an ordeal one could not avoid.

The legend of Jewish cowardice was firmly established throughout Europe by the nineteenth century. Centuries of social vulnerability and imposed estrangement from military life during an age of nationalism had created the impression that Jews were both unpatriotic and too fearful to risk their lives in war or even in the less martial conflicts of everyday life. Following the War of Liberation against Napoleon (1813–14) and the Great War of 1914–18, German Jews made a point of publishing documentary evidence that they had served with valor and in respectable numbers, but these arguments were powerless against the accumulated weight of folkloric beliefs about the ethnic character of the Jews. By 1903 Weininger's charge that the Jew is a coward was just a banality, although it is elaborated on with more subtlety (and more fancifully) in other passages. His insistence, for example, that the life of the Jew falls outside the basic experiential categories of human life leads to a claim that the Jew's insensibility to the precariousness of life makes him incapable of either courage or fear—a radical exile, indeed, and not merely from the ranks of virile heroes but from humanity itself. Heroism, after all, is alien to the Jew, whose proper role is to have brought the Aryan hero to a consciousness of himself (Weininger 1922, 434, 431, 405).

The alternative to Weininger's rigid and clichéd treatment of the cowardice issue was the more dialectical examination of the phenomenon of courage that was appearing in German Jewish publications at this time. Courage had long been accorded the status of an innate faculty that was associated with the Germanic hero and denied to the Jew. The preservation of Jewish male self-respect therefore required one of two solutions: either the Jew could assimilate to the traditional "virile" German identity—an option Walther Rathenau took to the point of the grotesque—or he could embark upon a revaluation of courage, transforming it from an innate and spontaneous virtue into an acquired and even rational faculty.

Weininger's violent antipathy to the male Jewish predicament prompted both an hysterical assimilationism and, on a more nuanced level, an argument that directly contradicted the contemporary Zionist view that the physically and characterologically stunted Jew could be transformed by altering the conditions of his existence. Only a superficial head, Weininger wrote, could believe that the human being is shaped by his environment; people change from the inside out, not the other way around (Weininger 1922, 409). Transfixed by the towering figure of Wagner and the whole Aryan mystique, Weininger was in no position to appreciate the Jewish challenge to the mystique of "courage" that surfaced on occasion in Zionist publications. It is even possible that Weininger had read Balduin Groller's essay in the Viennese paper *Die Welt* on "The Cowardice of the

Jews" (1900). Groller's analysis reproduces in neurological terms the medieval dichotomy that separated the knight from the numerous inferiors who could not aspire to his status: madmen, cripples, minors, paupers, traders, traitors, criminals—and Jews (Nerlich 1987, 22). Groller's point is that there is a coarse and predatory Jewish type whose nerves are tough and a gentler type whose nerves are not. To account for this dichotomy, he offers both hereditary and environmental arguments: the nervous disposition, he says, is both inherited biologically and transmitted by the humiliating circumstances of poverty. Here he offers what amounts to a constitutional alibi for Jewish cowardice, by defining it as a neurological condition. But his more interesting argument is that courage has a degenerate as well as a genuine form. The first is the courage of the predator or "bully" (*Raufmuth*) whereas the second is an "elevated ethical courage" (*hohen ethischen Muth*) of which Jews are fully capable when they must rise to the occasion (Groller 1900, 4). In a similar but more detailed analysis published in 1905, Elias Auerbach continues the critique of a courage (*Mut*) that is no more than an "inborn trait." Courage, he says, is "a relative concept," and it is fools who lack the rational restraints of more civilized people. Auerbach's dichotomy distinguishes between the often "reckless courage" (*Tollkühnheit*) that is "more a lack of inhibitions than a capacity for decisiveness" and an "acquired, learned" courage that is "under the constant supervision of an unobstructed consciousness" (Auerbach 1905, 21, 25). These challenges to the reigning masculine orthodoxy contrast starkly with the intellectual paralysis that afflicted the germanophilic Weininger when he contemplated the spectacle of uncourageous Jews. In one sense, then, Weininger's tragedy is that he forfeited an opportunity to become a more interesting Jew than the one he was. To put it bluntly, Otto Weininger was no Franz Kafka, a contemporary who was afflicted with the same Jewish male syndrome. The difference was that Kafka deflected his own terror into a literary creativity that was rooted in an honesty Weininger could not emulate.[13] Kafka embraced, however obliquely in his work, the Jewish predicament that Weininger fled in a panic.

Weininger's struggle with the problem of male norms is reflected in the conflicting impressions of those who knew him. Stefan Zweig's description of him conforms to the widespread stereotype of the ungainly and timid Jew: "He always looked as if he had spent the last thirty hours travelling in a railway coach, dirty, fatigued, his clothes rumpled. He walked in an awkward way, as if he were embarrassed, always keeping close to an invisible wall. His mouth under a small thin moustache appeared in some strange way painfully twisted" (Kohn 1961, 155). Weininger's friend Moriz Rappaport, however, left behind a very different picture, emphasizing Weininger's "tough [*zäh*] physical constitution" (meaning health rather than physique) and his conviction that his physical powers would never let him down: "he retained this proud feeling of absolute mastery over his own body until the very end." Rappaport also suggests that this self-image was not entirely imaginary: "hard on himself and strict toward others, possessed of an iron self-discipline, ready at any moment to put all of his talents and his very self on the line, he always kept his soldierly bearing [*soldatischen Habitus*]" (Rappaport 1907, VI, XIV). It would appear that the loyal Rappaport had persuaded himself that Weininger's fantasy self—the precise inverse of his portrait of the Jew—corresponded to an objective reality. In any case, there can be little doubt of Weininger's urgent need to believe that he carried himself with the bearing of a soldier, especially at a time when Jews were being burlesqued as quintessentially unmartial poltroons. Cultivated when self-consciousness about the racial implications of posture was widespread among European Jews, Weininger's "proud feeling of absolute mastery over his own body" offers an important clue for reconstructing his troubled state of mind. A year after Weininger's suicide, the novelist Jakob Wassermann described certain germanophilic Jews as "weaklings who come on strong" ("Schwächlingen, die sich stark stellen"; quoted in Koebner [1989, 67]), a formula that would seem to accord with Rappaport's sympathetic evocation of the body-conscious Weininger.

The preoccupation with posture—or *Leibespositur*, as an 1881 text calls it (Andree 1881, 27)—could even seep into the language of those one might expect to be least vulnerable to the aesthetic critique of the Jew. In 1910 a Polish Jew named Binjamin Segel published a scathing review of a series of unflattering articles on the *Ostjuden* (Eastern Jews) by Theodor Lessing, whose *Jewish Self-Hatred* (1930) happens to include a superficial chapter on Otto Weininger. Segel's positive reference to "straightforward and upright personalities" (*gerade und aufrechte Naturen*) shows that the vocabulary of posture had already taken on the unconscious form of metaphor among the very Jews it was meant to stigmatize (Segel 1910, 44). Indeed, the contemporary variations on the subtleties of the Jews' physical unattractiveness would fill an entire catalogue. This is why the review of one German novel in 1915 makes a point of noting Jewish characters who are "vital individuals who walk straight and erect without peering from side to side" (Bass 1915, 22)—an image that unmistakably recalls Stefan Zweig's picture of the awkward Otto Weininger. Small wonder, then, that Weininger writes about the "weakness" of the Jewish body, the "formlessness" of Jewish behavior, the Jew's lack of "hardness" and "élan" (*schwungvoll*) (Weininger 1922, 431n., 413, 433, 428), since the race consciousness of this period made the aesthetics of comportment a serious matter for Jew and gentile alike well into the twentieth century. In 1931, for example, the racial ideologist Hans F. K. Günther claimed that the Nordic man carries his body in a "characteristic way" (*eigene Leibeshaltung*) (Günther 1931, 159), while other German authors of the time equate the positive muscular tension of the body with force of will (Geuter 1984, 183, 184). The idea that there is a characteristic repertory of Jewish gestures has long been familiar to both Jews and anti-Semites. Although the issue is beyond the scope of this essay, one could continue this chronicle by demonstrating that self-consciousness about the form and movements of the body is a persistent and largely unacknowledged theme in twentieth-century Jewish writing.

Weininger's brief reference to Jewish physiognomy holds that the "uncertain facial expression" of the Jew is "the physiognomic correlate of an inner multiplicity" (Weininger 1922, 434). As this remark suggests, for Weininger the significant feature of the Jewish face was a transparency that stripped the Jew of his privacy, thereby eliminating the possibility of experiencing and projecting reserve and the *froideur* (coldness) of authority. The corporeal and characterological rigidity of the idealized Germanic type had its counterpart in the shifting, flowing, protean, spineless, voluble, and all-too-visible personality of the Jew. The eyes of the Jews were the window through which one saw the terrible concoction of their hatreds, dissatisfactions, and self-accusations (Bass 1913, 655). On his visit to the *Ostjuden* Theodor Lessing had seen Jews who had "the eyes of a beaten dog" (Segel 1910, 33). Physiognomy was thus a part of that *Habitus* that conveyed the dignity or the humiliation of the man who wore it.

Weininger's most subtle observations relate to the Jew's alleged lack of spontaneity, and here too he has tapped into a quasifolkloric body of European ideas of real cultural importance. This was a syndrome Weininger knew firsthand from countless hours of tormented self-examination; his friend Rappaport called him "the incomparable self-observer" (Rappaport 1907, XIV). In *Sex and Character* Weininger contends that the multifaceted nature of the Jewish personality deprives it of a chance to feel in a fresh and immediate way (yet another variation on the theme of the calculating Jew who is all intellect and incapable of real passion), and asserts that, unlike the Aryan male, the Jewish male is "not spontaneous" (*unmittelbar*) (Weininger 1922, 431, 426). Weininger's treatment of this stereotype is more interesting than the familiar cliché, because his free-associative processes diversified the theme of unspontaneous self-consciousness in ways the modern reader is likely to find unexpected and puzzling. In retrospect, however, one sees that the ideal of spontaneity, and the idea that it is absent in the Jew, account for the presence of several apparently random topics in the text. What is more, Weininger's free associations turn out to be quite unoriginal, since once again he has drawn on a set of interrelated themes on the Jew that are interwoven through European folklore.

Weininger's impassioned criticism of the inhibited Jew appears in various forms in the "Jewry" chapter of *Sex and Character*, and this is one way to understand his critique of Jewish family life. Because at the time the warmth and stability of the Jewish home enjoyed an enviable reputation among both Jews and anti-Semites, it was left to renegades like Kafka and Weininger to demystify this inner sanctum. But while these rebels shared an historical predicament, they did not share a common temperament, and this is reflected in their profoundly different attitudes toward the domestic scene. For Kafka, despite or because of his familial trauma, having a family was an unattainable, almost dreamlike goal, even if he experienced his own family as an unbearable confinement. For Weininger, the Jewish family, particularly the relationship between father and son, was an effeminizing (and therefore threatening) den of intimacy. The family, says Weininger, "is of female, maternal origin, and has nothing to do with the state, which is to say the formation of society"—an obvious reference to the stateless existence of the Jews and the powerlessness of a people who could not govern themselves. From this point Weininger centers on the diametrically opposed father-son relationships in the Jewish and Aryan homes, respectively. The "indogermanic male" never gets too close to his father, while it is only in the Jewish family that the son is absorbed into the family (*ganz tief in der Familie darinnensteckt*) in a way that precludes "comradeship" (*Freund und Freund*) between father and son (Weininger 1922, 412). For Weininger the Jewish family is a contemptible environment precisely because it is where "male camaraderie"— *Männerbund*—is sure to collapse into an effeminized relationship between men.[14] At the same time, his interpretation of the Jewish family and its inhibiting influence is only one perverse variation on a widespread if inchoate feeling about the constricting effects of Jewish domesticity. As a Jewish commentator noted in 1939, Jews are not comfortable with bacchanalia, and the lust of the Jew at an orgy is repressed by the haunting presence of his parents (*pudor judaïca* [Jewish modesty]) (Praag 1939, 172). As we have seen, the implications of this allegedly deficient spontaneity extended far beyond an incapacity for sexual license to other (and more public) forms of physical daring such as soldiering and dueling.

Weininger's fixation on spontaneity also explains his criticism of the Jews' failure to produce more dangerous criminals. At a time when Jews took pride in their unfamiliarity with violent crime, Weininger converted this ostensible virtue into the deficiency of an essentially undramatic human type over whom good and evil did not even bother to struggle. In this respect, the Jew lacks the "greatness" and therefore the stature to be either a "triumphant victor" on behalf of good (the old Crusader model) or an impressive servant of evil (the devil the Jews don't know). His veneration of the "radical stupidity" (*das Radikal-Dumme*) that he believed to be inherent in the genuinely masculine personality is yet another endorsement of the spontaneous impulse that is at the core of violent and predatory behavior. His derision of the Jew's estrangement from alcohol—an anti-Semitic theme that appears throughout the nineteenth and twentieth centuries—is at base a critique of the Jew's inability to experience intoxication. Weininger subscribed as well to the commonplace notion that the Jew was estranged from nature and therefore unable to experience glorious abandonment to its charms (Weininger 1922, 410, 410–11, 421, 429, 417, 427n.). The troubled Jewish relationship to the horse—vehicle and companion of medieval chevaliers, nineteenth-century cavalrymen, and modern English gentlemen—is only one aspect of the alleged separation of the Jews from the natural realm. Weininger's idealization of the horse as an "aristocratic" creature (Weininger 1907, 125) is therefore yet another sign of affiliation with the Aryan mystique and its many ramifications in the world of cultural symbols.

Weininger's analysis of Judaism, Hans Kohn wrote, "has nothing to do with reality" (Kohn 1961, 165). The categorical nature of this statement is likely to mislead Kohn's readers. On the one hand, it is true that Weininger libeled and otherwise distorted a Judaism of which he knew very little. But Kohn's assertion also suggests that the reality of being Jewish had nothing to do with Weininger's sometimes accurate and sometimes pathological analysis of the Jewish experience of his era. Suffice it to say that the historiography of the Jewish ordeals of the *fin de siècle*, including the Jewish confrontation with predominant male values and styles of behavior, remains inadequately developed to this day. The premise of this essay has been that Weininger's long service as a symptom of the *Zeitgeist* can be usefully applied to the study of how the Jews of Europe interpreted masculinity and the challenges it implied at a time when racial myth exercised its special tyranny. In addition, the case of Otto Weininger is a textbook example of Jean-Paul Sartre's dictum that "the Jew is one whom other men consider a Jew: that is the simple truth from which we must start" (Sartre 1965, 69). In fact, Jewishness is much more than the image of the Jew in the eye of the Other, and it is surprising that Sartre did not understand *this* "simple truth." Nevertheless, the value of Sartre's impoverished notion of Jewish identity is that it does in fact define the impoverished Jewishness of Otto Weininger and others like him. The purpose of Weininger's critique of Jewish masculinity, after all, was to effect his own disappearance as a Jewish male. Terrified by the critical Aryan gaze, Weininger tried desperately to achieve that state of invisibility we call total assimilation; or, in Anna Freud's famous phrase, "identification with the aggressor."

10 ✦

WEININGER AND NAZI IDEOLOGY

Barbara Hyams

Otto Weininger's popular scientific treatise of 1903, *Geschlecht und Charakter* (Sex and Character), lent itself in many ways to exploitation by *völkisch* and, slightly later, Nazi ideologues. Weininger, an apostate Viennese Jew who converted to Protestantism the day he became a doctor of philosophy in June of 1902, had attempted to define Jewish character in a single chapter of a work otherwise dedicated to defining male and female character and to suggesting a solution to the alleged moral depravity of the era. By drawing negative parallels between male Jews and "Aryan" women, Weininger appeared to fall victim to his contempt for women, who in his view were morally inferior beings driven either by a herdlike instinct to reproduce or by lasciviousness. Many people viewed his suicide at the age of twenty-three in the house in which a symbol of male "Aryan" genius, Beethoven, had died, as a desperate acknowledgment of unavoidable parallels between female character and Jewish male character.

Weininger's sensational suicide, the subsequent intellectual debate over his theories in Karl Kraus's influential periodical *Die Fackel* (The Torch) and elsewhere, and the popularity of his book, which went through twenty-five editions in roughly as many years, rendered Weininger for some a saint too ethical for this vile world and for others a tragic example of a Jew who could not overcome the ignobility of his race. Because *Sex and Character* was so popular in the first third of the century, *völkisch* and Nazi ideologues used him as a prime example of a tormented Jew who provided not just evidence but eloquent evidence of Jewish "inferiority."

Indeed, the Nazi view of Weininger was mostly a straightforward matter of exploiting the "Jewish self-hate" in a "racist classic."[1] However, Weininger proved to be a problematic figure for Nazi ideologues, because *Sex and Character*[2] was primarily about gender, not race, and its low opinion of women made manifest what was covert in Nazi ideology. As Annette Kuhn has demonstrated, "German fascism concealed its extreme antifeminism behind racist-biological rhetoric. Its *Weltanschauung* was overtly racist and implicitly antifeminist" (Kuhn 1988, 41).

As far as I can ascertain, *Sex and Character* was never banned during the Third Reich. Nazi men's reception of Weininger until 1943 tended to ignore his negative assessment of female character and motherhood while exploiting his condemnations of Jewish character. Their implicit point of agreement with Weininger's antifeminism was their belief that "superior" male intellect could analyze and control "Aryan" women's vulnerability to seduction by channeling it into socially desirable modes of behavior. The specific point of disagreement between Weininger and Nazi ideologues lay in their respective definitions of socially desirable behavior: for Weininger, it meant a spiritually motivated abstention from intercourse; for the Nazis, a racially motivated acceleration of selective breeding. Thus, since a number of Weininger's theses about women and motherhood contradicted some Nazi myths about the family, it eventually became opportune for Nazi men to discredit—by means other than censorship—Weininger's blatantly low assessment of women. Weininger's ideas were a point of contention between Nazi men and women, and Nazi men eventually attacked his specifically antifeminist ideas as a ruse to pacify "Aryan" women. Although it goes beyond the bounds of this article to discuss in detail Nazi women's motivations and experiences in creating and promoting a fascist state in "Greater Germany," the works of feminist historians such as Annette Kuhn, Claudia Koonz, Rita Thalmann, and Christina von Braun[3] provide a specific context within which to understand Weininger's reputation during the Third Reich.

However, one cannot understand Nazi women's and men's views of Weininger's treatment of the "woman question" without first addressing their views of his contribution to the "Jewish question." While Weininger sought to relativize his Jewish heritage in a footnote to the chapter on Judaism in *Sex and Character*—"The author notes at this juncture that he himself is of Jewish descent" (Weininger 1980, 406)—Nazi ideology and its precursors treated his conversion to Protestantism as an exemplary failure and prefaced all references to him with "the Jew." Most *völkisch* and Nazi Weininger reception falls under the rubric of "Jewish self-revelations" (*jüdische Selbstbekenntnisse*). Theodor Fritsch, the "creator of practical anti-Semitism,"[4] and Hans Jonak von Freyenwald (1941), for example, compiled anthologies of quotes taken out of context in which Jewish thinkers appear to support a blanket condemnation of Judaism and Jews.

Theodor Fritsch was a major contributor to the genre as both a writer and founder of the anti-Semitic Hammer publishing house in Leipzig. He quoted brief passages from Weininger under the heading "Jewish Character" in *Jüdische Selbstbekenntnisse* ([Jewish Self-Revelations], 1929). Other categories include "Masters of Perversity," "Judaism and Marxist Workers' Movement," "The Jew as Capitalist," "Jews as Rulers of Economic Life and Representatives of Shady Dealing," "Baptised Jews Remain Jews," "State Within a State," and "Complete World Domination." The 1919 and 1929 editions of Fritsch's book include fourteen identical quotes;

however, the 1919 edition cites a passage from *Sex and Character* that is not reprinted in the later edition. It is Weininger's only quote that ties purported Jewish character to purported female character and thus is the truest to his agenda in the chapter on Judaism: "The great talent of the Jews for journalism, the 'agility' of the Jewish spirit, the lack of a rooted and fundamental cast of mind—do these not hold true for Jews as well as women: they *are* nothing, and therefore they can *become* everything?" (Weininger 1903, 429). Fritsch's omission a decade later of this comparison between Jewish males and "Aryan" women is consistent with Nazi men's reception of Weininger until 1943.

Fritsch crafted the other fourteen quotations to exploit Weininger's self-hatred. The quotes focus on the following claims: that Jewish physical features have an apparent anthropological relatedness to Negroid and Mongolian features (Weininger 1903, 405; that "outstanding" people have been "almost always anti-Semitic" (Tacitus, Pascal, Voltaire, Herder, Goethe, Kant, Jean Paul, Schopenhauer, Grillparzer, and Wagner are cited [Weininger 1903, 406]); that the Jew excludes everything transcendent and has no feeling for mysteries, while the "Aryan" feels that the unfathomable lends life its meaning (Weininger 1903, 421); that Jews are only interested in the purely chemical aspect of medicine, not in the treatment of human beings as an organic whole (Weininger 1903, 422); that the Jew's ability to adapt to new requirements and host cultures is parasitic (Weininger 1903, 430); that the Jew believes in nothing and takes nothing and no one seriously (Weininger 1903, 431); that the Jew is frivolous and mocks piety (Weininger 1903, 431); that the Jew has no understanding of the concept of a state or citizenship (Weininger 1903, 410–11); that the notion that Jewish behavior is the product of historical misfortune is false (Weininger 1903, 413); that the Jew's belief in Jehovah and the teachings of Moses is merely belief in "the Jewish species and its vitality" (Weininger 1903, 416); that Jewish matchmaking is another proof of the Jews' lack of soul, since Jews more than any other people do not wed for love (Weininger 1903, 417); that since the "superior Aryan" wants to respect the Jew, anti-Semitism is not a pleasure nor an idle way of passing the time (Weininger 1903, 419); that the male Jew's total lack of humility explains his inability to understand grace and that his servile disposition leads to an immoral willingness to seek earthly affluence (Weininger 1903, 419–20); and that the Jew has no soul and therefore no belief in immortality, and that Judaism is not a religion of pure reason but of old wives' tales, materialism, slave consciousness, and impudence (Weininger 420–21).

Fritsch's quotation of the passage concerning the "superior Aryan" is particularly instructive, since it is lifted from a paragraph which, if cited in full, would attack the entire rationale for publishing "Jewish self-revelations" and challenge anti-Semites' refusal to accept apostate Jews as individuals. In fact, the ensuing paragraph in *Sex and Character* criticizes Fritsch himself in no uncertain terms: "The Jew's so crucial and so necessary recognition of the actual nature of *Jewishness* and *Judaism* would be the solution to one of the most difficult problems; Judaism is a much deeper riddle than many an Anti-Semitic Catechism believes, and ultimately it will never be completely dislodged from a certain inscrutability" (Weininger 1903, 419). Fritsch's *Handbuch der Judenfrage* (Handbook on the Jewish Question [1930, 1944]) was originally published in 1887 as *Der Antisemiten-Catechismus* (The Anti-Semitic Catechism).[5]

In *Sex and Character* Weininger explicitly confines himself to a discussion of the "singularity [*Eigenheit*] of Jewishness" as a state of mind. According to his definition, the most rabidly anti-Semitic "Aryan" exhibits "Jewishness," because part of "Jewishness" is a fixation on racial identity. By attempting to define "Jewishness" (*das Judentum* or *das Jüdische*) rather than "the Jews" (*die Juden*), he allows for the "triumph" of individuals over their racial heritage. However, as George L. Mosse points out, "As early as 1919 [Hitler] denied that anti-Semitism could be based upon one's feelings toward the individual Jew, unfavorable though this was bound to be. Instead, the evils for which the Jew stood were a 'fact' of his race."[6] While Weininger posited the Jew as a type, the non-believer, and consequently argued that, like Christ, one could *overcome* the Jew in oneself, the Nazi ideologue Alfred Rosenberg took advantage of Weininger's careless confusion of the Jew as a type, Jews as adherents of a religion, and Jews as a race. In his *Dietrich Eckart: Ein Vermächtnis* (Dietrich Eckart: A Legacy) of 1928, Rosenberg elaborated on the Jew's alleged lack of a soul. "To the Jew Weininger his own nation is like an invisible cohesive web of slime fungus (plasmodium), existing since time immemorial and spread over the entire earth; and this expansionism, as he correctly observes (without, of course, proving it), is an essential component of the idea, of the nature of Judaism."[7] In Rosenberg's view, Jews are by definition earth-centered, that is, incapable of overcoming themselves and ascending to spiritual heights. They thus exist as a counterweight to those peoples who are able to strive for salvation. As was often the case, Rosenberg expressed in pseudomystical terms that which Hitler stated baldly.

Most of the Weininger quotes in Hans Jonak von Freyenwald's *Jüdische Bekenntnisse aus allen Zeiten und Ländern* (Jewish Confessions from All Eras and Lands) of 1941 are identical to those in Fritsch's works, although they appear under a wider range of headings: "The Jewish People," "Race," "The Essence of Judaism," "Jewish Morality," "Assimilation and Baptism," "Anti-Semitism," "Marxism," "Means and Ways to Power," and "Messianism and World Rule."

In the section "on Jewish Morality," Von Freyenwald includes

Weininger's enigmatic assertion about Jewish male sexuality, which comes as no surprise, since the book was published by Julius Streicher's Der Stürmer publishing house: "The Jew is always more lecherous, hornier, if also oddly enough, perhaps in connection with his not actually antimoral nature, sexually less potent, and certainly less capable of all great pleasure than the Aryan man" (Freyenwald 1941, 417).[8] This odd balance of "more" and "less" serves a two-edged stereotype: the man who is driven by lustful designs yet who is physically[9] or morally incapable of the heights of feeling (a further indication of his lack of soul).

Weininger's brief discussion of the Jewish male's sexual appetite was by no means solely responsible for but added credence to the Nazi image of Jewish sexual insatiability: "In the popular culture and pornography of Germany, and Central Europe generally, the Jew often played a sexual role similar to that assigned the black male in the United States. He was presented as combining oversized genitals, insatiable appetites, and an irresistible approach" (Showalter 1982, 87). As Koonz (1987) and Braun (1990, 196ff.) point out, the male Jew was often portrayed as an economic bloodsucker *and* a seducer (the fat capitalist exploiting his secretary), and in caricatures his enormous nose symbolized a disproportionately large phallus. According to National Socialist ideology, Jewish lasciviousness had nothing in common with natural sensuality (Hahn 1978, 114). Ideologues like Rosenberg spread the misconception that the Talmud "obligates pious Jews to lead a sex life that is immoral, disgusting, and antisocial. The Jew is incapable of love. Since his physical urges are inseparable from his striving for power, his sexuality can only emerge as a deformation that plunges fellow human beings into torment and disaster."[10]

Two other Weininger quotes in Freyenwald's collection augment the themes in Fritsch's volumes: the Jew is someone who blurs the borders and categories between human beings (*Grenzverwischer*) and hence the "born Communist" (Freyenwald 1941, 417); and since "the spirit of modernity is Jewish," the present age is the highest point of Judaism since Herod (Freyenwald 1941, 440–41). Both of these additional quotes accentuate elements that Hitler made central to National Socialist ideology in *Mein Kampf*.

In his *Rassenkunde des jüdischen Volkes* (Racial Science of the Jewish People) of 1930, Hans F. K. Günther, who became one of the principal racial experts under the Nazi regime (Mosse 1964, 208, 302–3), explicated Weininger's statement that "the spirit of modernity is Jewish" as follows: Jews controlled the press and used the media to divert non-Jewish peoples from their spiritual values by substituting whatever values suited the needs of Judaism. Thus according to Günther, Weininger was a "highly gifted, perceptive critic of this spirit" (Günther 1930, 314). Günther also argued that modern city life in the West led to the assimilation that was corroding the biological safeguards that had traditionally protected the Jewish race. In a ploy to deliver a high-minded rationale for removing Jews from Western European societies, he concluded that Zionism was the one way to secure the future of Judaism, for only it could provide a means for Jews to turn their backs on the "modern spirit" and "individualism" and to emphasize family and *Volk*, eugenics and rural life (Günther 1930, 338). He recast Weininger's equation of the modern spirit with the Jewish spirit as a Nazi aversion to individualism. And, in a foregone conclusion, Günther speculated that the suicide of the "extraordinarily talented Jew" Weininger might have had something to do with his realization concerning the "dubiousness" of modern Judaism in the diaspora (Günther 1930, 320f.). The more brilliant Weininger could be made to appear, the more he posthumously condemned all Jews.

In a similar vein, Hitler's mentor Dietrich Eckart referred to Weininger as "the only decent Jew." Hitler recalled Eckart's remark during a conversation in December 1941 with Henry Picker in the Wolf's Lair: "Dietrich Eckart once told me that he had made the acquaintance of only one decent Jew, Otto Weininger, who took his life when he realized that the Jew lives from the destruction of other peoples" (Picker 1989, 79). In Eckart's posthumously published *Der Bolschewismus von Moses bis Lenin: Zwiegespräche zwischen Adolf Hitler und mir* (Bolshevism from Moses to Lenin: Conversations with Adolf Hitler), Weininger comes up in a discussion of the Old Testament. Eckart quotes Hitler as saying that "the Jew Weininger suspects that Christ too [i.e., in addition to Paul, whom Hitler has just described as a mass murderer] was originally a criminal, but my God, if a Jew says it a hundred times that doesn't necessarily mean that it has to be true" (Eckart 1923, 20). It is quite unlikely that Hitler ever bothered to read *Sex and Character*.

Using Weininger as a prime example, Nazi ideologues stressed the impossibility of Jews overcoming their "blood" through religious conversion. Georg von Schönerer had emphasized biological identity in 1885 (Weininger was five years old), adding a twelfth point to his hitherto non-anti-Semitic Linz Program of 1882: "The removal of Jewish influence from all sections of public life is indispensable for carrying out the reforms aimed at" (Pulzer 1988, 147). A 1942 article celebrating "One Hundred Years of Schönerer" credited Schönerer with "building the victorious road to Austria" for Hitler and for clearing up a false distinction between Jews and Christians: "What the Jew *believes* is all the same, in his *race* resides the dirty shame!" (Pichl 1942, 301–4). As Von Braun points out, Schönerer's portrayal of anti-Semitism as a "cleansing agent" made a great impression on Hitler.[11]

The Jewish theoretician Theodor Lessing had reinforced ¯blood imagery in *Der jüdische Selbsthaß* (Jewish Self-Hatred) in 1930. No Jewish writer of the period did more to secure Weininger's reputation as a self-hating Jew than did Lessing in this famous book. Featured in one of six case studies, Weininger emerges as a "Jewish Oedipus" who cursed his mother's blood (Lessing 1930, 82). According to Lessing, Weininger became obsessed with the belief that spirit is superior to nature, such that "woman" and "Jew" became synonymous with the "depths of nature" he feared and avoided. While Lessing pointed correctly to the tragic effect of Weininger's extremely polarized philosophy, he himself was caught up in the inflammatory racial rhetoric of his era. His most unfortunate pronouncement was that "no human being has ever freed himself from the constraints of his blood. No categorical imperative has ever obscured the voice of blood" (Lessing 1930, 91), which Nazi propagandists used to their best advantage (Kohn 1962; Janik 1987).[12]

Julius Streicher, editor of the notoriously anti-Semitic magazine for SA men, *Der Stürmer* (The Stormer), published from 1924 to 1945,[13] and Nazi *Gauleiter* of Nuremberg, popularized the racist eugenic belief that led to the criminalization of sex between "Aryans" and Jews: "A single act of intercourse between a Jewish man and an Aryan woman is enough to poison the woman's blood forever. Even if she marries an Aryan man, she will never bear pure Aryan children, but only bastards" (Westenrieder 1984, 31).[14] A lavishly illustrated text by Professor Theodor Pugel, a historian at the University of Vienna, expressed the same ideas somewhat less crudely in *Die arische Frau im Wandel der Jahrtausende: Kulturgeschichtlich geschildert* (The Aryan Woman in the Course of the Millennia) in 1936.[15]

In 1935, when *völkisch* notions about race were put into effect by Nazi laws such as the "Blood Protection Law" forbidding marriage and extramarital intercourse between non-Jewish and Jewish Germans, and the Marriage Health Law establishing hereditary biological standards for marriage between "Aryans" (Westenrieder 1984, 31), Robert Körber and Theodor Pugel edited *Antisemitismus der Welt in Wort und Bild* (The World of Anti-Semitism in Words and Pictures). In his concluding chapter, Körber, a popular anti-Semitic writer, stresses that one cannot adopt an ethnic identity or take it off "like a worn-out suit," insisting instead on "nationalism by blood only" (*Blutsvolkstum*). "Spare our people above all," he beseeches, "from the unfortunate figures of a Weininger and a Trebitsch, who could not overcome 'jewing' (*Judenzen*) despite their hating nothing more than their people of origin" (Körber and Pugel 1935, 316). Arthur Trebitsch (1880–1927) was an anti-Semitic Viennese Jew who published *Deutscher Geist und Judentum* (German Spirit and Judaism) in 1919 and also featured prominently in Lessing's study of Jewish self-hatred. As Sander Gilman notes, "Here was the Jew who bore witness to the truth of the accusation that it was the Jews who caused Germany's defeat [in

World War I]" (Gilman 1986, 249). Between Lessing and the Nazis, the stereotypes of Weininger and Trebitsch as self-hating Jews were assured.

Houston Stewart Chamberlain's *Grundlagen des* 19. Jahrhunderts (*The Foundations of the Nineteenth Century*) of 1899 served as a mutual point of reference for Weininger and Nazi ideologues. Weininger had met Chamberlain at sessions of the Viennese Philosophical Society and was thoroughly familiar with his highly celebrated work, which was one of the main sources for his views on Judaism. Citing the fourth printing of *The Foundations* in 1903, Weininger notes that Chamberlain's attempts to solve the "anthropological question" of the origin of Judaism had recently met with a great deal of controversy. His observation reflects the fact that Chamberlain's book, although rejected by many contemporary scholars as the work of a dilettante, nonetheless enjoyed enormous popular success.[16]

It has often been observed that Weininger chose to convert to Protestantism in the midst of the predominantly Catholic culture of Vienna. His decision underscores the fact that he felt most at home intellectually in the Protestant philosophical tradition upon which Chamberlain drew. Weininger was clearly inspired by Chamberlain's reading of Kant as "the first perfect pattern of the absolutely independent Teuton who has put aside every trace of Roman absolutism, dogmatism and anti-individualism," and who "can—whenever we please—emancipate us from Judaism: not by bitterness and persecution, but by once for all destroying every historical superstition, every cabalisticism of Spinoza, every materialistic dogmatism" (Chamberlain 1913, vol. 3, 490).[17] In *Sex and Character* Weininger underscored his intentions: "I shall emphasize once again, although it ought to be obvious: in spite of my adverse evaluation of the actual Jew, the last thing I have in mind is—on the basis of these or the following observations—to play into the hands of theoretical, or even worse, practical persecution of the Jews" (Weininger 1903, 417–418). Weininger's reading of Christ as the symbol of hope that individual Jews could "put aside" or "emancipate" themselves from "Jewishness" is an impassioned answer to Chamberlain's argument—so necessary for Chamberlain's synthesis of Christianity and "Aryan" identity—that Jesus had not been a Jew by "blood."[18] However, the evidence shows repeatedly that *völkisch* and Nazi ideologues dismissed this aspect of Weininger's argument, preferring to focus on the (self-hating) ways in which he agreed with Chamberlain, such as his reference to a section of *The Foundations* called "Consensus Ingeniorum," in which Chamberlain recites a consensus of anti-Jewish judgments among Cicero, Frederik the Great, Bismarck, Mommsen, Herder, and Goethe (Chamberlain 1913, vol. 1, 344–46).

In *Das Lebenswerk Houston Stewart Chamberlains in Umrissen* (The Life's Work of Houston Stewart Chamberlain in Outline) a tribute to Chamberlain published in 1927, the year of his death, Georg Schott cites the "Weininger case" as evidence for Chamberlain's claim that the Jewish race is "a crime against the holy law of life" (Schott 1927, 38). Schott stresses the "race question," quoting Weininger and Benjamin Disraeli as Jews who attest to its importance. Schott goes so far as to call Weininger a "martyr to his conviction" (Schott 1927, 96–97), thereby manipulating a prevalent view of Weininger's ethical integrity among intellectuals. He praises Chamberlain as an "inexorable judge and avenger for truth" who must feel like "a sword piercing the soul" to "a Jew of Weininger's inner constitution." Lauded as a martyr, Weininger "cannot blame" but rather must admire Chamberlain for his relentless campaign against Judaism—a campaign whose "high moral ground" Schott admonishes his fellow anti-Semites to emulate (Schott 1927, 109).

As a *völkisch* thinker, Oswald Spengler made a crucial distinction for later Nazi ideologues between culture and civilization, between a rooted (German) soul and (Jewish) rootlessness.[19] In Spengler's view, Jewish mysticism had produced "three more saints in the sense of Oriental Sufism—though to recognize them as such we have to see through a colour-wash of Western thought-forms" (Spengler 1928, 321). Weininger is the third of these saints, preceded by Spinoza and Baal Shem. Spengler labels Weininger's "moral dualism" and "death in a spiritual struggle [as] one of the noblest spectacles ever presented by a Late religiousness." Weininger's experience is said to be *Magian*, Spengler's term for those spiritual cultures in which man "belongs to himself alone, but something else, something alien and higher, dwells in him, making him with all his glimpses and convictions just a member of a consensus which, as the emanation of God, excludes error, but excludes also all possibility of the self-asserting Ego" (Spengler 1928, 235). The classification is only apparently problematic in relation to Weininger—Weininger's answer to Ernst Mach's "irretrievable self" being the restoration of Kant's "intelligible self"[20]—for Spengler cites a tradition of Magian fascination with Kant's thought.[21]

Spengler's respectful image of Weininger as a saint, albeit one whom Westerners could never fully understand, clashed with the flagrant anti-Semitism of the Weimar era. Like other *völkisch* and Nazi ideologues, Schott believed that Spengler's theories were not sufficiently anti-Semitic.[22] In his chapter "Spengler or Chamberlain?"—in which Chamberlain triumphs as the "Nordic" over the "Magian" character type—Schott classifies Weininger together with Spengler as "a Faustian spirit in a Magian soul." Such natures are "tragic," and their readers must learn to distinguish the "good" and "healthy" from the "insane" aspects of their genius (Schott 1927, 149).

✦ When National Socialism came to power, some of the Nazi Party's female adherents attempted to exert influence (Koonz 1987), in spite of the party's explicit history of excluding women from its top ranks (Franz-Willing 1962, 80; Thalmann 1984, 74). Rita Thalmann pinpoints a decisive moment in Nazi ideology in which Hitler left it up to party theoreticians like Rosenberg to justify women's subordinate role and at the same time to ensure their enthusiastic participation as mothers in the eugenic design of the future Germanic state. While Rosenberg drew on the "cultural pessimism of a host of misogynist thinkers from Schopenhauer to Wagner, Nietzsche, Houston Chamberlain and up through Otto Weininger" in his *Mythus des 20. Jahrhunderts* (Myth of the Twentieth Century) of 1930, he had to reconcile the call in cultural pessimism for a "return to chastity" with the aims of National Socialism (Thalmann 1984, 75). Thus, he claimed that in world history the creative-constructive world of the Apollonian "fathers" had triumphed over the orgiastic-destructive chaos of the Dionysian "mothers," thereby creating a "new" place of honor through marriage for the woman *as mother* within the Nordic-Apollonian principle. Lydia Gottschewski, a Nazi youth organizer since the 1920s and first appointed head of the Women's Front in 1933, accused Hans F. K. Günther of borrowing his views on women from Weininger and chided Rosenberg for his theory that Nordic man was the sole inventor of marriage (Thalmann 1984, 84; Koonz 1987, 142–43, 157). However, in any case Rosenberg's abstractions were too difficult for the average German. Consequently, Hitler made sure that key party concepts were also communicated in simpler language by himself and others (Thalmann 1984, 75–76; Diehl 1932).

The anthropologist Pia Sophie Rogge-Börner, who had been writing on gender and race since the early 1920s, "accurately perceived the danger of an all-male elite turning women into breeding machines" but "exalted racial thinking as long as it did not diminish women's participation in the master race" (Koonz 1987, 113). Rogge-Börner and some of her women Nazi friends wrote letters to Hitler in March 1932 and January 1933, demanding that the German people be led by the best and brightest of both genders. She took issue with Weininger's famous assertion about the relative abilities of men and women at the beginning of his chapter on Judaism: "Just because a Weininger has claimed that even 'the lowliest man is immeasurably superior to the most remarkable woman,' that's no reason to conclude that the majority of men are better suited to leadership positions than are the majority of women" (Rogge-Börner 1934, quoted in Thalmann 1984, 84). Hitler never answered her letter.[23]

Yet the National Socialists eventually did respond in an oblique form after the disaster in Stalingrad, since the policy of total war included gestures to increase women's sense of comradeship with men. As we have seen, Nazi ideology had always implicitly concurred with Weininger's contempt for women, but it needed them to produce the next "Aryan" generation (Koonz 1987, 59–60). Hitler's refusal to tap women as a reserve work force until late in the war and Himmler's cynical *Lebensborn* program, which provided prenatal care for unwed "Aryan" mothers and included plans for SS officers to impregnate vast numbers of "Aryan" girls, were both based on a view of women as breeding machines for the Third Reich (cf. Lilienthal 1985). It was only after Stalingrad that Hitler's deputies were able to override his opposition to drafting women into war work (Koonz 1987, 398).[24]

In the fall of 1943, a thirty-two-page pamphlet by Dr. Alexander Centgraf, "Ein Jude treibt Philosophie" ("A Jew Tries His Hand at Philosophy"), was published in Berlin (Kohn 1962; Janik 1987). In the preface, which is dated the end of August 1943, Centgraf, "currently in Kiev," admits that "many will ask whether it is actually necessary at this moment, when we are at the zenith of the greatest of all wars, to write a booklet of this kind. Who is still interested," he wonders, "in a twenty-three-year-old who has been dead for forty years [Weininger]—even if his book was a great success?" (Centgraf 1943) "Even if" is significant, for Weininger was apparently earmarked in the Nazi propaganda effort for the reasons I have stated above.

The "spiritual construction of Aryan culture," Centgraf explains, is a "fine weave" into which Weininger has smuggled a "Jewish thread." Centgraf sees a direct line between *Sex and Character*, Freud, and Magnus Hirschfeld, in all of whose writings "woman is branded as a person of low quality, and above and beyond that, is desecrated intellectually and spiritually. Above all today, when woman is employing her entire personality to fight with us for the political and spiritual conditions for a new Europe, we owe it to her as a comrade to thoroughly settle the score with *such a dangerous Jewish intellectual as Otto Weininger*" (Centgraf 1943 [emphasis added]).

Centgraf was probably relieved from active military duty in Kiev long enough to write this homage to German women because the Propaganda Ministry deemed it a good idea. He had studied journalism at the University of Berlin in the late 1930s. His doctoral dissertation, written under the direction of Professor Emil Dovifat (Benedikt 1986),[25] was published in 1940 as *Martin Luther als Publizist: Geist und Form seiner Volksführung* (Martin Luther as a Publicist: The Spirit and Form of His Leadership of the Volk).[26] As a friend of the Provostry of Berlin, he had also published a commemorative essay, *Luther und Berlin*, in 1939 for the four-hundredth anniversary of the Reformation.

The opening chapter of "A Jew Tries His Hand at Philosophy," entitled "A philosophical Prodigy," blasts Weininger's "dangerous definitions of women," which rob mothers of their dignity. Centgraf views

Weininger's call to ban mothers from the pedagogical tasks of childrearing as the "first stages of Bolshevist collective thinking," while at the same time accusing him of preparing the ground for "unbridled individualism" (Centgraf 1943, 6). However, Weininger's call for celibacy at the cost of the extinction of the human race receives Centgraf's harshest criticism: Weininger's "complete negation of the human race" is "Jewish" (Centgraf 1943, 7).

The second chapter, "No One Has Ever Freed Himself from the Constraints of His Blood,[27] declares Weininger's death a catastrophe for assimilated Jews, who had set for themselves the impossible goal of slipping into the protective covering of another race (Centgraf 1943, 9). Since the Jews have a different "spirit," they can never become Germans. Centgraf invokes the expertise of Theodor Lessing regarding Jewish self-hatred after citing Weininger's own prejudices about Jewish character (Centgraf 1943, 11). Weininger genuinely tried to become a Christian, Centgraf believes, but it was impossible for him to leave the "spiritual abyss of Jewishness" (Centgraf 1943, 13).

In Chapter Three, "The Demonic Nature of Sexuality: The Sexual Problem at the Core of Otto Weininger's Ideas," Centgraf explains that the Jew has deteriorated ontologically due to the demonic nature of sexuality; hence the predominance of Jews in sex research. Jews have less shame and less awe for the mysteries of life. Centgraf takes up the familiar theme of Jewish lasciviousness, then comes to the thrust of his argument: it is an outrage for a "Jewish philosophy" to place "Aryan" women on a par with the inferior Jewish race (Centgraf 1943, 17). In contrast, Centgraf praises the work of a Professor Mathilde Vaerting (1931) at the University of Jena on the psychology of the sexes, as "women must be consulted in order to gain a full picture of the psychology of the sexes" (Centgraf 1943, 20). Weininger's impertinent book, he laments, has done great damage to many immature young people in the first decades of the twentieth century by teaching them to undervalue women. Moreover, Bolshevism owes a great deal to its "apostle Weininger" for its view of woman as a "soulless machine" (Centgraf 1943, 21).

The fourth chapter, "A Jewish Prescription for Homosexuals of Both Sexes," is a homophobic attack on Weininger's theory of sexual gradations. Weininger, the "philosophical quack," has branded all famous women as lesbians and attempted to make "Aryan" heroes despicable by equating genius with homosexuality and perversion (Centgraf 1943, 24–25). Centgraf scoffs at Weininger's proposal to decriminalize homosexuality, and is alarmed by his suggestion that society mandate the pairing of contrasting "M" and "W" types, for the offspring would inherit their parents' imbalances (Centgraf 1943, 26). Weininger's "Jewish" agenda, he claims, is to corrupt and destroy "Aryan" morality (Centgraf 1943, 27).[28]

Centgraf's concluding chapter, "The Epistemological Cardinal Error in Dr. Weininger's *Sex and Character:* Truth Rather Than Jewish Arrogance," foresees the gradual emancipation of women and an accompanying increase in male objectivity toward women. He faults Weininger for his "one-sided" analysis of women. This, in and of itself, would be forgivable, Centgraf admits, since other psychologists and philosophers "have made the same mistake," but Weininger is guilty above all of "Jewish arrogance." Centgraf surmises that Weininger's "latent homosexual inclinations caused him to write a book that would violate woman's body and soul" (Centgraf 1943, 29). He rejects Weininger's argument that "man projects his own need for beauty and love onto soulless woman" as an idea borrowed from Islam (Centgraf 1943, 31): "When this incomparable war of destiny is behind us, should the European people degrade their women to soulless beings, to willing slaves to the desires of man, to slaves who can only hope to gain a soul from him? That would be poor thanks to all of the wives and mothers fighting as comrades side by side with men in two great wars for a newer, better future for our continent" (Centgraf 1943, 31). Centgraf accuses Jewish speculators of keeping *Sex and Character* alive by artificial means in order to pave the way for "sexual anarchy" and to "pit man against woman and woman against man" (Centgraf 1943, 32).

Centgraf has contorted the usual Nazi argument to serve Nazi ends, for Nazi idealogues typically blamed "Jewish intellect" for advancing the cause of women's emancipation. Women's emancipation, according to the prevailing Nazi argument, upset the social order by blurring borders between sexual spheres. Hitler had claimed in his 1934 speech to the Nationalsozialistische Frauenschaft that

> the phrase "emancipation of woman" is the product of Jewish intellect, and its content is stamped with that same intellect. During those truly good times in German life the German woman never found it necessary to emancipate herself. She controlled exactly that which nature freely gave her as her due to administer and preserve—just as the man in good times did not have to fear that woman would oust him from his position. . . . It is not true—as Jewish intellect would have us believe—that mutual respect is based upon the overlapping of sexual spheres of activity. On the contrary, such respect demands that neither sex encroach upon the sphere of the other (Hitler 1934, 376–77).

However, in this instance, Centgraf blames Weininger for his "arrogant Jewish" rejection of equal social status for women and men. Centgraf's task was in fact to lie about the actual sexist premise of National Socialism, which aimed to exploit women as a "means to the selective production and reproduction of the fascist body" (Kuhn 1988, 41). Even if Centgraf was naive—or frightened—enough to believe his own statements,[29] his naiveté was surely and cynically exploited.

As late as January 1945, Weininger's name appears in a major channel of Nazi propaganda to invoke yet again the dangers of "the Jewish essence." The *WeltDienst: Die Judenfrage/Internationale Korrespondenz* (World Service: The Jewish Question/International Correspondence), which was published bi-weekly in twenty-one languages, cites "the Jew Weininger's" definition of the Jew as one who contains all possibilities without actually *being* anything.[30] Jews are likened to species of animals whose biological characteristics include the ability to adapt to host cultures. Even Zionism is viewed disparagingly as the Jews' attempt to adapt themselves to European nationalism. The *WeltDienst* takes up the familiar refrain from prefaces to "Jewish self-revelations" that Jews themselves admit that their bad traits are not the result of centuries of oppression, but are endemic: "Jews themselves confirm it, and not just a few individuals like Otto Weininger at the turn of the century, but official Jewish organs, newspapers geared specifically toward Jews, like the Yiddish 'Tog' that appears in New York, or the 'American Hebrew,' which seeks to promote 'better understanding between Jews and Christians' " (*WeltDienst* 1945, 10). In the final frenzy of their war against the Jews, Nazi ideologues continued to milk Weininger's critique of "Jewish character" after they had already murdered millions.

III ✦
Weininger and
Modern Literature

11 ✦

A SCIENTIFIC IMAGE OF WOMAN? THE INFLUENCE OF OTTO WEININGER'S *SEX AND CHARACTER* ON THE GERMAN NOVEL

Gisela Brude-Firnau

Translated from the German
by Barbara Hyams and Bianca Philippi

Otto Weininger's *Sex and Character* still incites as much disgust and fascination in today's readers as when it was first published in 1903. Its significance is due largely to the history of its reception. Its large circle of readers included such illustrious names as Sigmund Freud, Ludwig Wittgenstein, Oswald Spengler, and James Joyce as well as numerous German-speaking authors who have by no means all been identified. The most well known are the authors of major novels from the first half of this century: Franz Kafka, Hermann Broch, Robert Musil, Heimito von Doderer, Stefan Zweig, Karl Kraus, and Franz Blei.[1] Weininger's work, stresses Heinz Politzer, "left a distinct mark on Kafka's generation, especially on those who, like Kafka, had learned to sympathize with the rampant misogyny of August Strindberg and were stimulated by Sigmund Freud's ardor to observe the mechanisms at work below the threshold of consciousness (Politzer 1966, 197).[2] Even Günter Grass describes the six-hundred-page opus as "the devil's work" and "a stroke of genius" (*Geniestreich*) (Grass 1989, 202).[3]

Along with those who carried on an earnest debate with Weininger, other critics took neither the book nor its author seriously. An anonymous reviewer of 1904 wrote: "It is a despicable book that has been set in front of us. Even if Strindberg's influence is unmistakable, no rational person would write a book such as *Sex and Character*. Had Weininger placed himself under the care of a psychiatrist in time, the German publishing industry would have been spared from such a disgrace, and the author would have been spared the bullet. It is incredible that there are people who still sing Weininger's praises despite his impudent book.[4]

How did this highly lauded yet "despicable book" come to be? The first part, regarded as positivistic and scientific, was presented as a doctoral dissertation to the faculty of the philosophy department at the University of Vienna. A year later the twenty-three-year-old author published it as a monograph, now expanded to include a psychological-speculative section. A few months later Weininger took his life. This contributed to *Sex and Character*'s status as a best seller for decades: the twenty-sixth German edition came out in 1926, the twenty-eighth in 1947 (Kohn 1962, 46), and there were numerous translations (Blomster 1969, 124).

The book struck the "nerve of the times"; it belonged to a kind of "philosophical journalism" (Lukács 1962, 88) that provided the bourgeoisie with a *Weltanschauung* until World War II. Weininger was quoted and reviewed. Accordingly, Georg Lukács included Weininger's work in the philosophy of life he considered to be the "ruling ideology of the entire imperialistic period in Germany" (Lukács 1962, 88). Weininger belongs among the early propagators of the irrational *völkisch* tradition: with a fanatical disdain for all materialism and everything "Jewish," he, like them, preaches a Germanic-Christian salvation myth. It is hardly surprising that his work was later appropriated by the Nazis and incorporated into their propaganda machine (Centgraf 1943).[5]

Last but not least, *Sex and Character* must also be understood as a reaction to the women's movement at the turn of the century, which threatened to bring about shifts in the social structure.[6] Yet, as we shall see, Weininger's ideas go far beyond the antifeminism of his time.

Under these auspices—the success of a best seller and the work's relation to its time—the influence of *Sex and Character* on the German novel and its portrayal of women is almost predictable. A comprehensive study of the broad spectrum of literary-historical Weininger reception has not yet been written. The present essay merely attempts to bring one aspect into sharper focus and to allude to others.

Since providing proof of Weininger's direct influence on other authors is more difficult and to some extent impossible because of his eclecticism, we shall begin by outlining the content of *Sex and Character*: Weininger's basic concern is an ethical one. His book is a confused attempt to construct a portrait of humanity that even outshines Kant's categorical imperative.

Weininger sees the central problem of all ethics in the relationship between the sexes. For him it is once again woman who is the cause of the problem; she embodies sexuality. Therefore, it is also she who impedes the ethical salvation of humanity and indeed the process of becoming authentically human altogether.

Given these premises, the question that runs throughout *Sex and Character* is: What is woman? How can she be defined in a biological, psychological, and ethical sense? In these terms, Weininger's work can be read as an early attempt to formulate a scientific understanding of woman. As hardly ever before, the entire conceptual and epistemological apparatus of contemporary science as well as examples from cultural history are employed to arrive at a complete definition of woman. The point of departure for this attempt is the thesis that all human beings have bisexual inclinations; in reality, neither "man" nor "woman" exists, but instead "all sorts of intermediate conditions between male and female—sexual transitional forms (Weininger 1906, 7).[7]

For heuristic purposes, the author erects two opposing constructs: an ideal man ("*M*") and an ideal woman ("*W*"). Using a far-reaching catalogue of examples encompassing religious history, the writings of the church fathers, and nineteenth-century philosophers, Weininger begins to give the terms *M* and *W* qualitative definition. Yet he does not spurn occasional recourse to such banal sayings as "the longer the hair, the smaller the brain" (Weininger 1906, 68).[8] Collectively, such popular sayings only support one firmly established a priori conclusion: all negative human characteristics belong fundamentally to type *W*. If they also show up as empirically verifiable traits in a man, this can be attributed to the share of *W* in the man's character. All ethical, creative, and intellectual values belong essentially to type *M*. The author is obviously as unconscious of the sophomoric arbitrariness of this definition as he is of the groundlessness of his further conclusions, for he makes hardly any distinctions between speculation and description. Instead he indulges in leaps of logic between the methodologically weak definition of type *W* and instances of real women. One would be tempted to suspect a logical sleight of hand if it were not one's obligation to impute ethical honesty to the author. However, the noncritical reader may hardly notice that the premise of a sentence frequently is based on the abstraction *W*, yet the sentence concludes with a statement about *das Weib*, that is to say, empirical women.

Weininger then measures and evaluates the definition of woman derived in this manner in relation to Kant's ethics, and concludes that in both thought and action woman is determined exclusively by her sexuality. Therefore she is, in the sense of a Kantian ethical absolute, thoroughly reprehensible. Since she is determined entirely by instinct, she also lacks any kind of distinct consciousness. However, in Weininger's view this very thing—distinct consciousness—is the fundamental precondition for genius, and thus something to which woman cannot lay a single claim. Since he considers genius to be the highest form of human consciousness and existence, woman is ultimately excluded from being human. Countless talents and other abilities that constitute human identity for Weininger are also incompatible with being a woman, namely logic, memory, and awareness of ethical responsibility. And, like Palström, he "astutely concludes that that which isn't permitted cannot possibly exist";[9] in the ethical-philosophical sense, woman is the undetermined one, a formless nothingness.

True to his initial query regarding the relationship between the sexes, Weininger now attempts to explain how woman, who is "without values," can inspire love in man. He decides—entirely caught in a web of compulsive conclusions—that man projects the values to which he aspires onto woman and loves only his own ideals in woman; that is, he loves only himself. According to Weininger, man completely ignores empirical woman, who functions solely as a means. In this way, profane love commits the harshest offense against the categorical imperative. In Weininger's judgment, "Love is murder" (Weininger 1906, 249).[10]

In a courageous metaphysical upswing, Weininger offers a solution to this moral entanglement: in the cosmic order of things, woman is relegated to an object for man, from whom she expects definition and meaning. She is her own impediment to becoming truly human because of her reliance upon instinct. For this reason, man must annihilate *das Weib*. By means of asceticism he must kill that which is female in woman, for only then can divine salvation be achieved in this world. As Weininger summarizes: "The question is not merely if it is possible for woman to become moral. It is this: is it possible for woman really to wish to realize the problem of existence, the conception of guilt? Can she really desire freedom? This can only happen by her being penetrated by an ideal, brought to the guiding star. It can happen only if the categorical imperative were to become active in woman—only if woman can place herself in relation to the moral idea, the idea of humanity. In that way only can there be an emancipation of woman" (Weininger 1906, 348–49).[11]

The ductus of the language and the stringent demands that nullify any comforting thoughts make one suspect that Weininger adhered to this absurdly extreme ethos as his own personal law. He could only resolve his Kantian conflict by means of self-obliteration.

As archaic and nonsensical as the message of *Sex and Character* may appear today, all the more telling is its literary reception. If we trace its course by way of representative authors, the following points emerge as indicators of Weininger's influence:

1. Positivistic proof directly in text or in correspondence of familiarity with Weininger's work
2. A rather consistently applied combination of those characteristics that Weininger designated as female appearing in a fictitious female character
3. The use of Weininger quotes, paraphrases, or otherwise unmistakable analogies.[12]

Two of these indicators are found in Kafka's work. Heinz Politzer was the first to discover that Kafka's female figures, above all in *The Trial*, are sketched as if according to Weiningerian formulas (Politzer 1966, 200).[13]

Heimito von Doderer can only be mentioned in passing as having "become acquainted [with Weininger] through Hermann Swoboda" (Wolff 1969, 275; cf. Doderer 1958, 190, 269, 274–75). However, the misogyny of both authors had to have deeper roots. It was merely articulated by Weininger and subsequently reverberated with greater intensity by Doderer.

Hermann Broch's understanding of Weininger was fundamentally determined by the ongoing debate of *Sex and Character* in *Der Brenner*, which was less concerned with the definition of woman than with the ethical-philosophical aspect of the book. Of all of Weininger's critics, Broch employed the most emphatic superlative when he apostrophized Weininger in August 1914 as the "most passionate moral philosopher since Kant" (Broch 1914, 689).[14]

Fifteen years later, the intensity of Broch's Weininger reception becomes fully evident in *The Sleepwalkers*. In Broch's trilogy, the conceptual foundation in the relationship between man and woman is Weiningerian, albeit not without critical or ironic refraction.

This is true for four couples. The "little whore" Ruzena, as Broch describes her (Broch 1957, 21), is reduced to Weininger's formula, which defines woman's existence in its entirety: she lacks the will and intentionality to make any decisions outside the realm of the erotic. Elizabeth von Baddensen seems to escape Weininger's terminological guillotine, but her image in Pasenow's consciousness is determined by Weininger: Pasenow uses her like a screen to conjure up a Madonna for himself. The concept of purely spiritual, salvational love is clearly seminal to his ethical-religious imagination. Only the reader is aware of the ironic-critical relativity of these hopes.

Broch defines the most important female character in Esch in a manner that sounds very much like a paraphrase of Weininger: "Mother Hentjen is for her part 'without values' and 'autonomous' right from the beginning, just as 'the feminine' or 'nature' as such is always without values."[15] Purged of all sentimental glorification, she embodies the

Weiningerian definition of motherhood: mindless, inert, oriented toward possession and materialism, determined and ruined by man. Weininger's thesis, according to which there is a latent whore in every mother, can be seen in Hentjen's indifferent surrender to Huguenau during the chaotic events at the end of the war.

The fatal chapter 13 of *Sex and Character* in which the Jew is equated with the conceptual abstraction of "woman" and condemned accordingly plays a decisive part in Broch's differentiation from Weininger. With the ridiculous claim to being "scientific" Weininger hardly differentiates himself from other anti-Semitic pamphlet writers of his time. Moreover, his personal point of departure as a converted Jew is disconcerting. As Theodor Lessing writes, explaining this "Jewish self-hatred," woman and Jew signified for Weininger "two different names for the ground of nature [*Naturgrund*] that he feared and avoided" (Lessing 1930, 91). Lessing fittingly labeled Weininger a "Jewish Oedipus."

Broch attempts to effect a resolution to Weininger's Judeo-Christian antagonism and ethical salvation myth by poetic means at the end of the trilogy as, in a kind of mythical union, the Jew Nuchem and the Christian Marie are bound as man and wife in spiritual love. Broch himself later criticizes the unreality of such gender metaphysics: "If I think back, on the first level it was an imperative to the Jew Nuchem: 'Do not let yourself be led astray by any fables, but stay true to the abstract book, remain a Jew, and stay true to your Torah.' On the second level, however, it is an imperative to the poet: 'Do not allow yourself to be seduced by the promise of salvation: Poetry cannot confer grace; rather, the path to grace is through knowledge.' "[16]

Broch's individual psychological debate with Weininger in *The Sleep-walkers* is translated into the sociopolitical dimension in the original 1935–36 version of *The Spell*[17] and leads to a decisive refutation. One can already see the signs of Broch distancing himself from Weininger in his 1914 essay "Ethics," in which he stresses that Weininger's Kant ethos is whipped "into dogmatism" (Broch 1914, 689) and thereby turns into unethical rigor. This dialectical reversal of values is the intellectual scaffolding of the 1935–36 edition of *The Spell:* "We are to live a chaste life so that the world may get better," is the postulate with which the wanderer Marius tries to make himself popular in the mountain village of Kuppron. His demand for asceticism, together with his aggressively antifemale and by extension anti-Semitic stance, proves him to be a figure largely inspired by Weininger (Broch 1987, 8).[18]

Broch only indirectly employs Weininger's perjorative equation of the Jew with woman: Wetchy, the commercial agent and sole non-Catholic of the village, conforms in virtually every detail to the literary caricature of the Jew indelibly drawn by Wilhelm Heinrich Riehl, Gustav Freytag, and

Wilhelm Raabe, and described by George L. Mosse as follows: "It held the Jew to be without a soul, without the humble German virtues, and consequently uprooted . . . . In contrast to the German soul, which acted as a filter between man and cosmos, the soul of a Jew was an insensitive, materialistic thing" (Mosse 1964, 126–27). Marius attempts to press Wetchy into this stereotype—in which Broch substitutes urban ways for Jewishness—in order to direct the villagers' hatred and dissatisfaction toward him. Marius's diatribes read like *völkisch*/National Socialist propaganda; the antifeminist component evokes Weininger: "They insinuate themselves and tempt us with their wheeling and dealing like women, yes, like women, for they only pose as men, and though they still may manage to grow beards, those beards cannot hide the womanly greed staring from their flaccid faces." (Broch 1988, 351).[19]

Discrimination against Wetchy and his exile from the village are subplots with concrete and timely significance. Marius's confrontation with Mother Gisson, which takes on cosmic dimensions with the death of the old peasant woman, remains in the foreground. This cosmic conflict between a perverted male principle and an idealized female principle must be seen as the actual myth that is functioning behind the scenes of the peasant milieu of the novel. Until now it has proved difficult to identify one myth running through the work: is it about Demeter or the earth mother, about an affirmed or a negated "mysticism of the soil" (*Bodenmystik*)? The diverse, so eclectically assembled mythological allusions become comprehensible if viewed as set pieces that are meant to conceal Broch's ongoing reckoning with Weininger's salvation myth, for Weininger had recently "elevated male-female dichotomy into a cosmic principle," as Mosse stresses (Mosse 1964, 215).[20] In the ritualized murder of Irmgard, Broch shows the murderous consequences of Weininger's postulates made absolute. The abstruse doctrine of purity and salvation that Marius preaches like a madman in a trance or a demagogical agitator of the masses shows how very far Broch distances himself from Weininger. At this juncture he refers to the totalitarian potentiality that is inherent in every form of dogmatism.

Unfortunately, this interpretation loses credibility through Broch's cliché-strewn conception of the female characters: Mother Gisson's death bears an embarrassing resemblance to the Assumption. Agatha is exclusively the naive pregnant woman caught up in her dreams. Irmgard remains the weak-willed, loving victim. Even the pediatrician Barbara, clearly intended as a counterweight, is too good to be true. There is an overabundance of female virtues, virtues that coat the women like a shiny varnish. The women enter into battle against a metaphysical principle, indeed not one corresponding to the Weiningerian M ideal, but rather to the historical and sociological consequences that ensued from Weininger's doctrines about male superiority. Another reason why Broch's female characters are far removed from reality is that historically the majority of German women most certainly did not oppose the National Socialist movement.

As we gain distance over time, we are able to see a greater parallel between Broch's *The Sleepwalkers* and Robert Musil's *The Man Without Qualities* than their authors were once willing to acknowledge. One of the—thus far scarcely examined—analogies between the works lies in the influence of Otto Weininger on Musil's monumental novel.[21]

If we read *Sex and Character* alongside *The Man Without Qualities*, we find in Musil's work a more peripheral, less conceptually fundamental confrontation with Weininger; the conceptual mechanisms of the young rigorist, and Musil, with his "gliding logic of the soul," were completely different forms of thought. Therefore, in Musil's novel Weininger's conceptual patterns are merely integrated as representative time-bound material into the consciousness of particular characters. This is demonstrated in the first short episode of *The Man Without Qualities*, for it is conceived like a fictional paraphrase of Weininger: a not precisely identified "lady" and her "escort" happen upon the scene of a traffic accident. The contrast between their respective observations of the same event demonstrates the difference between male and female spheres of thought and experience. This difference is first portrayed through particular narrative modes: the "lady's" reactions—pity, indecisiveness, and relief— are presented through indirect discourse. The discourse of her "escort"— technical explanations, statistical details, and original observations—is expressed exclusively as direct speech. The narrator's irony-laden offer of identification stands in contrast to the neutral information about the "escort." This contrastive technique as well as the willful ignorance of the "lady," who gratefully accepts her male counterpart's interpretation and valuation of the experience, is characteristic of Weininger's analysis of "male and female consciousness," which he analyzes in Chapter Three: female consciousness consists of inarticulate, feeling-bound complexes of thought, whereas male consciousness shows "greater decisiveness in . . . judgments." Weininger stresses that "wherever a new judgment is to be made (not merely something already settled to be put into proverbial forms), it is always the case that the female expects from the man the clarification of her data, the interpretation of her henids" (Weininger 1906, 101).[22]

The attentive gaze with which the "lady" responds to the decisive quality of male consciousness finds its explanation in Weininger: "A psychological proof that the power of making judgments is a masculine trait lies in the fact that the woman recognizes it as such, and that it acts on her as a tertiary sexual character of the male. A woman always expects definite convictions in a man, and appropriates them" (Weininger 1906, 195).[23] This definition of supposedly gender-specific consciousness is a determining factor for various female characters in Musil's novel, which is similar to Weininger's work in theme but not in its ethical judgments.

Above all, Musil's psychological profile of the charming, man-hungry society matron Bonadea corresponds to Weininger's definitions, as she continually fluctuates between the poles of "whore" and "mother." Now and then, a societally imposed feeling for "manners and morals" awakens in her a sporadic attack of conscience: "For the woman unfaithfulness is an exciting game, in which the thought of morality plays no part, but which is controlled only by the desire for safety and reputation," as Weininger pronounces in a corresponding passage (Weininger 1906, 221).[24]

Almost the entire retinue of negative female characteristics described by Weininger comes to life in Bonadea's unsuccessful attempt to seduce Ulrich in Chapter 63. The narrator makes the following comment on the pretext she uses as an entrée to Ulrich: "She always believed many things at once, and half truths made it easier for her to tell lies" (Musil 1979, vol. 1, 307).[25] In Weininger's logistic terminology, the same sentence appears as: "A creature that cannot grasp the material exclusiveness of A and not A has no difficulty in lying; more than that, such a creature has not even any consciousness of lying, being without a standard of truth" (Weininger 1906, 149).[26]

The basic constellation of the scene is also compatible with Weininger's theories: "The female principle is, then, nothing more than sexuality; the male principle is sexual and something more" (Weininger 1906, 90).[27] *M* possesses—as Ulrich demonstrates—the ability to distance himself from both his mental as well as his physical urges, whereas Bonadea is entirely at their mercy.

Even Bonadea's interest in the Collateral Campaign, a mere pretext for her singular objective of winning Ulrich for herself, is in keeping with Weininger's assertion that "when the female occupies herself with matters outside the interests of sex, it is for the man she loves or by whom she wishes to be loved. She takes no real interest in the things for themselves" (Weininger 1906, 89–90).[28]

Both the far-reaching "devaluation of sexuality"[29] in *The Man Without Qualities* and the way in which female characters are mirrored in Ulrich's consciousness frequently bring Weininger's formulations to mind. Yet *Sex and Character*'s importance for Musil should not be overestimated: as Corino's work on Musil and psychoanalysis makes very clear, his underlying childhood experiences and family constellation were of greater significance. For Musil, like Kafka, Weininger may only have had the function of raising his awareness and of confirming preformulated ideas.

Musil's differentiation from Weininger is most obvious when Weinin-

gerian values show up in his novel as time-bound judgments and precon-
ceived notions, such as in the letter in which Professor Hagauer replies to
Agathe's request for a divorce. In it he categorizes her as an intellectually
and consequently morally deficient type, for "the irregular form of
behaviour manifest in his wife could be associated with a fairly general
type of inferiority that was simply feminine, in other words, it could be
termed 'social imbecility' " (Musil 1979, vol. 3, 338).[30] For Weininger, the
purported "connection between logic and ethics" is the fundamental link
that holds his case against women together. Thus he does not view her as
immoral but simply as amoral: "Woman resents any attempt to require
from her that her thoughts should be logical. She may be regarded as
logically insane" (Weininger 1906, 150).[31] Lindner also receives prompts
from Weininger when he resolves to concern himself "solely" with
Agathe's ethical improvement. He explains unctuously "that I serve you as
a brother, wishing at the same time to awaken in woman herself the
antidote against woman,"[32] which corresponds to Weininger's plea for the
"emancipation of the female from the female" (Weininger 1906, 343).[33]

In these and similar cases, the woman is judged and condemned in the
realm of commonly held truisms, that is, in the narrow compound of
socially accepted standards. The corresponding phrases are often tellingly
introduced with "people say" (*man sagt*). Ulrich alone transcends this level
with the insight that "definite rules were contrary to the essential nature of
morality" (Musil 1979, vol. 3, 154).[34]

Agathe reacts to Hagauer's written diagnosis much as a noncritical
female reader would react to Weininger's book: she allows herself to be
defined within the categories of her judge, for "her behaviour struck her
now as so entirely that of someone who was really not quite responsible for
her actions" (Musil 1979, vol. 3, 340).[35] She appears to have accepted her
own condemnation right down to her choice of words when she asks, "So
what it does come to is that I'm a moral imbecile?" (Musil 1979, vol. 3,
349).[36] And as Ulrich appears to confirm this, her self-esteem collapses, and
she decides to take her life. Musil thus demonstrates clearly how an
external judgment turns into self-condemnation.

"She [woman] possesses no personal value, she is devoid of man's
sense of value of his own personality for itself" (Weininger 1906, 202)[37]—as
Sex and Character synopsizes the seldom articulated presupposition of
those who believe in male superiority. Agathe's intention to commit
suicide demonstrates how in individual cases, such generally and silently
accepted propositions can ultimately degenerate into hardened roles, and
finally into murderous, obsessive compulsions. If the author had not
needed the character of Agathe later in the novel, she would have become,
next to Broch's Irmgard, the second literary offering to Weininger.

Musil's reckoning with Weininger occurs through the character

Clarisse, in whose mind "the contents of the times had gotten all mixed up." Her obsessive demand for "pure love" appears to be the ironic counterpart to Weininger's metaphysically exorbitant postulate demanding an end to sexuality altogether, for "there is no possibility of establishing the kingdom of God on earth" (Weininger 1906, 343).[38] Clarisse echoes this in a secularized form: "And the world will never get any better until there are such lovers!" (Musil 1979, vol. 3, 291).[39]

Above all, the imagery connected with Clarisse, who becomes ever more overtly schizophrenic, points to Weininger: "every person has an animal that he inwardly resembles,"[40] she proclaims analogously to Weininger's claim that "certain people embody specific animal-like possibilities."[41]

In his "Animal Psychology" Weininger sees close parallels between women and birds "physiognomically as well as characterologically," while for him worm and snake "are related to the hunchbacked criminal."[42] In a similarly abstruse and forced relationship, Clarisse sees a blackbird and "a fat caterpillar that it was devouring": remembering her earlier conversation about Moosbrugger, she experiences at the sight of it "an ineffable correspondence of interior and exterior experience" (Musil 1979, vol. 3, 308).[43] "Every form of life in nature corresponds to a human quality. Every possibility in human beings corresponds to something in nature,"[44] wrote Weininger, who had suffered similarly from schizophrenia in the last few months of his life (cf. Abrahamsen).

As the examples have clearly shown, Musil takes a number of stances toward Weininger in his fiction. The character Bonadea shows that several of Weininger's claims were based on his observations of women in the Viennese leisure class of his time. Insofar as Musil interprets Bonadea's "one-sided" behavior in the final analysis as "ambition" (Musil 1979, vol. 3, 263; 1970, 889), he illustrates, in contrast to Weininger, that it had not so much to do with an existential standard of behavior as with a psychosexual potency that lacked any other means of expression because of the social conditions for women in those times. Musil thereby rejects Weininger's primitive, generalizing conclusions. Through Hagauer, Agathe, and to some extent Ulrich, however, he shows how these views belonged to an unreflected *opinio communis* prior to World War I and how they reified into ruinous, obsessive compulsions. By integrating Weininger's imagery into Clarisse's consciousness, which moves increasingly into a reality of its own, he emphasizes the insane elements in this paradigm.

Weininger and the consequences are with us to this day. Even in Günter Grass's *Dog Years*, which was written sixty years after *Sex and Character*, the book figures as a document of German anti-Semitism (Grass 1989, 36–37, 109–10, 202–4, 216, 262). And in 1976 *Sex and Character* was translated into French as an example—however eccentric—of German philosophizing (Amery 1976, 429). By virtue of the sheer number of novels in which Weininger's influence may be ascertained, there is a danger of overestimating the intellectual significance of his work. A more realistic evaluation is possible only if we first become cognizant of the biographical and historical conditions in which *Sex and Character* was created: Weininger gave eloquent expression to his family-influenced and pubescent animosity toward women, which he stylized into scientific knowledge with the help of some examples from cultural history and data from the natural sciences. In so doing, he articulated subliminal fears to which his epoch was quite susceptible. His work remains a "singularly grandiose error"[45] that made history.

12 ✦

WEININGER IN A POEM BY APOLLINAIRE

Jeffrey Mehlman

It is one of the enduring commonplaces of French literary history that after the protracted *askesis* of Mallarméan "symbolism," French poetry underwent a fundamental renewal at the beginning of the twentieth century in Apollinaire's opening of French verse to the undisciplined heterogeneity of a world Mallarmé had done his heroic best to hold at bay.[1] What has not been observed is that no sooner did Apollinaire open his great poem "La Chanson du mal-aimé" than he reproduced—in one of his most memorable images—the very components of Otto Weininger's crackpot synthesis in *Sex and Character:* bisexuality, misogyny, and anti-Semitism. The poem's action—or passion—is set in 1903, the year of Weininger's suicide, the year in which Apollinaire found himself abandoned by his English lover, Annie Playden.[2] Here then is the beginning of Apollinaire's long poem:

> Un soir de demi-brume à Londres
> Un voyou qui reassemblait à
> Mon amour vint à ma rencontre
> Et le regard qu'il me jeta
> Me fit baisser les yeux de honte
>
> Je suivis ce mauvais garçon
> Qui sifflotait mains dans les poches
> Nous semblions entre les maisons
> Onde ouverte de la mer Rouge
> Lui les Hébreux moi Pharaon
>
> Que tombent ces vagues de briques
> Si tu ne fus pas bien aimée
> Je suis le souverain d'Egypte
> Sa soeur-épouse son armée
> Si tu n'es pas l'amour unique (Apollinaire 1965, 46)

One half-misty night in London / I happened to meet a tramp resembling my love / And the way he glanced at me / Made me lower my eyes in shame. // I followed him / his hands in his pockets, whistling / Between the houses we seemed / Open billow of the Red Sea / He the Hebrews, myself Pharaoh. //

Let the waves of bricks crash down / If you were not well loved / I am the sovereign of Egypt / His sister-wife, his army / If you are not my only love.

The poet, in his despair at the faithlessness of his woman, finds himself following a provocative young male tramp down a London street. An initial and unresolved ambiguity is presented by the notion that the tramp resembled his love, which might mean Annie herself or his love experience in what he had come to regard as all its sordidness. In any event heterosexuality has given way to homosexuality, and the poet's fury at the situation takes the odd form of comparing the street of red brick buildings down which he pursues his young prey to the Red Sea through whose parted waters he, in the role of Pharaoh, chases the tramp, in the role of the Hebrews. Whereupon the poet dissolves the image in a burst of fury at the woman, claiming that he is indeed the king of Egypt (or for that matter his incestuous wife or his whole army) if the love he had for her was not true. The proposition that is, is: may the sea of red bricks come crashing down on me with all the force of the subjunctive *tombent* if what I say is not true. Or more abstractly: may my metaphor be true if my poem is false. That last statement puts Apollinaire's proposition in the situation of what philosophers call "counterfactual self-referentiality," the kind of uncontrollable self-contradiction (e.g., "I'm lying") that is the bane of many, if not every, coherent system of thought.[3]

The content of Apollinaire's "counterfactual" proposition is vintage Weininger. Thus the anger against a woman is quirkily actualized as a fury against Jews, wherein we encounter that homology between Jews and women that is the heart of the "Judaism" chapter of *Sex and Character*.[4] Moreover, the crossing of the Red Sea, Apollinaire's exemplum, "with the consequent thanks of cowards to their Savior," in Weininger's phrase, happens to be singled out by the Austrian as the quintessential episode of Jewish history (Weininger 1906, 323). In addition, both rages—against women and against Jews—are vented in Apollinaire as in Weininger in the context (or as an instantiation) of bisexuality. The human condition is "permanently bisexual," in Weininger's words (Weininger 1906, 7), even as the image of the male tramp "resembling my love" implies that Apollinaire's heterosexual experience was either always already or ultimately homosexual—that is, bisexual. Finally, both Weininger's and Apollinaire's fantasies were destined to abject failure. Even before the Austrian committed suicide, the indifference to the end of the human race in which his calls to total sexual abstinence at the close of *Sex and Character* would result constituted something of a suicide *in petto*. And in the case of Apollinaire, the poet's identification with a pharaoh doomed to a watery death serves a similar function. Thus the core of "counterfactual self-referentiality" in Apollinaire's image, a kind of unconscious that cannot quite be contained by his poem, appears to mediate nothing so much as the dominant fantasy of Weininger's book. It is a circumstance, moreover, that the opening sequence in the poem is far from exhausting.

For "La Chanson du mal-aimé" is a kind of Nietzschean carnivalization, or "refabulization," in Pierre Klossowski's coinage, of the poet's sentimental life (Klossowski 1963, 194). "I am, at bottom, all the names of history," wrote Nietzsche, and Apollinaire's major poem all but follows that maxim (Klossowski 1963, 221). Specifically, Apollinaire's sentimental disaster is negotiated through a series of unhappy kings whose stories intersect with his own. The first, we have seen, is Pharaoh chasing the Jews to his own discomfiture across the parted waters of the Red Sea. The second, more obscure than the first, is a seventeenth-century Ottoman sultan pursuing a band of Ukrainian Cossacks ("les Cosaques Zaporogues") he is intent on converting to Islam. Now the Cossacks—"drunk, pious, and thieving"—bitterly reject the sultan's proselytory advances and as such figure the faithfulness of the poet toward his faithless lover. But what the Cossacks are faithful to above all is the Ten Commandments:

Je suis fidèle comme un dogue
Au maître le lierre au tronc
Et les Cosaques Zaporogues
Ivrognes pieux et larrons
Aux steppes et au décalogue (Apollinaire 1965, 50)

I am as faithful as a dog / To his master, ivy to the trunk / And the Zaporozhian Cossacks / Drunk, pious, and thieving / To the steppes and the Decalogue.

So we have passed from Pharaoh pursuing the Hebrews through the Sinai desert to a sultan pursuing a raucous band faithful to the Ten Commandments. Plainly the two episodes, however different, are versions of each other.[5] The aggressive, shaming glare of the tramp in the initial Pharaoh sequence is here amplified in the Cossacks' contemptuous taunt of the sultan, who makes his first appearance in the following stanza:

Portez comme un joug le Croissant
Qu'interrogent les astrologues
Je suis le Sultan tout puissant
O mes Cosaques Zaporogues
Votre Seigneur éblouissant (Apollinaire 1965, 51)

Bear as a yoke the Crescent / Pondered by astrologists / I am the all-powerful Sultan / Oh my Zaporozhian Cossacks / Your dazzling lord.

The third line of the stanza all but recycles the line quoted above from the earlier sequence: "je suis le souverain d'Egypte." The sultan's overture is greeted with scorn and ends with an interpolated poem, "Réponse des

Cosaques Zaporogues au Sultan de Constantinople," in which the Cossacks give voice to the violence of their contempt:

> Plus criminel que Barrabas
> Cornu comme les mauvais anges
> Quel Belzébuth es-tu là-bas
> Nourri d'immondice et de fange
> Nous n'irons pas à tes sabbats (Apollinaire 1965, 52)

> More criminal than Barabbas / Horned like the evil angels / What Lord of the Flies are you down there / Fed on excrement and mud / We won't attend your revelries . . .

Thus begins the amplification, in the second sequence, of the tramp's hostile glance in the first. But this brings us to a major difference between the two, for if Apollinaire seemed to identify with Pharaoh (against the Jews) in the first sequence, he speaks his fury above all in the persona of the pursued band, the Cossacks, in the second. At one level, this is entirely appropriate, of course, since what is at stake is providing the poet a vehicle to vent his rage . . . against a woman. But since the two sequences are transformations of each other, it is somewhat unsettling to see the poet identifying first with the ineffectively pursuing potentate, then with the pursued (and "faithful") band. Unless, of course, the undergirding reality of bisexuality were related to this capacity to occupy either position in the scenario.

A further difficulty is presented by the fact that the Cossacks, whatever their fidelity to the Ten Commandments, and however homologous their position to that of the Hebrews in the initial sequence, were notorious anti-Semites. But that dilemma is in part resolved by a stanza whose repetition at key junctures of the poem makes it something of a refrain. It is, for instance, repeated immediately after the interpolated curse of the Cossacks against the proselytizing sultan:

> Voie lactée ô soeur lumineuse
> Des blancs ruisseaux de Chanaan
> Et des corps blancs des amoureuses
> Nageurs morts suivrons-nous d'ahan
> Ton cours vers d'autres nébuleuses (Apollinaire 1965, 53)

> Milky Way, o luminous sister / Of the white streams of Canaan / And of the white bodies of women in love / Dead swimmers will we follow painfully / Your course to other nebulae?

The poem, in its evocation of the Milky Way, opens up to the universe itself, but only, it turns out, to return to the Hebrews of the "counterfactual" core at the poem's beginning. For the Milky Way brings us to the "white streams of Canaan," a land said to be flowing with milk and honey.

Now the key words in the stanza are "nageurs morts," for on the one hand they provide an image of drowning in the treacherous waters of Jewry, thus linking the refrain to the experience of Pharaoh pursuing the Jews across the Red Sea. But, on the other, the words, at first hearing, appear to refer to the "white bodies" of the desired women ("amoureuses"), for white is the color conventionally assigned to corpses. So the waters of Jewry are those in which the poet, like Pharaoh, encounters disaster, but they are also the fluid—or blank—medium in which a whiting out occurs: pursuer and pursued, male and female, become indiscernible. Here we broach the constitutive medium of bisexuality, which lay at the heart of the initial episode and seemed to lie at the horizon of the second, with its apparent switch of the poet's identification from pursuer to pursued. Bisexuality, fury at woman, and the threat posed by the Jews: it is as though in Apollinaire's "refabulization" of his sentimental existence, the one name, which he may not have known, that he might well have included in his catalog of identifications was that of Otto Weininger. Again it is as though the defeat constituted by Weininger's project were all but enacted by Apollinaire's poem. If an intuition of "the starry vault above me and the moral law within me," in Kant's words, as quoted by Weininger, were the stuff of "Aryan" genius (Weininger 1906, 161), Apollinaire all but offers a parody of that formulation in his reference to the Decalogue (which Weininger termed "the most immoral book of laws in the universe," [Weininger 1906, 313]) and a Milky Way always already aflow toward the promised land of the Jews. Judaism remains the medium in which disaster threatens.

The final unhappy king in Apollinaire's series stages a further encounter with Weininger. For he is none other than the benefactor-king whom Wagner called his "Parsifal," Ludwig II of Bavaria (Pourtalès 1927, 114):

> Destins destins impénétrables
> Rois secoués par la folie
> Et ces grelottantes étoiles
> De fausses femmes dans vos lits
> Aux déserts que l'histoire accable
>
> Luitpold le vieux prince régent
> Tuteur de deux royautés folles
> Sanglote-t-il en y songeant
> Quand vacillent les lucioles
> Mouches dorées de la Saint-Jean
>
> Près d'un château sans chatelaine
> La barque aux barcarols chantants
> Sur un lac blanc et sous l'haleine
> Des vents qui tremblent au printemps
> Voguait cygne mourant sirène

Un jour le roi dans l'eau d'argent
Se noya puis la bouche ouverte
Il s'en revint en surnageant
Sur la rive dormir inerte
Face tournée au ciel changeant (Apollinaire 1965, 58, 59)

Destinies, destinies beyond comprehension / Kings rocked by madness / And those shivering stars / False women in your beds / In the deserts history assaults // Does Luitpold the old prince regent / Tutor to two mad kings / Sob when thinking about it / As the fireflies flicker / Golden flies of the solstice? / By a castle without chatelaine / The bark with singing barcarolles / On a white lake beneath the breath / Of breezes trembling in the spring / Sailed a dying siren swan. // One day in the silvery water the king / Drowned himself, then open-mouthed / Floated back / On the shore to sleep inert / His face turned toward a shifting sky.

The two mad kings were Ludwig II of Bavaria and his brother Othon; Luitpold had himself declared regent and may indeed have driven Ludwig to his apparently suicidal death by drowning in 1886. With a drowned king, we return to the initial sequence of Pharaoh drowned in his disastrous pursuit of the Hebrews. Moreover, even as the image of Pharaoh mediated a homosexual encounter, the current passage is rife with allusions to Ludwig's homosexuality. The phrase "fausses femmes dans vos lits" may, as Roger Lefevre suggests, indicate the deceitfulness of women, but the mention of "bed" is additionally an allusion to gender fakery (Apollinaire 1971, 60). Similarly, the insistence on a "castle without chatelaine" seems an allusion to Ludwig's sexual proclivities. What is most striking, however, is the extent to which the waters in which Ludwig goes to his death seem to flow directly from the land of milk and honey. For the "white lake" (*lac blanc*) in which Ludwig dies is a version of the "white streams" (*blancs ruisseaux*) of Canaan" in the orienting refrain. The "trembling stars" (*grelottantes étoiles*) and "fireflies" (*lucioles*) may be superimposed on the Milky Way (*Voie lactée*), even as the "inert" body washed ashore seems nothing so much as one of the "dead swimmers" of the refrain. So it is once again in the waters of Jewry, raging against deceitful women (*fausses femmes*), lusting after "fake" women (*fausses femmes*) in his bed, that the poet-king goes to his ruin. Weininger again: bisexuality, misogyny, anti-Semitism.

But the alleged threat of Judaism becomes clearer still in the context of the name most intimately associated with Ludwig, Richard Wagner, the author of *Judaism in Music,* and of the name Wagner frequently used in referring to Ludwig, Parsifal. For even as young Parsifal saves the ailing Fisher King, Amfortas, Ludwig, in saving Wagner from debtor's prison, in bankrolling his career after 1864, no doubt earned his nickname as redeemer (Pourtalès 1924, 44).

Wagner's *Parsifal*, of course, was the touchstone of art for Weininger. In *Sex and Character* he refers to it as "the greatest work in the world's literature" (Weininger 1906, 344). So it is worthwhile recalling its plot in the culminating encounter of Weininger and Apollinaire we are staging. Wagner's "sacred drama" transparently effects a retreat from what Weininger's self-described first reader, Sigmund Freud, would call a positive Oedipus complex to a negative one, from heterosexuality to homosexuality.[6] Young Parsifal's triumph is over his own lust as incarnated in the wildly hysterical figure of Kundry, who is a reincarnation of Herodias, we are told, and no doubt, operatically, an anticipation of Strauss's (that is, Oscar Wilde's) Salome. She has, moreover, as Weininger reminds us, shades of Ahasuerus, the Wandering Jew (Weininger 1906, 319). It is no doubt this conflation of threatening woman and Jew that led Weininger to see in her "probably the most perfect representation of woman in art" (Weininger 1906, 319). Now Kundry, who emerges in odd communion with Parsifal's own deceased mother, had earlier seduced Amfortas, leader of the knights of the Grail. As a result he lost—to Kundry's master, the evil magician Klingsor—the sacred spear of the Grail, from which he suffered a devastating, unhealable wound. Thereafter the land lies fallow, Amfortas fails to perform the rituals of the Grail, and his own father, Titurel, lacking the sustenance of the Grail, will die as a consequence. In short, Amfortas lusts after a maternal woman, loses his spear, suffers a symbolic castration in the process, and is responsible for the unintended death of his father. He is Wagner's Christian Oedipus. Or rather Wagner's Christian solution to what is all too un-Christian in Amfortas lies with Parsifal, who rejects Kundry's advances, swears off heterosexual lust, recaptures Amfortas's lost spear, and touches its tip to Amfortas's side in a concluding, healing gesture. Heterosexuality has been decisively rejected, and Parsifal is free to enter the grand homosexual brotherhood of the knights of the Grail.

One perceives the basis for Weininger's enthusiasm for Wagner at the end of *Sex and Character*. If Wagner, as he asserts, was "the greatest man since Christ's time" (Weininger 1906, 344), it was no doubt because he was able to make good on a promise at the beginning of his book that Weininger himself never quite managed to redeem: a demonstration of "the possibility that homosexuality is a higher form than heterosexuality" (Weininger 1906, 66). For such, I would suggest, is the upshot of Wagner's swan song, *Parsifal*.

We return now to Wagner's other "Parsifal," Ludwig II, as he figures at the end of Apollinaire's poem. Before drowning, Ludwig, in his secluded swan castles of Hohenschwangau and Neuschwanstein, staged his own retreat *through Wagner* from heterosexuality to homosexuality. Engaged early on to his cousin Princess Sophie, daughter of Maximilian of Bavaria, he could write to her, "You must know that I do not have many years to live, that I will leave this earth when the horror will have occurred, when my star will no longer shine, when he will no longer be, the faithfully beloved friend . . . . The principal object of our relations has always been, you will agree, the strange and moving destiny of Richard Wagner" (Pourtalès 1927, 71). Finally, on October 10, 1867, he would call off his engagement and consecrate his life as a homosexual (Pourtalès 1927, 83). But with a kingly retreat from heterosexuality to homosexuality before drowning, in a context of anti-Jewish sentiment (Kundry as Wandering Jew), Ludwig, the last of Apollinaire's unhappy kings, reproduces precisely the fate of the first: Pharaoh, about to succumb in a Red Sea (as opposed to Ludwig's "white lake") in the course of a homosexual pick-up.

There is a fundamental anomaly in Weininger's *Sex and Character* that Apollinaire's series of unhappy monarchs—Pharaoh, the sultan, and Ludwig—may help to unravel. For the insistence on a biologically based and irreducible bisexuality in all human beings would seem to have been a liberatory gesture. If there is something of the female in every male and of the male in every female, how confident, after all, might one be in any rigidly defined hierarchy of gender? Yet Weininger's metaphysics withdraws with a vengeance everything that his would-be biology was prepared to concede. For of all the insults heaped upon women in the name of Weininger's understanding of Kant, the culminating one—after his insistence that women are "without logic," "non-moral," without soul, without genius, "mindless," ontologically untruthful—is that at bottom "woman is nothing" (Weininger 1906, 148, 151, 186, 188, 253, 264, 294). Thus a pseudobiological bisexuality serves to introduce a ruthless metaphysical homosexuality. Or to strip Weininger's argument of its ideological pretexts, bisexuality is the cover used to advance a rigidly misogynistic form of homosexuality. The anti-Semitic motif of the penultimate chapter ("Judaism") may seem gratuitous, but to the extent that a Jewish male is traditionally regarded as Jewish through his mother, the Jew in one may be said to be the woman (or mother or Kundry) in one. And anti-Semitism, which for Weininger is as much an outward projection of Jewish self-hatred as sadism is a deflection of primary masochism for Freud, is perhaps above all a castigation of the woman-Jew in a fundamentally homosexual self. Proust, who was not a misogynist but spoke of Jews and homosexuals (or "inverts") as "accursed races," (Proust 1961, 615) hated himself above all *in his Jewish mother* and to that extent may not have been that far removed from Weininger.[7]

Apollinaire's kings, by combining the anti-Semitic and misogynistic motifs, and moving from the bisexual tenor of the Pharaoh image to the homosexual valence of Ludwig, subliminally stage the reading of Weininger proposed in the preceding paragraph. But to link the thought of

Weininger to a certain strand in the masterpieces of Apollinaire or Proust is to broach the grisly fascination of Weininger: the possibility that the elaborate dream of Western culture might have as its nightmare subtext a synthesis such as that proposed by Weininger.[8]

✦ "La Chanson du mal-aimé" is the record of Apollinaire's season in hell and in many ways represented for the poet a road not taken. The poem, with its hints of homosexuality and suicide, is prefaced by a verse statement distancing the poet from the episode and alluding to his new love (in 1908), Marie Laurencin:

> Et je chantais cette romance
> En 1903 sans savoir
> Que mon amour à la semblance
> Du beau Phénix s'il meurt un soir
> Le matin voit sa renaissance (Apollinaire 1965, 46).

> And I sang this romance / In 1903 without knowing / That my love, like / The beautiful Phoenix, should it die in the evening / Next morning sees its rebirth.

Moreover, Apollinaire, whose real name was Kostrowitzky, was not only not Jewish but something of a philo-Semite.[9] The image of him as the gentle "flâneur des deux rives" that tradition has preserved is as far from that of the tortured Weininger as might be imagined. And yet the logic of the unhappy king series in his major poem—with its tripartite synthesis of bisexuality, rage against a woman, and anti-Semitism—remains, which is why a minor episode in the poet's life is worth evoking. In the *Mercure de France* of June 13, 1913, Georges Duhamel, reviewing Apollinaire's *Alcools*, wrote: "A truculent and dizzying diversity takes the place of art in the assembling of objects. Through the holes in his shabby shop, one can barely make out the ironic look of the merchant, who has something simultaneously of the Oriental Jew, the South American, the Polish gentleman, and the *facchino*" (Bieder 1947, 17). The principal result of the article was that Apollinaire was soon referred to throughout the French press as "the Jew Apollinaire." The poet, furious, was prepared to challenge Duhamel to a duel had not André Billy, their mutual friend, stepped in to mediate. It appears that it was precisely the word "Jew" that infuriated the poet, for he proceeded to seek public acknowledgment that he was not a Jew. The result was the following document, which one commentator, Joseph Bieder, has termed a "certificate of Aryan birth" (Bieder 1947, 17):

> Paris, 7 March 1914
> In an article in his journal *Maintenant*, M. Arthur Cravan has written "the Jew Apollinaire." Our friend Guillaume Apollinaire, who is not the slightest

bit Jewish, asked us to call on M. Cravan and request that he correct his error. Here is the passage from his letter concerning our mission:

"Having very little *amour-propre* [vanity], I hereby declare, contrary to what I had allowed to be understood in my article on the "Exposition des Indépendants," appearing in my journal *Maintenant*, that M. Guillaume Apollinaire is not a Jew, but Roman Catholic."

Since that rectification appears to have satisfied our friend Guillaume Apollinaire, we have acknowledged receipt of M. Arthur Cravan's letter and, as agreed between him and yourself, we herewith cosign it in the present notarized form so that it may be published in the press, and declare the incident closed.

Cluade Chéreau
Artiste peintre

Jérôme Tharaud
Homme de lettres
Chevalier de la Légion d'honneur

Thus in 1913 did Apollinaire obtain—and go through the trouble of obtaining—a notarized confirmation of the fact that he was in no way Jewish. As Bieder observed in 1947, this was a document that would have stood him in good stead during the years of the Nazi occupation. But is not the very trouble to which he went a reminder of the poem just analyzed, the season in hell in which he found himself drowning (as Pharaoh, as Ludwig of Bavaria) in the waters of sexual disorientation and Jewry? It may be suggested that his certificate of Aryan birth was an effort to put all that definitively behind him. The paradox, of course, lay in the fact that in so doing, he was putting the greatest of his poetic achievements behind him as well.

Unless, of course, one decides that the result of Apollinaire's effort (and document) is that one does not have to be Jewish to experience Jewish self-hatred. Part of the grisly humor of Weininger's Platonic sense of the Jew is precisely that: "When I speak of the Jew I mean neither an individual nor the whole body, but mankind in general, in so far as it has a share in the Platonic idea of Judaism" (Weininger 1906, 306). Apollinaire apparently was the first Frenchman to mention the work of Freud in a literary journal (Roudinesco 1990, 76). Perhaps this non-Jew deserves as well the dubious honor of having been the first to inject a dose of "Jewish self-hatred" into the higher reaches of French literature. Mystification, after all, as Marcel Raymond observed, was Apollinaire's constant temptation (Raymond 1969, 229).

✦ Apollinaire died in Paris just prior to the signing of the armistice ending World War I. His most spectacular legacy, of course, beyond his own poetry, was that passion for literary experimentation that he was no doubt the first to call "Surrealism" (Raymond 1969, 229). But there were others who were poets *in Apollinaire*. Here, for instance, is a fragment of a text about a railroad center, first published in 1970:

> Il y ceux qui viennent de Varsovie avec de grands châles et des baluchons noués
>
> Il y a ceux qui viennent de Zagreb les femmes avec des mouchoirs sur la tête
>
> il y a ceux qui viennent du Danube avec des tricots faits à la veillée dans des laines multicolores
>
> il y a ceux qui viennent de Monte-Carlo
>
> ils étaient au casino
>
> ils sont en frac avec un plastron que le voyage a tout cassé
>
> ils ont des ventres et ils sont chauves
>
> ce sont de gros banquiers qui jouaient à la banque

> There are those who come from Warsaw with large shawls and knotted bundles / there are those who come from Zagreb the women with kerchiefs on their heads / there are those who come from the Danube with their nighttime knitting in multicolored wool / there are those who come from Monte Carlo / they're in dresscoats with their shirt fronts broken by the trip / they are overweight and bald / these are the big bankers playing at banking. . . .
> (Delbo 1970, 1:13)

The litany, the randomness, the cosmopolitanism, the lack of punctuation, the reference to Monte Carlo, the primitivist pleasure in repeating words (*banquiers . . . banque*), the futurist interest in railroad travel and the arbitrary assemblages it can effect—all seem to be inspired directly by Apollinaire's great poem "Zone." The railroad center, however, was not Apollinaire's Gare Saint-Lazare (1912), but Auschwitz, where the poem's author, Charlotte Delbo, was imprisoned during World War II. It is as though the century to which Apollinaire was intent on opening French poetry when he seized on the Weiningerian synthesis in "La Chanson du mal-aimé," comes to a certain end (or destination) in Delbo's moving trilogy, *Auschwitz et après*.

Did Delbo realize as much? *De profundis* she meditates on just how ravaged her experience in the camp has left her: "Why was I left only memory? And my memory comes up with only clichés. Mon beau navire, o ma mémoire' . . . Where are you, my real memory, my earthly memory?" All she can remember, that is, is a line about memory from "La Chanson du mal-aimé":

> Mon beau navire o ma mémoire
> Avons-nous assez navigué
> Dans une onde mauvaise à boire (Delbo 1970, 47)

My handsome ship o my memory / Have we steered enough / In waters bad to
drink? . . .

The allusion to our unhappy kings (Pharaoh, Ludwig) drowning in waters
"bad to drink," losing the battle that Weininger too lost, is but a line away.
For which reason, we can do no better than conclude with verse out of
Auschwitz, penned by Delbo to a friend, from the second volume of her
trilogy, *Une Connaissance inutile:*

> Nous étions ivres d'Apollinaire
> et de Claudel
> vous souvient-il?
>
> C'est le début d'un poème
> dont je voulais me souvenir
> pour vous le dire.
>
> J'ai oublié tous les mots
> ma mémoire s'est égarée
> dans les délabres des jours passés
> ma mémoire s'en est allée
> et nos ivresses anciennes
> Apollinaire et Claudel
> meurent ici avec nous (Delbo 1970, 2:34).

We were drunk with Apollinaire and Claudel, do you remember? It's the
beginning of a poem I wanted to remember to tell you. I've forgotten all the
words; my memory has gotten lost in the ruins of days past; my memory has
strayed off and our old intoxications, Apollinaire and Claudel, die here with
us.

13 ✦

KAFKA AND WEININGER

Gerald Stieg

Translated from the German
by Barbara Hyams

Nowadays decency would seem to forbid mentioning the names Kafka and Weininger in one breath, but historical truth forces one to commit such a sacrilege. In certain respects, the differences between the two are vast: Franz Kafka "had the ability to transform himself into the most insignificant man,"[1] and for that reason was "the greatest expert on power,"[2] whereas Otto Weininger's texts provide a philosophical directive whose swaggering surpasses Zarathustra in content if not in tone. Kafka was haunted by suicidal thoughts his whole life and wanted to take his life's work with him to the grave, even though it is what kept him alive, whereas Weininger masterfully orchestrated his posthumous fame—so that his book *Sex and Character* could live, he shot himself in a "consecrated place," the house in which Beethoven had died. He did not delude himself: Indeed, his book became the philosophical best seller of the first third of the century, and if many of his ideas had not taken on terrible political gestalt in 1933, it would most certainly have had many more printings and popular editions (!) (Le Rider 1985).

Yet Kafka did not delude himself either. On January 28, 1922, shortly before he began writing *The Castle*, he made the following note to himself about his position in the world: he describes himself as having "been forty years wandering from Canaan" in the desert, where he was the "most insignificant and timid of all creatures," as he had been in the patriarchal-bourgeois Canaan. Thus he sees himself in every context as the "most insignificant," but he also knows that in contrast to Canaan, in the *desert* "it is possible even for the humblest to be raised to the heights as if with lightning speed." (He would not be himself if he did not also immediately append, "though they can be crushed forever as if by the weight of the seas" (Kafka 1949, 213–14; 1954, 564f.).

Both Kafka and Weininger underwent "a kind of Wandering in the Wilderness in reverse": instead of seeking the land, or even remaining in the land "where milk and honey flows," they used desert monks as their models. Consequently, each of them has something of the stylite about him. In this endeavor they are by no means alone. The Benedictine-Occidental *ora et labora* is shattered: intent upon remaining in Kafka's and Weininger's purview, Ludwig Wittgenstein (the most monk-like of all), Karl Kraus, Trakl, and Rilke bear witness to it. For all of them, writing is their "form of prayer," for them, prayer and work are one.

This monkish sacralization of writing is a constituitive trait of Viennese modernism that is *truly* deserving of the name. The process has something heart-wrenching about it: appearing long before *Dialectic of Enlightenment*, which used World War II as illustrative material, it was nothing more and nothing less than a lament over the bankruptcy of the Enlightenment. The apparently unstoppable and irrevocable secularization process of the eighteenth century that Sigmund Freud still wishes to validate in *The Future of an Illusion* in 1927 has culminated in a powerful movement of *resacralization*.

The "sacrifices for the dead" that Weininger and Kafka concocted for themselves and their work are probably the most astonishing attestations to this process. By comparison the diverse aesthetic cults that arose in the aftermath of George seem simply ridiculous, although from a purely historical perspective, something comparable is being played out. (Moreover, Kafka, like Karl Kraus, was thoroughly receptive to the gospel of the "stern master" George [Kafka 1958b, 301 (September 1921)].

So the poets formed a gallery of "stylites." Weininger and Kafka (in a very particular sense, one can look at Karl Kraus as the connecting link between them) are exemplary *monks*. They share a radicalness of experience in the world that is dictated to them by *angst:* they are afraid of the *others*. Their *others* are first of all women. On a more abstract plane, the *others* are the intermediaries who disturb the *praying man* in his solitude. Weininger believed that in his urge toward monkhood he had compre- and appre-hended once and for all the identity of these interlopers: the women *and* the Jews. His thinking becomes murderous: the salvation of the world depends on "overcoming" *the* woman and *the* Jew. It results—one can formulate this without applying rhetorical brakes—in a demand for the suicide of all mankind, in which both fascistic Papini and friendly Cioran followed his lead (cf. Le Rider 1985; Le Rider and Leser 1984). In the face of such grand projects, one must look at Kafka's assessment of his private situation, written on January 31, 1922: "Hence it is a defensive instinct in me that won't tolerate my having the slightest degree of lasting ease and smashes the marriage bed, for example, even before it has been set up" (Jan. 31, 1922) (Kafka 1949, 217).[3]

In such sentences Kafka appears as a Weininger in private, as a private monk in a negative theological undertaking that proposes to "treat" Weininger's philosophical claim on a "world scale." This total disavowal and condemnation of the "pleasure principle" becomes a violent drive in

Weininger's case to compress the manifold, i.e., anti-monkishness (the monk is the "monachos" who easily confuses "alone" with "singular") into a higher unity. Kafka's urge to "smash the marriage bed" is terrible but harmless, because he is only thinking of this for himself, as opposed to Weininger's demand to "do away with" women and Jews in the name of the (holy) *spirit.*

The biographical material indicates that the Jews Kafka and Weininger suffered equally from their Jewishness and their sexuality. The "monkish" aspirations of both only take on their full import when one confronts them with their "temptations."

In 1923 Karl Kraus, who had been Weininger's highly conscious advocate against defamation by the liberal bourgeois Viennese press and as such had influenced Kafka, published the following poem by the nineteen- (or twenty-one)-year-old Weininger:

Filled with longing and carefully hidden,
Stealing my way through the darkest night,
I laugh at all that your law has bidden,
Burning, voluptuous, yet full of fright.

This is the road I have often wandered
To her, the Goddess who knows no shame,
The road desire bade me to follow,
And I was weeping when home I came.

May darkness reign on the road I follow;
May God turn day into darkest night,
Make the windows and mirrors empty, hollow,
Leave not a shimmer, no trace of light.

And, scornful still, the ancient terror
Steals darkly ahead of the dear delight.
Oh, redden the cheeks of Sinful Error
That I may serve him, free of fright (Abrahamsen 1946, 84).[4]

The third stanza is a great *poem of prayer.* It corresponds to the following in Kafka's diary and letters:

Coitus as punishment for the happiness of being together. Live as ascetically as possible, more ascetically than a bachelor, that is the only possible way for me to endure marriage. But she? (Kafka 1948, 296 [August 14, 1913]).[5]

And as it was then, so it has always remained. My body, sometimes quiet for years, would then again be shaken to the point of not being able to bear it by this desire for a small, a very specific abomination, for something slightly disgusting, embarrassing, obscene, even in the best that existed for me there was something of it, some small nasty smell, some sulphur, some hell. This urge had in it something of the eternal Jew, being senselessly drawn, wandering senselessly through a senselessly obscene world (Kafka 1953, 164 [letter to Milena concerning the "first night," August 9, 1920]).[6]

It is beyond question that such texts are treating something besides the private sphere and that the epoch itself is being heard. The fact that the "sexuality-Judaism" syndrome could be concentrated in such a private form may help us of the present generation to understand what an overwhelming influence Weininger had on his own. The uncanny part is that in such writings the most dreadful aspects of the political propaganda of National Socialism seem to present themselves in the most private sphere, internalized to the point of self-torture. It is not a Jewish "family matter" that is at stake but rather a kind of historical humus. Consider that Weininger's thinking exercised the strongest of influences upon Lanz von Liebenfels's periodical "for blonds and masculinists," *Ostara*, which started in Vienna in 1905. Weininger was the most ardent—but by no means the only—disavower of two emancipation movements: those for *Jews* and *women*. He could tolerate them in one single form: as emancipation *from* Judaism and *from* femaleness.

From a critical point of view, what I have said up to this point belongs in the broad realm of analogies and associations that are convincing in themselves, but do not necessarily carry the strength of *proof*.

A weighty argument contradicts my enterprise: in Kafka studies, whose gigantic proportions are legendary, Weininger plays a completely subordinate role. There are standard works (Brod 1937; Emrich 1958; Sokel 1964; Wagenbach 1964) in which he is purely and simply ignored; Binder (1966) takes him more seriously, but is too caught up in his biographical puzzles. He is only taken truly seriously by Politzer (1965), who personally experienced Weininger's milieu. Yet strangely enough, Politzer confines his analysis to the figure of Leni in *The Trial*. Politzer was Max Brod's collaborator, and therefore Brod's strategy to stifle the name of Weininger thoroughly must be taken as an act of repression.[7]

My thesis, then, is that Weininger's possible "influence on Kafka," or the "parallel" between Weininger and Kafka, fully unfolds for the first time in *The Castle*, which is a novel about Judaism *and* sexuality. In this essay I do not intend to discuss both aspects in their reciprocal relationship to one another, but rather to put the accent on the pole of sexuality. Since it is well known that the dear Lord lurks in the details, I will begin with a textual explication of *The Castle* in which both poles appear to be nearly inseparable.

After his first futile attempt to enter the Castle under his *own* steam, the Land-Surveyor K. is drawn into the magnetic field (one may certainly speak in terms of "elective affinities") of Barnabas's family. People suggest to him that this is where he belongs. But he does not believe it, does not *want* to believe it, and prefers to go to the Herrenhof Inn. He goes there on the arm of the Jewish whore, Olga, in the belief that he is heading toward a *higher* goal. (In his plot scheme, Kafka made a very telling "Freudian slip": at first he wrote *Castle* instead of *Herrenhof* [Kafka 1982, 82].) Although she arrived on K.'s arm, the whore is left to her usual fate: Klamm's servants will relish her in the stables. There is a lot to be said about Olga's story that actually has less to do with sexuality than would at first seem to be the case. (She is the little coin with which the Barnabas family tries to buy its freedom. The fact that this "coin" correlates to the equation of Jew with woman turns Olga into a Weiningerian paradigm.) Yet Olga has a sister, Amalia, the paragon and incarnation of nunlike chastity. Amalia is the embodiment of the Weiningerian ideal of pure self-abnegation and emancipation *from* sexuality. K.—the monk—is her utopian bridegroom. (One also could say that: Amalia represents emancipation *from* Judaism, insofar as it refers to those particular clichés that were considered "typically" Jewish.)

Aside from a letter of April 1921 that contains a comment that presupposes Kafka's acquaintance with Weininger's work but provides no substantive leads (Kafka 1958b, 276), our attempt to connect the two is confined to weaving a tapestry of *associations and analogies* so tightly that the speculative character of our hypothesis can claim great probability. This process has to do with a kind of "securing of clues" that has already been achieved with respect to the same topic as it relates to Elias Canetti's *Auto-da-Fé* (Pöder 1985, 57ff.). Therefore, I am excluding from my analysis the wide-meshed concluding chapters of *Sex and Character* from which the book's fatal posthumous fame stems. Since these two chapters— "Judaism," Chapter XIII; "Woman and Mankind," Chapter XIV—can be taken as the spiritual common property of the era, the fact that *The Castle* is also infected by them requires no extensive proof. What I am endeavoring to do is to tighten the net of analogies to a measurable degree of possibility by limiting the field of observation and comparison to Weininger's posthumously published work *Über die letzten Dinge* (On Last Things),[8] and the subplot of "Frieda" in Kafka's *The Castle*.

Weininger's *Über die letzten Dinge* first appeared in 1904 and was reprinted in 1907, 1912, 1918, 1919, 1920 and 1980. It is noteworthy that *Geschlecht und Charakter* not only went through an astonishing numbering of printings, but that in the years immediately following World War I, the rate of new printings for both works is almost the same. (*Geschlecht und Charakter* appeared in 1918, 1919, 1920 in two printings, and 1921.) Kafka's sole reference to Weininger is apparently the result of this "boom." Nevertheless, it would be incorrect to limit ourselves to this period. Naturally, Kafka was familiar with Weininger's thought by way of the "Fackel," and I'd also like to refer at this point to another source of Kafka's Weininger reception:

Max Brod and Kafka met in Riva with Carl Dallago, who was prominently involved in the intensive Weininger debate that commenced in the journal "Der Brenner" in 1912.[9]

These brief references to Weininger reception have been made to demonstrate

- that there was extremely intensive interest in his work immediately following the publication of Kraus's *The Last Days of Mankind;*
- that this phenomenon was also true for Weininger's *Über die letzten Dinge.* This posthumous work is distinctive because here Weininger has completely forsaken the dissertation genre of *Sex and Character* in favor of more *literary and radicalized* forms of thought.

His more literary approach is shown in Weininger's more and more frequent use of the *aphorism* to express his thoughts. His radicalization manifests itself everywhere, but especially in two areas: (1) intensified interest in the Wagner cult, as seen through his use of Wagner's *Parsifal* in his discussions; (2) heightened involvement of the morality cult in his series of aphorisms "On the One-Directionality of Time and Its Ethical Significance." The common thread is Weininger's masculine ideal of the restless Faustian seeker.

The Castle can be read as a variation on the Faust or Parsifal myth. Mythical substrates are present everywhere in Kafka's novel in an extended state of decay (e.g., in the beer-drinking god Klamm and Bürgel, who embodies the Greek god Chios). If *The Castle* is read in this way—that is, as a novelistic fable about "seeking" and "pathfinding,"—then the story of Frieda takes on a meaning that far exceeds the biographical coffeehouse framework of the "Herrenhof" and refers to a philosophical-cultural context in which Weininger is its figurehead.

These claims are intended to be made plausible on the strength of the following three examples:

- Weininger's interpretation of sexuality in *Parsifal*
- Weininger's thoughts about the one-directionality of time
- Weininger's comments on the "spatialization" of consciousness.

1. WEININGER'S INTERPRETATION OF *PARSIFAL*

Weininger's interpretation of Wagner's *Parsifal* seems significant from the outset because this work belongs to the tradition of great myths about seeking and pathfinding to which *The Castle* belongs. As such, one parallel comes immediately to our attention: Parsifal is portrayed as the "pure fool," and K. is treated again and again as a *child* or a *simpleton* by the *experienced* characters in the novel. Parsifal's search for the Grail and K.'s search for the Castle are also easy comparisons. During his search for the Grail, Parsifal meets an obstacle, the seductive woman Kundry.

Weininger's commentaries go as follows: "Man's morality understands sexual intercourse as sin";[10] "Woman is no longer meaningful when man is chaste";[11] "Kundry *in* Parsifal (it's *yearning* that prevents him from reaching the Grail, i.e., the moral, the divine). . .";[12] "To be sure, Kundry would have to die already in Act II, since Parsifal resists her."[13]

Thus, Weininger sees Kundry—the W(oman) principle itself—as present in the heroic M(an); however, this principle is constructed by Weininger to be *surmountable*.

Weininger's condemnation of Goethe's *Faust*, which he rates far below *Parsifal* because it concludes with "Woman, eternally,/shows us the way" (Goethe 1984, 305),[14] must be seen in this context as well. For him—and Kafka stands very close to him in this respect—the opposite is true: the feminine pulls man down into the *obscenity* that was discussed above. The union between K. and Frieda is consummated in garbage.

Weininger expresses the same idea on a less metaphysical plane when he writes: " 'Gander, find your goose' means *get married*, but then don't set the Kingdom of God as your goal."[15] It is a monk's turn of phrase that played an underground role in Kafka's attempts to marry. There is, however, a qualitative difference between Kafka and Weininger, since Kafka held marriage (at least theoretically) quite high in the hierarchy of *ethical goods*, while Weininger appears to address it as a primitive nod to convention, indeed, as a bestial stage in the development of humanity. Yet, in Kafka's life as well as *The Castle*, marriage, or more precisely the matrimonial strategies themselves prove to be an obstacle on the path to the Castle, a *losing one's way and a wrong track* that leads away from the goal that, for Kafka, is often identical with the "sacralization" of writing.

It is only hesitantly that I dare include in this context one of Weininger's most bizarre utterances, which seems to be echoed in *The Castle:* "Kundry's laughter crosses over into Judaism. The metaphysical sin of the Jew is to smile over God."[16] Thus for Weininger, Kundry embodies the negative twice over: as woman *and* Jewess. Now the story of Frieda is set from its very beginning under the law of *laughter and smiling*. It begins with the laughter of the Jewess Olga (a paradigmatic Kundry figure) over K.'s question about Frieda's relationship to Klamm. (At this moment, Klamm is still Frieda's [false] god). The subject of God and Eros is handled most ironically of all in the episode with *Klamm's brandy*. The drink, which purports to be a heavenly essence, transforms itself through actual enjoyment into something "fit for a coachman" (*kutschermäßiges*), that is, into something that everyone possesses, regardless of the higher expectations that they have attached to it. This scene clearly shows the proximity of Freud, the greatest ironist that God and religion have encountered in the twentieth century. In *The Castle*, the Jewish sin of "smiling over God" is omnipresent as the Freudian "Ecclesia supra cloacam."

Weininger's "unethical" woman appears in two forms that emerge in *The Castle:* (1) the *human* (i.e., the whore), and (2) the *bestial* (i.e., the mother). The significance of prostitute and mother figures (among them, the enigmatic Madonna-like girl from the Castle) is clear, as well as is the meaning of the unusual role of the "female monk" (*Mönchin*) Amalia. (I am consciously employing Trakl's androgynous term, for there is relatively great certainty about his relationship to Weininger. See Doppler 1971, 43–54). She is the true anti-Kundry. K.'s path is ambivalent in contrast to that of his heroic bride, Amalia. K. will come closer to the ascetic ideal: Frieda leaves him, and he himself throws the assistants out of the temple.[17]

2. ON THE ONE-DIRECTIONALITY OF TIME AND ITS ETHICAL SIGNIFICANCE

Weininger's discussion of *Parsifal* is complemented by his complex of considerations on the problem of the human experience of time, which is integrated in his series of aphorisms collected under the title "On the One-Directionality of Time and Its Ethical Significance."[18]

Weininger's thinking on this question can be summarized as follows: TIME passes in one direction (*Einsinnigkeit*),[19] that is, it flows toward a GOAL. The *ethical* person is duty-bound to obey this law of time and therefore to be constantly SEEKING. (The Faust and Parsifal themes are closely tied to the theme of time.) The greatest temptation that threatens mankind (man?), according to Weininger, is belief in the CIRCULARITY OF LIFE, the eternal repetition. For Weininger, sexuality belongs exclusively to the drive toward repetition, which assumes eternal sameness. The ethical man-person breaks out of this circle in order to have a goal toward which he can strive.

A few of Weininger's considerations on this issue can be employed directly for an interpretation of *The Castle*, especially the Frieda theme. In order to do this, a bit of textual interpretation is necessary.

Weininger hates circular motion, even in the galaxy. Circular motion and retrograde motion are ethically unbearable for him. He looks for "vulgar" analogies to planetary circular motion and finds the following example: "Spinning around in a circle is senseless, purposeless; someone who spins around on his tiptoes has a self-satisfied, ridiculously vain, commonplace nature."[20] In *The Castle* there is an extreme example of this in the miserable smugness of Momus (i.e., the *sense*less scoffer), the tip of whose tongue runs in a circle round "his slightly parted lips" in the chapter, "Waiting for Klamm" (Kafka 1974, 134; 1968, 90). With this allegorical mouth gesture, Momus's "return" is converted by Kafka into his *own* regressive "reason" (*Vernunft*), which has not allowed itself to be thrown off track by K.'s "foolishness." The apparently "enlightening" impulse of this antagonism toward the "disturber of the peace" is completely devaluated by the gesture and reduced to what it really is: an expression of the self-complacency of the completely hermetic, controlled course of events that sees itself as impervious to every interruption of the circle. K., however, interrupts the *circles*.

In Weininger's case, such reflexion on time culminates almost compulsively in the following type of observation: "Dance is female motion, and indeed, it is above all the motion of prostitution."[21] In contrast to this "female" motion, which becomes a gestalt through the roundelay ring of peasants around Olga, Weininger posits the "male" attitude toward time, which is that of the WANDERER, he who travels toward his goal, driven by unexplicit yearning for a higher ethical good (e.g., Gralsburg).

In opposition to the "senseless" and directionless circling of sexuality, Weininger juxtaposes the never-abating strivings of human will:

> The *one-directionality of time* is thus identical to the fact that the human being is a deeply willing being. *The ego as will is time.*
>
> The realized ego would be God: the ego on the *path* to self-realization is will.
>
> Will is something between non-being and being; its *path* goes from non-being to being (for all will is the will to freedom, to value, to the absolute, to being, to idea, to God).[22]

It goes without saying that sexuality is assigned to Platonic non-being. As abstract as this approach may sound, it could be K.'s approach during his search for access to the Castle. In the same context, Weininger says something about time that applies to Kafka's *Castle* not only thematically but also aesthetically:

> "Life is a kind of journey through the realm of the innermost ego, a journey, to be sure, from the narrowest interior regions to the most comprehensive, freest overview of the universe."[23]

This *spatialization* of consciousness and those forms of it that are manifested through time are *the* essential artistic method that Kafka uses in *The Castle*.

By comparing the previously mentioned aspects of Weininger's thinking about time and sexuality, we obtain an important key to *The Castle*. To document this convincingly, we must take a very precise look at the "love scene" at the Herrenhof.

3. "... FRIEDA HAD TURNED OUT THE ELECTRIC LIGHT"

A kind of interrogation and hide-and-seek precedes the famous passage from *The Castle*, "Frieda had turned out the electric light" (Kafka

1974, 53),[24] in which Kafka gave up on first-person in favor of third-person narrative. The landlord would like to oust the *stranger* from the inn; Frieda plays along in order keep the *stranger* there, no matter what the cost. The controlling authority, who is uncertain about K.'s presence and apparently fears it, has scarcely left the room when the *light* goes out.

Frieda consummates a conscious exchange: Klamm's passive mistress becomes a lover, K. her beloved. She exchanges the position, respect, and protection that Klamm had provided for free love with K. She yields fully to this love, this "rapture," this unconscious and timeless swooning ("time must have seemed endless to her in the prospect of her happiness" [Kafka 1974, 53]);[25] she is thus freed from the one-directionality of time and therefore is nothing more than a vessel for the blissful moment. She is also *speechless:* "she sighed rather than sang some little song or other."[26]

The antigrammatical zeugma of singing and sighing corresponds perfectly to Frieda's deteriorating consciousness. K. doesn't immediately follow Frieda in her path to unconsciousness: he remains "absorbed in thought," that is, conscious. Frieda starts up at this, for indeed K.'s manner is at absolute odds with her condition. She "began to tug at him like a child,"[27] which once again offers a grammatical interference: who is the object, who the subject, i.e., who is the child? (The zeugma is never innocent.) That which follows eradicates the difference, for K. and Frieda become a couple ("embraced each other").[28] This course of events is portrayed as K.'s transition to a reflective position in a rolling (circular) motion, which is perceived as a "state of unconsciousness" and ends with K.'s Grail-like search for the Castle being degraded to a "thud" on the forbidden door. In the act of love K. loses consciousness—consciousness of the path that he wants to pursue. Instead of the proper path, there is a sense- and goal-less circular motion. This circular motion is not merely senseless but obscene; it is consummated in puddles of beer and refuse.

Weininger's and Kafka's assessments of coitus are absolutely identical. Another passage in *The Castle*, the episode about Klamm's *brandy*, may serve to corroborate this finding:

> "the perfume was so sweet, so caressing, like praise and good words from someone whom one likes very much, yet one does not know clearly what they are for and has no desire to know and is simply happy in the knowledge that it is one's friend who is saying them" (Kafka 1974, 132).[29]

This is where Kafka *defines* the essence of love as the negation of knowledge. If the promises of the perfume become reality, then the drink "burns" (just as Frieda's body *burned*), and the "heavenly" (*himmlische*) drink becomes something "fit for a coachman" (*kutschermäßigen*).

In this passage, there is not only an exemplary presentation of a *disappointment* following "delusion" (*Blendung*), but the context sheds a telling light on the Frieda chapter and gives Pepi's brandy—she has "no other" (!) than bestial sexuality—its true significance.

K.'s encounter with Frieda (it is carried out through glances, whereas when Pepi seduces K., he closes his eyes!) is clearly marked off from the animalistic sexuality of the locale (where the bestial roundelay, into which Frieda is nearly drawn, takes place). Here the scene is set for something apparently quite different, namely, individual love. Yet in Kafka's use of images the act of love itself is hardly differentiated from what happens in the stables. "Obscenity," "puddles of beer," "stables," and "drink fit for a coachman," supplement one another to draw a (Swine)ingerian picture of sexuality.

K. spends quite distinctive time *there*, i.e., at the obscene site. Kafka invented brilliant sentences to describe it. (Something comparable can only be found in the starkly contrasting vision of isolation at the end of the chapter, "Waiting for Klamm").

> There hours went past, hours in which they breathed as one, in which their hearts beat as one, hours in which K. was haunted by the feeling that he was losing himself or wandering into a strange country, farther than ever man had wandered before, a country so strange that not even the air had anything in common with his native air, where one might die of strangeness, and yet whose enchantment was such that one could only go on and lose oneself further (Kafka 1974, 54).[30]

In this sentence, the most violent oppositions are teamed: "breathed as one, in which their hearts beat as one," are expressions of the greatest familiarity, of a complete sense of being at home. Yet in the same sentence homeland transforms itself into the most foreign, most suffocating Other. Intimacy becomes the farthest outpost, love that promises hearth and home becomes the most senseless, pathless enticement. I do not hesitate to draw upon etymology: sexuality is *sense*-less, and therefore *path*-less and *goal*-less, perversion, as Kafka formulated it in his description of intercourse: "it had in it something of the eternal Jew, being senselessly drawn, wandering senselessly through a senselessly obscene world."[31]

Love, or at least consummated sexual union, proves to be the wrong path. "Strangeness" and "losing himself" are the key words of the sentence. If one considers that the entire novel is a tremendous variation on the *path* theme, this judgment takes on enormous significance. The fusion of extreme hope and extreme hopelessness—losing one's way approaches *insanity* (*Irrsinn*)—in a sentence about love makes it the sum and substance of *The Castle*. In the face of such sum and substance, in which an extremely reactive consciousness creates language, that which follows may seem almost trivial.

From the *rapture of love* there is a gradual return to the everyday consciousness from which K. and Frieda had cut all ties. Frieda admits to this (senseless?) break; she exchanges Klamm for the Land Surveyor. K., on the other hand, sees Frieda's body by the dawning light as a now worthless pawn in his possession. The first glimmer of morning makes it obvious to K. that he had lost his way in the night. He believes that he has lost something; Frieda thinks that she has won him. In the present context, one can also note that

- The assistants who were sent by Galater were also on hand during the act of love.
- Olga returns from the stables, she says to K., "Why did you not *come home* with me?"[32] It is a terrible sentence, for it connotes 1) that K. sent Olga into the stables, and 2) that instead of "going home," K. cast himself through his night of love with Frieda into nothing but *strange country*, while the path back to Olga's house offered him a *homeland*.
- In the morning K. does not proceed with Frieda's bundle on his search for the Castle, but takes it instead to the originating point of the journey, the "Bridge Inn," Frieda's "womb," the foremother Gardena. The *bed* will be the predominant object in his place of residence.
- In this bed, the instrument of mothers and whores, the lost Parsifalistic and Faustian seeker K. *wastes* the entire day sleeping.

The Castle is a novel about the path to the holy. The path quickly proves itself to be a labyrinth. Sexuality is consciously used by Kafka as one of the labyrinthian paths. In the process, Kafka makes an almost transparent reference to Weininger and Wagner, or Weininger's interpretation of Wagner's *Parsifal* and *Tristan*. K.'s and Frieda's "night of love" is an obvious parody of *Tristan*. In the construction of the novel, the detour/path through Eros seems like a wrong way à la Weininger, indeed even more than that, like a *regression*. For the lost way of the night that led to false quarters ends with a return to the point of origin, to the great mother in the Bridge Inn who will give her all to throw obstacles in K.'s *path* (progress?). He has her to thank for a day lost to sleeping. Woman robbed him of sleep in the night, woman robs him of the day.

We cannot rule out the possibility that the analogies presented here rest only on coincidence. Even if that were the case, coincidence would provide a not-so-insignificant key to one of the innumerable doors of the Castle. Why shouldn't coincidence for once bear the name of Weininger instead of Bürgel?

14 ✦

WEININGER AND THE BLOOM OF JEWISH SELF-HATRED IN JOYCE'S *ULYSSES*

Marilyn Reizbaum

James Joyce's connection with Judaism has been a source for some discussion since he made Leopold Bloom the "hero" of *Ulysses* (1922). The novel has received either praise or blame, and has been interpreted variously on the basis of conclusions drawn in this matter. Among those who have seen Joyce's representation of the Jew as antipathetic is Maurice Samuel, noted Jewish author and translator; in an article of 1929, citing passages from the "Circe" chapter, he asserts that Joyce treated Bloom in a loathsome and malevolent manner, and that he seemed to exhibit a "cosmic loathing for the little Jew, Bloom" (Samuel 1929, 14).[1] The notion that Joyce harbored hatred for the Jew and an extension from that to a consideration of Joyce as anti-Semite is voiced quite tellingly by Robert M. Adams: "Sentimentalists who simplify Bloom the Jew into a pathetic and admirable little man who forgives his enemies and so is apotheosized into the perfect Christian hero would do well to face the sizeable element of anti-Semitism in Joyce himself. This element is not distinct from powerful feelings of self-loathing" (Adams 1972, 104n.).

What is striking about both Samuels's and Adams's assessments of what are inherent and complex ambiguities in the presentation of Bloom are their assumptions about Joyce's own affinities in this regard. If we use the text of *Ulysses* to document Joyce's connection with Judaism, then we are faced with might seem to be irresolvable ambiguities; or we might be able to interpret them as artistically significant—Bloom as Jew or non-Jew or non-identifying Jew, Bloom as loathsome or heroic. A more profitable way of approaching these ambiguities and their significance is by examining a source that Richard Ellmann mentions in his biography of Joyce. Ellmann claims that this source—Otto Weininger's *Geschlecht und Charakter* (1903)—contains theories that Joyce generally believed, especially as they pertain to women (Ellmann 1982, 477). Ellmann does not make clear how well Joyce knew the book, and he does not discuss in any depth the relevance of Weininger's theories to Joyce's concepts of Jews. In fact, one cannot be certain from Ellmann's documentation that Joyce even read the book.[2] Nevertheless, the literature (by which I mean the intellectual documents exchange of the period) attests to the popularity of Weininger's ideas about Jews and women, as does the frequency with which the book was reprinted.[3] Assuming that Joyce used this source, I believe that it can be of at least heuristic value to examine Weininger's theories and how they might inform Joyce's work. For whether Joyce used Weininger, he plainly used the themes, and his development of them reveals an apprehension that adapts and departs from Weininger's own theories.

In his book Weininger expounds upon what he sees as the inferiority of women and the inhumanity of Jews. A kind of metaphorical link is set up between the two, and it is this link which Joyce gathered up to use in *Ulysses*. Weininger based his theory about the inferiority of women on what he saw as a fundamental relationship between sex and character. He saw every human being as a combination of both sexes, in which the male is the positive, productive, logical, conceptual side capable of genius, and the female is the negative side, incapable of any of these virtues. Woman has only two functions, according to Weininger—prostitution or procreation. The ideal woman accepts her role as being dependent on the phallus, and her only emancipation is achieved in the ending of coitus.

Since the Jew, according to Weininger's dubious yet historically informed anthropological observations, is "weiblich" (womanish or feminine), he theorizes that the Jew too is the negative side of every human being.[4] In the rest of his proof, Weininger rehearses the litany of discriminatory commonplaces about Jews: the Jews have no redeeming qualities; they believe in nothing and therefore are useless. Because they are undirected, they gravitate toward all destructive institutions and beliefs—communism, anarchism, materialism, and atheism. What is peculiar to Weininger's theories is the notion that Jewishness is a state of mind or being, a psychological constitution, rather than a religious or cultural attribute:

> I do not refer to a nation or to a race, to a creed or to a scripture. When I speak of the Jew I mean neither the individual nor the body, but mankind in general, in so far as it has a share in the platonic idea of Judaism. My purpose is to analyze this idea.
>
> That these researches should be included in a work devoted to the characterology of the sexes may seem an undue extension of my subject. But some reflections will lead to the surprising result that Judaism is saturated with femininity, with precisely those qualities the essence of which I have shown to be in the strongest opposition to the male nature. It would not be difficult to make a case for the view that the Jew is more saturated with femininity than the Aryan, to such an extent that the most manly Jew is more feminine than the least manly Aryan (Weininger 1906, 306).

The kinds of connections between race and sex that Weininger makes appear most prevalently and climactically in the "Circe" chapter of *Ulysses*, which in a way enacts the realm of the psyche. Bloom appears there in a series of stereotypes, some of which are directly associated with his Jewishness—as womanish, degraded—externalizations of a self-regard he exhibits throughout the novel. Rather than reproducing or representing Weininger's theories literally, however, the chapter dramatizes the psycho-dynamic of self-hatred, linked here with gender and race. The Jew, in this case, Bloom, internalizes the plight of being an outcast and accepts the sense of the self that others have determined and foisted upon him.[5]

If Joyce knew Weininger's book, he might also have known that Weininger was a Jew who converted to Christianity and then committed suicide at the age of twenty-three, in the very year the book was published. He might have seen Weininger as a man who, when confronted with his origins, theorized a way out that seemed to reinforce those origins and his dread of them. To Joyce, Weininger's philosophies may have appeared to be an expression of his subconscious. In fact, the study of Weininger's work has almost invariably entailed biographical investigation, seemingly mandated by the circumstances of his life and death. Since Theodor Lessing's ground-breaking work, *Der jüdischer Selbsthaβ* (1930), Weininger has become the exemplar of the condition of Jewish self-hatred. His notions represent, by the example of his life as well as by history, a prevalent dynamic within a psychoanalytic framework that can be used, as the "Circe" chapter exhibits, both rhetorically and characterologically.

In the section of "Circe" where Bloom embarks upon his series of transformations, Dr. Dixon is reading Bloom's "bill of health:" "Professor Bloom is a finished example of the new womanly man. His moral nature is simple and lovable. Many have found him a dear man, a dear person. He is rather a quaint fellow on the whole, coy though not feeble-minded in the medical sense" (Joyce, 1986, 1798–1801). Bloom is *weiblich*, but it is impor-tant to note that he is a *"new* womanly man." (It is equally important to note the double entendre in the word "finished." Just as Stephen is, according to his self-description later in the episode, a "most finished artist," at once polished and impotent, so Bloom here is exemplary of qualities that make him a "dear man" while he too is impotent. This may also be a clue to his rehabilitation within the context of the chapter; he is "finished" with the "old" womanly man and ushering in the new.) Joyce seems to rewrite the Weiningerian model that reproduces the historical figuration of racial or cultural inferiority in stereotypes of the feminine (just before Dixon, "Dr." Punch Costello has identified Bloom as Jewish by his smell—"*fetor judaicus*" while using B's urine to discover he's pregnant) not so much by using parody, but by decoding this series of condemnatory pronouncements upon Bloom.

One way that this decoding is achieved is through the use of the fantastic. This womanly man is about to give birth, an act of regeneration that Joyce's texts regularly celebrate and interrogate as the biological analogue of artistic immortality; it is an act so devoutly to be wished that it is embodied within the church's doctrine of the Trinity, allowing for the fathering of the wor(l)d and emptying the mother of the (pro)creative function. Thus another way to read Bloom's feminization or capacity for childbirth is as a symbolic enactment of this kind of appropriation, keeping in place the logical and conceptual side that a complete feminization would preclude in Weiningerian terms. But this description of Bloom as "coy though not feeble-minded in the medical sense" suggests that he is not governed totally by his intellect; to be coy is metonymically to be woman and therefore, in (not exclusively) Weiningerian terms, intellectu-ally inferior. To be coy is also to be uncommitted and flighty, a stereotypi-cally feminine disposition that here signals that stereotype as well as Bloom's gender position. What makes Bloom "dear" both as a man and as a person, a distinction that points to the gendering of attributes, is that the strength of his intellect could be said to be enfeebled by his emotional, or "other,"capacities. In other words, the intellectual is devalued, or valued differently. We see this borne out later in "Circe" when Stephen and Bloom come together—when "extremes meet" (Joyce 1986, 15.2098). Lynch's "cap" invokes and disrupts the Arnoldian distinction between Hellenism and Hebraism—"Jewgreek is greekjew" (Joyce 1986, 15.2099)— and at once characterizes Stephen's analysis of this relation as tautological and illogical—"Woman's reason" (Joyce 1986, 15.2098). Finally Stephen's analysis breaks down in the face of this illogic and becomes elliptical; he cannot "finish." Here sex and race both become determinants of intellec-tual prowess. Logos, however, does not accommodate or account for the fantastic, the mystical, the cosmic, the realm of Stephen's and Bloom's meeting.

These extensions, which are not immediately logical, lead us to Joyce's notion of lineage. It is useful to note that "*geschlecht*" may mean "race" as well as "gender," allowing these concepts to collapse together in Joyce's (and Weininger's) creation of character. Bloom gives birth to a kind of mini-Europe, producing eight white and eight yellow (exotic or metal-lic) children, who run the economic world (Joyce 1986, 1820–31). But then "A Voice" questions the origins of Bloom and his brood: "Bloom, are you the Messiah ben Joseph or ben David?" "You have said it," Bloom answers "darkly" (Joyce 1986, 15.1833–36). This invocation of the messianic doctrine in which there are two messiahs—one who will prepare the way for the messianic age, another who will enact it—calls up the relationship between the Christian and Jewish messianic traditions, a relationship that is variously represented in the literature. Bloom's answer to this query repeats Jesus' answer to Pilate's question—"Are you the king of the Jews?"—which in turn had been prompted by the elders' report that Jesus had identified himself as the messiah of the house of David (Luke 23:3).[6] Bloom's response, like Christ's, makes the question into a statement, so that in this case either Messiah will do (Jew or Christian/Bloom or Jesus). Perhaps more to the point here, the only distinction is accorded by dogma rather than lineage.[7] With this distinction gone, Stephen and Bloom may become familial by virtue of a line of descent from Bloom that is comically disrupted by a sexual and linguistic error: "*Leopoldi autem generatio*. Moses begat Noah and Noah begat Eunuch and Eunuch begat O'Halloran and O'Halloran begat Guggenheim and Guggenheim begat Agendath . . ." (Joyce, 1986, 15.1855–69). This is Joyce's line—a sort of jumble of association that is more synchronic than linear, putting a new gloss on race.[8] At the same time, an acknowledgment of the distinction made between races and religions points up the split within Bloom—Jew and non-Jew, the self and the alien self; what is dogmatic is reproduced through internalization.

It is with these ideas of the "new womanly man" and the Joycean notion of lineage (sex and character, race and character) that we may most profitably look at Bloom's relation to the Circean Bella/Bello figures and at the final section of "Circe" in which Bloom meets his son, Rudy/Stephen. In "Circe" the sexes take turns being both dominant/sadistic and subservient/masochistic. These extremes are separated out and embodied in the figments Bella and Bello. Their interaction with Bloom in part dramatizes or (en)acts his relationship with Molly. Weininger's theory states that each person is made up of both female and male, and therefore both are always present. Joyce has, however, altered this distribution, and in doing so decodes as before the essentialism of certain kinds of gendering—what signals their sex are the accouterments of gender. Bella has olive skin, which signals the exotic (i.e., Jewish) element that Joyce so often evokes and that we associate with Molly; she wears a dress and earrings; and she has a "sprouting mustache." What establishes her sex is only the linguistic signal—"she." In her "fan's" (synechdochic) interaction with Bloom we see an inversion of roles in Bloom's relationship with Molly:

THE FAN
(*Flirting quickly, then slowly.*) Married, I see.
BLOOM
Yes . . . Partly, I have mislaid . . . .
THE FAN
(*Half opening, then closing.*) And the missus is master. Petticoat government.
BLOOM
(*Looks down with a sheepish grin.*) That is so.

(Joyce 1986, 15.2754–62)

When the Bello side comes out, the positions are more than reversed. What was a characterization of Bloom's externalized submissiveness—the "sheepish grin"—and an externalization of his internal condition—"the missus is master"—now becomes literalized when the "man" (with "bobbed hair") takes over. Bello turns Bloom both into a woman (with "large male hands") and an animal ("pet"), the latter aligned with the former and, in the parallel with *The Odyssey*, emblematic of the submission to desire or seduction (Circe transforms the men into hogs and thus "unmans" them). In Bello's equation, to be unmanned or impotent/castrated is to be woman(ish)/inadequate. The Bello side of Bloom "finishes" him off, "embodying" his feelings of impotence and self-hatred:

> BELLO
>
> What else are you good for, an impotent thing like you? (*he stoops and, peering, pokes with his fan rudely under the fat suet fold of Bloom's haunches*) Up! Up! Manx cat! What have we here? Where's your curly teapot gone to or who docked it on you, cockyolly? Sing, birdy, sing. It's as limp as a boy of six's doing his pooly behind a cart. Buy a bucket or sell your pump. (*loudly*) Can you do a man's job?
>
> BLOOM
>
> Eccles street . . . .
>
> BELLO
>
> (*Sarcastically.*) I wouldn't hurt your feelings for the world but there's a man of brawn in possession there. The tables are turned, my gay young fellow! He is something like a fullgrown outdoor man. Well for you, you muff, if you had that weapon with knobs and lumps and warts all over it. He shot his bolt, I can tell you! Foot to foot, knee to knee, belly to belly, bubs to breast! He's no eunuch. A shock of red hair he has sticking out of him behind like a furzebush! Wait for nine months, my lad! Holy ginger, it's kicking and coughing up in her guts already! That makes you wild, don't it! Touches the spot? (*He spits in contempt.*) Spittoon!
>
> (Joyce 1986, 15.3127–3144)

In both cases, Bella and Bello, the locus of desire/consequence is Molly, the woman. Bloom, the Jew, the voyeur, the displaced, confronts his stand-in—Blazes Boylan—and images the role he plays in the scenario, as Molly does hers later in the "Penelope" section. And in both cases what is revealed is the character(ization) of such historical linking of sex and race.

Furthermore, we can see another twist on The Odyssey that marks a departure from as well as a manipulation of Weininger's theories. Odysseus uses the drug "moly" to ward off Circe and to save himself and his men from destruction (from being "unmanned"). Here too Molly is transformative in Bloom's realm of desire and fantasy, although she represents, like Penelope within the Odyssean myth, both prohibition and antidote. Bloom's confrontation with his origins, his desire, and his "death" are staged, and this sets up a parallel between Bloom and Weininger in a personal and parodic sense. The Bello in him consigns him to death, and while it is suggested that it is his guilt that kills him (for sexual desire and apostasy), he is given a Jewish funeral (no flowers) by "The Circumcised" (which he tearfully attends), pointing to, as with the accouterments of gender, the signifiers of race (Joyce 1986, 15. 3218–40). He seems to emerge absolved and, in a parody of resurrection, enlightened— "(*crawls jellily forward under the boughs, streaked by sunlight, with dignity*) This position. I felt it was expected of me. Force of habit" (Joyce 1986, 15.3241–3).

It seems at least ironic that Jewishness and womanishness become states of mind that destroyed Weininger yet save Bloom. And while Bello sends Bloom to his "death," Bloom puts Bello to his, or, in other words, banishes him from the text. It is within the realm of the textual that this can occur, although we may be reminded that it is the textualization of Weininger's fears and notions about race, sex, and character that prompted his suicide, or literalized his death.

Finally, what is proposed as possible within the Joycean outline of lineage and sexuality, ironically informed by Weininger's own theories— the reunion of Molly and Bloom with each other and with a lost son (Stephen takes the place of Rudy)—seems viable only in the fantastical realm of "Circe." The family epic is countered by a kind of anti-*nostos* (homecoming) in the last three chapters of the novel, in which the rhetoric of sexual and cultural difference takes on mythic proportions and comes between the characters. Joyce's probable adaptation of Weininger's ideas dramatizes both the illogic in and the historical power of those ideas, if not, as some of the critics have suggested, the psychobiography of these two writers.

15 ✦

JAMES JOYCE'S WOMANLY
WANDERING JEW

Natania Rosenfeld

The want of definitiveness in the ideas of women is the source of that "sensitiveness" which gives the widest scope to vague associations and allows the most radically different things to be grouped together. And even women with the best and least limited memories never free themselves from this kind of association by feelings. For instance, if they "feel reminded" by a word of some definite colour, or by a human being of some definite thing to eat—forms of association common with women—they rest content with the subjective association, and do not try to find out the source of the comparison, and if there is any relation in it to actual fact. The complacency and self-satisfaction of women corresponds with . . . their intellectual unscrupulousness . . . and . . . their want of the power to form concepts. This subjection to waves of feeling, this want of respect for conceptions, this self-appreciation without any attempt to avoid shallowness, characterise as essentially female the changeable styles of many modern painters and novelists. Male thought is fundamentally different from female thought in its craving for definite form, and all art that consists of moods is essentially a formless art.—Otto Weininger, *Sex and Character*

Judaism is the abyss over which Christianity is erected.—Otto Weininger, *Sex and Character*

When James Joyce wrote *Ulysses,* he had read two pseudoscientific books about women and Jews. One, according to Richard Ellmann, was Otto Weininger's *Sex and Character,* from which Joyce borrowed "a pet theory . . . that Jews were by nature womanly men" (Ellmann 1982, 463). The second was a volume in the Contemporary Science Series edited by Havelock Ellis: *The Jews: A Study of Race and Environment,* by Dr. Maurice Fishberg, published in 1911.[1] The extent to which Joyce drew on either of these works in his writing is difficult to ascertain. Weininger's characterization of woman as amoral, illogical, passive, animalistic, and both soul- and egoless corresponds to Joyce's description of her in a well-known letter to Frank Budgen as "perfectly sane amoral fertilisable untrustworthy engaging shrewd limited prudent indifferent *Weib* [woman]" (Joyce 1975, 285). While both Joyce's notions and Weininger's are fairly standard misogynist fare, Joyce's use of the German *Weib* suggests that he may have read Weininger in the original.[2]

Daniel Fogel posits that Joyce drew on Fishberg's discussions of alcohol consumption and suicide among the Jews in his characterization of Leopold Bloom (Fogel 1979). According to Fishberg, there are virtually no Jewish alcoholics, and the incidence of suicide is high only among Jews who have migrated westward. Thus Bloom is noted by the other characters in *Ulysses* for his abstemiousness, and Bloom's Hungarian-Jewish father is known to have committed suicide in Ireland. With his penchant for curious and absurd detail, Joyce may also have recalled Fishberg's paragraphs on the frequency of constipation and hemorrhoids among Jews when he made Bloom worry about both ailments in the outhouse (Joyce 1986, 56).

Joyce's portrait of Bloom, thrice-baptized and uncircumcised, perhaps owes something as well to Fishberg's lengthy discussions of assimilation. In the pivotal chapter of his book, "Assimilation *versus* Zionism," Fishberg dismisses the latter as Jewish self-ghettoization. Joyce was interested in Zionism: his Trieste library included Theodor Herzl's *Der Judenstaat* and a collection by H. Sacher, *Zionism and the Jewish Future* (Ellmann 1977, 112, 126). But he appears to have been as little a Zionist as he was an Irish patriot. In *Ulysses*, he has Bloom burn a Zionist leaflet (Joyce 1986, 580). Bloom thinks of Palestine as "a barren land, bare waste" that "could bear no more. Dead: an old woman's: the grey sunken cunt of the world" (Joyce 1986, 50). Fishberg correspondingly writes that Palestine is essentially infertile, although it provides good pasturage for cattle (Fishberg 1911).

Fishberg's solution to the problems of modern Jewry—in particular, the problem of anti-Semitism—is assimilation. He counters the charge that assimilation is "race suicide" by claiming that the Jews are not a race but an ethnic group characterized solely by certain "peculiarities" handed down from generation to generation. If only they would abandon these "peculiarities" (dietary laws, dress, etc.) and be baptized, Jews would be accepted and respected by their fellow citizens in all nations. The same claim, common among writers on "the Jewish problem" at the end of the century, is made by Otto Weininger, in mystical and high-flown language, in "Judaism," the penultimate chapter of *Sex and Character.* Weininger, too, refers to Jewish "peculiarities" and disparages the Zionist movement:

> "Before Zionism is possible, the Jew must first conquer Judaism.
>
> To defeat Judaism, the Jew must . . . understand himself and war against himself. So far, the Jew has reached no further than to make and enjoy jokes against his own peculiarities. Unconsciously, he respects the Aryan more than himself" (Weininger 1906, 312)

Weininger places the Jew in the same position vis-à-vis the superior "Aryan" that woman occupies in relation to man. Thus, just as men and not women rightfully govern the world, "the true conception of the State is foreign to the Jew, because he, like the woman, is wanting in personality" (Weininger 1906, 307). The Jew too is materialistic, incapable of distinguishing good from evil, and rooted in his sexual and reproductive functions: "It is the Jew and the woman who are the apostles of pairing to bring guilt on humanity" (Weininger 1906, 329).

Yet, just as woman's sole value is in bringing forth children, the one virtue of Judaism is the fact that it has produced the Christian Messiah—and that it may still produce another:

> Judaism is the abyss over which Christianity is erected . . . .
>
> Perhaps [Christ] was, and will remain, the only Jew to conquer Judaism. . . . It may be, however, that there still lies in Judaism the possibility of producing a Christ, and that the founder of the next religion will pass through Jewry.
>
> The Jewish nature has no other metaphysical meaning than to be the spring from which the founders of religion will come. Their tradition to increase and multiply is connected with this vague hope, that out of them shall come the Messiah. The possibility of begetting Christs is the meaning of Judaism (Weininger 1906, 329).

Like both Fishberg and Weininger, James Joyce disparaged Zionism; like Weininger, he also disparaged women, considering them incapable of intellection. He adopted Weininger's theories about the femininity of Jews in his creation of Leopold Bloom, a protagonist with androgynous characteristics. Joyce was not, however, an anti-Semite, nor can he unequivocally be termed a misogynist. In his story of an assimilated Jew and his Jewish-born Catholic wife, Joyce seems to aggrandize the views of Weininger (and, to a lesser extent, Fishberg)—most notably in the "Cyclops" chapter—only to turn them on their heads.

In *Ulysses*, as in *Sex and Character*, woman is pure flesh, but instead of representing negation, she is "*der* [*sic*] *Fleisch der stets bejaht* [the flesh that always affirms]" (Joyce 1975, 285). Joyce here deliberately misquotes Goethe's Mephistopheles: "Ich bin der Geist der stets verneint [I am the spirit that always negates]." He reverses Weininger's spirit-flesh hierarchy by alluding to a male "spirit" whose essence is negation and making the body of a woman fundamentally affirmative. In his letter to Budgen, Joyce says that "*Penelope* is the clou of the book. . . . It begins and ends with the word *yes*. It turns like the huge earth ball . . . its four cardinal points being the female breasts, arse, womb and cunt expressed by the words *because, bottom* . . . , *woman, yes*" (Joyce 1975, 285).

If Molly's life-affirming cunt represents origins, her arse embodies ends: it is the pillow on which the wandering Jew rests his head at night; he kisses it as the faithful, arriving in Palestine, kiss the ground. A man-child, Bloom issues at morning from Molly's bed, returning to it in the dark hours to be reborn the next morning, when his wife will cook him eggs. Bloom's day is an allegory of Jewish history: the expulsion from Zion, the adventures and persecutions of the Diaspora, the return to the place of origin. However, the anti-nationalist Joyce replaces Zion with the body of a woman. The substitution is not inappropriate: in Hebrew the word for homeland, *moledet,* means "she gives birth."

Molly in her bed is evoked throughout the novel by references to Plumtree's Potted Meat: a symbol of flesh within a container, womb or tomb. The first such reference occurs in the chapter "Lotus-Eaters":

> —Wife well, I suppose? M'Coy's changed voice said.
> —O, yes, Mr Bloom said. Tiptop, thanks.
>   He unrolled the newspaper baton idly and read idly:
>   *What is home without*
>   *Plumtree's Potted Meat?*
>   *Incomplete.*
>   *With it an abode of bliss.* (Joyce 1986, 61)

The advertisement that just happens to catch Bloom's eye at this moment is a summary of his hopes, difficulties, and dilemmas. "Home" is incomplete without a wife in bed: the irony of M'Coy's question is that Molly plans to share hers with Blazes Boylan in the afternoon. The brand name suggests another "home": in the chapter "Aeolus," Stephen Dedalus tells a story called "*A Pisgah Sight of Palestine* or *The Parable of the Plums.*" Plumtree's Potted Meat thus stands both for woman's flesh and for the Jewish dream of a homeland.

Already before this moment, in the chapter "Calypso," Joyce links two kinds of *Fleisch:* womanflesh and animal meat. The chapter famously begins: "Mr. Leopold Bloom ate with relish the inner organs of beasts and fowls." This statement jolts the reader from the neo-Platonism of Stephen Dedalus to the bodily desires of the middle-aged Jew. Like Weininger's woman, Bloom is preoccupied with food, and food reminds him of other things. In the butcher shop, his attention wanders from the meat to the Zionist leaflet that Dlugacz, the Jewish pork butcher, uses as a wrapper, to the body of the "nextdoor girl" who is buying sausages:

> The ferreteyed porkbutcher folded the sausages he had snipped off with blotchy fingers, sausagepink. Sound meat there: like a stalled heifer.
>   He took a page up from the pile of cut sheets: the model farm at Kinnereth on the lakeshore of Tiberias. Can become ideal winter sanatorium. Moses Montefiore. I thought he was. Farmhouse, wall round it, blurred cattle cropping. . . . A young white heifer. Those mornings in the cattlemarket, the beasts lowing in their pens, branded sheep, flop and fall of dung, the breeders in hobnailed boots trudging through the litter, slapping a palm on a ripemeated hindquarter, there's a prime one, unpeeled switches in their hands. . . . The crooked skirt swinging.
>   To catch up and walk behind her if she went slowly, behind her moving hams. Pleasant to see first thing in the morning (Joyce 1986, 48–49)

As if Bloom's consciousness determined his world, no sooner does he compare the nextdoor girl to a "stalled heifer" than he spots the Zionist leaflet with its picture of cattle grazing. His absorbent mind blurs the two images into a pornographic scenario à la Leopold von Sacher-Masoch—one that is realized later in "Circe," when Bloom plays cow to Bella Cohen as breeder. Finally, Bloom denotes the woman *as* meat by referring to her thighs as "hams."

The address of "Agendath Netaim: [Zionist] planters' company" is a certain Bleibtreustrasse 34 in Berlin. *Bleib treu* means "stay faithful," an injunction that Bloom ignores in both his religious life (he relishes ham, for instance) and his sexual life. Although his reflections on the barrenness of Palestine lead inevitably to contrasting daydreams of Molly's "ample bedwarmed flesh," (Joyce 1986, 50) Bloom is temporarily preoccupied with various other women's bodies and is carrying on an epistolary affair.

The exchange of sentimental, pseudopornographic letters between Bloom and Martha Clifford recalls a similar incident in Joyce's own life.[3] When he and Nora were living in Zurich in 1918, Joyce conceived a voyeuristic passion for a woman who lived across the way. In the first of four letters to this woman, he described his initial impression of her:

> You were dressed in black, wearing a big hat with waving feathers. The colour suited you very well. And I thought: a pretty animal.
>
> Because there was something frank and almost shameless in your allure. Then, as I watched you, I noticed the softness and regularity of your features, and the gentleness of your eyes. And I thought: a Jewess. If I am wrong, you must not be offended. Jesus Christ put on his human body: in the womb of a Jewish woman (Joyce 1966, 433).

The passage is redolent of Weiningerian ideology. The woman is an "animal" who must not be offended if Joyce thinks her Jewish, because the Jews possess the one virtue of having brought forth Christ. In "Eumaeus," Bloom tells Stephen of his run-in with the citizen: "He called me a jew and in a heated fashion offensively. So I without deviating from plain facts in the least told him his God, I mean Christ, was a jew too and all his family like me though in reality I'm not." Stephen replies by alluding to the Vulgate: "et ex quibus est Christus secundum carnem" (and from that race is Christ, according to the flesh) (Joyce 1986, 525). In the one instance of Christ's birth, both Judaism and woman's flesh are instrumental, indeed indispensable.

Joyce must have relished the discovery that the object of his desire was named Marthe *Fleischmann:* "Flesh-man." The name itself is androgynous, since in the Joycean scheme of things, woman, not man, is flesh. Moreover, the suffix does not fit a woman. In a list of *"the circumcised"* in "Circe," Joyce humorously includes *"Minnie Watchman,"* whose masculine patronymic echoes Marthe Fleischmann's and whose appearance on a list of men further suggests androgyny.[4] Conversely, he emphasizes his protagonist's feminine characteristics by giving him a flowery last name and the middle name Paula.

Ellmann describes Joyce's elaborate staging of his first encounter with Marthe Fleischmann as follows:

> On February 2, 1919, his birthday, Joyce prepared a strange ritual to celebrate Candlemas, which also falls on that day. . . . He wrote [Marthe Fleischmann] a letter, dating it *Marias Lichtmesse*, as if to infuse a touch of mariolatry into his sexual approach. She replied that she could see him in the late afternoon . . . . Early that day Joyce [borrowed] a handsome ceremonial candlestick, lighted during the Jewish festival of Chanukah, and so appropriate to his conjecture about Marthe's ancestry. He brought it to Frank Budgen's studio, and explained that Marthe would be coming later in the day.
>
> When Budgen [hesitated] to assist his friend's infidelity, Joyce replied severely, "If I permitted myself any restraint in this matter it would be spiritual death to me." Rather than feel guilty of spiritual murder, Budgen gave in. There were further preparations. Budgen's paintings were fine as decor, but what was missing was a nude with ample buttocks. The painter had to whip up a charcoal drawing on the spot . . . .
>
> Marthe arrived. . . . Eventually [Joyce] took her home. He and Budgen met later that night, and he confided, "I have explored the coldest and hottest parts of a woman's body." (Such scientific lechery would be mocked in the *Circe* episode.) He did not claim to have had sexual intercourse with Marthe, and Budgen's estimate was that, as Bloom says of Gerty MacDowell, she had been "fingered only" (Ellmann 1982, 451).

Joyce played both director and protagonist in this peculiar dramatization of his pet obsessions. He set the stage and then walked onto it to enact not merely a sexual encounter, but his own rebirth—both *in spiritu* and *in carne*. For by emphasizing the coincidence of his birthday with *Marias Lichtmesse*, he equated Marthe Fleischmann with his mother. As for the fetishization of her bottom—and of female posteriors in general—implied by Budgen's commissioned drawing, Brenda Maddox has suggested that Joyce maintained an infantile association between defecation and childbirth fairly late in life.[5]

The themes that dominated Joyce's rather peculiar extramarital affair recur throughout *Ulysses*. In the chapter "Scylla & Charybdis," Bloom manifests an analogous fascination with the female anus. Like Joyce, he transfers his erotic desires to an artistic representation of woman—in this case, the statue of Venus in the library. If Joyce associated the anus with childbirth, he also associated childbirth with creative power. Early in "Scylla & Charybdis," he suggests that male genius is nurtured by women and mimics pregnancy—"What useful discovery did Socrates learn from

Xanthippe?" John Eglinton asks. "Dialectic, Stephen answered: and from his mother how to bring thoughts into the world" (Joyce 1986, 156). Shakespeare's composition is also likened, by Buck Mulligan, to parturition (Joyce 1986, 171).

As for fatherhood, Stephen both echoes and subverts Weininger when he tells his listeners:

> Fatherhood, in the sense of conscious begetting, is unknown to man. It is a mystical estate, an apostolic succession, from only begetter to only begotten. On that mystery and not on the madonna which the cunning Italian intellect flung to the mob of Europe the church is founded and founded irremovably because founded, like the world, macro and microcosm, upon the void. Upon incertitude, upon unlikelihood. *Amor matris*, subjective and objective genitive, may be the only true thing in life (Joyce 1986, 170).

Stephen's remark that "the church is founded . . . upon the void" recalls the sexual metaphor implicit in Weininger's statement that "Judaism is the abyss over which Christianity is erected" (Weininger 1906, 328). In saying that the church is *not* founded on the Madonna, however, Stephen contradicts both himself and Weininger. By his very word choice, Stephen leads us inevitably back to the mother's body. If fatherhood is a *void*, what remains to flesh out our notion of origins but the empty space of the womb? Stephen's definition of *amor matris* as "the only true thing in life" indeed privileges the feminine "abyss." As the song that Bloom remembers in "Sirens" tells us, "the hand that rocks the cradle rules the world" (Joyce 1986, 236).

It is Bloom's own identification with the feminine that distinguishes him from other men. To Molly, the distinction is a positive one: "yes that was why I liked him because I saw he understood or felt what a woman is" (Joyce 1986, 643). The "Cyclops" episode, however, presents the Weiningerian view with a vengeance. The mock-description of the Citizen, a parody according to Gifford of "Irish revival legendry," also reads like a satire on Weininger's ideal "Aryan" man: "The figure seated on a large boulder at the foot of a round tower was that of a broadshouldered deepchested strong-limbed frankeyed redhaired freelyfreckled shaggybearded widemouthed largenosed longheaded deepvoiced barekneed brawnyhanded hairlegged sinewyarmed hero" (Joyce 1986, 243). This prepossessing figure is a rabid anti-Semite, with whom the narrator of "Cyclops" is ideologically in collusion. The latter speaks of Bloom in the most primitive and hateful tones: "So they started talking about capital punishment and of course Bloom comes out with the why and the wherefore and all the codology of the business and the old dog smelling him all the time I'm told those jewies does have a sort of a queer odor coming off them for dogs about I don't know what all deterrent effect and so on. . . ."

And then he starts with his jawbreakers about phenomenon and science and this phenomenon and the other phenomenon" (Joyce 1986, 250).

Although Weininger does not stoop to allege the existence of a "Jewish smell" (a notion that *is* discussed and discounted in Fishberg's book), he more than implies an affinity between Jews and animals. The Jew is soulless, fundamentally irreligious, mired in the material world and his own sexual functions: this is as much as to say that he is subhuman. He is also incapable, Weininger maintains, of faith or mysticism, and is thus attracted to the sciences.

The brunt of the anti-Semitic virulence in the "Cyclops" episode is directed at Bloom's manhood:

—Yes, says J.J., and every male that's born they think it may be their Messiah. And every jew is in a tall state of excitement, I believe, till he knows if he's a father or a mother.

—Do you call that a man? says the citizen.

—I wonder did he ever put it out of sight, says Joe.

—Well, there were two children born anyhow, says Jack Power.

—And who does he suspect? says the citizen.

Gob, there's many a true word spoken in jest. One of those mixed middlings he is. Lying up in the hotel Pisser was telling me once a month with a headache like a totty with her courses. Do you know what I'm telling you? It'd be an act of God to take a hold of a fellow the like of that and throw him in the bloody sea. Justifiable homicide, so it would (Joyce 1986, 277).

The narrator's condemnation of Bloom in this passage virtually echoes the frightening, apocalyptic final paragraph of Weininger's "Judaism" chapter. "The decision must be made," writes Weininger, "between Judaism and Christianity, between business and culture, between male and female, between the race and the individual, between unworthiness and worth, between the earthly and the higher life, between negation and the God-like. Mankind has the choice to make. There are only two poles, and there is no middle way" (Weininger 1906, 330). Weininger's words anticipate the rhetoric of Nazism; the "decision" he projects is the one made by Hitler three decades later. Although Joyce could not have foreseen the Holocaust, he appears to have understood both the implications of Weininger's rantings and the naiveté in Fishberg's calls for assimilation. Baptized or not, a Jew is always a Jew in the eyes of the "citizens" among whom he lives; he never escapes being viewed as a foreigner ("that foreign gentleman," Gerty McDowell calls Bloom [Joyce 1986, 313]), and his foreignness poses a threat to patriots and racial purists. The chauvinism that Joyce portrays in "Cyclops" is not only national and racial but sexual as well; thus the Jew is denigrated as being outside *all* categories, including those of gender. Bloom is a "mixed middling," a motherfather who suffers monthly headaches like a menstruating woman.

While Joyce seems actually to have believed in Jewish androgyny, he endorses the notion in order to valorize it. Unlike Weininger, he does not equate "manwomanliness" with a kind of sterile hermaphroditism that, must be eradicated because it is threatening to society. On the contrary, it is Bloom's capacity to empathize with women that sets him apart from the boorish citizens of Dublin and dignifies him in the eyes of the reader. The menial tasks he performs for his wife are labors of love, the principle denied by his fellow-citizens and of which Bloom becomes, in "Cyclops," the apostle:

> Gob, he'd adorn a sweepingbrush, so he would, if only he had a nurse's apron on him. And then he collapses all of a sudden, twisting around all the opposite, as limp as a wet rag.
> —But it's no use, says he. Force, hatred, history, all that. That's not life for men and women, insult and hatred. And everybody knows that it's the very opposite of that that is really life.
> —What? says Alf.
> —Love, says Bloom. I mean the opposite of hatred . . . .
>
> . . .
>
> —A new apostle to the gentiles, says the citizen. Universal love (Joyce 1986, 273).

Both here and later in the chapter, the citizen refers sarcastically to Bloom as the new Messiah. Joyce, however, revises the implications of Weininger's contention that the next savior will "pass through" Judaism by taking this to mean not that the Jew's only salvation lies in conversion to Christianity but that Christian salvation depends upon a Jew. Thus the "limpness" and effeminacy that the "Cyclops" narrator ascribes to Bloom become positive values. Bloom's world vision, unlike that of the citizen and his friends or of Stephen Dedalus's confraternity, is itself androgynous; it encompasses both sexes: "That's not life for men and women . . . ."

Bloom's belief that love is life also implies an identification with women, who are posited again and again in *Ulysses* as creators: fatherhood, we recall, is founded on a void; *amor matris* is "the only true thing in life." In "Oxen of the Sun," Bloom is the only man among the assemblage at the lying-in hospital to spare a sympathetic thought for the suffering Mrs. Purefoy. In the hallucinatory "Circe" chapter, he is transformed into a birth-giving female by the sinister Bella/Bello Cohen, a figure already anticipated in Bloom's butcher-shop fantasies of flagellating cattle-breeders and in his sado-masochistic correspondence with Martha Clifford. It is in fact in his portrayal of the masculinized Jewess, rather than that of the womanly Jew, that Joyce seems to subscribe to Weininger's misogynist, and perhaps also anti-Semitic, ideologies. The Jewish women Joyce fabricates—among them Marthe Fleischmann, whom he barely knew and who was actually a Gentile—represent inversions of Weininger's portrait of the Jew. Or rather, for Weininger all Jews are, in effect, women, while in Joyce's view Jews share and exchange gender. If the "limp" Bloom is heroized as the apostle of love, Bella Cohen on the other hand is a monstrous *femme fatale* with power over men's lives. Joyce ascribed similar powers to Marthe Fleischmann: her fleshly favors amounted, as he told Budgeon, to his spiritual rebirth. By calling her an animal, he also associated her with the bestiality of Circe. As both muse and midwife, she represented God the Father as well as the mother of Christ, inspiring or impregnating the writer so that *he* could give birth. Joyce thus ironically committed the very act that he condemned throughout *Ulysses:* usurpation. Frightened by woman's awesome creative capacities, he attempted to appropriate them, taking the credit away from the mother who made him. His statement to Budgen—"If *I* permitted myself any restraint... it would be spiritual death to me" [*my italics*]—denies Marthe Fleischmann any agency in their encounter.

If Bloom, like Joyce, becomes "a finished example of the new womanly man" (Joyce 1986, 403) and learns to give birth under the tutelage of Bella Cohen, his androgyny is its own reward. It is his empathy for women that enables him, ultimately, to return to Molly's bed at day's end. The reader ought not to imitate Joyce's inequity in the Fleischmann affair by crediting Bloom alone for his successful return: it is, after all, Molly's own choice to continue sharing her bed with him. And this choice is based largely on the fact that, unlike the other men of her acquaintance, Bloom "understood or felt what a woman is."

Thus the very thing that according to Otto Weininger *prevents* the Jew from establishing a homeland leads to that homeland in *Ulysses.* Already in "Calypso," Joyce links Zion to the female body. The connection is elaborated in the course of the book and focused upon a specific anatomical part, the female fundament. This first becomes explicit in the "Nausicaa" chapter, when Bloom rests and ruminates after his voyeuristic orgasm. He envies the rock that Gerty McDowell sat on and the chairs under the women he saw earlier in the library. He thinks of "Jerusalem artichokes" and of Blazes Boylan: "I am a fool perhaps. He gets the plums, and I the plumstones" (Joyce 1986, 308). He then falls into a dream that ends with the words "sleep wander years of dreams return tail end Agendath swoony lovey showed me her next year in drawers return next in her next her next" (Joyce 1986, 312). This is the first time in the novel that Bloom rests from his wandering. His postorgasmic nap anticipates his ultimate return to Molly's bed, and Gerty McDowell's tail end is the precursor of Molly's arse, the "Jerusalem artichoke" of Bloom's private Zion. His very last words hark back to "Aeolus" when Bloom, thinking of his dead father, recalls the Jewish liturgical phrase "Next year in Jerusalem" (Joyce 1986, 101).

The connection is reiterated in "Circe" following Bloom's anal parturition. Stephen Dedalus, holding forth about music, tells his audience that "the fundamental and the dominant are separated by the greatest possible interval which. . . . Interval which. Is the greatest possible ellipse. Consistent with. The ultimate return" (Joyce 1986, 411). His allusion to the two poles of the diatonic scale refers also to the two cultures impersonated by Dedalus himself and by Bloom, who have finally come together: "Jewgreek is greekjew. Extremes meet" (Joyce 1986, 411). This mingling of identities in turn reflects the androgynous mingling of Leopold Bloom and Bella/Bello Cohen, and is summed up as the distance that Bloom has nearly traversed between the place of origin and the place of return: Molly's cunt and Molly's arse.

At the end of "Ithaca," the wandering Jew has made it home at last. He lies with his head against Molly's "posterior female hemispheres, redolent of milk and honey" (Joyce 1986, 604). At rest beside her flesh, Bloom has in a sense *become* Molly. Earlier in the chapter, Joyce emphasizes his fascination with water, in contrast to Stephen Dedalus's distrust of "aquacities of thought and language" (Joyce 1986, 550). When Bloom turns on the faucet, he becomes a kind of source, like Molly, who gets her period during the "Penelope" monologue. And in "Circe," of course, he has experienced the act of childbirth.

It is Molly who has the final word. Her reiterated "Yes" might be read as Joyce's answer to Weininger. The Jew and the woman represent not negation but the principles of life and love: both of them are sources of creation. "They can't get on without us," (Joyce 1986, 635) Molly thinks of men, subtly subverting Weininger's disparaging statement that "Judaism is the abyss over which Christianity is erected." Indeed, her remark extends to Christians as well, for it is in the final chapter that we find out for the first time that Molly is "jewess looking after [her] mother" (Joyce 1986, 634). We cannot know from this whether Lunita Laredo was in fact Jewish, but the association stands: without Jews, without mothers, the world could not perpetuate itself.

After finishing *Ulysses*, James Joyce began a workbook that eventually became *Finnegans Wake*. The book was divided into sections, each named after one of Joyce's previous works. The section titled "Penelope" resumes the voice of Molly Bloom: "I'll be glad when it stops (menses)?: bolt the door: Moses couldn't put stops in Torah dictated so fast" (Joyce 1961a, 163). In *Ulysses*, Leopold Bloom had been associated with the figure of Moses; here Molly's menstruation is the equivalent of Moses' inspired writing. Moses, as Stephen Dedalus recalls, after leading his people on their Odyssey through the desert, was permitted merely a "Pisgah sight of Palestine" (Joyce 1986, 122). While Joyce concurred with Maurice Fishberg and Otto Weininger in rejecting statehood as a realistic Jewish option, he endorsed the rest of their arguments in order to subvert them. If Joyce's figure of the Jew is a "mixed middling," it is his very androgyny that makes him deserve a Zion of his own in any nation he inhabits. Himself an exile, Joyce depicted Bloom and Molly as citizens of the world who carry their home, like a womb, within them. While Weininger condemned the "middle way," Joyce understood the ability to navigate between two poles as the essence of love and the only real "life for men and women."

16 ✦

MOLLY *IS* SEXUALITY: THE WEININGERIAN DEFINITION OF WOMAN IN JOYCE'S *ULYSSES*

Elfriede Pöder

SOME REMARKS ON LITERARY WEININGER RECEPTION

In 1979 Gisela Brude-Firnau established three criteria that must be fulfilled for us to refer legitimately to a particular writer's Weininger reception: (1) that a writer's knowledge of Weininger can be proved either directly from the person's text or correspondence; (2) that a female character in any given work of fiction must correspond rather consistently to the combined characteristics that Weininger defined as feminine; and (3) that there are Weininger quotations, paraphrases, or other obvious analogies in a writer's text (Brude-Firnau 1979, 139).[1]

It seems that the second criterion, above all, must be considered with special care, since it enables us to distinguish between a writer's adherence to the representational convention of femininity within patriarchy and a writer's actual indebtedness to Weininger's *Sex and Character*. This distinction is of special significance, since *Sex and Character* is as much an individual contribution to the question of feminine (and masculine) sexual identity as it is a most explicit articulation of the patriarchal concept and status of femininity/woman. In *Sex and Character* femininity/woman signifies everything that must function as the Other in patriarchy (Simone de Beauvoir), and it signifies everything that Luce Irigaray in particular has deconstructed as the suppressed, excluded, and desired for subtext of patriarchal culture. Emphasis therefore should be placed on the combination of feminine characteristics that constitute Weininger's concept of the all-sexual and mentally inferior essence of the feminine/woman as well as on his notion of feminine essence. Merely misogynous and/or reductionist images of the feminine are instances of Western patriarchal tradition in general; they are not Otto Weininger's invention.

Finally, I would like to suggest a further criterion for judging a writer's Weininger reception: intertextuality.[2] This criterion could even substitute for the first rather positivistic one, so that a writer's text can be regarded as an instance of Weininger reception if it fulfills criteria two and three and if the text's author is known to work intertextually. Moreover, hunting for extraliterary material will hardly be necessary if we accept the criterion of intertextuality and thus work more strictly within the literary field.

SEX AND CHARACTER: OTTO WEININGER'S CONCEPT OF FEMININITY/WOMAN

In *Sex and Character* Otto Weininger attempts to elaborate a concept of the "absolute female" and the "absolute male" from a psychological, philosophical, and partly natural sciences approach. But although he states at the beginning of his investigation that neither the absolute male nor the absolute female principle can be found in reality, and that they always exist in mixed forms, he contradicts his own statement throughout his work by basing his abstract propositions on observations about real women, as well as by constantly mixing phrases like the "absolute female" and "female principle" with the term "woman" so that his statements refer as much to real women as they refer to an abstract concept of femininity/ woman (Brude-Firnau 1979, 138). Before Weininger sets out to deduce typical female characteristics, he establishes a crucial and basic difference between the "female" and "male" consciousness: the female is closer to the "henid" state than the male. By "henid" Weininger means the not yet clarified, confused state of mental and psychical data. According to him, "the male has the same psychical data as the female, but in a more articulated form; where she thinks more or less in henids, he thinks in more or less clear and detailed presentations" (Weininger 1906a). Weininger's basic assignment of the feminine to "a lower grade of consciousness" (Weininger 1906a, 99) allows him to establish his main thesis about the female: her lack of an intelligible ego, which is the consequence of her incapacity for logical thinking: "The absolute woman . . . cannot take the proposition of identity, or its contradictory, or the exclusions of the alternative, as axiomatic. . . . And so it appears that woman is without logic" (Weininger 1906a, 148); "The absolute female knows neither the logical nor the moral imperative. . . . The absolute female has no ego" (Weininger 1906a, 186).

Woman's lack of an intelligible ego consequently expresses itself as the female trait of giving "the widest scope . . . to vague associations" and of grouping together "the most radically different things" (Weininger 1906a, 190). All subsequently deduced female characteristics are expressions of the basic proposition that women lack an intelligible ego. Woman's two most important characteristics, according to this proposition, are irrationality and contradiction, and their exclusively sexual identity. The characteristics of irrationality and contradiction manifest themselves in a specifically female mode of thinking, namely, as "sliding and gliding through subjects," and as superficially "tasting of things" (Weininger 1906a, 191).[3] Woman's thought is an "extravagant and dainty method of skimming that has no grasp of accuracy" (Weininger 1906a, 191). As women do not have any identity in the mental sphere, only one possible identity is left for them: sexuality. "The female principle is, then, nothing more than sexuality" (Weininger 1906a, 90). "A woman's sexuality is not limited to periods of time nor to localized organs. . . . A woman is . . . nothing but sexuality, because she is sexuality itself" (Weininger 1906a, 92).

Like a woman's lack of an intelligible ego, her lower state of consciousness expresses itself in the flowing, associative, and irrational mode of thinking; her identity as sexuality expresses itself in her preoccupation with sexual matters: "the female, moreover, is completely occupied and content with sexual matters, whilst the male is interested in much else, in war and sport, in social affairs and feasting, in philosophy and science, in business and politics, in religion and art" (Weininger 1906a, 89). According to Weininger, woman's preoccupation with sexual matters is proved by the fact that her otherwise disconnected and uncontinuous memory is able to recall and imagine love scenes most accurately (Weininger 1906a, 124); the power of her imagination of course stems exclusively from her sexual life (cf. Weininger 1906a, 118). Consequently, "all that the real woman recalls of her life" (Weininger 1906a, 124), apart from actual sexual experiences and reexperiences ("the condition of sexual excitement is the supreme moment of a woman's life" [Weininger 1906a, 88], is her lovers, their proposals, their presents, their compliments, "every phrase by which a lover has impressed her" (Weininger 1906a, 124). Small wonder that the "exactness" (Weininger 1906a, 124) of women's memory in sexual matters expresses itself in the "shamelessness . . . in which they talk of being loved" (Weininger 1906a, 203).

Another manifestation of the all-sexual identity of woman is her narcissism, her "obsession with her own body." Of course this preoccupation is not an expression of her identity, nor does it reflect self-interest and self-contained pleasure, but it is her "desire to feel that her body is admired, or rather sexually coveted, by man." Her narcissism only "comes to its full measure . . . in the effect that her body has on man" (Weininger 1906a, 201).

Her inability to think logically and her lack of an intelligible ego, revealed in contradictions, disconnectedness, vague associations, and indefiniteness/flow, coupled with her exactness and shameless preoccupation with sexual matters, finally lead to the "actual essence of woman" (Weininger 1906a, 259). Since women "are careless as to the individuality of their sexual complement" (Weininger 1906a, 220), their sexuality is not an individual self-manifestation nor an expression of interest in the other, but the manifestation of sexuality itself. Sexuality is the "transcendental function" of the woman; "her personal sexuality is only a special case of this universal, impersonal instinct" (Weininger 1906a, 260). The "superindividual" aspect of sexuality in women defines their "nature" as "impersonal instinct," which equates their ontology with the more unconscious being of plants and animals: "as a matter of fact, women are sisters of the flowers, and are in close relationship with animals" (Weininger 1906a, 290).[4]

JOYCE'S WEININGER LEGACY

Few scholars have investigated James Joyce's Weininger reception in the novel *Ulysses*. Richard Ellmann was the first to mention Joyce's familiarity with *Sex and Character* (Ellmann 1982, 463). According to Ellmann, Joyce not only knew *Sex and Character*, but, like Weininger, he even set out "labouring to isolate female characteristics, from an incapacity for philosophy, to a dislike of soup" (Ellmann 1982, 463; see also Reizbaum 1982, 230). Although Ellmann mentions Joyce's indebtedness to Weininger both with regard to Weiningers's theory of Judaism and his theory of femininity/woman, he only applies Weininger's theory of the Jew as "womanly man" in *Ulysses* (Ellmann 1982, 463).

Thus the main critical focus of Joyce's Weininger reception has pertained to Weininger's theory of the Jew.[5] However, this is misleading, since Weininger's definition of the Jew as a "womanly man" is a by-product of his focus on the "absolute female." The fact that Joyce also deals with the (male) Jew as a "womanly man" further indicates how well Joyce knew Weininger's text.

Nonetheless, Weininger's concept of femininity/woman is the primary subject of *Sex and Character* and therefore should always be considered in any discussion of a writer's indebtedness to this work.

Thus a closer look at Joyce's female character Molly Bloom reveals the Weininger legacy in *Ulysses* to be much wider than Weininger's concept of the "womanly man" suggests; rather, the close and frequently explicit parallels between Joyce's literary presentation of Molly and Weininger's concept of woman/femininity imply Joyce's thorough knowledge of *Sex and Character*. Molly's prevailing traits even suggest that Weininger's concept of woman was something like a blueprint for the construction of the most fully delineated female character in *Ulysses*. This, however, is not to deny that it is "Joyce's language . . . [that] makes Molly so alive" and that "Molly's frankness and her use of four-letter words were of course revolutionary" (Unkeless 1982, 150). In its own way Weininger's *Sex and*

Character too was quite a "revolutionary" undertaking, considering the radicalism of some of his ideas (not least his presentation of women as having sexual feelings) and the frankness with which he discussed them.

The following comparison of Joyce's female character Molly and Weininger's theory of the feminine will help not only to distinguish between Weininger reception and the representational convention of patriarchal tradition, but to determine the extent to which Joyce's "Penelope" deviates from the particular moral imperative that underlies *Sex and Character*.

MOLLY'S FEMININE IDENTITY

Our very first image of Molly prior to "Penelope" is mediated through Bloom's perception of her; thus she appears as a "male" image of the "female":

> A sleepy soft grunt answered:
> —Mn.
> No. She did not want anything. He heard then a warm heavy sigh, softer, as she turned over and the loose brass quoits of the bedstead jingled (Joyce 1961b, 56).

Molly's answer to Bloom's question ("Mn") and the adjectives "sleepy," "soft," "warm," "heavy," and "softer" applied to the nouns "grunt" and "sigh" remind us of the cat Bloom talks to in an earlier passage of the novel. Consequently, Bloom's image of Molly evokes a combination of sexuality (the bed) and animalism, as utterances and movements linguistically recall the image of the cat.

Before we are actually confronted with Molly's authentic point of view in "Penelope," she is present either in the form of Bloom's conscious perception of her or as subtext in *Ulysses*. As subtext, she also signifies Bloom's subconscious and unconscious carnal and sexual desires, since he associates her primarily in the sexual context of body warmth and nourishment. Even when Bloom thinks of her as a singer, he cannot avoid associating Molly with her love affair with Boylan (cf., for example, Joyce 1961b, 75, 171–73, 319).

All the images of Molly prior to "Penelope" are signaled as male perceptions or associations. However, "Penelope" is presented exclusively from Molly's point of view, which suggests that Joyce wanted to create the illusion of a woman's own inscription of the feminine. As Molly reduces herself to mere sexuality in "Penelope," she also reproduces the previously "male"-signaled images of the feminine. Therefore, we must bear in mind that the subtext "Molly" triumphantly emerges and unfolds in the last chapter of *Ulysses*. In "Penelope," heretofore only subconscious and unconscious male sexual desires are finally established as the text proper.

Joyce presents all of "Penelope" as a silent soliloquy,[6] which indicates that Molly's thinking is illogical, disconnected, and associative, and thereby emphasizes her mental inferiority, or within Weininger's theory, her less developed "female" consciousness. The most outstanding characteristics of Molly in "Penelope" are her obsession with sexuality (Unkeless 1982, 156) and her predilection for contradictory statements.[7] Molly's contradictions are most obvious when she, for example, talks about her inability to masturbate and then states a few sentences later that she has "to finish it off" herself; or when she talks about the cruelty of war "killing any finelooking men there were" and at the same time says that she loves "to see a regiment pass in review the first time I saw the Spanish cavalry at La Roque it was lovely" (Joyce 1961b, 749).

Molly's sexual obsession becomes apparent in her minutely detailed recollections of love affairs and in how these memories frequently excite her anew, especially when she remembers specific sexual practices with Bloom or Boylan: "yes I think he made them a bit firmer sucking them like that so long he made me thirsty . . . ill get him to keep that up and ill take those eggs beaten up with marsala fatten them out for him" (Joyce 1961b, 753); "I was coming for about 5 minutes with my legs round him . . . and my tongue between my lips up to him the savage brute Thursday Friday one Saturday two Sunday three O Lord I cant wait till Monday" (Joyce 1961b, 754). Molly's primary interest in sexuality is not only revealed in her "frankness and her use of four-letter words" (Unkeless 1982, 156) but also in the fact that every topic other than sexuality that she introduces, be it politics, motherhood and fatherhood, art, money, religion, or dresses, finally works its way around to the recollection or anticipation of sexual experiences.

A further important aspect of Molly's sexuality is her narcissism. Joyce inscribes the female body—supposedly from a woman's point of view—as the object of male desire; Molly admires/contemplates parts of her body only because she thinks them sexually attractive to males: "I bet he never saw a better pair of thighs than that look how white they are the smoothest place is right there between this bit here how soft like a peach God I wouldn't mind being a man and get up on a lovely woman" (Joyce 1961b, 770).

The workings of Molly's mind reveal a strange discrepancy. On the one hand, she is completely incapable of considering topics other than sexuality in elaborate detail; her mind associates things vaguely, without troubling over accuracy and logical development. On the other hand, her memory shows a surprising obsession with details when it considers sexual matters, such as the exact positions and techniques in episodes of love-making (e.g., Joyce 1961b, 739, 742, 753, 754), exactly how long her orgasms lasted (Joyce 1961b, 754), how often her partners came (Joyce 1961b, 742), and her lovers' phrases (Joyce 1961b, 742, 758, 782), presents (Joyce 1961b, 742, 758), and compliments (Joyce 1961b, 753, 755). Inaccuracy, disconnectedness, vague associations, and indolence characterize Molly's mind only when she deals with nonsexual matters; it is capable of accuracy, persistency, and even logic when it focuses on sexual matters. In Weininger's concept of "woman's essence" as well, woman's general lack of an intelligible ego goes hand in hand with her specific obsession with sexuality.

Finally, Molly's prevailing use of the pronoun "he" causes confusion over the individual identities of her lovers, if not their total relativization, in the minds of both readers and Molly (cf. the very end of *Ulysses*, where Molly confuses Bloom on Howth with Mulvey on Gibraltar, and her statement "and I thought well as well him as another" [Joyce 1961b, 783].[8] It is thus exclusively Molly's reexperiences of past and anticipation of future sexual intimacies that form the subject of "Penelope." Her indifference about the individuality of her lovers as well as her preoccupation with sexuality shifts the focus from a character's personal attitudes toward sexuality to Molly as the embodiment of sexuality. Molly *is* sexuality.

IS MOLLY A WEININGERIAN WOMAN? READING *SEX AND CHARACTER* "THROUGH PENELOPE"

The preceding presentation of Weininger's concept of femininity/woman makes it quite easy to identify Molly as a literary embodiment of the Weiningerian woman. Moreover, some of Weininger's pronouncements on women, such as "The female is soulless and possesses neither ego nor individuality" (Weininger 1906a, 207) and "Man is form, woman is matter" (Weininger 1906a, 293), are echoed in Molly: "he says your soul you have no soul inside only grey matter" (Joyce 1961b, 742).[9] Weininger's equation of the "female" with flowers also turns up at the end of "Penelope": "he said I was a flower of the mountain yes so we are flowers all a woman's body yes" (Joyce 1961b, 732; cf. Joyce 1961b, 783).

An accumulation of Weininger's roster of female characteristics appears at the very end of "Penelope," culminating in Molly's famous experience of sexual union, which Weininger defined as "the supremest moment in a woman's life" (Weininger 1906a, 296): "and first I put my arms around him yes and drew him down to me so he could feel my breasts all perfume" (Joyce 1961b, 783).

It seems, then, that what Weininger pseudotheoretically[10] isolated as feminine characteristics served Joyce in his construction of Molly's identity in *Ulysses*. Both Weininger and Joyce reduce the feminine to sexuality; both characterize a woman's (a female character's) mind and memory in the same way; and, both mystify a woman's (a female character's) identity as sexuality. Indeed, Molly's sexuality and consciousness overlap so completely with those of the Weiningerian woman that she provides an instance *par excellence* of literary Weininger reception.

However, if we recall Weininger's attitude toward woman's essence, then we must also recognize that "Penelope" diverges considerably in spirit from the Weininger text.

Weininger feared the "female" principle in general and pitied women, who were *per definitonem* damned to embody it. He feared the fluent, irrational, chaotic "female" principle that could at any time take an active part in men and thus endanger, even preclude, any further "true"— in the Weiningerian sense—cultural achievements. He pitied, even detested, women's all-sexual identity because it kept them forever the object of male desire. Finally, since Weininger saw women as, after all, human beings, their inevitable object status meant the most horrible degradation of the idea of humanity, and it was the ultimate responsibility of moral men to liberate themselves and women from the shackles of human sexuality (cf. Chapter XII, "The Nature of Woman and Her Significance in the Universe" and especially Chapter XIV, "Woman and Mankind," in *Sex and Character*).

In "Penelope" Molly's identity is presented as neither a dangerous force nor a degrading state of being. Rather, Molly's reiterated "yes" functions as a joyous affirmation of her sexual identity.

This sexual identity is powerfully mystified at the very end of *Ulysses*. In the final pages of "Penelope," the text quickly moves from romantic scenes, picturing the sea and mountains and Andalusian girls, and Molly as flower (yet undeflowered) to her final dissolution into an embrace with Mulvey, whom she confuses with Bloom. *Ulysses* ends with Molly's ecstatic absorption in sexual union.

The circle closes. Molly is left at the beginning of all the sexual intimacies that await her.

In the context of *Ulysses*, the circularity implied at its end makes female sexuality the end to and perhaps even the source of all male endeavor and achievement. In this respect, feminine sexuality in Joyce's *Ulysses* achieves the (Goethean) status of a muselike force that enhances patriarchal dominance.

Joyce's powerful mystification of feminine sexuality at the end of *Ulysses*, his stylization of it as a (male) life-affirming, life-inspiring force—as powerful as nature (Molly as flower)[11]—presents a view of the status of feminine identity that is diametrically opposed to that of Weininger.[12] So in this respect, "Penelope" diverges sharply from *Sex and Character* in light of Weininger's radical moral agenda. However, "Penelope" does not break through the representational conventions of patriarchal tradition precisely because Molly is yet another reductionist (Molly's purely sexual identity) and misogynous (Molly's incapacity for logical thinking) image of femininity. It is this representational convention in which the author of *Sex and Character* and the author of *Ulysses* have—independently of one another—an equal share.

17 ✦

SVEVO AND WEININGER (LORD MORTON'S MARE)

Alberto Cavaglion

Translated from the Italian
by Nancy A. Harrowitz

A few pages from the conclusion of the chapter "The Wife and the Mistress" in his most important novel, *The Confessions of Zeno* [*La coscienza di Zeno*], Italo Svevo lets slip one of those scientific quotations in describing Zeno's last goodbye to Carla that occur frequently. At this point in the story, the adultery has ended darkly with the return of the hero to the family nest. Carla is happily engaged to a musician and is content in the thought that her lover has finally decided to alleviate the sadness of his wife. In the past, Zeno had been careful not to correct misunderstandings. Not even now, during this pathetic ceremony of farewells, does he find the strength to explain to Carla that the woman with whom he shares an already exhausted conjugal life is not the beautiful Ada, whom Carla assumed to be the wife, but her sister Augusta, with her "crossed" eye and her figure of a "healthy nurse." Trembling with desire, Zeno abandons himself to a "babbling without sense." The scene is among the most exhilarating in the novel. The protagonist confesses to still being in love with Carla, notwithstanding everything: he claims his male prerogative ("she didn't know how much mine she was and it was as if she no longer had the right to take care of herself"). Then he adds to himself, in a rather elliptical manner: "In my head the scientific proof of what I want to say was rumbling around, in other words, Darwin's famous experiment on the Arabian mare. But thank heavens I'm almost sure I never said anything about it" (Svevo 1986, 270).

Now let's take a look at the Darwinian experiment that Zeno finds it convenient to keep on the tip of his tongue (but would he really have been capable of keeping quiet?). To which work of Charles Darwin's is it necessary to turn? The answer is found in *The Variation of Animals and Plants under Domestication* (1868), where Darwin chronicles the misadventures of an Arabian mare. One must, however, pay careful attention to avoid falling in a trap. Svevo is creating a smokescreen here to confound us and to impede us from arriving at his real source of inspiration, for only with great difficulty could *The Variation of Animals and Plants Under Domestication* have been the book he had in mind. Here, as in many other situations in *The Confessions of Zeno*, the critic must patiently surrender and submit to the capricious tricks of a writer who likes to put a spoke in somebody's wheel.

One must therefore proceed with caution; first it is necessary to report exactly what Darwin wrote:

> In the case often quoted from Lord Morton, a nearly purely-bred Arabian chestnut mare bore a hybrid to a quagga; she was subsequently sent to Sir Gore Ouseley, and produced two colts by a black Arabian horse. These colts were partially dun-colored, and were striped on the legs more plainly than the real hybrid, or even than the quagga. One of the two colts had its neck and some other parts of its body plainly marked with stripes. Stripes on the body, not to mention those on the legs, are extremely rare—I speak after having long attended to the subject,—with horses of all kinds in Europe, and are almost unknown in the case of Arabians. But what makes the case still more striking is that in these colts the hair of the mane resembled that of the quagga, being short, still and upright. Hence there can be no doubt that the quagga affected the character of the offspring subsequently begot by the black Arabian horse (Darwin 1896, 435).[1]

The reference in *The Confessions of Zeno* is not necessarily clearer in the light of this citation. If Zeno had listed the genetic laws of Lord Morton to Carla, or rather if he had delineated the hypothesis of "telegony" (procreation from a distance), as Darwin defines it a little farther on in his own text, his ties to the loved woman would have become indissoluble and irreversible. So authoritatively endorsed, the supremacy of Man would have been clear: in the children that Carla would have legitimately borne in the future, at least a few exterior characteristics of her former lover (Zeno) would have been manifested. Those children would have had signs in some way comparable to the stripes noted by Lord Morton and recorded by Darwin. A sign of guilt, one could say. It is legitimate to suppose that Zeno was thinking more of psychological traits, or better yet neurotic ones, that of plain and simple stripes.

Thus Zeno would be impersonating the male quagga, the unaware musician Vittorio Lali, Carla's fiancé, would be playing the part of the Arabian stallion, and the seductive Carla, as in an incantation, would be transformed into a chestnut mare. These would be the protagonists in an inopportune hippologic digression, in case Zeno had overcome his resistance and decided to express out loud that which was going through his mind during the memorable walk in the public gardens of Trieste.

What makes us most suspicious, however, is the heavily misogynist tone that the episode, thus clarified, comes to assume. Was Svevo really such a scrupulous student of Darwin's work? My impression is that the presence here of the first modern evolutionist is a little overestimated. One can add that, contrary to what many commentators have written, in *The Variations* and in the *Origin of the Species* Darwin tells the story of Lord Morton's mare in an accidental fashion. It is with circumspection and also with a little diffidence that a serious scientist like Darwin reports the data in his possession.[2] He had no intention of betting on the Arabian mare the same exact amount of cultural energy that Otto Weininger, in *Sex and Character*, wanted to place. Here we face the definitive solution to the enigma and are sure of having found Svevo's primary source.

"Maternity and Prostitution" is without a doubt the chapter in *Sex and Character* that was the most read and commented upon by Svevo, who, in another part of *The Confessions of Zeno*, speaks of nothing less than Weininger's "genial theories." "Paternity," writes Weininger, "is a miserable deception; for it always must be shared with an infinite number of things and men. . . . White women who have had a child with a Negro later often bear children to a white man, yet the children manifest unmistakable characteristics of the Negro race. Flowers that have been pollinated with one type of pollen often, after many subsequent pollinations of different types, bear fruit that resembles the species with whose pollen they were once commissioned" (Weininger 1903, 307). At the end of this delirious, drunken telegony, enraptured before such a multicolored array of gynecological strangenesses, Weininger cites of course the case of Lord Morton's mare, which, "after having borne once the quagga's bastard, had much later two colts by an Arabian stallion, who bore evident signs of the quagga" (Weininger 1903, 307).

In the Braumüller edition of *Sex and Character*, almost certainly the one that Svevo owned, Lord Morton's entire report to the Royal Society, which Darwin cites only in passing, is published. Weininger also furnishes a little telegonic bibliography (for example, he mentions Augustus Weismann, the late nineteenth-century theorist of telegony, among others). It is thus legitimate to fantasize about the state of excitement with which Svevo immersed himself in reading the report, which must be recognized as the most authentic point of contact between Svevo and Weininger. This document is reproduced here almost in its entirety:

My Dear Sir,

I yesterday had an opportunity of observing a singular fact in Natural History, which you may perhaps deem not unworthy of being communicated to the Royal Society.

Some years ago, I was desirous of trying the experiment of domesticating the Quagga, and endeavoured to procure some individuals of that species. I obtained a male; but being disappointed of a female, I tried to breed from the male quagga and a young chestnut mare of seven-eighths Arabian blood, and which had never been bred from: the result was the production of a female hybrid, now five years old, and bearing, both in her form and in her colour, very decided indications of her mixed origin. I subsequently parted with the seven-eighths Arabian mare to Sir Gore Ousley, who has bred from her by a very fine black Arabian horse. I yesterday morning examined the produce, namely, a two-years old filly, and a year-old colt. They have the character of the Arabian breed as decidedy as can be expected, where fifteen-sixteenths of the blood are Arabian; and they are fine specimens of that breed; but both in their color, and in the hair of their manes, they have striking resemblance to the quagga. Their colour is bay, marked more or less like the quagga in a darker tint. Both are distinguished by the dark line along the ridge of the back, the dark stripes across the fore-hand, and the dark bar across the back part of the legs. The stripes across the fore-hand of the colt are confined to the withers, and to the part of the neck next to them; those on the filly cover nearly the whole of the neck and the back, as far as the flanks. The colour of her coat on the neck adjoining to the mane is pale, and approaching to dun, rendering the stripes there more conspicuous than those on the colt. The same pale tint appears in a less degree on the rump; and in this circumstance of the dun tint she also resembles the quagga. . . . These circumstances may appear singular; but I think you will agree with me, that they are trifles compared with the extraordinary fact of so many striking features, which do not belong to the dam, being in two successive instances, communicated through her to the progeny, not only of another sire, who also has them not, but of a sire belonging probably to another species; for such we have very strong reason for supposing the quagga to be.

I am, my dear Sir,
Your faithful humble servant,

Morton.   (Morton 1893, 20)

Be it in the form of a deliberately masked allusion, the spirit of Lord Morton is raised in *The Confessions of Zeno*. For love of completeness, I must specify that ideally Zeno and Carla's walk in the public garden has to be linked to the earlier walk of Zeno and Guido Speier, for it was then that Zeno evoked Weininger's work in clear terms and without word plays: "I held onto those theories and I perfected them with the reading of Weininger."[3] Although it is still claimed that this is the crucial moment of Svevo's encounter with Weininger, we now know that this is only a prelude to an even more grotesque comedy that culminates in the courting scene with Carla. Thus ends the career of Zeno Cosini the libertine. It is in this sense that the theories of Weininger can constitute "a comfortable companion."

It is often noted today that old age and illness are two essential components of Svevian poetics; both have already been sufficiently appraised by critics. The case of Weininger, however, demonstrates that the tie between science and literature should be deepened. A tortured relationship made up of attraction and repulsion, it is increasingly difficult to understand the more it emerges and the more one succeeds in unmasking narrative exponents like the one of Lord Morton. One thing must be said immediately to avoid misunderstandings: it is useless to hope that some new avant-garde scientist or some great innovator will jump from the pages of Svevo. Svevo's discovery of Freud is important because of its uniqueness in a text bristling with obsolete references: Darwin in his most vulgate and tired form, chemistry in its most spectacular phenomenon explained through the tractate of Wilhelm Ostwald, the electrophysiology of Johannes von Müller and Ernst Brücke. When Svevo finds himself in the position of mentioning a scientific tractate, he more willingly leans on a text that is not strictly orthodox—in other words, a text like *Sex and Character*.

The figure of Otto Weininger harmoniously inserts itself in *The Confessions of Zeno* in an accumulation of citations, just as Lord Morton's mare finds its place in the rather craftsmanlike stable where tools and medicines of various types, such as the salts of Karlsbad (purgative energies adapted by Zeno in the last part of the novel) and vesicant pomades, coexist. Rather than scientificity, it is a maniacal curiosity for the teratological aspects of nature and of science that is displayed here. Svevo has an impertinent vocation for paradoxes and adores clashing approaches. It is within such a context that his encounter with Weininger and thus with Lord Morton's mare occurs. The political and philosophical interests found in the first Italian Weiningerians, such as Giuseppe Prezzolini and the critics from *La Voce*, are not found in Svevo. Even Scipio Slapater, who, like Svevo, is from Trieste, submits to the fascination of *Sex and Character*, which becomes a way for him to get away from the provinces, to "Italianize" himself, by getting rid of the image of the "dilettante Sigfrid." None of this interested Svevo, just as he lacked interest in the self-destructive aspect of Weininger's thought, that feeling of Jewish self-hatred that was to have so much success in the twentieth century in Italy, not just in Trieste. It was Umberto Saba who suffered from that self-hatred in Trieste at about the same time, not the ironic and distracted Svevo, despite the otherwise lucid analysis of Svevo written by one of his most attentive critics, Giacomo Debenedetti, whose own relationship to Judaism was tormented and Weiningerian (Debenedetti 1929).

Without a doubt, as time goes on, Svevo's work slowly assumes the shape of a magic wonderland, a continent still to be explored. Weininger certainly is a part of this continent, but he is defrauded of his polemical and cutting weapons. This Svevian Weininger is a tamed one, made more sympathetic and innocuous. The literary critic alone cannot explore this unknown continent. A collaboration with a biologist, an ethologist, a zoologist, an officer of the cavalry, besides of course a psychoanalyst, becomes necessary. Rather than the marriage of philosophy to art, it is the marriage of science to literature that "produces beautiful children," according to the formula devised by Svevo that now, after the episode with Carla has been clarified, becomes more comprehensible. One of the most fascinating aspects of this Ariostesque wonderland that is *The Confessions of Zeno* is the presentation of minor characters, be they pureblood Arabs or nonexistent Cerusians. One thing is certain: Svevo's novel almost always has to do with a fairytale itinerary through the relics of European positivist culture.

Already undermined by the Mendelian revolution (and today by modern hematic testing, used by juvenile courts to determine paternity), at the end of the twentieth century the prosopopoeia of Lord Morton seems to be a really good case of gynecological archeology or, better yet, a Dickensian humorous artifice. In an age in which people discuss and divide in factions over genetic engineering and that other genre of "procreation from a distance," in vitro fertilization, the distance that separates us from the mentality of the Royal Society and from Weininger is ideologically abysmal but literarily still perceptible and functional. The notion of procreation from a distance was a rather diffused *topos* in early twentieth-century Italian literature. For example, in his novella "Un consulto legale" (A Legal Consultation), published in 1903, Luigi Capuana wrote:

> There is the question of children introduced surreptitiously, as we lawyers say, into the family. The situation is dubious. I know from physiologists who claim to have discovered a great artifice of nature to impede this inconvenience. According to them, a woman is fertilized, once for life, by the first man who possesses her. In this case, there are no adulterine children possible. The children of the second husband belong, physiologically, to the first. . . . The wisdom of nature is infinite; it seems that she has taken the most solid preoccupations against the malevolence of individuals. In this case, what can the husbands complain about? They are reassured in advance. It happens, to use legal language, that there is a turbulent moment of possession; really nothing (Capuana 1903, 129).[4]

It is difficult if not impossible to demonstrate that Capuana was struck by the ideas of Weininger (who died a suicide in that same year, 1903). But the fact remains that the experiment of Lord Morton circulated in the culture of the time and reaped quite a few victims.

We are left with a few perplexities, a few questions of different kinds. One would first like to satisfy curiosity and finally arrange for an illustrated edition of *The Confessions of Zeno,* useful today more than ever—perhaps even more than the many annotated editions that are coming out. What did a quagga really look like? What kind of stripes did it have? Could one relate it to a striped hippogriff, or would it be easier to imagine it as an ideal model for a veterinary atlas? And finally, how does one imagine the "Isabellian" colts born to the coupling of Carla with her fiancé? In the hypothetical "fourth novel" of Svevo, which has remained dispersed among thousands of pages of notes, what space could one of these "Isabellians" have had? Could it have been something similar to a classic character from serial novels: the Secret Son? It is not surprising that in all this confusion *Sex and Character* functions like a cornucopia: it is part of the Italian rules of the game imposed by the kaleidoscopic fortune of its ambiguous philosopher.

The last issue we would like to raise is a subject of real concern. Many years after the publication of *The Confessions of Zeno*, other readers of Darwin and Weininger will demonstrate that they do not have the self-control that Zeno shows in his encounter with Carla. With fateful results, many pseudoscientists of the 1930s will abandon themselves to certain nonmetaphorical excursions into the "polluted" gardens of eugenics and racial doctrines. And there Svevian irony becomes only a nice memory.

18 ◆

WHORES, MOTHERS, AND OTHERS: RECEPTION OF OTTO WEININGER'S *SEX AND CHARACTER* IN ELIAS CANETTI'S *AUTO-DA-FÉ*

Kristie A. Foell

Otto Weininger's wide-ranging influence on many of the leading minds of his time is well established, yet his impact extended decades after his death (cf. Le Rider 1982, 1985; Janik 1985; Wagner 1981, 152–166), as Elias Canetti's 1931 novel, *Auto-da-Fé* (*Die Blendung*), clearly shows (Pöder 1984, 1985).[1] Canetti knew Weininger's work well when he began his novel; in the canon of works read by Canetti and his friends as teenagers, Weininger ranks with Arthur Schopenhauer and Karl Kraus, who was Canetti's personal idol in his youth and who had supported Weininger from the beginning (cf. Le Rider 1985, 147–61; Stieg 1983). Canetti records that Weininger was considered "high literature," and that he and his friends committed parts of Weininger's *Sex and Character* (Geschlecht und Charakter) to memory—especially the misogynistic passages (Canetti 1978b, 90, 136). Yet Canetti repeatedly asserts that he is not a misogynist and has recently shown himself reluctant to be associated with Weininger.[2] The question, then, is not whether Canetti was influenced by Weininger, but how he was influenced, particularly whether his reception of Weininger was unquestioning or critical. In the following analysis of Canetti's *Auto-da-Fé*, I will summarize the role played by Weiningerian idealization in the protagonist Kien's "courtship" of his maid Therese, and ask whether the portrayal of Therese can be read as Canetti's critical response to Weininger's concept of Woman ("*W*"), based on some of the satirical techniques employed in the novel.

DECEIVER AND DECEIVED: BLIND IDEALIZATION OF THE NEGATIVE WOMAN

In Weininger's exclusively negative view of women, all idealizations of women are simply male projections, and he speculates about why men are reluctant to surrender their falsely idealized views of women (Weininger 1903, 298). Weininger refers to the worship of the Madonna (*Madonnenkult*) as follows:

> Therein lies such a projection of all the values that transcend the temporal limitations of the individual onto a woman, who is in herself entirely worthless, that one can scarcely bear to unveil the true nature of this process .... One would rather swear on the feminine sense of "shame," rhapsodize on feminine "pity," interpret the young chit's downcast eyes as an eminently moral phenomenon, than surrender along with these lies the possibility of using the woman as a means to the ends of one's own higher strivings (Weininger 1906, 249; my translation).[3]

Essential to Weininger's view is the assumption that women have no positive traits that might lead to male idealization. In *Auto-da-Fé*, the housekeeper Therese illustrates this principle: she swindles her way into marriage with her employer, the reclusive Sinologist Peter Kien, and is partially responsible for his development into a full-fledged misogynist. Ignorant, greedy, deformed, promiscuous (at least in her thoughts), treacherous, and violent toward Kien, Therese is a paradigm of negativity. Kien initially attributes Therese's character and behavior to her social status as housekeeper, consigning her to the category of the illiterate and unrefined (Canetti 1978a, 37; 1985a, 35). After elevating Therese to his own class by marrying her, however, Kien can no longer criticize her on these grounds. Instead, he begins to view her primarily as a representative of her gender rather than of her social class. In Kien's mind, as well as in the thematic structure of the novel, she comes to stand for Woman in general; he concludes that all women must be like her.

Canetti's characterization of Therese draws heavily on the schematization of femininity laid out by Weininger, for as Pöder has briefly noted, "the presence of the Weiningerian idea of femininity could be demonstrated with the example of the figure Therese as completely as [the Weiningerian idea of masculinity] with the example of the figure Kien; Weiningerian criteria of femininity are apparent in Therese's sexual arousal and gliding movements, characteristics Canetti uses as Leitmotifs, as well as in Therese's unarticulated, associative speech" (Pöder 1985, 70).[4]

Of the two types into which Weininger divides "*W*"—mothers and whores—Therese has most in common with the whore. Therese's correspondence to "*W*"-as-whore is reflected in her undiscriminating and insatiable sexual cravings. Weininger writes: "Both types [the mother and the whore] are actually indifferent to the individuality of the sexual complement. The one takes any Tom, Dick or Harry who serves her as a means to a child . . . the other is ready to yield herself to any man who stimulates her erotic desires" (Weininger 1906, 220).[5] Therese's goal is clearly the latter, erotic enjoyment, the goal of the whore. It is certainly not the mother's goal of procreation, as indicated in the scene on the tram in which she declares "children last" (with a meaningful glance at her husband) (Canetti 1978a, 51; 1985a, 50). In keeping with the Weiningerian model, her pursuit of erotic pleasure is indiscriminate: she sets her sights first on tall, bony, slit-mouthed Kien; then, disappointed by his failure to consummate the marriage, she attempts to use his money to ensnare a slippery eel of a furniture salesman; finally, she submits to the attentions of the muscular but brutal caretaker of Kien's apartment building, who has already beaten his wife and daughter to death. For the reader who fails to make the connection to Weininger's whore, Kien himself makes it explicit by equating her with the prostitute "wife" of the pimp, Fischerle's (Canetti 1978a, 185–86; 1985a, 202).

While on the one hand corresponding to what Weininger calls the "constitutional untruthfulness of women," the ruse Therese uses to trap Kien into marriage is especially evocative of the Weiningerian whore (Weininger 1906, 264; my translation).[6] Weininger asserts that the whore only feigns love toward a child because the man finds this behavior appealing: "Even when she is still a child, children are a torment to the absolute whore; later she at most uses the child as a means to enact an illusory idyll between mother and child, which is calculated to tug at the heartstrings of the man and lure him into her net" (Weininger 1906, 219–20; my translation).[7]

Therese adopts exactly such an "idyllic" posture in order to lure Kien—except that she feigns love for a book rather than a child, since books are what is most important to Kien. When he lends Therese the oldest, most dog-eared volume in his library, she carefully wraps the book in two separate covers, "as though she were dressing a child." Kien is duly impressed. In a later scene, Therese's supposed unselfishness and *caritas* inspire religious feelings in Kien: "She had compassion, not for men (there was nothing in that) but for books. The weary and heavy-laden could come to her. The meanest, the most forsaken and forgotten creature on the face of God's earth, she would take to her heart. Kien left the kitchen in the deepest perturbation. Not one word more did he say to the saint" (Canetti 1978a, 46).[8] But the narrator clearly indicates that Therese is acting for Kien's benefit (Canetti 1978a, 48; 1985a, 47). Kien the scholar, who prides himself on his intelligence and knowledge, is deceived by a simple contrivance; Therese is a charlatan whom he falsely idealizes.

Kien maintains this hyperidealized view of Therese on their wedding night. Assuming that the fifty-eight-year-old Therese fits his stereotypical notion of a newlywed woman—innocent, afraid of sex, and in need of guidance from her husband—Kien takes great pains to pile his divan with books so as to lure the "book-lover" Therese to the bed. When she strides into the room, undresses, and sweeps his beloved books off the bed, Kien is distraught: "A terrible hatred swelled up slowly within him. This she had dared. The books! . . . Kien plunged out of the room in long strides, bolted himself into the lavatory . . . automatically let his trousers down, took his place on the seat and cried like a child" (Canetti 1978a, 59).[9]

The Freudian overtones of the foregoing scene, which begins in the bedroom and ends on the toilet, are obvious. But Kien's emotional distress also stems from the shaking of what he thought were fundamental truths about women. His idealization of Therese is, as Weininger says, part of his need to functionalize her in the service of his higher ideals (represented by his library). The reader understands his true motivations when he exclaims: "I will marry her! She is the heaven-sent instrument for preserving my library" (Canetti 1978a, 47).[10] If the "whore" Therese uses books as a means to gain the man, Kien uses the woman as a means to maintain his books. This is exactly the type of functionalization of the other against which Weininger, read in the most positive light, sought to warn. Kien's disillusionment could be the first step in the process of freeing the human race from sexual divisions and exploitation, which Weininger ultimately hopes to achieve with his book. But Kien is not equal to this challenge; he does not fulfill the high expectations Weininger sets for the male.

SATIRE AND EMPATHY

Not only is Kien unequal to the ideals Weininger holds for men, but he may be read as an indictment of the very masculine ("M") ideal Weininger proposes. While Weininger's "M" is clearly satirized in Kien, it is harder to determine whether the satire of Therese serves to distance the author of *Auto-da-Fé* from Weininger or to confirm Weininger's ideas. I will discuss three methods of satire used in *Auto-da-Fé:* exaggeration, the hypocrisy standard (Kernan's "dullness"), and a demonstration of the theory of socially determined behavior that Weininger sought to deny.

In Elfriede Pöder's interpretation, Canetti discredits "M" through satirical exaggeration. She perceptively enumerates the ways in which Kien either falls short of or exaggerates Weininger's claims for the male, and concludes that "by taking Weininger literally, Canetti drives his masculine ideal to an absurd extreme" (Pöder 1985, 68). In another example of exaggeration, Weininger's claim that "M" possesses an unchanging ego identity (Weininger 1906, 158; 1903, 204–5) is ridiculed when Kien turns himself to stone as a defense against Therese, sitting immobile in front of his desk all day long (Canetti 1978a, 154–66; 1985a, 165–78). He thus abandons the very scholarly work that had formed the basis of the identity he attempts to solidify and protect. By exaggerating Kien's (and Weininger's) ideal of masculine character to the point of absurdity, Canetti calls the very desirability of the Weiningerian ideal into question.

Are the same satirical methods applied to Weininger's "*M*" through Kien—exaggeration and exposure of shortcomings—brought to bear on "*W*" through Therese? Therese is certainly an exaggeration of "*W*"; her drooling salaciousness when she is finally seduced by Benedikt Pfaff, for example, seems a literalistic grotesque of Weininger's statement that the whore "slurps up pleasure to the last drop."[11] However, since Weininger does not endow "*W*" with any positive qualities, it is questionable whether this approach is as subversive as in Kien's case. Since Weininger maintains that the "absolute woman" has no identity, no existence to begin with, Therese has no ideal to frustrate, and an exaggeration of "*W*" would be like squaring the quantity zero (cf. Weininger 1906, 186, 207, 286; 1903, 240, 269, 383). The satirical method of exaggeration, if used to take an already negative view to an extreme (as opposed to exposing a positive view as questionable by means of the extreme), poses the danger that the extreme will be seen as reality. The *reductio ad absurdum* cannot be a means of satire when the object of satire (here Weininger's "*W*") is itself an absurd exaggeration.[12]

In his classic work on satire, Alvin Kernan writes that "the point of these attacks is not that man is 'a carnivorous production,' but that he tries so ridiculously to pretend that he is not. . . . This compulsive hypocrisy is the most evident quality of the world which satire constructs, and the first activity of the satirist is exposing it" (Kernan 1965, 204). Applying this attitude to Therese, we may conclude that she is satirized not because she is ugly, but because she thinks herself beautiful; not because of her indiscriminate sexual appetite, but because she continues to portray herself as a "virtuous" woman; not because she is stupid and uneducated, but because she reveals, in her railing against the fact that others "don't learn anything," that she considers herself more intelligent or educated than others (Canetti 1978a, 37; 1985a, 35).

Canetti's observations on Alma Mahler-Werfel, widow of the composer, at their first meeting in 1933, recorded in his *Play of the Eyes*, make his application of the hypocrisy standard explicit: "After one look at her I was aghast; everyone talked of her beauty; the story was that she had been the most beautiful girl in Vienna and had so impressed Mahler, much older than herself, that he had courted her and taken her for his wife. The legend of her beauty had endured for over thirty years. And now she stood there, now she sat heavily down, a slightly tipsy woman, looking much older than her age" (Canetti 1985b, 59–60; my translation).

The phrase "sat heavily down" hints at the heavy thighs, spreading hips and waistline, loss of agility, and graceless movements of someone whose body can no longer carry out every movement it may be asked to perform. Canetti is shocked at the contrast between rumor and reality caused by the passing of time, but his comment could still be read sympathetically were it not for the fact that Alma herself seems completely unaware of her own aging.

As her first "trophy," the score of Gustav Mahler's Tenth Symphony, opened to the inscriptions to "Almschi," is pointed out to Canetti lying in its glass case, Canetti writes: "I read these words in the handwriting of a dying man and looked at the woman to whom they had been addressed. Twenty-three years later, she took them as if they were meant for her now. . . . She was so sure of the effect of his writing in the score that the vapid smile on her face expanded into a grin" (Canetti 1986, 52; 1985b, 60).

With the mention of her grin, the picture of Alma blends into Canetti's description of Therese, and one wonders whether his negative reaction to the real woman, Alma, was partly predicated on her external resemblance to the woman he had recently created in *Auto-da-Fé*. It is even possible that Alma herself was one of the models for Therese; at least one contemporary was fond of pointing out the similarities between Alma and Weininger's "W" (Berg 1987, 243).[13] Yet this passage also reveals that what Canetti is most critical of in Alma, as in Therese, is the self-deception of a fat, haggard old woman who seems to think she is still the belle of the ball. According to Kernan, such self-deception is what makes the object of satire deserve satirical treatment: the failure to perceive the contrast between one's self-image and reality is a form of stupidity or dullness, a bubble that always deserves to be burst. This method of satire applied to women, however, is in keeping with Weininger, who also aims to point out the discrepancy between positive views of womanhood and what he perceives as a negative reality.

In its effort to show clear-cut good and evil, the satirical stance is often reductive; Canetti's discussion of Alma Mahler allows this stance to infiltrate a genre (autobiography) that is not usually satirical. This is perhaps unfair to Alma, who records that it was Gustav Mahler himself who tyranically cut off whatever artistic potential she might have had by forbidding her to compose, thus effectively relegating her to the domestic sphere and to the vicarious enjoyment of men's accomplishments (Mahler 1973, 22–23).[14] Alma's account shows her concrete reason for reducing her own worth to the "merely" physical and sexual: she is not incapable of creating (as Weininger would have it), but forbidden to do so. What Canetti refers to as Alma's "trophies," then, could be seen instead as her only outlet for recognition, rather than as a kind of threatening female vampirism.

While Canetti is either unaware of, or chooses to omit from his account, anything that would mitigate or explain Alma Mahler's personality and behavior, he does paint Therese in some depth through her internal monologues. In so doing, he moves to a more complex plane of satire, what Northrop Frye defines as its fourth phase—the "ironic aspect of tragedy"—which "looks at tragedy from below, from the moral and realistic perspective of the state of experience," and "supplies social and psychological explanations for catastrophe" (Frye 1957, 237). Weininger denies economic and social influences on gender differences, insisting that these differences, and particularly the inclination to prostitution, are innate and biologically determined. Weininger argues that the "limited fertility" of prostitutes proves the biological/deterministic origins of prostitution in the nature of women and makes it unnecessary even to consider the role of social conditions, which he summarizes as "the poverty of women and the economic stress of a society arranged by males, . . . the difficulty of women succeeding in a respectable career, or . . . the existence of a large bachelor class with the consequent demand for a system of prostitution" (Weininger 1906, 216).[15] Canetti, by contrast, graphically illustrates the ways in which both "whores" and "respectable" women are exploited by men. It is Therese herself who notes that she is more exploited in her new position as the lady of the household (*"Frau im Haus"*) than she was in her earlier "lowly" position as housekeeper, which at least guaranteed her an income (Canetti 1978a, 74–79; 1985a, 76–80). As unpalatable as Therese may be, her dependence on Kien's bank account even after their marriage, the necessity of her conniving and wheedling every penny out of him, is a realistic portrayal of the situation of many married women in this period.[16] The inclusion of this perspective is in itself an argument against Weininger's essentialism.

Canetti's insight into the forces motivating Therese goes beyond the merely economic. In an inner monologue, Therese's associative thought processes lead her to remember what may be a rape scene involving her stepfather:

> He wanted me, too, but I didn't fancy him. I only humored him to annoy the old woman. Everything for my children, she used to say. She looked a picture that time she came home from work and found her man with her daughter! Nothing had happened yet. The butcher tried to jump out of bed. I grabbed tight hold of him, so he couldn't get away until the old woman came right in and up to the bed. She did take on! Hunted him out of the room with her bare hands. She hugged hold of me, howled and tried to kiss me. But I didn't care for that and scratched her.
>
> "No better than a step-mother, that's what you are!" I screamed. To her dying day she thought he'd done me wrong. He never did. I'm a respectable woman and never had anything to do with men (Canetti 1978a, 57).[17]

Therese's childhood memory is neither corroborated nor denied by information supplied by the narrator. Instead, the reader has access to the same type of information a psychoanalyst might have: the subjective, affect-laden memories of the "patient." The manner in which Therese tells or recollects her story corresponds closely to what Freud, in the clinical background to his *Dora* essay, says can be expected of hysterics: "The connections—even the ostensible ones—are for the most part incoherent, and the sequence of different events is uncertain. Even during the course of their story patients will repeatedly correct a particular" (Freud 1963, 31; 1942a, 174). The central event itself is in doubt: at first reading, Therese seems to have been the victim of an attempted rape by her stepfather, from which her mother saved her. A second glance, however, reveals that Therese cooperated to some extent in order to annoy her apparent savior, her mother ("I only humored him to annoy the old woman"). If Therese's objective in going along with his attack is not to sleep with her (step)father but to annoy her mother, then the entire Electra complex, which Freud had such trouble with, is made subject to the same type of agonic motivations as the Oedipal struggle between father and son in which the mother is merely an item of barter. Here it is the father, his status reduced by a "step," who is the object of exchange between mother and daughter.

In this case, the struggle between mother and daughter is also that between mother and whore. Therese's mother appears to be a mother type after the Weiningerian model: "Everything for my children, she used to say." Therese derides her mother for this motherly solicitousness, yet the worst insult she can think of is to call her a stepmother, reproaching her with lack of concern for her children. In the Weiningerian model, a woman is concerned with one of two things: children or sexual pleasure. If the mother is not a real mother, then she must be more concerned with the man (as a means to pleasure) than with her children, thus making her a rival. Weininger comments specifically on the mother-daughter relationship: "The best test case [of the difference between whore and mother] is the relation to the daughter. It is only when there is no jealousy about her youth or greater beauty . . . but an identification of herself with her daughter so complete that she is as pleased about her child's admirers as if they were her own, that a woman has a claim to the title of perfect mother" (Weininger 1906, 219).[18] The whore type relies on the mother type to give way to her wishes; when Therese states, early in the book, that "you can't get along with women" (Canetti 1978a, 26),[19] she is essentially confirming the Weiningerian postulate that the mother in pure form does not exist (Weininger 1906, 219, 222; 1903, 287, 290). Every woman is a rival.

Because of the shifting narrative perspective in *Auto-da-Fé*, it is especially difficult to speak with any confidence of Canetti's intentions (cf. Pankau 1990, 147). If the one incident that offers a social or psychological explanation for Therese's negativity is true (within the world of the novel), then it offers a counterargument to Weininger. If it is not true, however, then Therese's memory may be seen as a Freudian *Wunschvorstellung,* or "fantasy," along the lines of the Electra complex. Therese's memory would then not be a real memory at all, but an event she wishes had happened and disguises as an unsuccessful rape in order to keep herself blameless. By making Therese, the apparent victim, the creator of the imagined attack (or an accomplice if it was real), such an interpretation would also follow in the footsteps of the by-now infamous *Dora* case, in which Freud assumes that Dora should have been sexually excited by Herr K's advances. Such a reading severely mitigates the power of this incident to explain Therese's Weiningerian negativity in accordance with Frye's fourth phase of satire. Whether the figure of Therese is a critique or an affirmation of Weininger thus remains open to debate.

VICTIMS AND HEROINES

Therese repeatedly states that she has not been raped, that she has never even slept with a man. Yet her actions seem to give the lie to her assertions, for she behaves as someone who has internalized the mentality of the victim and of the violence done to her: she both victimizes Kien (the episode in which she beats Kien up in bed, is a clear substitute for sexuality [Canetti 1978a, 143–53; 1985a, 153–64]) and allows herself to be victimized by Pfaff. Therese's final position as Pfaff's willing victim places her in relationship to another victim of Pfaff, one who has no choice.

Benedikt Pfaff's prehistory leaves no doubt that he abuses his wife and child, the former to the point of death: "Sometimes he had to wait a full five minutes for his food. Then his patience would break down and he would beat her even before he had finished eating. She died under his hands. But all the same she would certainly have pegged out of her own accord in the next few days. A murderer he was not" (Canetti 1978a, 368).[20] The story of Pfaff's wife's death and his abuse of his daughter are related as objective fact by a third-person narrator. Pfaff's perspective is integrated just enough to reveal his motivations, but not enough to convince the reader of the justness of his position. Although there is room for doubt in Anna's story as to the details of her sexual molestation—that is, whether the father actually has intercourse with her or "merely" derives sexual pleasure from beating her—the identity of perpetrator and victim in this family saga is hardly in doubt. Since the daughter has been trained in her father's rituals from earliest childhood,[21] there can be no question of her provoking the attacks or desiring them. The fact that Anna does not run away from her father cannot be seen as cooperation, since her father's strict control over both the family money and her experience with the outside world deprives her of the mental and material resources for escape. She can only hope pathetically for rescue from outside: the grocery clerk (Ritter Franz), whom she fancies as her knight in shining armor. When this source of help vanishes from the horizon, she rebels in the most courageous way available to her: she confronts and accuses her father, reclaiming her own name, and is beaten bloody as reward for her courage.

Although Anna's resistance changes nothing in her external situation, she may be said to have appropriated both the phallus and the *nom du père* at this point; more precisely, she has renounced them. The clearest phallic symbol in this narrative, the "love cigarette" (*Liebeszigarette*) given to Anna by her grocery clerk-knight, represents Anna's hope of gaining mastery over her situation *within the patriarchal order*, using one man (the lover) as defense against another (the father). It functions as a talisman for Anna, sustaining her hopes of rescue, at least until Franz blunders his attempt to steal the grocery's cash register. Although it is the father who disposes of the physical remains of the tattered cigarette while Anna lies unconscious, her hope in the phallus has disappeared before this point. Anna literally renounces the *nom du père* by taking back her own name, Anna, associated with the mother, and shedding the name "Poli" given to her by her father. Figuratively, Anna is no longer impressed by the trinity of authority her father represents: "himself as policeman, himself as husband, himself as father," representing the "father state" (*Vaterstaat*), God the Father (the church, which sanctions marriage), and the biological father (Canetti 1978a, 337).[22] Anna's renunciation of the patriarchal trinity shows a woman undertaking the task of emancipation of which Weininger considered only men to be capable. Weininger demands that the male withhold the phallus from the female, since she has neither the self-awareness nor the self-control to renounce it herself. Anna does, and Canetti's portrayal of her may be taken as a counterargument to Weininger.

Particularly in the story of Anna, and possibly in that of Therese as well, Canetti exposes the social origins in the patriarchy of what both Freud and Weininger took for attributes of an unchanging feminine constitution. *Auto-da-Fé*'s presentation of women does what Frye says a satire should do: it sets "ideas and generalizations and theories and dogmas over against the life they are supposed to explain" (Frye 1957, 230). In so doing, it shows women, their situations, and their motivations to be a good deal more varied and complex than Weininger's reduction of "*W*" to the principle of "pairing."

Of these two young female victims, Anna and Therese, Therese is the one who escapes—and lives. Yet she does not escape, since the cycle repeats itself in her identification with the aggressor, leading her to beat her husband, attempt to seduce other men, and allow herself to be abused. Therese's later actions toward Kien and other men may be seen in the light of what Alice Miller has called reactivity, the repetition of the role assumed by the traumatizer in a real childhood trauma (Miller 1984, 6, 12, 22–23). Anna, whose victimization externally appears to be total, since she dies as a result of her misuse, is actually the one who frees herself psychologically from the structure of oppression.

Perhaps the most deep-reaching similarity between Canetti's novel *Auto-da-Fé* and Weininger's thought is the valuation of death over life. Therese is the only one who experiences the traditional narrative "happy" ending: she is united with Pfaff, and both are set up as shopkeepers. It is the happiness of mediocrity, bought at the price of Therese and Pfaff spying on each other. Despite the absence of procreation, Therese's Astartean figure, her "will to live" (*Lebenstüchtigkeit*), and her interest in sex all qualify her as a symbol of the immoral principle of life in Weininger's sense (cf. Weininger 1906, 345–47; 1903, 457–59). By contrast, the moral figures in the book, those who have renounced—Kien, Anna, and others (such as the fishwife)—all meet with tragic ends. Kien's end is particularly ambivalent, both grand and insane, laughable and awe-inspiring, a fulfillment and a threat. It is an end after Weininger's own heart: a suicide, a choice to follow the pure (but possibly deluded) logic of books rather than join in the illogic of human life. Yet Kien's end is not a choice, and not pure, since it is the result of his growing paranoia, his emotions gone awry. As both a satire and a compelling realization of the Weiningerian call to purity, Kien's death is emblematic of the ambivalent presence of Otto Weininger in *Auto-da-Fé*.

19 ✦

MEMORY AND HISTORY: *THE SOUL OF A JEW* BY JEHOSHUA SOBOL

Freddie Rokem

The Soul of a Jew, subtitled *The Last Night of Otto Weininger*, by the Israeli playwright Jehoshua Sobol, premiered at the Haifa Municipal Theatre in Israel in October 1982 (Sobol 1982, n.d.).[1] This psychological historical play focuses on the internal struggle of Otto Weininger, the Jewish Viennese philosopher-outcast, during the night of his suicide in 1903. At the same time, it very clearly plays out the discussions concurrently going on in Israel, with its first performance less than half a year after the Israeli invasion of Lebanon in June 1982. The psychological anatomy of Weininger's Jewish soul in turn-of-the-century Vienna, as dramatized by Sobol, thus also reflects the contemporary Israeli soul at a time when the use of force and power no doubt overshadowed the traditionally accepted Jewish humanistic values. Sobol has based his analysis on Weininger's ideas about the psychological dichotomy between male/Aryan and female/Jewish in order to make a clear and critical statement about the complexity of the state of the contemporary Jewish/Israeli soul.

What characterizes Sobol as a playwright is that he, in the words of Aristotle, "takes real events as the subject of [his] poem." History, that is, real events, is the basis of his plays, but in order to be transformed into theater, these events must be artistically and theatrically narrated.[2] Otto Weininger, the central figure of *The Soul of a Jew*, is torn by ambivalent feelings arising from his fear of hostile, anti-Semitic surroundings on the one hand, and his wish to act with dignity and humanistic values on the other. Weininger's solution to his internal spiritual conflicts between budding Zionism, growing anti-Semitism, the eternal conflicts with his parents, and his wish to find his authentic sexual identity was suicide.

The play starts with the sound of a bullet in the dark, and what appears on the stage after that is an expressionistic exposé of what goes on in the mind of Otto Weininger during his last hours before death. During this time some of the more significant events from his own life supposedly return to him, and the play depicts these flashes of memory. Sobol's awareness of his technique is revealed in his stage direction defining the time of the play: "The real time of the play is the night between October

3 and October 4, 1903. The internal time (the duration) of the play is from
the early childhood of Otto until his suicide on the eve of October 4,
1903."[3] In the play these "memories" are arranged in such a way as to
recount Otto's spiritual history. By the time of the final scene, in which we
see the death of Otto Weininger in "real" time—not as an internal memory
realized on the stage as a flashback but as an external event—various
aspects of his short life have been presented and reviewed.

In compounding this scenic flashback from the actual life of Otto
Weininger, Sobol selected from amongst a large amount of historical
source material. I shall not analyze the relationship between the dramatic
script and these sources here, but it is important to emphasize that the
aesthetic principle that has guided Sobol in his treatment of them is that
history is translated into theater through the transformative power of the
memory of the individual hero. In fact, recollection itself is an important
aspect of his heroism. This is perhaps more clearly developed in the *Ghetto*
plays[4] than in the case of Otto Weininger, but in all of Sobol's plays
salvaging the past is perceived as an act of giving meaning to the present
and the future, even if this past is immersed in death and destruction.

Sobol places the dramatic action of his play and his fictional reconstruction of the historical Otto Weininger at the focal point of three central
forces or ideologies that originated in Austria at the turn of the century and
that in different ways have formed modern Jewish consciousness. The first
of these forces is psychoanalysis, which in the play is not only conceived as
Freud's notion of the introspective search of the soul—in this case the
Jewish soul—but also as the central organizing principle of Sobol's
retrospective narrative technique. The second is the strengthening of
anti-Semitism as an ideology and a political force, which is represented by
the mayor of Vienna, Karl Lueger. As we know from our post–World War II
perspective, this ideology led to the gas chambers of Lueger's compatriot,
the Führer of the Third Reich. The third force is the first buds of political
Zionism, which appeared as the utopian idea of enabling the Jewish
people to create their own history and as a means of saving the Jewish soul
from the threat of that extinction. Zionist ideas originated through the pen
of another Viennese, Theodor Herzl, and these ideas, as we also know,
were realized in the establishment of the state of Israel. It is thus the
"birth" of the Israeli Jewish soul in the crosscurrents between these forces
and their early "childhood" development that Sobol "analytically" constructs from our contemporary perspective.

Sobol, as in the three plays of his *Ghetto-triptych*, in *Palestinait,* and in
Solo, often presents a protagonist who through his own life and experiences focuses on a centrally "located" historical event or process that in
turn offers a critical analysis of the present-day social and political situation
in Israel. By remembering their own subjective past, Sobol's heroes

become representatives of a collective experience, and this creates a narrative in which the memories, the subjective experiences of an individual, is recapitulated (and theatrically relived) in the present and thereby transformed into a more objective historical version of the past. Several of Sobol's plays, with *The Soul of a Jew* being only one example, are based on the complex dialectical tensions between the "subjective" and "objective" dimensions of the past, not only from the point of view of the individual hero but also with regard to the terms of the narrative structures created by Sobol.

A personal subjective memory is the creative force that transforms objective history into a work of art. On the ideological level the adaptation of the historical material has been carried out by the playwright,[5] while on the level of plot as a fictional device the responsibility for the arrangement of the material has been passed on to the recollecting hero. The shot from Otto's pistol triggers a flash of memories that are the "stuff" from which the play itself is made. This device contains several important aspects. First, the theater becomes the "scene" for remembering the past. The recollections from the past are also an educational "scene," a source of ideological learning and moral instruction. It also becomes a means of reevaluating certain historical situations. The clearest example of this probably occurs in Sobol's play *Ghetto*, where the role of the Jews who collaborated with the Nazis in order to survive has gained, if not growing respect, at least a deeper understanding. In *The Soul of a Jew*, by placing Otto Weininger, whom Hitler called "the only acceptable Jew" and an "Aryan Jew" (cf. Picker 1989, 79), in the center of his drama, and characterizing him as a "Jewish Soul," Sobol achieves a similar effect by forcing his audiences to reevaluate some aspects of the canonized past.

The basic hermeneutical principle of Sobol's theater is that history does not exist as an objective truth, separated from an individual and the mechanisms of memory. History instead depends on *individual* recollection, and the implicit claim is that if we do not remember and confront even the most controversial aspects of our past, our present will become distorted. The dimension of the present as history recollected gives both a moral and an aesthetic dimension to Sobol's plays, almost in complete accordance with the Romantic notion of this concept, including its pathetic and sentimental aspects. This subjective hermeneutics of history also contains a potential weakness, especially in connection with the performative aspects of the theater. The subjective conception of the past can, on the stage, easily be discredited if something unreliable is introduced in the presentation.

The initial point of departure for the recollection of the past is therefore of utmost importance. The idea that during the moments of dying the most important moments in one's life flash by one's inner eye, which is the device used by Sobol in *The Soul of a Jew*, has often been used in expressionistic "Soul," or "*Ich*," drama. Since the moment of death is supposedly very short, this device extends and expands it into a dramatic action presenting the spiritual history of the individual. Immediately after hearing the shot we see Weininger trying to enter the apartment of Beethoven, where the historical Weininger actually ended his life with a bullet. Through several of the clues given in this first scene, we understand that it takes place the evening before he ended his life. In the penultimate scene of the play, the same bullet is heard again, this time signifying that we have returned to the point of departure, and as mentioned above, the last scene shows the death of Weininger from a real external perspective, with his parents and friends present.

In the Haifa production of *The Soul of a Jew* in 1982 the initial shot was not carried out. The audience was instead given the impression that the play started in "real" time. However, when Otto Weininger's Double, looking exactly like him but played by a woman, appeared in the mirror (scene 3) and started to talk to Otto (scene 5), exactly repeating what Otto said, it became clear that this performance freely mixed the real with the fantastic, and that it was actually a flashback that was being presented. The Double represents the female aspects of Otto's torn soul, which on the ideological level of the play represent the Jewish and humanistic aspects. In the short scene between Otto and his friend Berger inserted between the two appearances of the Double, the fantastic-imaginary aspects of her appearance are further emphasized.

> OTTO: Tell me, Berger. What would you do if your Double turned up right here and now?
>
> BERGER: What... Who!?
>
> OTTO: There's one person in the world who knows everything about you. Also things you've never told a soul, and never will tell anyone.
>
> BERGER: Do you mean a real living person or an idea?
>
> OTTO: When you talk, he watches you. He observes you from the point beyond your death.... What would you do if he would jump up from the ground right this minute, and appear in front of you? (Sobol 1982, 28).

This exchange ironically refers to the psychoanalytic process that Sobol's flashback technique reconstructs, but it also explains the mystical appearance of the Double behind one of the mirrors of the room. Berger's distinction between a person and an idea even presents a key to the allegorical dimensions of the play—the torn Jewish Soul as the concrete dilemma of Otto Weininger as well as an idea that can be applied to all Jews and in particular to the contemporary Israeli scene.

When Otto meets his feminine Double on his way to the meeting with Sigmund Freud, the objective credibility of the events is further undermined:

DOUBLE: Didn't you notice me following you down the street? I even passed you once when you stopped to talk to yourself.

OTTO: I was talking to Berger. (*The Double bursts out laughing*). I was talking to Berger!

DOUBLE: You'll have to start to pay attention. You walk down the street talking to yourself and imagine that you're meeting people! (Sobol 1982, 53).

The irony of this exchange is of course that in terms of the objective historical reality Berger exists, while the Double is the figment of Otto's imagination.

Several clues enable us to understand that the events are presented from Otto's subjective perspective. The scenes with his student friends have a higher degree of objectivity than those with the Double and his parents, where the subjective perspective has completely distorted the memories. The scene where the teacher Tietz appears first as Strindberg and then as Moebius, the critic of Weininger's work, each time transforming himself by removing a mask, presents both memories of fantasies during the last moments before death as well as a possible recollection of a trick actually played by Tietz. The scene between Weininger and Freud, based on some historical evidence, even though Sobol was not certain if this meeting ever really took place, shows how Sobol elaborates a fantasy relating to Otto's past without making it clear whether this fantasy is triggered by Otto's real past or originates during the last moments of his life as a fantasy about a fantasy that has actually not occurred.

It is impossible to say what the perception and effect of the different layers of the play would have been if the Haifa production had started with the shot as prescribed in the stage directions, but Sobol clearly intended a somewhat different dramatic/theatrical convention to that used by the director Gedalia Besser in his production. If Sobol's version is more like the expressionism of the Strindbergian dream-play genre, where the fantastic is the governing norm of the arrangement of the events, Besser's production is more like a Strindbergian chamber-play, where the frame is real and reality and fantasy can coexist on the stage, at any given moment moving from one to the other without warning.

The initial shot was apparently implemented in all of the foreign performances of *The Soul of a Jew*. In the Düsseldorf/Munich version directed by Jean Claud Kuner, this was done slightly differently than the text stipulates. After Adelaide, the concierge of the Beethoven apartment where Otto commits suicide, has left the room, Otto is on his own. There is a long silence during which he slowly takes out his pistol and holds it toward his temple, while the backdrop is suddenly lifted, and his friend Clara and the teacher Tietz enter. At this point they are already flashes of memory. This interpretation, emphasizing the suicide by making it visible, clarifies a point that could remain vague if we only hear the shot, as indicated in the text. By cutting out the shot, the Haifa performance emphasized the historical, more objective side of the play, while the written play and the foreign performances emphasized the subjective aspect of Weininger's individual memory.

This conclusion is also confirmed by the different productions of *Ghetto*, where the foreign stagings clearly emphasized the subjective dimension of remembering the past, in some cases even to a greater extent than in Sobol's text, while the Haifa production, which was also directed by Besser, emphasized the more objective aspects of the historical past. It is both interesting and intriguing that the Israeli productions stress the objective, indisputable, evidence from the past, while the foreign productions, like the plays themselves, situate the past in the subjective regions of memory. Presented as subjective memory, the past is perhaps less obliging and even less demanding for the spectator. The objective point of view, on the other hand, is indisputable—entirely noncontroversial, and perhaps Besser felt Sobol's choice of subjects was provocative enough and therefore chose the more objective form of theatrical presentation.

The Soul of a Jew develops two different perspectives of time. The first, as mentioned and analyzed above, is the perspective from the point of view of the time that passes between the shot and the actual death, the night of agony, during which Weininger's past is recalled from his own subjective memory. The second temporal perspective points toward the future in terms of the action depicted and toward the present in terms of the audience's reality in Israel and in Europe, and in particular in relation to the present situation of Israel and the Jewish people. The play and its different productions create a strong clash between the subjectivity of Weininger's memories and fantasies, and the reality of the audience. We know that between Otto and us lies the Holocaust and the events that have led to the present situation in Israel. This clash heightens the dialectic relationship to the past through the "media" of subjective memory and objective history. Several sections in the play refer more or less directly to the future, of which Otto as an historical figure is unaware, but which constitutes the present-day reality of Sobol and his audiences.

Otto Weininger's lifetime coincides on the one hand with the birth of political Zionism under the leadership of another Viennese Jew, Theodor Herzl, and on the other with the birth of various anti-Semitic tendencies. As is well known today, this is the anti-Semitism that would lead to the Holocaust under the leadership of another Austrian, Adolf Hitler, while the Zionist movement would lay the foundation for the Jewish state. In all of his important decisions during the play, Weininger considers his Jewish identity to be his weaker, more feminine part, while his Aryan, German identity signifies a masculine, almost ruthless aspect of his soul. Clara, one of Otto's friends, wants to convince him to leave Austria for Palestine with her, and for Otto, who feels that "Judaism has finished its function thousands of years ago" (Sobol 1982, 39), Zionism, the national movement of the Jews, is the "last remnant of nobility still left in Judaism" (Sobol 1982, 38).

At a later point in the play, just before the second shot is heard, Otto has a painful fantasy in which the Double appears dressed as a soldier (the meaning of the Hebrew word *kalgas* used here is even stronger than a mere soldier) shouting, "March, Jew!" (*Marsch Jude!*). Otto defends himself against this nightmare as well as from his friends who urge him to become a Zionist in order to solve his own problems as well as the problems of the Jewish people by saying that "Zionism is not a solution. I warned you that the results of that adventure will be terrible. That you will return to the Diaspora if you do not conquer the Judaism that is within you" (Sobol 1982, 106). When his friends Clara and Berger do not understand what he means, Otto develops this idea further: "Zionism has been striving towards something that is opposed to Judaism. Judaism had to be overcome and conquered from within, and be gotten rid of once and for all, in order for the Zionist realization to become possible indeed. You have not done that at all. It is no wonder then that Judaism has conquered Zionism within you and in this victory it is leading you to destruction" (Sobol 1982, 107).

Several points in this passage and others like it in the play require clarification. The first concerns Sobol's use of tenses, which are extremely difficult to render in English because of the strange mixture between the past and the future with regard to what Zionism will be doing—1904—and has already done—1982. In terms of Weininger's own time, where he functions somewhat as a prophet, he foresees the Holocaust. It is quite a strong statement to claim that Judaism has to be destroyed for Zionism to succeed, but in historical terms it is indisputable that the Holocaust was a strong factor in obtaining international recognition of the Jewish state.

In considering the passage in contemporary Israeli terms, we should keep in mind that this play was first performed during the autumn of 1982, when the Israeli army in Lebanon had conquered large parts of Beirut and implemented policies through the use of military force. What Sobol's play is indirectly arguing in this context is that Zionism is gradually erasing its Jewish roots, that is, losing its humanistic values and becoming completely dependent on brutality and power.

For the French translation of *The Soul of a Jew* Sobol made a few additions to this speech to clarify the complex ideological issues further.

Directly after the end of the previous passage quoting Otto, in the French version he continues:

> Zionism is striving towards something which is opposed to Judaism! In order to realize Zionism it was [*sic!*] necessary to uproot Judaism from within and to depart from it. In order to secure the victory of Zionism over Judaism, its most dangerous enemy, it was necessary to absorb the Aryan spirit and to develop the Aryan soul. If Judaism will not win the battle over Zionism, obstruct it, it will mean the end of the Jewish state and the return to the Diaspora, the most liked and natural place for the survival of Judaism. I told you! I warned you![6]

Here what was more or less implied in the original version has become completely explicit.

In *The Soul of a Jew* Sobol developed a discourse in which Nazi Germany and present-day Israel are discussed and analyzed with the same terms, that is, the same terminology is used to discuss the development of anti-Semitism in the German-speaking world and the policies of the state of Israel, in particular during the war in Lebanon in 1982. This terminology is based on a series of dichotomies in which the concepts on each side of the equation are more or less overlapping: Aryan versus Jewish, masculine versus feminine, strong versus weak, brutal versus humanistic, and so on. Otto's torn soul, which is "Jewish" in a more inclusive sense than the use of the term "Jewish" in the dichotomy, is in a state of constant struggle between the two poles, which is why he is not able to survive. From our present-day perspective Otto's Jewish soul is the same Jewish soul that is a direct quotation from the Israeli national anthem:

> As long as inside the heart
>
> The Soul of a Jew is yearning,
>
> In the direction of the Orient
>
> An eye is looking towards Zion

with the implicit question added as to whether the present-day Israeli *nefesh* (soul, spirit, or character) will manage to survive in its struggle between the two poles. In today's Hebrew the word *nefesh* also has the connotation of being soft-hearted and overly moral in the expression *yefei-nefesh*, which is used by the right-wing to characterize the attitude of leftist "submission." In the context of the play this is of course ironic, because none of this is known when the action takes place.

However, Sobol does not claim, at least not directly, that today's Israelis are actually like Nazis or behave in the same way.[7] But since he analyzes the fate of the Jewish people as the direct result of the Holocaust as initiated and carried out by the Germans, it is, in this limited context, possible to use the same terminology or the same universe of discourse. Sobol has described the spiritual development and profiles of the two peoples, with special reference to the ideological background and roots of Nazism and Zionism. The fact that both of these movements developed in Vienna at the turn of the century and in a sense "clashed" in the individual soul of Otto Weininger enables Sobol to develop a historiosophic idiom whereby the two national movements are comparable and interact within a comprehensive dynamic historic model. In the Israeli context this model of a dramatic-historical-ideological discourse is naturally heavily loaded intellectually as well as emotionally, even if the express aim of Sobol and other left-wing writers and intellectuals in using it was first of all to warn against the possibility of its realization in the conflict between the Israelis and the Palestinians.

When *The Soul of a Jew* was first performed in Israel, almost all of the critics emphasized the immediate relevance of the production. Here I shall only give a few typical examples. Giora Manor, the critic of the *Mapam* left-wing daily newspaper, wrote that

> the real achievement of the performance and the play is to bring the main features of Otto Weininger's special thought scenically to the spectators . . . and while he was arguing with Zionism he reached some conclusions that suddenly seem extremely pertinent during the autumn of 1982. The essence of life in Israel after the war in Lebanon, the basic problems of our existence, are reflected in Weininger's declaration that a Jewish state is impossible unless it ceases to be Jewish (Manor 1982).

Michael Handelsaltz, in the liberal newspaper *Ha'aretz*, underlined this further by claiming that "the play had something to say to the audience present in the hall during that evening, and it had the means with which to say it in the most effective way. . . . In *The Soul of a Jew* some dismal truths are said about Israeli reality, and there is no choice but to relate to them" (Handelsaltz 1982).[8] The critic in *Ma'ariv*, Elyakim Yaron, was even more explicit, arguing that "Sobol is a political playwright, and his last play as well is a salient political-social play. The ideas of Weininger serve as a 'filter' for Sobol through which he examines the basic questions of our national identity, here and now" (Yaron 1982).

Several public voices were gradually raised, especially among religious groups and right-wing intellectuals, who felt uneasy about the implicit comparison between the tormented Jewish soul of Otto Weininger and the spirit of the state of Israel.[9] Religious Knesset member Chaim Drukman even went so far as to claim that Sobol's play would induce anti-Semitism if performed outside of Israel. In the heated debate that followed his statement, left-wing/liberal Yossi Sarid argued that "art is not deodorant."

The first time *The Soul of a Jew* was performed outside Israel was when the Haifa production was performed at the Edinburgh Festival and afterward in London during the autumn of 1983. The play fit exceptionally well into the festival's preoccupation that year with turn-of-the-century

Vienna. The production was on the whole given good reviews, with Michael Billington of *The Guardian*, for example, claiming that "Mr. Sobol clearly finds in Weininger a handy means of opening the debate between Judaism and Zionism and of indirectly criticizing the modern Israeli state for its betrayal of the Zionist principles. But it is hard to get involved with such a palpably demented protagonist" (Billington 1983). This revealed the same understanding as the Israeli critics, but with less personal involvement and identification with the self-destructive hero.

The reaction in Germany and Austria to *The Soul of a Jew* underwent an interesting development. After the German tour of the Haifa production in May 1985, the *Süddeutsche Zeitung* published an enthusiastic review analyzing Sobol's technique of historization and distancing, claiming that "the manner in which it is embedded in the spiritual situation, how the signs of disintegration in Vienna of 1900, the infamous Lueger anti-Semitism, the first signs of the destruction of the Jews, and Theodor Herzl's Zionist utopia for the rescue from habit and routine, are all brought in, is highly intelligent—with the distance of a joke, the torn parts are put together and turned into sensuous theater" (Niehoff 1985).

However, when the play was produced by German theaters, it was probably difficult to find theatrical tension and ideological relevance, and the reviewers on the whole concentrated on its formal qualities. After the performance of the Kuner production, the tone of the *Süddeutsche Zeitung* changed completely, saying that Sobol "simply wanted to blow off some of the most crude Weininger quotations for his compatriots, and for this purpose he needed a semitheatrical package. So he glued together some flashy original quotations and the scenic arrangements of a feature film" (Skasa 1986). The *Abendzeitung* even called it a piece that does not contain interesting material for the actors (Seidenfaden 1988). Urs Jenny, in *Der Spiegel*, however, acknowledged Sobol's skill of composition by calling the play "a thorough, effective theater collage" (Jenny 1985). German theater critics tended to stress the play's literary qualities rather than its ideological and political implications, and on the whole they were not pleased by what they had seen on the stage.

It is difficult for me, who has not seen them, to say why the two German productions in Düsseldorf/Munich and Hamburg were not well received by the critics.[10] By searching for its literary qualities instead of looking at the play as part of a complex process of confrontations with the past through the present, something apparently was lost in the theatrical communication. Whether this was due to the expectations of the critics or took place in the performances themselves I am not able to say. One possible reason for the mixed reception in Germany could have been that it is still quite controversial to depict anti-Semitism on the German stage, even if this is done in the form of an analysis of its historical roots, and in particular if the purpose of such a depiction is to evoke and discuss a contemporary social reality. According to the hermeneutic mechanisms of memory and history that the play raises, it is evident that it has to be directed and performed with some kind of intention to comment on a contemporary social or ideological reality. In a context where anti-Semitic sentiments still exist this can be problematic, in particular if the production does not take a clear stand concerning the issues raised in their historical or contemporary context. We must, of course, remember that the play was written for an Israeli audience, warning against a situation in which the Israelis were the aggressors, namely the war in Lebanon. What will a German audience make of this warning? Will it be understood as a criticism of the local German profascist and anti-Semitic tendencies, or will it serve as an additional argument in the *Historikerstreit*[11] against the exceptional nature of the Holocaust?

The production of *The Soul of a Jew* at the Volkstheater in Vienna in November 1988, which was given the title *Weiningers Nacht*, clearly confronted this issue, and this version, directed by Paulus Manker, who also played Weininger, was very favorably received. For this production Sobol added some newly written scenes aimed at specifying the direct social context of the play not only in the Vienna of the turn of the century but in the Vienna of today as well. The purpose of these additions was to point, at least indirectly, to the Nazi past of the Austrian president, Kurt Waldheim. Instead of Clara telling Otto that she has been to the theater, at the opening of act 2, in the new Austrian version she says she has visited the Parliament. According to the new stage direction, "The doors open and outside the statue of Karl Lueger, the Mayor of Vienna, can be seen" (Sobol 1988), and Clara's recollection of the Parliament comes alive on the stage. Lueger steps down from his pedestal and gives one of his famous anti-Semitic speeches. This statue is one of the well-known sights of Vienna, and after the speech the "statue" returns to its original position and the stage closes. The past is still talking. It is evident that this production, in its present-day context, is intended to emphasize and point directly to the fact that individuals who had Nazi sympathies during World War II, and in the case of Kurt Waldheim even more than that, can still hold official positions. This clearly shows that Sobol sees theater as a process of reacting to a concrete political-ideological situation, and that he contextualizes his text so that in performance it will not only bring out the past but reflect on the present as well.[12]

In 1990 Paulus Manker directed a film based on his Vienna production in which he also plays the leading role. In the film several scenes showing Otto as a child (played by a child actor) were added to underscore the more objective status of memories, a technique that is possible in the medium of film through the use of flashbacks. Recollection through flashback is very different depending on whether it is an adult actor who plays the character as a child or whether we actually see the child. In the film version of *Weiningers Nacht* the two approaches were mixed.

Another distinct feature of the film, which I imagine also reflects the tendency of the Vienna theater production (which I did not see), is the almost total disappearance of the arguments concerning the present situation of the Zionist project in relation to traditional Jewish humanistic values. Instead, the film carries a much more universal message in which the Jewish identity of the protagonist has been transformed into a trope or a symbol for his struggle against intolerance and hypocrisy. Manker's Weininger fights the constrictions and aggressions of his family and the sentimental images, such as the "schmaltzy" music of his Viennese surroundings, to emphasize the fact that his primary aim is simply to be a human being. The old anti-Semites, like Lueger, appear as ghosts from the past who prevent the hero from realizing his human potential, and when he fails there is no other way out than suicide. This message is very different from the criticism of the suicidal, self-destructive tendencies of contemporary Israeli life and politics that was so strongly emphasized in the Israeli production of the play.

The meanings a play can assume in different contexts are very difficult to predict. Sobol wishes to comment on and criticize the contemporary reality through the fictionalization of historical material. In the Israeli context the purpose of this subjective form of presenting history is to warn about the possible dangers in the future. But what does a play showing the sources and effects of anti-Semitism mean on a German stage? This issue was very much on the public agenda of the German-speaking world when *The Soul of a Jew* had its German premiere in Düsseldorf in December 1985. Only a few months previously, on the night of October 31, 1985, the performance of the Rainer Werner Fassbinder play, *Garbage, the City, and Death*, had been stopped at the Schauspielhaus in Frankfurt by the local Jewish community.[13] The productions of *The Soul of a Jew* did not raise any of the comprehensive issues regarding the place and function of anti-Semitism in contemporary Germany. Jacques Le Rider, however, considers the provocation implicit in Sobol's play to be much more threatening than that in Fassbinder's play: "Compared with it [*The Soul of a Jew*] I find the Fassbinder piece to be quite harmless. For the first time in [postwar] Germany a Jew is shown negatively and called names on the stage, and it is done by an Israeli" (Le Rider 1986a). Sobol's position seems to be that precisely because he is an Israeli he can allow himself to be outspoken concerning the most burning issues, those that, according to his understanding, matter most for the future of the Israeli society.

By placing the action of *The Soul of a Jew* in the cradle of the consciousness of the modern Jew and Israeli—Vienna at the turn of the century, where Herzl, Freud, and the first modern anti-Semites all grew up—Sobol can address a number of crucial issues. Otto Weininger's torn soul is the constantly revolving prism reflecting the historical and psychological forces through which the hero's past can be relived and made significant in the present. For Sobol the theater even functions as a collective psychoanalytic process bringing the spectators back to their collective past and investigating its relevance and significance in the present. Sobol's theatrical ideal is to make the subjective memories of the individual hero and the collective, public dimension of the historical past (and present), which the spectators supposedly are familiar with, communicate on the theatrical stage. This is the point where the dialectic process between *history* and *memory* is activated in a concrete historical situation. In his "Theses on the Philosophy of History," completed in the spring of 1940, Walter Benjamin has approached this complex dialectics by expressing his own keen awareness that also those who are dead continue to write their own as well as our history: "To articulate the past historically does not mean to recognize it 'the way it really was' (Ranke). It means to seize hold of a memory as it flashes up at the moment of danger. . . . Only that historian will have the gift of fanning the spark of hope in the past who is firmly convinced that *even the dead* will not be safe from the enemy if he wins. And this enemy has not yet ceased to be victorious (Benjamin 1969, 255).

Notes ✦

CHAPTER 1   *A Critical Introduction to the History of Weininger Reception*

1. For a perspective on how commonplace conversion was among Jews in *fin-de-siècle* Vienna, see Endelman (1987) and Rozenblit (1983). Beller points out that the highly influential Schorskean approach to the period "is usually to claim that . . . the flowering of Viennese culture at the turn of the century was the response of a class rather than primarily that of a religious or ethnic minority" (Beller 1989b, 4). In Beller's view, however, Jewish secular and religious culture are the key to understanding the period. Also see Beller's essay in this volume (Chapter 6).

2. Giovanni Sampaolo has rediscovered a second version of *Geschlecht und Charakter*, published a few months after Weininger's suicide, which contains over two hundred modifications of the first version. In 1992 Sampaolo published an Italian translation of this text that takes both versions into account and thus makes an important contribution to Weininger studies (Weininger 1992).

3. For a discussion of anti-Semitism and misogyny and their interrelation in the works of two nineteenth-century Italian authors, see Harrowitz (1994a). For a historical analysis of their interrelation in twentieth-century Germany, see Bridenthal, Grossmann, and Kaplan (1984), and Heinemann (1986). On the convergence of stereotypes of the Jew and the woman in European modernism, see Braun (1992, 1993) and Gilman (1985, 1992a).

4. For a full account of "fantasies of feminine evil" in this period, see Dijkstra (1986). On the political uses of sex, see also Showalter (1982) and Koch (1986).

5. See Stieg's essay "Kafka and Weininger," in this volume (Chapter 15).

6. Cf. Pusch (1984) and Janssen-Jurreit (1976, 1982). Marion A. Kaplan, one of the most innovative scholars of modern German-Jewish history, notes that in Jewish history too "masculine actors and male arenas have been virtually the only ones that mattered." In her work on the Jewish middle class in imperial Germany, Kaplan provides a model for the synthesis of German, Jewish, and women's history (Kaplan 1991). Ruth Klüger, an Austrian-born American Germanist and survivor of Auschwitz, notes many instances in her life in which Jewish males implicitly or explicitly subordinated Jewish female experience to their own experience of Jewish culture and of anti-Semitism (Klüger 1992).

7. On the crisis of male gender identity in twentieth-century Europe, see Le Rider (1993b), Widdig (1992), Dijkstra (1986, esp. 210–34), Mosse (1985), Wagner (1981), Nitzsche (1980), and Theweleit (1977, 1989).

8. For an extensive discussion of these issues, see Harrowitz (1994b).

9. See the respective essays by Rodlauer and Janik in this volume (Chapters 3 and 4).

10. On the Freud-Fliess estrangement over the Weininger-Swoboda affair, see Jones (1953, 315–18), Sulloway (1979, 223–37), and Le Rider (1985). For documents pertaining to the controversy, see Fliess (1906), Swoboda (1906), and Pfennig (1906).

11. See Schnedl-Bubeniček (1981).

12. Cf. his 1938 analysis of anti-Semitism in *Moses and Monotheism* (Freud 1955–74, Vol. 23) and "A Comment on Anti-Semitism" (Freud 1955–74, vol. 23, 287–293).

13. See Bahr (1993).

14. See, for example, Zweig (1960) and a particularly irreverent work by Wickham (1929).

15. Cf. Koonz (1987), Thalmann (1984), and Mosse (1985; 1966) esp. "The Bonds of the Family," "The Ideal of Womanhood," and "The Foundation: Racism"; 1964, esp. "Racism"). Also see Pugel (1936), especially the chapter on "Die deutsche Frau im Kampfe gegen das Judentum und den Bolschewismus" (The German Woman in Battle Against Judaism and Bolshevism).

16. In this light, cf. Katherine Arens's reading of the struggles of Karen Horney in her essay on characterology for this volume (Chapter 8).

17. In Klein's view, Weininger was correct in seeing an analogy between women and Jews in his society, insofar as "any subject group which for generations has lived in close contact with the dominant class would develop—with variations, of course, according to circumstances and dispositions—similar psychological traits" (Klein 1946, 58–69).

18. The story behind Abrahamsen's scholarship is quite dramatic. Beginning the work in his native Norway in the early 1930s, he had nearly completed it when the Germans invaded the country in 1940. Abrahamsen escaped to the United States with part of the manuscript and was reunited with the rest of it when his family was able to join him in 1941. One of Abrahamsen's most valuable contributions to the history of Weininger reception was to record his own correspondence with Freud, Lucka, and Weininger's sister Rosa. Abrahamsen's primary concern was with Weininger's state of mind while writing *Sex and Character* and in the months prior to committing suicide. He diagnosed Weininger's mental conflicts as "schizophrenic" in a broad sense.

19. For studies in connection with specific authors, see the following: Wittgenstein (Mayr 1970; Mulligan 1981; Smith 1985; Janik 1985; Le Rider 1990a; Gabriel 1990), Trakl (Doppler 1971), Musil (Corino 1973), Stein (Katz 1978), Doderer (Jaffe 1979; Le Rider 1986b), Kafka (Mulligan 1981); Stieg 1987 [translated for this volume]), Schnitzler (Jaffe 1979; Arens 1986), Kraus (Wagner 1981; Stieg 1983; Unglaub 1988), Svevo (Cavaglion 1982; Scandiana 1983), Joyce (Reizbaum 1982 [revised for this volume], Joly 1982; Byrnes 1990), Strindberg (Perrelli 1983; Sokol 1987; Unglaub 1988), Canetti (Stieg 1983; Pöder 1985; Pankau 1990), Lawrence (Delavenay 1984), Sternheim (Nabbe 1984), Altenberg (Schoenberg 1987), Broch (Marlock 1993) and the German novel in general (Brude-Firnau 1979 [translated for this volume as Chapter 11]; Labanyi 1985).

20. See Sobol (1984, 1987, 1989). On the play's reception in Israel, see Ofrat (1983), Feldman (1987), Rokem (1989), and Shteir (1990). For a Viennese perspective, cf. Fritsch (1986) and Marschall (1987). For studies of the play's Jewish themes in contemporary German and Austrian contexts, also see Morgenstern (1989) and Skloot (1989).

21. Cf. Mosse's treatment of the influence of the *völkisch* idea on German Jewry: "Young Germans talked about the 'new German'; young Jews spoke of the 'new Jew' in exactly the same terms. Jews also wanted to opt out of bourgeois society, to escape from the alienation which industrialism had brought. At the same time, they wanted to be rid of any association with a stereotype that might link them with the very capitalist and urban society against which they were fighting" (Mosse 1970, 81).

22. Cf. Janik (1987, 88): "nearly all that we tend to find obnoxious in his thought was commonplace in the social reform programme, biology and sexology of his day."

23. Janik attributes the "philosophical assault upon the concept of rationality" to a host of figures including Heidegger, Wittgenstein, Collingwood, Polanyi, Kuhn, Lakatos, Toulmin, Koyré, and Butterfield (Janik 1986, 76).

24. Janik (1987, 80) has also launched an attack on a widespread tendency to use the stock concept "Jewish self-hatred," to help "explain the worrisome, even repellent, anti-liberal and anti-modernist currents of the Viennese *fin de siècle*." He criticizes Le Rider and Gay (1978), among others, for slipshod usage, but pins the main blame on Theodor Lessing: "The simple fact about Theodor Lessing's account of Weininger in *Der jüdische Selbsthass* [1930] is that it is based upon a racism which is just as crude as anything that the most vulgar Nazi ideologues might have asserted. For Lessing Weininger's problem was rooted in hatred for his blood" (Janik 1987, 80).

25. Considered lost after World War II, an early draft of Weininger's dissertation, entitled "Eros und Psyche," was rediscovered in Vienna's Archiv der Österreichischen Akademie der Wissenschaften in the 1980s. See Rodlauer (1987).

CHAPTER 2 *"The Otto Weininger Case" Revisited*

Unless a citation to an English-language edition is given, all quotations from French and German authors have also been translated by Ms. Foell.

1. I am taking this opportunity to add a postscript to the gigantic bibliography of Weininger reception:

Gottfried Benn mentions Weininger several times, for example, at the beginning of his essay "Das Genieproblem." Franz Blei evokes Weininger in his pamphlet directed against Karl Kraus, "Der Affe Zarathustras." A reference to Weininger attributed to Max Nordau probably comes instead from R. Nordhausen. Hans Mayer wrote the following about Weininger in his well-known book *Aussenseiter*: "Max Nordau, writing in Berlin's *Vossische Zeitung*, spoke of a 'shot in the dark' when he reported on Otto Weininger to a larger readership for the first time: shortly after the latter had shot himself on October 4, 1903, in Vienna's

Beethoven house" (Mayer 1975, 118). However, Nordau's article cannot be located in the *Vossische Zeitung*. Mayer's information probably arises out of a confusion with the article "The Shot in the Dark" ("Der Schuss im Nebel"), an account of *Geschlecht und Charakter* written by R. Nordhausen and published in the journal *Münchner Neueste Nachrichten* (November 5, 1903). I owe these references to Dr. Richard Landwehrmeyer, Genraldirektor of the Staatsbibliothek-Preussischer Kulturbesitz in Berlin.

Ferdinand von Saar writes in a letter of July 25, 1905, addressed to Camill Lederer: "I still owe you my hearty thanks for Weininger's book. He was really a genial fellow—but also an *overwrought* Jew. There are passages of great, deep thought in the book. But also much that points to mania" (quoted in Saar 1987, 147).

Rudolf Steiner evokes Otto Weininger in two lectures: first on July 29, 1916, when he states, "What is expressed as intuition and imagination in Weininger's work, these are real ideas of the future!" (Steiner 1978, 11ff.); then on August 19, 1918, when he refers to *Über die letzten Dinge* as "notes that are extraordinarily interesting because they are plainly imaginings of astral perception" (Steiner 1967, 46ff.). I owe this information to Thomas Meyer, Zurich.

2. Strindberg to Gerber, December 8, 1903, quoted in Weininger (1919, 101); and Weininger (1980, 651): "Dies zynische Leben war ihm zu zynisch?" On the relationship between Strindberg and Weininger, cf. Unglaub (1989, 121–50) (an interesting article despite certain gaps in information about Weininger).

3. Sloterdijk (1983, 479ff.): "Die Liebesehe: . . . das Körperliche im äussersten Falle als 'Ausdruck' der seelischen Passion hingenommen . . . Dieser erotische Laienidealismus: . . . Der Bürger ist, in sexuellen Dingen wie in vielen anderen, ein Beinahe-Realist . . . und diese Spannung ist es, die den bürgerlichen Mann besonders empfänglich macht für sexualzynischen Witz, schmutzigen Schlüssellochrealismus und Pornographie . . . Daher das zynische Lächeln."

4. Artaud (1956, 171): "Le Solitaire a vengé le Mal venu des ténèbres de la Femme, par la force qu'il vient de reinventer. La force qu'il à mise a se detacher lui a rendu une force inverse. / Et c'était une force de mort. / Notre Destin à tous est un Destin de Mort. Un cycle du Monde est achevé."

5. Artaud (1971, n. 76, 24). (This part of the work, "Le Rite du Peyotl chez les Tarahumaras," was written at Rodez in 1943.): "quelque chose d'affreux qui monte et qui ne vient pas de moi, mais des ténèbres que j'ai en moi. . . . Et bientôt c'est tout ce qu'il y aura: ce masque obscène de qui ricane entre le sperme et le caca."

6. Artaud (1956, 159 n. 77): "Cela veut dire qu'une *Initiation supérieure* sera le fruit de cette Mort et que tout ce qui est de la sexualité sera brûlé dans cette Initiation supérieure, sone feu changé en Initiation. En vue de remettre partout la Suprématie absolue de l'Homme."

7. Cf. Politzer (1966); Binder (1976, 374ff.).

8. Kafka, *Tagebücher 1910–1923*, in Kafka (1976, 231): "Der Coitus als Bestrafung des Glückes des Beisammenseins. Möglichst asketisch leben, asketischer als ein Junggeselle, das ist die einzige Möglichkeit für mich, die Ehe zu ertragen. Aber sie?"

9. Kafka, letter of August 9, 1920, in Kafka (1983, 197): "Mein Körper, oft

jahrelang still, wurde dann wieder geschüttelt bis zum Nichtertragen-Können von dieser Sehnsucht nach einer kleinen, nach einer ganz bestimmten Abscheulichkeit, nach etwas leicht Widerlichem, Peinlichem, Schmutzigem: noch in dem Besten, was es hier für mich gab, war etwas davon, irgendein schlechter Geruch, etwas Schwefel, etwas Hölle. Dieser Trieb hatte etwas vom ewigen Juden, sinnlos gezogen, sinnlos wandernd durch eine sinnlos schmutzige Welt."

10. Freud (1942b, 43): "In nicht fachlichen Kreisen wird die Aufstellung der menschlichen Bisexualität als eine Leistung des jung verstorbenen Philosophen O. Weininger betrachtet, der diese Idee zur Grundlage eines ziemlich unbesonnenen Buches (Geschlecht und Charakter, 1903) genommen hat. Die oben stehenden Nachweise mögen zeigen, wie wenig begründet dieser Anspruch ist."

11. Pontalis (1973, 20).

12. Weininger (1980, 403ff.): "Es könnte nicht wundern, wenn es manchen scheinen wollte, bei dem Ganzen der bisherigen Untersuchung seien 'die Männer' alzugut davongekommen. . . . Diese Beschuldigung wäre ungerechtfertigt. Es kommt mir nicht in den Sinn, die Männer zu idealisieren. . . . Es handelt sich um die besseren Möglichkeiten, die in jedem Manne sind. . . . Es gibt, wie schon öfter hervorgehoben, Männer, die zu Weibern geworden, oder Weiber geblieben sind."

13. "Freud (1948, 30): "dass auch die Mehrzahl der Männer weit hinter dem männlichen Ideal zurückbleibt."

14. For a systematic reconstruction of Lawrence's sexual metaphysics, see Lévy-Valensi (1962).

15. Bataille (1957, 22): "Nous supportons mal la situation qui nous rive à l'individualité de hasard, à l'individu périssable que nous sommes. En meme temps que nous avons le désir anguissé de la durée de ce périssable, nous avons l'obsession d'une continuité première, qui nous relie à l'être . . . Cette nostalgie commande chez tous les hommes les trois formes de l'erotisme."

16. Weininger (1904, 184): "Es gibt kein Ich, es gibt keine Seele. . . . Das 'intelligible Ich' ist nur Eitelkeit."

17. Weininger (1919, 60 n. 31): "Der Hass gegen die Frau ist immer nur noch nicht überwundener Hass gegen die eigene Sexualität."

18. Cf. Lévy-Valensi (1962, esp. Chap. 4: "La Connaissance, le péché et let salut chez Schopenhauer et chez Lawrence").

19. Schopenhauer (1976, 724): "Weil im Grunde die Weiber ganz allein zur Propagation des Geschlechtes da sind und ihre Bestimmung hierin aufgeht."

20. Schopenhauer (1976, 447): "Das Judentum hat zum Grundcharakter *Realismus und Optimismus*, als welche naheverwandt und die Bedingungen des eigentlichen Theismus sind."

21. Baudelaire (1976, 581): "J'entends par progrès la diminution progressive de l'âme et la domination progressive de la matière."

22. Baudelaire (1975b, 706 n. 37): "De l'infamie de l'imprimerie, grand obstacle au développement du Beau./ Belle conspiration à organiser pour l'extermination de la Race Juive./ Les Juifs, *Bibliothécaires* et témoins de la *Rédemption*.

23. Groddeck (1966, 258): "Wie das Glied gespalten wird, um dem Manne den weiblichen Geschlechtsteil zu geben, so wird die Vorhaut fortgeschnitten, um alles Weibliche an dem Abzeichen der Männlichkeit zu beseitigen; denn die

Vorhaut ist weiblich, sie ist die Scheide, in der die männliche Eichel steckt. . . . Bei den Juden liegen die Dinge anders: Wenn sie die Vorhaut abschneiden . . . so beseitigen sie damit die Zwiegeschlechtlichkeit des Mannes, sie nehmen das Weibliche an dem Männlichen fort. Damit verzichten sie zugunsten der zwiegeschlechtigen Gottheit auf ihre angeborene Gottähnlichkeit; der Jude wird durch die Beschneidung Nur-Mann."

24. Groddeck (1966, 258ff.): "Nimmt man den Mann als das, was er ist, ein an sich leistungsbedürftiges, unfreies, tausendfach vom Alltag gebundenes Wesen, das nur hie und da der Erhebung fähig ist und nur für die kurze Zeit der Erregung, dessen dauernde Kraft nicht in der Erregung, sondern in der Bindung an das Gesetzliche liegt, so kommt man zu dem Schluss, dass der Jude soweit wie irgend möglich das Weibliche verdrängt hat."

25. Weininger (1980, 407 n. 19): "Es gibt Arier, die jüdischer sind als mancher Jude."

26. Weininger (1980, 407 n. 19): "So erklärt sich, dass die allerschärfsten Antisemiten unter den Juden zu finden sind."

27. "Allerweltsjude," quoted in Stieg (1976, 257).

28. Bahr (1907, 69): "Das Tüchtige, das Grosse, die Kraft des Judentums mag [die Wiener Stadt] nicht. Aber der Jude, der es nicht mehr sein will, der Verräter seiner Rasse, der sie verlässt, der Schausspieler einer fremden, ist ihr verwandt. Das Künstliche dieser ausgerissenen Existenzen, die, von aller Vergangenheit entleert, gierig sind, sich jede Gegenwart, jede Zukunft einzupumpen, die nur Schale sind, die sich täglich anders aufblasen, gar nicht zu sein, aber alles zu scheinen fähig, hat den Wiener immer verlockt. Er findet an ihnen sich selbst. Wenn man das Wort so nimmt, kann man sagen, dass er durch und durch verjudet ist. Er war es schon, bevor noch der erste Jude kam."

29. Quoted in Schur (1975, 552): "Man wehrt sich in jeder Form gegen die Kastration, hier mag sich noch ein Stückchen Opposition gegen das eigene Judentum schlau verbergen. Unser grosser Meister Moses war doch ein starker Antisemit und macht kein Geheimnis daraus. Vielleicht war er wirklich ein Ägypter."

30. Quoted in Major (1986, 56).

31. Janik (1983, 1985). On Weininger's "Jüdischer Selbsthaβ," Janik (1987) has set forth theses that seem unacceptable; I find Sander Gilman's interpretation more convincing (Gilman 1986).

32. Taguieff (1988, 12): "la croyance que le racisme est essentiellement une théorie des races, distinctes et inégales, définies en termes biologiques, et en conflit éternel pour la domination du monde."

33. Taguieff (1988, 105): "le mot 'race' ne peut plus être pris pour l'indicateur exclusif, ou par excellence, des modes de racisation."

34. [Translator's note: Cf. also Karl Lueger's famous statement, "Wer Jude ist, bestimme ich!" ("I'll decide who is a Jew.")]

35. Taguieff (1988, 168): "Nous parlons de race juive par commodité de langage, car il n'y a pas, à proprement parler, et du point de vue de la génétique, une race juive . . . La race juive est avant tout une race mentale."

36. Cf. Le Rider (1985, Chap. 3, "Ein Experimentalroman").

37. Rodlauer (1987). Several unedited documents have been published in Le Rider 1986a. Several other manuscripts are preserved in the archives of the Leo Baeck Institute in New York (including a card addressed to Artur Gerber as well as a text about Weininger by Artur Gerber).

38. The complete text of the *Wiener Fassung* was published in 1988 in the program book of the Volkstheater (Sobol 1988), along with a documentary dossier assembled by Paulus Manker. (This volume is distributed by Europaverlag, Vienna.) An analysis of Sobol's play, inspired by the Hamburg production, appears in Le Rider (1986a).

39. Several allusions in Sobol's play remind us that Leopold Weininger, Otto's father, was the son of Salomon Weininger (1822–1879), a goldsmith and art forger, who died (so claims the *Allgemeines Lexikon der bildenden Künstler*) in the Stein prison (on Salomon Weininger, cf. Thieme and Becker, 1942; S.V. Oettinger 1879, 278; Kurz 1967). Stephen Tree passed on to me a copy of a letter in which Eugene Kellert (the husband of one of Otto Weininger's sisters) writes to Eva Weininger in London on November 25, 1988: "In a church in a Carinthian village, there was an altar from the 14th century, and the congregation ordered a copy of it for another church. The copy was as excellent as the original, but he [Salomon] had delivered the duplicate and kept the original for himself . . . He was sentenced to a *short* imprisonment. He did *not* die there." At the beginning of the same letter, Kellert writes: "Leopold was a fanatic for truth. He had testified against his father. He hated liars."

If these anecdotes are accurate, they would establish a parallel between Otto Weininger's "family novel" and Sigmund Freud's. It is known that Josef Freud (the brother of Sigmund's father, Jacob Freud) was arrested in June 1865 for holding false bank notes. Sigmund Freud evokes this episode with veiled words in his *Interpretation of Dreams* ("the dream of the uncle"). In Otto Weininger's case, his grandfather Salomon's "hidden fault" may have contributed to the "ethical fanaticism" of *Geschlecht und Charakter*.

CHAPTER 3   *Fragments from Weininger's Education* (1895–1902)

1. This text is an abridged version of Hannelore Rodlauer's introductory essay to Rodlauer (1990, 11–51).

2. Weininger insisted on the translation of this term as "not darkly glowing." See Rodlauer (1990, 6 n. 4).

3. The forty-sixth to forth-eighth Annual Reports of the Royal and Imperial State Gymnasium in Vienna's Eighth District were reviewed (school years 1895–96 to 1897–98).

4. According to the school's Annual Report for 1897–98.

5. [Translators' note: Weininger's early manuscripts are among the papers Rodlauer has published along with *Eros und Psyche*, and which she introduces in the present essay.]

6. [Translators' note: Literally "The Times"; we will be using the German title throughout.]

7. Mach to Alexius von Meinong, cited in Haller and Stadler 1988, 24.

8. Kraft (1880–1975); Ph.D., University of Vienna, 1903 (dissertation, "Perception of the External World"); tenured in theoretical philosophy, 1914; See Kainz (1976, 519–57).

9. Kassowitz (1842–1913) was, according to Lesky (1978, 367), "the best-known personality" among Viennese pediatricians of this period, although most of his theories have been disproved. He was the director of the Vienna Children's Clinic, where the young Freud worked. On Kassowitz as a biologist, see Lesky (1978, 370).

10. Especially in the main body of *Sex and Character*.

11. Weininger wrote to Artur Gerber on August 12, 1902: "I am now convinced that I was indeed born to be a musician. More than anything else, at least. Today I discovered a specific musical fantasy in myself that I would never have believed I had." On August 17, he no longer saw a future for himself as a philosopher: "This journey has led me to the realization that I am not a philosopher, either. Really not! But *am* I anything else? I gravely doubt it—" (Weininger 1903).

12. This often cited work exerted great influence on Weininger. [Translators' note: The German title translates "Woman as Criminal and Prostitute." The original Italian title is *La donna criminale, la prostituta e la donna normale* ("Criminal Woman, the Prostitute, and the Normal Woman")]

13. Wiener Stadt- und Landesbibliothek, Handschriftensammlung, Inventory no. 107, 949.

14. Jodl wrote his dissertation on Hume; for the revised version, see Jodl (1872).

15. Weininger paraphrased many passages from Moll's article (Moll 1900a) in both *Eros und Psyche* and *Geschlecht und Charakter*.

16. Freud realized his project (which was a long time in preparation, as the letters to Fliess show) with his *Three Essays on the Theory of Sexuality* (published 1905), in which he also mentions Weininger.

17. Chamberlain's letters to Kassner from 1900 to 1906 are published in the latter's memoirs (Kassner 1938).

18. Reviews by Theobald Ziegler in *Die Zeit*, no. 262, October 7, 1899; no. 263, October 14, 1899; no. 318, November 3, 1900.

19. Soergel and Hohoff (1963, 706 [in connection with Oswald Spengler's *Decline of the West;* see Spengler 1922, 1928]): "Similar remarks can be made about Houston Stewart Chamberlain's work on the foundations of the nineteenth century (first published 1898). Like Spengler's theses, Chamberlain's have lost their credibility because of the fondness the Nazis showed for them. Spengler and Chamberlain were writers of astounding influence, not because they had important ideas, but because they understood how to make the world comprehensible from one particular standpoint. Otto Weininger's brilliantly written book *Sex and Character*, which demonstrated the spiritual and moral inferiority of woman, provides an example from the area of sexual psychology."

20. At the time Weininger was promoted to doctor of philosophy he was twenty-two, and not—as Jodl writes—twenty-four.

21. Ferdinand Tönnies said the following in his review of volume 2 of Wundt's *Logik* 2: "The *psychology* of our century is essentially a "psychology *without* a soul"; it purports to be nothing further than an empirical description of *facts*. It does not relapse into the animistic-teleological method, which derived psychological or even physical events from sensation or will as their causes. . . . On the other hand, these nineteenth century tendencies *persist* in the negation of all teleological causality and the harmonious world view such causality brings with it; at the same time, these tendencies *theoretically* restore the priority of the organistic and, with it, the psychological-metaphysical view" (Tönnies 1901, 183)

22. Cf. Miguel de Cervantes Saavedra. *The History and Adventures of the Renowned Don Quixote*, Book 1, Chapter 1.

23. Cf. the first sentence in this essay.

24. [Translators' note: The German word *Löser* evokes the related word *Erlöser*, which means the "redeemer" or "messiah."]

25. Wittgenstein wrote to G. E. Moore on August 23, 1931, that "I can quite imagine that you don't admire Weininger very much, what with that beastly translation and the fact that W. must feel very foreign to you. It is true that he is fantastic but he is great and fantastic. It isn't necessary or rather not possible to agree with him but the greatness lies in that with which we disagree. It is his enormous mistake which is great. i.e., roughly speaking if you just add a '~' to the whole book it says an important truth." (Wittgenstein 1974, 159).

CHAPTER 4   *How Did Weininger Influence Wittgenstein?*

1. I have discussed the importance of Wittgenstein's later philosophy for the analysis of skill in working life in Janik (1988, 53–66; 1989a, 6–17).

2. I am deeply indebted to Dr. Hannelore Rodlauer for information about the unpublished manuscripts and letters that she has unearthed in the Austrian Academy of Sciences and the National Library. These materials will definitively show how little Weininger has been understood by both his supporters and his enemies. See Rodlauer (1990, 11–51), an abridged version of which comprises Chapter 3 of this book.

3. Lest this seem all too curious, Rodlauer has established that Wilhelm Jerusalem, the Viennese forerunner of all these figures, was Weininger's Greek teacher and a sort of mentor to him.

4. Here Weininger seems to take his clues from Ludwig Feuerbach, although there are no references to Feuerbach in Weininger's book. The fact that Friedrich Jodl, Weininger's *Doktorvater* (dissertation advisor), edited Feuerbach's collected works may well have something to do with the Feuerbachian elements in this part of Weininger's work.

5. I owe this information to Reinhard Merkl, to whom Popper admitted a positive evaluation of Weininger at the same time that he fully distanced himself from Weininger's alleged antifeminism and anti-Semitism.

6. On the importance of what is "striking," see Wittgenstein (1953, vol. 1, 129).

CHAPTER 5   *Weininger and Lombroso: A Question of Influence*

All translations of Lombroso are by the author.

1. The readings of Lombroso in this essay are revised from my book on Lombroso and Serao (Harrowitz 1994a, chaps. 2–3).

2. This edition was put together just before Lombroso's death by his daughter Gina Lombroso-Ferrero and is a summary of his theories. The volume was first published in 1911, two years after his death. Lombroso wrote the introduction, which provides a valuable contextualization of his theories within the discipline of criminology. Savitz points out that the issue of who was translated played an important role in which texts were influential in the development of American criminology. The Lombrosian school was quickly and frequently translated, while the French school was poorly represented in translation, and thus many of the latter texts remained unavailable to American criminologists, the majority of whom were unskilled in foreign languages.

3. Lombroso and Ferrero ([1893] 1903). Although Lombroso did co-author this text with the young historian Guglielmo Ferrero, who later was to marry Lombroso's daughter Gina, Lombroso was very clearly the senior author with ultimate responsibility for the text, and he alone wrote the preface.

4. Lombroso and Ferrero (1903, 490): "quel fondo d'immoralità che latente si trova in ogni donna"; "quel fondo di malvagità che è latente in ogni donna."

5. Lombroso and Ferrero (1903, 499): "la maternità è—quasi diremmo—essa stessa un vaccino morale contro il delitto e il male."

6. Lombroso and Ferrero (1903, 358): "ma se la donna primitiva non fu che di raro assassina, fu, come provammo sopra. . . sempre prostituta, e restò tale quasi fino all'epoca semi-barbara; quindi anche atavisticamente si spiega che la prostituta debba avere più caratteri regressivi della donna criminale."

7. Lombroso and Ferrero (1903, 334, 330): "si direbbe la laringe di un uomo. E così nella laringe, come nella faccia, come nel cranio, spicca il carattere speciale a queste, la virilità"; "distribuzione virile del pelo."

8. Lombroso and Ferrero (1903, 350): "Però, anche nelle ree più belle il carattere virile, l'esagerazione della mascella, degli zigomi, non manca mai, come non manca in nessuna delle nostre grandi cocottes, sicchè hanno tutte un'aria di famiglia che avvicina le peccatrici Russe a quelle che stancano le vie delle nostre città, sieno esse in cocchi dorati o in umili cenci. E fate che la giovinezza scompaia, e allora quelle mandibole, quegli zigomi arrotondati dall'adipe, sporgono gli angoli salienti e ne rendono il viso affatto virile, più brutto di un uomo, e la ruga si approfonda come una ferita, e quella faccia piacente mostra completamente il tipo degenerato che l'età nascondeva."

9. Lombroso and Ferrero (1883, 133): "Dimostrare come la menzogna sia abituale e quasi fisiologica nella donna sarebbe superfluo, tanto è perfino nella leggenda popolare"; "le donne dicono sempre il vero, ma non lo dicono mai intero (Toscania)"; "le donne—dice il Dohm—si servono della bugia come il bue delle corna."

10. Lombroso and Ferrero (1893, 465): "E si capisce come la chiacchiera del delitto sia più frequente nella donna che nell'uomo, perchè essa deve supplire a

tutti quei mezzi usati dal maschio a ravvivare l'immagine del delitto, come il disegno e la scrittura, che vedemmo mancare alla donna. La donna parla spesso de' suoi delitti, come l'uomo li dipinge, o li scrive, o li scolpisce nei vasi, ecc."

11. Lombroso (1894, 5). "Ne provavo quel disgusto che coglie anche il meno impaziente scienziato quando deve studiare le più ributtanti secrezioni umane. Il decidere se un odio fra popoli possa essere giustificato, nei nostri tempi, è già certo un odioso e doloroso compito; e non è agevole acconciarvisi."

12. Lombroso (1894, 6): "mi garantiva anche contro il pericolo, massimo in tali quistioni, della parzialità."

13. Lombroso (1894, 7): "l'aiuto di tali mastri sorti nelle nazioni più ricche di antisemiti e di filosemiti mi era nuova arra della rettitudine e dell'imparzialità del giudizio per chi dubitasse dello strumento che da poco tempo maneggio."

14. Lombroso (1894, 12): "la segregazione dell'abitato, la dissonanza degli usi, dei cibi, dei dialetti, la concorrenza nei commerci che fomentava gelosie, aumentava disparità reali e apparenti, rendendo desiderabile ed utile ai privati, se non al paese, il loro avvilamento; e infine la epidemia psichica che diffonde e centuplica gli odi e le leggende."

15. Lombroso (1894, 13): "certo contribuì pure alla persecuzione il carattere degli stessi perseguitati."

16. Lombroso (1894, 14): "gli stupidi riti delle azime Pasquali; i quali, divergendo da tutti quelli in uso fra i popoli in cui vivono, destano naturalmente il ridicolo e la ripugnanza che cresce coll'esagerata importanza che gli ortodossi vi annettono"

17. Lombroso and Ferrero (1903) "una stigmata grave di degenerazione è in molte criminali-nate la mancanza dell'affetto materno."

18. Lombroso (1894, 107): "Agli ebrei a lor volta tocca persuadersi come molti dei loro riti ormai appartengono ad altre epoche e per le loro inutili stranezze (azime, p. es.; circoncisione) fanno sospettare ai profani di costumi di cui essi stessi hanno il massimo ribrezzo. Se tutte le religioni hanno modificato le loro essenza, non che la loro veste, a seconda dei tempi, perchè non dovrebbero modificarne essi almeno la vernice? perchè non rinunciare a quel vero ferimento selvaggio che è la circoncisione, a quei molteplici feticci della scrittura sacra o di alcuni dei suoi periodi, che essi spargono nelle proprie case e persino legano sopra il proprio corpo, precisamente come gli amuleti, conservando senza saperlo quell'adorazione delle lettere che ne ebbero i primi scopritori e che hannno ancora i selvaggi?"

19. *Mezuzot* are small objects placed on the doorframe of houses where Jews live, containing an important prayer from the book of Deuteronomy.

20. Even as famous and important a figure as Theodor Herzl, known as the father of Zionism, became an important protagonist in the debates regarding the favorability of assimilation. As Steven Beller asserts, "Herzl wanted to free the Jews from what he saw as the dehabilitating state of being outsiders in a hostile society, and hence make Jews normal as it were" (Beller 1989b, 208).

21. Katz (1980, esp. 4–6) assesses various kinds of reactions to antisemitism in the second half of the nineteenth century on the part of the Jewish community.

22. Lombroso (1894, 24, 26): "Un altro bacillo epidemico"; "i germi del morbo."

23. Lombroso and Ferrero (1903, 223): "Presso gli Ebrei, prima della redazi-

one definitiva delle tavole della legge, il padre aveva diritto di vendere la figlia ad un padrone che ne facesse la propria concubina per un tempo stabilito dal contratto di vendita: e la figlia venduta in quel modo per profitto di suo padre, non ricavava alcun vantaggio personale dall'abbandono forzato del proprio corpo, tranne il caso in cui il padrone, dopo averla fidanzata al proprio figlio, volesse sostituirla con un altra concubina. Gli Ebrei trafficavano insomma della prostituzione delle loro figlie."

24. The model for this sort of father–daughter exploitation does exist. As Robert Oden maintains, the Greek historian Herodotus, source for most of the information on cultic and sacred prostitution, "refers in passing to the Lydian custom by which parents turn their daughters into prostitutes who thereby earn dowries for themselves" (Oden 1987, 141). This is a similar if not exact rendition of the version Lombroso comes up with regarding the Jews, since here the Lydian daughters end up with a dowry. Herodotus influenced most of the other early writers and thinkers on the topic of sacred prostitution, and Lombroso was probably familiar with his work either directly or indirectly. This possible source for a similar story does not of course explain why Lombroso would attribute this tradition to the Jews instead of the Lydians.

25. For more discussion of this point, and of Weininger reception in Italy, see Cavaglion, 1982.

26. According to Lombroso's theories, religious rituals and practices do not stand up to the scrutiny of positivism or measurement, although it should be noted that Lombroso confines his attacks on the "ridiculousness" of religious practice to Judaism. Both Weininger and Lombroso seem to deny Judaism a theological content, as they focus on attacking religious practices as if these practices were disassociated from theology.

CHAPTER 6   *Otto Weininger as Liberal?*

All translations are by the author.

1. For a full-scale study that takes the traditional approach, see Le Rider (1982). Weininger's portrayal as an exemplary Jewish self-hater stems from Lessing (1930, 80–99). Other negative dismissals include Gay (1978, 195–96); and Schwarz (1979, 278–79). A much more subtle account is given in Kohn (1961, 165–68), Janik (1987).

2. One illustration of the survival of this approach was a notorious British Conservative campaign poster that had a picture of a West Indian man with the caption, "I'm not black; I'm British." The recent battle in France over the wearing of veils by Muslim girls in French public schools is another example.

3. The phrase "second emancipation" is used by Ludwig Speidel in a review of Theodor Herzl's play *Das neue Ghetto* in *Neue Freie Presse,* January 16, 1898, 1.

4. A good example of the attempt at restructuring is Joseph Wertheimer's "Verein zur Beförderung der Handwerke unter den inländischen Israeliten," discussed in Mayer (1918, 301–2).

5. Both Chamberlain and Bahr took this approach. Chamberlain saw Jewish revolutionary socialists as typical Jews, while he thought that the rabbi who looked after his community was not Jewish at all. (Chamberlain 1899, 450–51). Bahr contrasted the "real Jew" with the camouflaged Reform Jews in Vienna (Bahr, 1906, 69).

6. This second essay, entitled "jber die Grenzen der jüdischen intellektuellen Begabung," was written in 1904, after Weininger's *Geschlecht und Charakter* was published (1903). There is, however, no evidence that Gomperz read Weininger, and there is enough continuity between his views of 1881 and 1904 to suggest that he had held these opinions for some time. The similarity between certain of Gomperz's attitudes and those of Weininger is, nevertheless, striking.

7. All following page references will be to the English translation (Weininger 1906). However, a proper understanding of Weininger's work can be gained only by reading the original German version, *Geschlecht und Charakter*, as the English translation is compromisingly bowdlerized.

8. Weininger cites the example of New Zealand's enfranchisement of women, stating that it is based on ethical principles, but that New Zealand's bad experiences confirm the inadvisability of enfranchisement on the grounds of utility.

9. This inconsistency was noted early on by, among others, the women's emancipationist Rosa Mayreder (Mayreder 1913, 23–24). Mayreder was sympathetic to Weininger's attempt to demonstrate the innate bisexuality of all individuals, although she saw his effort as ultimately a failure. She did recognize Weininger's attempt to differentiate between "women" and "Woman." However, she did not see his occasional blurring of the difference as the oversight that it is and thus did not perceive the full emancipatory message that *Geschlecht und Charakter* contained in its final chapters.

In many other respects Mayreder, with her plea for granting the "abnormal" female full equality with men and her general affirmation of the need to treat human beings as individuals regardless of group affinities, is very close to Weininger (Mayreder 1913, 36, 74–89). The political individualism of both puts them firmly in the liberal camp.

10. Cf. Spackman (1989, 73–77). Basing her critique largely on the work of Gaston Bachelard, Barbara Spackman shows the assymmetry implicit in aestheticist theories of poetic androgyny, whereby the male poet gains his creativity from the subordinate part of his psyche, the feminine anima that is his poetic reverie, and then molds this with his dominant, conscious animus. This being so, however, the female cannot be a poet, because her dominant psychic component is already the anima, and thus she is all reverie, with no androgynous component of animus, which would be necessary for her to be capable of formed thought. Hence the "feminine" character of anima, of reverie, is praised, as it applies to men; women remain, in this interpretation, unconscious beings. It might be remarked that such an asymmetric approach to sexual androgyny, where the feminine principle is praised as the source of creativity but empirical women are denied the faculty of reason, can be seen very strongly in the writings of Weininger's contemporaries, such as Karl Kraus and Frank Wedekind. "Lulu" can indeed be seen as the archetypal representation of this view of Woman.

CHAPTER 7   *Otto Weininger and Sigmund Freud: Race and Gender in the Shaping of Psychoanalysis*

1. See the letter to Sándor Ferenczi of October 6, 1910, in which Freud wrote: "Since Fliess's case, with the overcoming of which you recently saw me occupied, that need has been extinguished. A part of my homosexual cathexis has been withdrawn and made use of to enlarge my own ego. I have succeeded where the paranoiac fails" (Jones 1955, vol. 2, 83; see also Koestenbaum 1989, 17–43).

2. In the 1950s there was a simple reversal of argument about the meaning of Jewish creativity. After the Holocaust, Silvano Arieti, certainly the most widely influential psychoanalyst after Freud to deal with the question of creativity, reverses the process, as he focuses on this issue and the (for him) related question of the nature and meaning of schizophrenia (Arieti 1950, 1976). Arieti is fascinated by the relationship between madness in its mid-twentieth-century manifestation, schizophrenia, and the creative. His interest lies in examining the relationship between Freud's sense of creativity as stemming from the primary processes of psychic development, as reflected in the mechanisms of the dream, and higher forms of psychic organization. For Arieti the clue to the meaning of creativity lies in the psychopathological structures of the schizophrenic, who organizes the world along quite different structures than does someone of "normal" consciousness: "The seriously ill schizophrenic, although living in a state of utter confusion, tries to recapture some understanding and to give organization to his fragmented universe. This organization is, to a large extent, reached by connecting things that have similar parts in common. Many patients force themselves to see similarities everywhere. In their relentless search for such similarities they see strange coincidences; that is, similar elements occurring in two or more instances at the same time or at brief intervals. By considering these similarities as identities they attempt to find some clarity in the confusion of the world, a solution for the big jigsaw puzzle" (Arieti 1977, 7). As this statement shows, Arieti is expanding upon but continuing Freud's model of the creative.

But there is also an extraordinary subtext in Arieti's corollary to Freud's argument. For Arieti, an Italian Jew whose study *The Parnas* is one of the most moving accounts of the psychological destruction of Italian Jewry, the Jew becomes the prototypical creative individual (Arieti 1979). Arieti creates a category labeled the "creativogenic culture," which encourages the innovation of creativity. Qualities such as the availability of cultural means, openness to cultural stimuli, stress on becoming and not just on being, tolerance for diverging views, and freedom following repression all provide the matrix for the creativity. It is of little surprise that for Arieti the exemplary creative individuals are the Jews. The exemplary Jews whom he chooses as his example of the truly creative are the scientists, especially the medical scientists. He tabulates the relationship of Jewish recipients of the Nobel Prizes to German, French, Italian, and Argentinean recipients, and determines that "Jews exceed in all categories with the exception of the Peace Prize, where they are surpassed by the French and the Argentineans. If we examine the five fields in which prizes are assigned, we notice that the greatest Jewish contributions are in the fields of medicine and physics (Arieti 1976, 327–28). (The slipperiness of this undertaking can be judged by examining Hermann (1978), where the "Jewish" prize winners are suddenly identified "German" prize winners. The ideology behind both of these categorizations is clear.) Of course, Arieti can offer no working definition of the "Jew." He rather constructs an ontological category quite similar to that of Weininger, simply reversing the poles of his argument. For Arieti, the creative becomes the Jewish state of mind, and the Jew becomes creativity incorporated. But again this is a specific form of the creative—science and specifically the science of medicine—Arieti's own self-definition.

   To contrast Arieti and Freud on the concept of creativity is to confront a world in which the question of Jewish particularism is repressed or qualified when creativity is addressed and one in which it is celebrated. Both views are answers to the charge that Jews, through perverse sexuality, are different, mad, and inherently uncreative. Today, we have sufficient distance from the wellsprings of this turn-of-the-century debate about the creative and its sequelae to see how Freud and his followers such as Arieti found themselves confronted with a need to provide a rationale for their own creativity in their construction of the world. What is the truly creative in this context thus becomes the writing of the scientists in their striving to define the creative.

CHAPTER 8   *Characterology: Weininger and Austrian Popular Science*

   1. This could also be proved with a second institutional example from Vienna. See the case of the herpetologist Paul Kammerer (Koestler 1971/73) and the discussion in Arens (1986).

CHAPTER 9   *Otto Weininger and the Critique of Jewish Masculinity*

   1. "For Weininger," Sander L. Gilman notes, "the Jew is always the male" (Gilman 1986, 245). Gilman investigates this point in a later volume of essays (Gilman 1991b).

   2. Contrasting treatments of the stage Jew and Jewess long antedate Weininger's era: "But from the outset a distinction must be drawn. The Jewess enjoyed an extraordinary immunity from attack; she was as much lauded as the Jew was reviled. The stage Jewess was always beautiful, and was always inteded to be loveworthy" (Abrahams 1898, 257). For a biting critique of the Jewess employing the familiar repertory of deficiencies traditionally directed against the Jewish male, see Sachs 1916–17, a young Jew who finds German girls more carefree, "natural," and so on.

   3. In fact, Weininger calls the Jewess the ultimate incarnation of the idea of woman—"keine Frau der Welt die Idee des Weibes so völlig repräsentiert wie die Jüdin" (Weininger 1922, 425). [no woman in the world represents the idea of woman as completely as the Jewess.]

   4. As Frederick R. Karl has noted, Weininger's "attack on women is associated with the so-called womanish aspect of himself—his own sense of himself as a weak male; his attack on Judaism is part of his low estimate of himself as a Jew; his opposition to the Zionist movement is to remove heroism from Jewish affairs, so as to justify his own low profile as a Jew; his assault on whatever he feels

to be degenerative is connected to his own need to defend the true faith, a kind of Knight Templar of the modern spirit. Weininger has located in himself all these weaknesses and then projected them on society and culture, using women as the chief scapegoats. Modernist artists accomplished the obverse. Searching out personal weaknesses, projecting those weaknesses as salient ingredients of their culture, they constructed alternate modes of perception. Weakness, thus, becomes not a source of debilitation, but a source of new sight, new sensory experience, new experiences" (Karl 1985, 89).

5. On one occasion Weininger does single out the "male" Jew, saying that "there is no (male) Jew who does not, however apathetically, suffer on account of his Jewishness, which is to say, on the deepest level, due to his lack of belief" ("und es gibt denn auch keinen (männlichen) Juden, der nicht, wenn auch noch so dumpf, an seinem Judentum, das ist, im tiefsten Grunde, an seinem Unglauben, litte") (Weininger 1922, 434). Weininger's evasive strategy for dealing with the humiliations of the Jewish male is evident in his claim that the root cause of his suffering is a lack of religious faith.

6. Jews often encountered discrimination in a number of European armies, most notoriously in the Dreyfus Affair in France. While Jews were allowed to join the officer corps in southern Germany and Austria-Hungary, in Prussia they could not (Deák 1990, 133).

7. See, for example, one Dr. Jeremias, whose views are quite typical of this period. Unlike some Zionist "self-critics," Dr. Jeremias rejects the idea that the "*physiologische Misère*" resulting from centuries of ghetto life affected only Eastern European Jews. Undersized bodies, flat feet, varicose veins, hemorrhoids, and other disorders afflict, he says, European Jewry as a whole (Jeremias 1901, 4). This essay is a response to Balduin Groller, who had called the idea of Jewish physical inferiority a "fable" Jews had taken over from anti-Semites (Groller 1901, 4).

8. Jacques Le Rider, citing Weininger's definition of Jewry as "a psychic constitution," argues that Weininger's argumentation "has almost nothing to do with [racial] biology" (Le Rider 1985, 194).

9. Not surprisingly, this physical portrait of the Jew appeared in certain Nazi texts decades after Nordau and Rathenau (among others) called for a more physically presentable Jewry (Schneemann 1966).

10. Rathenau's notorious text, published in 1897 under a pseudonym, is "Höre, Israel!" (Rathenau 1965). Its most famous passage criticizes the inferior bodies and physical ineptness of the Jews, whose appearance and deportment compare poorly with the military bearing of the German male.

11. This well known early text on this subject is Lessing (1930), which includes a disappointing chapter on Weininger. The standard treatment is Gilman (1986).

12. Denis de Rougemont, for example, says Columbus was "probably of Jewish origin" (Rougement 1965, 21).

13. In addition to Kafka's own *Letter to His Father* and the biographical studies by Max Brod (Brod 1937) and Elias Canetti, the indispensable commentary on Kafka's struggle with the masculinity issue is Pawel (1984, 202–05).

14. On Weininger's relationship to his father, Hans Kohn wrote: "Weininger's rejection of Judaism did not spring from a revolt against his Jewish father.

Nothing is known to us of any conflict between father and son. On the contrary, after Weininger's death his father wrote about him in *Die Fackel*, a periodical edited by Karl Kraus, in a very dignified and sympathetic way. The father was an enthusiastic admirer of Wagner's 'Parsifal' and before his death left his Jewish community. . . . The situation was entirely different in the case of Weininger's contemporary Franz Kafka, whose early rejection of Judaism, which only changed later, can perhaps be explained by his negative relationship to his father" (Kohn 1961, 165–65n).

CHAPTER 10 *Weininger and Nazi Ideology*

Many thanks to Dr. Antje Gerlach at the Berlin Center for Anti-Semitism Research, to the Memorial House of the Wannsee Conference, and to the New State Library of Berlin for their friendly assistance with their respective collections. All English translations are by the author, except where expressly noted otherwise.

1. Mosse (1966, 76f) calls *Sex and Character* "a classic not only of Jewish self-hate but also of racist literature."

2. Weininger's posthumously published *Über die letzten Dinge* (On Last Things) is never quoted by Nazi ideologues.

3. Koonz (1987) has become a standard work on both National Socialist policy toward women and women's responses to life in the Third Reich. For a preliminary study on the European cultural history of hostility toward women and Jews, see Braun (1992, 1993). Also cf. Jakubowski (1991).

4. See Fritsch (1887, 1919, 1929, 1943). A biographical note in his *Handbuch der Judenfrage*, first published in 1930, proudly refers to Fritsch as "der Schöpfer des praktischen Antisemitismus" (the creator of practical anti-Semitism). Fritsch also published under a number of pseudonyms such as Thomas Frey, Fritz Thor, and F. Roderich-Stoltheim.

5. The *Handbuch* also contains an appendix of "Jewish Self-Revelations" in which two of the same quotations appear, also under the rubric "Jewish Character."

6. See Mosse (1964, 302), who in turn cites Deuerlein (1959, 203).

7. Rosenberg (1928, 214–19), quoted in "The Earth-Centered Jew Lacks a Soul" (Mosse 1966, 75–78). Also see Rosenberg (1930).

8. The phrase "and certainly less capable of all great pleasure" did not appear in the first edition, but was added to subsequent editions.

9. Another aspect of Weininger's portrayal of Jewish male sexuality has to do with body image. Cf. John M. Hoberman's essay in this volume (Chapter 9).

10. Richard Wagner is the source of both Rosenberg's and Weininger's assertions. See Rosenberg (1933, 15), quoted in Koch (1986, 72).

11. For an explication of the significance of blood imagery in anti-Semitism, see Braun (1990, 153).

12. See Janik (1987, 80): "The simple fact about Theodor Lessing's account of Weininger in *Der jüdische Selbsthass* is that it is based upon a racism which is just as crude as anything that the most vulgar Nazi ideologues might have asserted. For Lessing Weininger's problem was rooted in hatred for his blood."

13. Also see Bytwerk (1983).

14. The same racist tone is appearing again in neo-Nazi publications; for example, "A vagina that has been sullied by a Jew remains a cesspool. No Aryan broom can sweep it clean," which appeared in an issue of the *Skinhead-Zeitung*, was quoted in "Bestie aus deutschem Blut" (Beast of German Blood), the cover story in *Der Spiegel* (50/1992) 30.

15. See in particular Pugel's chapter "Die deutsche Frau im Kampfe gegen das Judentum und den Bolschewismus" (The German woman in battle against Judaism and Bolshevism).

16. However, as Jacques Le Rider notes, it also impressed more subtle thinkers, such as Karl Kraus (Le Rider 1985, 23, 144, 190–91, 201, 217). Also see Rodlauer's (1990) discussion of Chamberlain and Weininger, and the abridged translation of the work in this volume (Chapter 3).

17. On the Chamberlain-Kant connection cf. Mosse (1964, 94).

18. Cf. Braun (1990, 157).

19. See Mosse (1964, 6; 1970, 15, 36, 57, 162, 243 n. 68).

20. See Beller (1989b, 222). Regarding the last months of Weininger's life, during which he rejected the Kantian self, see Kohn (1962, 41–42).

21. Cf. Spengler in the passage on Jewish saints: Kant's "abstract kind of thought has always possessed an immense attraction for Talmudic intellects" (Spengler 1928, 321).

22. Cf. Spengler (1928, 318): "But all this has nothing to do with the silly catchwords 'Aryan' and 'Semite' that have been borrowed from philology."

23. Rogge-Börner also made a bid to become national director of women's affairs, but was disqualified because she was independent and charismatic (Koonz 1987, 140). Her journal, "Die deutsche Kämpferin" (The German Woman Fighter), was banned in 1937 when it was perceived as too critical of National Socialist policies toward women (Thalmann 1984, 85f).

24. Also see, for example, Buresch-Riebe (1942), and articles in the *Völkischer Beobachter* (Berlin edition) such as Sachisthal (1943), "Berliner Mädel" (1943) and "Nationaler Ehrendienst (1943).

25. Dovifat, who began his career in the Weimar era and ended it as a renowned professor at the Free University of Berlin and founding editor of the journal *Publizistik*, provides yet another example of "inner emigration" during National Socialism. Although his academic freedom was curtailed at the University of Berlin because his loyalty to the state was under suspicion, he was allowed to teach, and he managed to inspire enthusiasm among young Nazis and fledgling critics of the regime alike. Benedikt reports that in 1982 one of Dovifat's former doctoral students, Elisabeth Noelle-Neumann, recalled his general principle that "the first and last three pages of a dissertation had to make National Socialist arguments, and that he referred to these pages among his trusted inner circle as 'wrapping paper' " (Benedikt 1986, 202). On the controversy surrounding Noelle-Neumann, see Bogart (1991) and Lederer (1993). Dovifat's most controversial publication during the Third Reich was a 1937 analysis of political orators and oratory in which he wrote of Hitler: "Just as he can explain with technical rationality the principles of leading the masses, so too does he vividly and warmly look beyond the primary substance of the masses for the *Volk*, which he wants to

convince, to turn into a believer, and thereby transform. . . . Everything is folksy, eager to instruct, presented with tireless clarity, not speaking beyond the *Volk*, but rather of and for the *Volk*" (Dovifat 1937, 138). While it is easy to read such statements after the fact as veiled criticisms, Dovifat never openly resisted the Nazi state.

26. Centgraf had the appropriate Nazi credentials to write a diatriabe against Weininger. His dissertation topic, which casts Martin Luther in the light of a charismatic German leader who engaged in "propaganda for the masses" with his books and leaflets (Centgraf 1940, 5), is completely in line with Houston Stewart Chamberlain's view of the Reformation as "the most decisive of all political acts." Chamberlain's views served as the ideological foundation for subsequent *völkisch* interpretations of Luther (cf. Brosseder 1972, 98–101). Centgraf comments in a lengthy footnote on Luther's infamous treatise of 1543, "On the Jews and Their Lies": "Luther makes . . . practical suggestions on how to do battle with the Jews and shows himself *here especially to be the innovative and path-breaking communicator of timeless importance for and influence on the German nation*" (Centgraf 1940, 34f.).

27. The title is a quote from Theodor Lessing's *Der jüdische Selbsthaβ* of 1930.

28. Magnus Hirschfeld regularly came under attack for his sexual preference and for his scientific studies on homosexuality. *Der Stürmer*, for example, accused homosexuals like Hirschfeld of creating "a Jewish conspiracy to destroy marriage and the family" (Showalter 1982, 100).

29. Centgraf continued to publish after the war, but under the pseudonym of N. Alexander Centurio. He devoted himself to the sixteenth-century prophetic visions of Nostradamus, a longstanding fascination he had in common with many prominent Nazi leaders, Goebbels among them. Centgraf/Centurio translated and interpreted the prophecies in the "first complete German edition" in 1953 as *Nostradamus, der Prophet der Weltgeschichte* (Nostradamus, The Prophet of World History). The book is still available today in the Goldmann Verlag *Esoterik* series (Centurio 1991). Centgraf/Centurio defines National Socialism as "a strange mixture of romanticism and brutality" (Centurio 1991, 198). He mentions Jews only in the context of Nostradamus's biography, noting that Nostradamus's paternal ancestors were Sephardic Jews who fled religious persecution (Centurio 1991, 13), and in the context of the still unresolved Arab-Israeli conflict in the Middle East. According to Centgraf/Centurio's reading of 1,45, "Hitler did away with all parties that criticized the system. He set up concentration camps in which dogs were also set on the unfortunate victims. With ancient cruelty of a sadistic nature, the inmates of these camps were tortured and killed. As a result of the crimes of the Nazi Party, the world is thrust into division and despair" (Centurio 1991, 202). Interpreting Nostradamus's prophecies about the years 1942–45, in Verse 5,96, Centgraf/Centurio writes, "Hitler . . . spilled, for the sake of his insane goals, the blood of six million Germans. All opposition to the politics of violence was stifled by the Gestapo" (Centurio 1991, 211). While Centgraf/Centurio has no difficulty recalling that *Germans* were subject to National Socialist brutality, he apparently cannot face up to the mass murder of *European Jews* to which he contributed indirectly at the very least.

30. This issue contains two anonymous essays, "Das jüdische Wesen" (The Jewish Essence) and "Juden zeichnen sich selbst" (Jews Portray Themselves), which refer in passing to Otto Weininger.

CHAPTER 11   *A Scientific Image of Woman? The Influence of Otto Weininger's* Sex and Character *on the German Novel*

This essay appeared originally as Brude-Firnau (1979). It is printed here for the first time in English translation by kind permission of its author, Gisela Brude-Firnau, and its new copyright holder, K. G. Saur Verlag.

1. On the Freud-Weininger relationship and Freud's accusation of plagiarism, see Abrahamsen (1946, 43), Fliess (1906), and Freud (1955, 5; 1953, 135); on the influence of Weininger on James Joyce refer to Ellmann (1959, 477). I would like to thank John E. Woods, who gave me this reference during the Amherst Colloquium. For Karl Kraus, see Kraft (1956, 73–94); also see Blei (1903), Goldmann (1971, 68), and Kohn (1961).

2. Politzer (1965, 288–89): "prägte sich der Generation Kafkas ein, besonders jenen Zeitgenossen, die sich für die Weiberfeindschaft August Strindbergs empfänglich gezeigt hatten oder von Sigmund Freuds Ehrgeiz angefeuert waren, die unterschwelligen Mechanismen des Seelenlebens zu beobachten."

3. The phrases "Brain child" and "stroke of genius" (*Geniestreich*) in reference to Weininger's work appear as early as p. 36 of Grass's novel. See Blomster (1969).

4. Anonymous (1904). Quoted in a forty-eight-page prospectus of *Sex and Character* provided by the publisher Wilhelm Braumüller as a supplement to the twelfth edition: "Es ist ein niederträchtiges Buch, das wir vor uns haben. Mag auch der Einfluß Strindbergs unverkennbar sein, ein Buch wie *Geschlecht und Charakter* schreibt kein vernünftiger Mensch. Hätte Weininger sich rechtzeitig in die Behandlung eines Psychiaters gegeben, so wäre der deutsche Büchermarkt vor einer solchen Schande und der Verfasser vor dem Revolver bewahrt geblieben. Unbegreiflich aber ist es, wie es Leute gibt, die Weininger trotz seines frechen Buches noch Loblieder singen."

5. Weininger's critique of Judaism was used as late as 1939 in an anti-Semitic German radio broadcast (cf. Abrahamsen 1946, 122).

6. On Weininger's significance for the women's movement, see Klein (1946, 53–70).

7. Weininger (1910, 9): "unzählige Abstufungen zwischen Mann und Weib."

8. Weininger (1910, 84): "Je länger das Haar, desto kürzer der Verstand."

9. Morgenstern (1965, 263): "schließt er messerscharf, daß nicht sein kann, was nicht sein darf."

10. Weininger (1910, 334): "Liebe ist Mord."

11. Weininger (1910, 472): "Nicht die Frau heilig zu machen, nicht darum kann es so bald sich handeln. Nur darum: kann das Weib zum Problem seines Daseins, zum Begriff der Schuld redlich gelangen? Wird es die Freiheit wenigstens wollen? Allein auf die Durchsetzung des Ideales, auf das Erblicken des Leitsternes kommt es an. Bloß darauf: kann im Weib der kategorische Imperativ lebendig werden? Wird sich das Weib unter die sittliche Idee, unter die Idee der Menschheit, stellen? Denn einzig das wäre Frauen-Emanzipation."

12. "Unmistakable analogies" are a contestable point, since frequently used sources, such as the works of Nietzsche, Schopenhauer, or the earlier writings of Freud, may be equally pertinent. For this reason, I will apply this indicator only to the imagery in *The Man Without Qualities*.

13. In contrast to Politzer, see Bödecker (1974, 104–5).

14. For other reviews, see Dallago (1912) and Ebner (1919). On Broch's Weininger reception, see Durzak (1968, 11–23) and Lützeler (1973, 36–37).

15. Broch (1957, 26): "Mutter Hentjen, die ihrerseits von allem Anbeginn 'wertfrei' und 'autonom' ist, wie eben das 'Weibliche' oder die 'Natur' als solche immer wertfrei ist."

16. Broch (1957, 348): "Denke ich zurück, so steht auf der ersten Ebene eine Aufforderung an den Juden Nuchem: 'Laß dich von keiner noch so zarten Legendenhaftigkeit verführen, sondern bleib beim abstrakten Buch, bleib ein Jud, bleib bei deiner Thora.' Auf der zweiten Ebene jedoch ist es eine Aufforderung an den Dichter: 'Laß dich nicht vom Heilversprechen verführen: Dichtung vermittelt dir keine Gnade, vielmehr liegt der Gnadenweg in der Erkenntnis.' "

17. See Broch (1988). Only the first version of the novel, except as noted by its translator, H. F. Broch de Rothermann, is available in English. Cf. Broch de Rothermann's "Brief Genesis of the Novel" and "Translator's Note" in Broch (1988, 387–91).

18. Marius is specifically called a "foe of mothers" (Broch 1987, 67); he attacks Agatha publicly as a "witch."

19. Broch (1969, 405): "Wie die Weiber schmeicheln sie sich heran mit ihren Geschäften, ja, wie die Weiber, denn sie tun ja nur so, als ob sie Männer wären, weil ihnen der Bart im Gesicht hängt, aber die Weiberhabsucht in ihrem weichen Gesicht können sie damit nicht verdecken."

20. The doctor/narrator's passive complicity in the murder of Irmgard has been interpreted in various ways. Furthermore, the narrator's susceptibility to demagogic seduction—analogous to a criticism often levied against Weininger—is related to his youthful fanaticism for chastity. Cf. the second version of Broch (1969, 16).

21. I would like to thank Professor Ingo Seidler for pointing out during the Amherst Colloquium that Weininger is mentioned a number of times in Musil's unpublished manuscripts. Sporadic reference to Weininger also appears in the following secondary literature on Musil: Roth (1972, 57), Appignanesi (1973, 84), and Corino (1973, 154, 177).

22. Weininger (1910, 129): "wo immer ein neues Urteil zu fällen, und nicht ein schon lange fertiges einmal mehr in Satzform auszusprechen ist, daß in solchem Falle stets W von M die Klärung ihrer dunklen Vorstellungen . . . erwartet."

23. Weininger (1910, 252): "Ein psychologischer Beweis für die Urteilsfunktion ist dieser, daß das Urteilen vom Weibe als männlich empfunden wird, und wie ein (tertiärer) Sexualcharakter anziehend auf dasselbe wirkt. Die Frau verlangt vom Manne stets bestimmte Überzeugungen, die sie übernehme."

24. Weininger (1910, 289): "Für die Frau ist der Ehebruch ein kitzelndes Spiel, in welchem der Gedanke der Sittlichkeit gar nicht, sondern nur die Motive der Sicherheit und des Rufes mitspielen."

25. Musil (1970, 258): "Sie glaubte immer mehreres gleichzeitig, und halbe Wahrheiten erleichterten ihr das Lügen."

26. Weininger (1910, 193–94): "Ein Wesen [i.e., die Frau], das nicht begreift oder nicht anerkennt, daß A und non-A einander ausschließen, wird durch nichts mehr gehindert zu lügen; vielmehr gibt es für ein solches Wesen gar keinen Begriff der Lüge, weil ihr Gegenteil, die Wahrheit, als das Maß, ihm abgeht." Ulrich muses correspondingly over Agathe: "but she hasn't the slightest idea what Truth means!" ("aber sie weiß doch gar nicht, was Wahrheit bedeutet!" [Musil 1970, 1797]).

27. Weininger (1910, 113): "W ist nichts als Sexualität, M ist sexuell und noch etwas darüber."

28. Weininger (1910, 112–13): "W befaßt sich . . . mit außergeschlechtlichen Dingen nur für den Mann, den sie liebt, oder um des Mannes willen, von dem sie geliebt sein möchte. Ein Interesse für diese Dinge an sich fehlt ihr vollständig."

29. Corino (1973, 132): "Abwertung der Sexualität."

30. Musil (1970, 952): "ziehen sittliche Mängel nach sich, spricht man doch von moralischem Blödsinn."

31. Weininger (1910, 192): "Die Frau erbittert die Zumutung, ihr Denken ausnahmslos von der Logik abhängig zu machen. Ihr mangelt das intellektuelle Gewissen. Man könnte bei ihr von 'logical insanity' sprechen!"

32. Musil (1970, 1353): "daß ich Ihnen brüderlich dienen, gleichsam im Weibe selbst das Gegengewicht gegen das Weib . . . erwecken möchte."

33. Weininger (1910, 463): "Emanzipation des Weibes vom Weibe."

34. Musil (1970, 797): "feste Regeln dem innersten Wesen der Moral widersprächen."

35. Musil (1970, 954): "ihr Verhalten kam ihr so sehr wie das eines wirklich nicht zurechnungsfähigen Wesens vor."

36. Musil (1970, 961): "Es bleibt also dabei, daß ich moralisch schwachsinnig bin?"

37. Weininger (1910, 261): "So kann sie [die Frau] eben keinen Wert an sich selbst besitzen, es fehlt ihr der Eigenwert der menschlichen Persönlichkeit."

38. Weininger (1910, 466): "es ist keine Möglichkeit für eine Aufrichtung des Reiches Gottes auf Erden, eh dies nicht geschehen ist."

39. Musil (1970, 912): "Und die Welt wird sich nicht eher bessern, als es solche Liebende gibt!"

40. Musil (1970, 1473): "jeder Mensch hat ein Tier, dem er innen ähnlich sieht."

41. Weininger (1907, 126): "daß gewisse Menschen spezielle Tier-Möglichkeiten verwirklichen."

42. Weininger (1907, 128): "zum buckligen Verbrecher Beziehungen [aufweisen]."

43. Musil (1970, 926): "eine unaussprechliche Übereinstimmung des inneren Geschehens mit dem äußeren." Clarisse views Rachel as a "gazelle and queen of snakes" (Musil 1970, 1473).

44. Weininger (1907, 114): "Jeder Daseinsform in der Natur entspricht eine Eigenschaft im Menschen. Jeder Möglichkeit im Menschen entspricht etwas in der Natur."

45. Brann (1924, 26): "ein einziger grandioser Irrtum."

CHAPTER 12   *Weininger in a Poem by Apollinaire*

All translations are by the author.

1. See, for instance, Raymond (1969, 233): "Far from wanting to abolish the random [*le hasard*], like Mallarmé, Apollinaire worshiped it."

2. For Apollinaire's biography, see Steegmuller 1963.

3. Hofstadter (1985, 7) links such propositions to Gödel's "incompleteness theorem": Gödel "was able to show that in any mathematically powerful axiomatic system S, it is possible to express a close cousin to the liar paradox, namely, " 'This formula is unprovable within axiomatic system S.' "

4. Weininger (1906, 309): "The homology of Jew and woman becomes closer the further examination goes."

5. French literature would have to wait for Romain Gary's memorable *La Danse de Genghis Cohn* (1967) to find its next conflation of Jew and Cossack. Oddly enough, Gary was, like Apollinaire, of East European origin, raised on the French Riviera, and given to mystification. See Catonné (1990, 43).

6. See Freud's letter of March 13, 1938, to D. Abrahamsen (Abrahamsen 1946, 4).

7. For a discussion of Proust's maternal identification and its relation to Judaism, see Mehlman (1974, chap. 1; 1983, 968–82).

8. Thus Anthony Kenny, reviewing Ray Monk's biography of Wittgenstein (Monk 1990), does not hesitate to list Weininger as one of the two "major intellectual influences" on the "greatest philosopher of the twentieth century" (*New York Times Book Review*, December 30, 1990, 9). He then proceeds to offer a somewhat edulcorated version of Weininger's theses, omitting, unlike Monk, the mention of anti-Semitism entirely. And yet, when one reads in Wittgenstein's *Vermischte Bemerkungen* (Wittgenstein 1977, 144) that "when you can't unravel a knot, the most intelligent thing you can do is realize it; and the most suitable recourse is to recognize it [Anti-Semitism]," it is hard not to recall the celebrated ending of his *Tractatus:* "Worüber man nicht sprechen kann, darüber soll man schweigen" [What we cannot speak about, we must pass over in silence]. Anti-Semitism, then, as the unspeakable limit of philosophy.

9. "I like Jews," he would write in "Le Passant de Prague," (Apollinaire 1902).

CHAPTER 13   *Kafka and Weininger*

This essay appeared originally as Stieg (1987). It is printed here for the first time in English translation by kind permission of its author, Gerald Stieg, and the Österreichischer Bundesverlag.

1. Canetti (1982b, 49): "dem es gegeben war, sich ins Kleine zu verwandeln."

2. Canetti (1969, 86): "der größte Experte der Macht."

3. Kafka (1954, 568): "Darum ist es ein Abwehrinstinkt, der die Herstellung des kleinsten dauernden Behagens für mich nicht duldet und zum Beispiel das Ehebett zerschlägt, ehe es noch aufgestellt ist."

4. Sieh mich gebeugt mit lockerm Schritte

In Mauernähe ängstlich gehn,
Verhöhnend dein Gebot der Sitte.
Nach Füßchen und nach Busen spähn.

Das ist der Weg, der längst bekannte,
Zu ihr, der Göttin ohne Scham,
Den ich so oft zu gehen brannte
Und reuig weinend wiederkam.

O Gott, in alle Spiegel schlage
Vernichtend deine Faust hinein,
Das klare Licht entzieh dem Tage,
Dem Bache nimm den Widerschein!

- Und höhnisch schleicht das alte Bangen
Der heißbegehrten Lust voran. -
O!!! Gib dem Laster rothe Wangen,
Daß ich ihm angstlos fröhnen kann (Weininger 1923, 158).

5. Kafka (1954, 315): "Der Coitus als Bestrafung des Glücks des Beisammenseins. Möglichst asketisch leben, asketischer als ein Junggeselle, das ist die einzige Möglichkeit für mich, die Ehe zu ertragen. Aber sie?"

6. Kafka (1983, 197f.): "Und so wie es damals war, blieb es immer. Mein Körper, oft jahrelang still, wurde dann wieder geschüttelt bis zum Nichtertragen-Können von dieser Sehnsucht nach einer kleinen, nach einer ganz bestimmten Abscheulichkeit, nach etwas leicht Widerlichem, Peinlichem, Schmutzigem; noch in dem Besten, was es hier für mich gab, war etwas davon, irgendein kleiner schlechter Geruch, etwas Schwefel, etwas Hölle. Dieser Trieb hatte etwas vom ewigen Juden, sinnlos gezogen, sinnlos wandernd durch eine sinnlos schmutzige Welt."

7. I am not afraid to compare this silencing to religious practices of suppressing the name of God or the devil.

8. Passages are cited from Weininger (1904); English translations are by Barbara Hyams.

9. For more on this point, see Stieg (1976).

10. Weininger (1904, 89): "Die Moralität des Mannes empfindet den Geschlechtsverkehr als Sünde."

11. Weininger (1904, 89): "Das Weib hat keinen Sinn mehr, wenn der Mann keusch ist."

12. Weininger (1904, 89): "Kundry in Parsifal (das Sehnen ist's, das ihn verhindert, zum Gral, d.i. zum Sittlichen, Göttlichen zu kommen)."

13. Weininger (1904, 89): "Kundry müßte freilich schon im II. Akt sterben, da Parsifal ihr widersteht."

14. Cf. Weininger (1904, 89): "All of that places Wagner far above Goethe, whose last words, after all, were only about the 'Eternal Feminine,' the salvation of man through woman." ("Das alles stellt Wagner hoch über Goethe, dessen letztes Wort doch nur das vom 'Ewig-Weiblichen,' die Erlösung des Mannes durch das Weib war")

15. Weininger (1904, 91): " 'Suche dir Gänser die Gans' heißt heirate, aber dann steck dir nicht das Reich Gottes zum Ziel."

16. Weininger (1904, 91): "Das Lachen der Kundry geht aufs Judentum. Die metaphysische Schuld des Juden ist Lächeln über Gott."

17. The role of the assistants deserves in-depth consideration. It would be meaningful to see the circumstance of their being sent by Galater as directly connected to the Epistle of Saint Paul to the Galatians. In *The Castle*, they represent the "Galatian principle" (i.e., "pleasure principle") that was severely condemned by Paul. I believe that taking biblical "sign" names seriously (Barnabas, Galater) leads us quite a bit closer to our goal.

18. Weininger (1904, 93–109): "Über die Einsinnigkeit und ihre ethische Bedeutung."

19. Translator's note: There is no single English translation for "Einsinnigkeit." Weininger constructed the noun to express his interpretation of teleology. "Ein," of course, refers to oneness, to singularity, and "sinnig" ranges in meaning from "ingenious, clever," to an ironic "appropriate, apt," to a poetic "thoughtful, delicate." "Sinnigkeit," then, can mean "ingenuity, cleverness," ironic "appropriateness, aptness," or "thoughtfulness, delicacy" (Springer 1974, vol. 2, 1406). Gerald Stieg italicizes the root "Sinn," which encompasses the five senses, mind, wits, consciousness, sexual desires, thought, feeling, sense, meaning, significance, and direction—in short, a veritable complex unto itself of matters that preoccupied Weininger.

20. Weininger (1904, 97): "Sich im Kreis zu drehen ist sinnlos, zwecklos; jemand, der sich auf der Fußspitze herumdreht, selbstzufriedener, lächerlich eitler, gemeiner Natur."

21. Weininger (1904, 98): "Der Tanz ist eine weibliche Bewegung, und zwar vor allem die Bewegung der Prostitution."

22. Weininger (1904, 104):

"Die *Einsinnigkeit der Zeit* ist sonach identisch mit der Tatsache, daß der Mensch zutiefst ein wollendes Wesen ist. *Das Ich als Wille ist die Zeit.*

Das realisierte Ich wäre Gott: das Ich auf dem *Wege* zur Selbstrealisierung ist Wille.

Der Wille ist etwas zwischen Nichtsein und Sein; sein *Weg* geht vom Nichtsein zum Sein (denn aller Wille ist Wille zur Freiheit, zum Wert, dem Absoluten, zum Sein, zur Idee, zu Gott)."

23. Weininger (1904, 108): "Das Leben ist eine Art Reise durch den Raum des inneren Ich, eine Reise vom engsten Binnenlande freilich zur umfassendsten, freiesten Überschau des Alls."

24. Kafka (1968, 37): "Schon hatte Frieda das elektrische Licht ausgedreht"

25. Kafka (1968, 37): "die Zeit war wohl unendlich vor ihrer glücklichen Liebe."

26. Kafka (1968, 37): "sie seufzte mehr als sang irgendein kleines Lied."

27. Kafka (1968, 37): "fing an wie ein Kind ihn zu zerren."

28. Kafka (1968, 37): "umfaßten einander."

29. Kafka (1968, 89): "der Geruch war so süß, so schmeichelnd, so wie man von jemand, den man sehr lieb hat, Lob und gute Worte hört und gar nicht genau

weiß, worum es sich handelt, und es gar nicht wissen will und nur glücklich ist in dem Bewußtsein, daß er es ist, der so spricht."

30. Kafka (1968, 38): "Dort vergingen Stunden, Stunden gemeinsamen Atems, gemeinsamen Herzschlags, Stunden, in denen K. immerfort das Gefühl hatte, er verirre sich oder er sei so weit in der Fremde, wie vor ihm noch kein Mensch, einer Fremde, in der selbst die Luft keinen Bestandteil der Heimatluft habe, in der man vor Fremdheit ersticken müsse und in deren unsinnigen Verlockungen man doch nichts tun könne als weiter gehen, weiter sich verirren."

31. Cf. Kafka's letter to Milena of August 9, 1920 (Kafka 1953, 164).

32. "Warum bist du nicht mit mir nach Hause gegangen?"

CHAPTER 14   *Weininger and the Bloom of Jewish Self-Hatred in Joyce's* Ulysses

This essay is a revised version of Reizbaum (1982). The author would like to thank Indiana University Press for permission to reprint it here.

1. "Cosmic" seems almost an apt description of the strength of Samuel's response to Joyce's portrayal of Bloom. I include here a bit more of the passage from which this characterization comes: "somehow Stephen emerges from all this undefiled in the eyes of the reader. *His* madnesses are those of poets. Bloom's are those of a wretched, indecent little person, none the less so because there is something pathetic in the way he clings to the young Irishman. Joyce's malevolence can do no more. By the time the scene closes the worst that can be revealed concerning human beings, the most loathsome, has been unfolded about the figure of Bloom. One should not be personal, but one cannot help feeling that for the character of Bloom, the Jew, Joyce harbors a mad, insatiable hatred. As he sees into the soul of Stephen with the mercilessness of great love, he sees into the soul of Bloom with the mercilessness of hate" (Samuel 1929, 14).

2. Ellmann writes that Joyce "borrowed" Weininger's theory that Jews are by nature womanly men (Ellmann 1982, 463); this view is endorsed and enlarged upon by Ralph Robert Joly, who points out that Italo Svevo, often cited as a prototype for Bloom, may have told Joyce about Weininger to whom, Joly claims, Svevo was often compared. Although their documentation for such claims is largely speculative, one can safely imagine that Joyce would have encountered Weininger's work, regardless of whether Svevo told him about it. *Geschlecht und Character* was reprinted eighteen times between 1903 and 1919, and many can attest to its popularity and the prevalence of these theories of "psychobiology." Further, Joyce's notebooks make reference to Weininger (VI, C.7–267), and while the date of this notation cannot be firmly established, it at least confirms without doubt that Joyce knew of Weininger.

3. As this collection attests, there has been a great resurgence of interest in Weininger's work among, for example, feminists and Germanists, *fin-de-siècle* Vienna and Jewish scholars: Viola Klein's *The Feminine Character: History of an Ideology* (1946), Sander L. Gilman's *Jewish Self-Hatred* (1986) and *Difference and Pathology* (1985), and Peter Gay's *Freud, Jews, and Other Germans* (1978) are a few of the sources. And see my own "James Joyce's Judaic 'Other': Text and Context" (1985).

4. For example, Sander Gilman discusses this historical link of figuration of the Jew in stereotypes of the feminine in both *Jewish Self-Hatred* (1986) and *Difference and Pathology* (1985).

5. In an article on Jewish self-hatred, Allan Janik critiques the theorization around this "stock concept"; he sees it "not only as a form of decadence but a type of dangerous cultural pathology presaging, perhaps, the eventual triumph of Nazism" (Janik 1987, 75–76).

6. For this source, see Gifford (1988, 481 [entry 15.1836]).

7. The Messiah ben Joseph appears in the Talmudic writings as a herald to the Messiah ben David who will bring about the messianic age. Since the former is from the house of Ephraim, he is often represented in the literature as a symbolic embodiment of the reunification with the ten tribes of Israel. In the Book of Zerubbabel, written around the beginning of seventh century B.C., this martial figure is pitted against a satanic king of Rome whom the whole world—except the Jews—believe to be God. This is of course resonant of Christ's stand against Rome. Zerubbabel is from the apocalyptic literature from the Middle Ages. It is a pseudoepigraphical work of the last ruler of the house of David. It is collected in Adolf Jellinek's *Bet Ha-Midrash*, Jerusalem: Bamberger and Wahrmann, 1938. The set is in six volumes and it is the standard edition for these texts—rabbinic and post-rabbinic apocalyptics. The linguistic error here appears in the word "Agendath," which we first encounter in the "Calypso" chapter (Joyce 1986, 4. 191). It is part of the title, *Agendath Netaim*, which should read *Agudath Netaim*, translated from the Hebrew as "Planter's Company," an organization promoting land development in Palestine during the early years of the Zionist movement. Bloom reads of this company's propositions of land for sale in Palestine in the newspaper at Dlugacz's (The Porkbutcher) that he uses to wrap meat Bloom buys. There has been much speculation about this mistransliteration from the Hebrew (see Reizbaum 1990, 217–8n. 16). Dr. Fritz Senn has pointed to the word "agenda" within "Agendath" as perhaps having some import for Bloom's sense of history and identity; this idea works particularly well in the discussion of lineage.

CHAPTER 15 *James Joyce's Womanly Wandering Jew*

1. Ira Nadel discusses Fishberg's influence on Joyce at a number of points in his *Joyce and the Jews* (1989).

2. In the March 1918 issue of *The Little Review*, in which the first installment of *Ulysses* appeared, there was also an article by Ford Madox Hueffer, the second in his series of essays titled "Women and Men." The article is devoted largely to an analysis of the astounding popularity of *Sex and Character* and a debunking of Weininger's theories, which, Hueffer claims, debunk themselves instantly upon intelligent examination.

3. Ellmann writes that Marthe Fleischmann, to whom Joyce wrote letters using Greek instead of Roman *e*'s, is "in part the prototype of Bloom's penpal Martha Clifford, to whom, as Joyce emphasizes, Bloom is always careful to write with Greek *e*'s"—as well as being one of the prototypes for Gerty McDowell (Ellmann 1982, 449–50).

4. In a footnote to Chapter 22, Louis Hyman informs us that "Minnie

Watchman, my great-aunt, is recorded in *Thom's Directory* for 1905 as the tenant of 20 St. Kevin's Parade, as her husband, Jacob Leib, was in Dundalk in 1904 setting up a business. She wrongly appears in the *Directory* with the prefix 'Mr.,' and Joyce, by including her name in a list of the circumcised, was probably having his own little private joke on the *Directory*" (Hyman 1972, 329).

5. In her biography of Nora Barnacle Joyce, Maddox refers to a pornographic letter in which Joyce fantasizes about watching a "fat brown thing" slide out of Nora's bottom and remarks: "Somewhere between his training at the hands of his mother and his experience at Clongowes Wood, where he was afraid of wetting the bed and where bullies could push boys into the cold slime of the 'square ditch' (the cesspit), Joyce came to find everything associated with excretion unusually pleasurable. Moreover, if the Freudian view be taken—that the unconscious associates defecation with spending money or with childbirth—Joyce had formidable influences within his own home. His father's wild extravagance was the very opposite of anal retentiveness; Joyce himself linked his father's 'spendthrift habits' with his own and with 'any creativity I may possess.' As for his fertile mother, fat brown things popped from her body with a regularity that must have awed her impressionable eldest child" (Maddox 1988, 102).

CHAPTER 16   *Molly* Is *Sexuality: The Weiningerian Definition of Woman in Joyce's* Ulysses

All translations are by the author.

1. For an English translation of Brude-Firnau's essay, see Chapter 11.

2. Cf. Barthes (1979, 77): "Every text, being itself the intertext of another text, belongs to the intertextual, which must not be confused with a text's origins: to search for the 'sources of' and 'influence upon' a work is to satisfy the myth of filiation. The quotations from which a text is constructed are anonymous, irrecoverable, and yet *already read:* they are quotations without quotation marks." Also see Broich and Pfister (1985).

3. The French philosophers and psychoanalysts Helene Cixous and Luce Irigaray characterize feminine thinking and writing in exactly the same way as Otto Weininger does here. Unfortunately, both Cixous and Irigaray fail to politicize their concepts, which leads to biologism in Cixous's case and to a mystification of the patriarchal concept of "woman" in Irigaray's. Cf. especially Cixous (1977, 1980) and Irigaray (1985).

4. Weininger also establishes the oppositional types of "mother" and "prostitute," a familiar typology that is reflected in *Ulysses* in the chapters "Oxen of the Sun" and "Circe." Molly's thoughts too frequently move between the two Weiningerian poles of "female" identity: motherhood and prostitution. However, motherhood is one topic among others that enters Molly's mind and finally works its way around to her sexual fantasies.

5. To my knowledge, only Ralph Robert Joly (1982) and Marilyn Reizbaum (1982) discuss Joyce's Weininger legacy in greater detail. Both concentrate exclusively on Weininger's theory of the Jew. [Editors' note: Pöder's article was

completed prior to Natania Rosenfeld's submission to this volume (see Chapter 15).]

6. Cf. Steinberg (1969, 192): "Penelope, however, represents Korzybski's fourth, or verbal level. At this higher level above that for which I would like to reserve the term 'stream-of-consciousness,' an author presents the ruminations of a character who has organized his thoughts into language, translating the matters of paramount importance in his stream of consciousness into language patterns. At this level, the character is speaking to himself."

Irrationality, disconnectedness, and vague associations would be common features of the preverbal level. If they are outstanding features of the verbal level, they are certainly intended to characterize and emphasize any character's specific mode of thinking. The device is thus a conscious qualifier. Also cf. Unkeless (1982, 155): "Joyce's derision of Molly is not predominantly bitter; however, his comedy is based on a supposition that a woman's method of thinking is irrational and disconnected. Even if Molly's sentences can be punctuated, even if each statement follows the one before it 'realistically' within the stream of consciousness technique, and even if scholars can find patterns in Molly's thoughts, Joyce intends the sentences to be flowing and elusive, and the statements to be illogical."

7. Joyce depicts Molly's characteristic trait of contradiction linguistically through the liberal use of oppositional word pairs in her speech patterns.

8. As Bernard Benstock remarked (personal communication), Molly need never specify each of her lovers by name because *she* always knows to whom she is referring. Still, Molly often contemplates a specific sexual practice that simultaneously evokes two different lovers; this works precisely because she uses the unspecified pronoun "he" and thus shifts the focus from the sexual intimacies with one lover in particular to sexual intimacy in general, thereby blurring the identity of her lovers. In "Penelope" Joyce brilliantly exploits the polyreferential possibilities of the personal pronoun "he."

9. Although Molly is quoting Bloom, who disputes the immortality of everyone's (i.e., "your") soul in this statement, the comment, embedded as it is in the "Penelope" text, functions as a direct address to Molly.

10. For readers who are interested in the details of Weininger's pseudoscience, Jacques Le Rider's monograph on Weininger will be of special interest, especially the chapter entitled "Weininger und die Plagiatsaffäre, Moebius, Fließ, Freud und andere" (Le Rider 1985, 78–101).

11. Cf. Hayman (1970, 164): "By his magnificent language, he [Joyce] transforms Molly into the rolling earth, amoral, indifferent. . . . Joyce depicts Molly's transcendence more by making her become a life force or woman's essence than by creating her to be analogous to Mary, Eve, or Penelope." Since proper names always carry the notion of complex identity, I want to be more precise here by substituting "feminine sexuality" for "Molly." In "Penelope" it is feminine sexuality that is stylized as life force.

12. The Molly Bloom text therefore does both: it agrees with and departs from *Sex and Character*. Both in its degree of conformity with and departure from the "foster" text, "Penelope" is a rather striking incidence of intertextuality in *Ulysses;* it is even more so, since the *Sex and Character/*"Penelope" dialogue

continues throughout the entire chapter. For an analysis of Karl Kraus's similarly stylized affirmation of feminine sexuality in the modern Austrian tradition, see Wagner (1981).

CHAPTER 17   *Svevo and Weininger (Lord Morton's Mare)*

All translations of Weininger (1903) are by Barbara Hyams.

1. Darwin found this information in *The Philosophical Transactions of The Society of London*, (Morton 1893).

2. Steven Jay Gould overestimates the importance of Lord Morton's experiment in relation to Darwin's thought (Gould 1983, 376–80). For an initial overview of all the available material but without reference to Weininger, see Burckhardt (1979).

3. For further discussion of the relationship between Svevo and Weininger, and an interpretation of this episode, see Cavaglion (1982).

4. I am grateful to Tonino Tornitore for this reference.

CHAPTER 18   *Whores, Mothers, and Others*

This article is condensed from Ms. Foell's book, *Blind Reflections: Gender in Elias Canetti's "Die Blendung"* (Riverside, CA: Ariadne Press, 1994) and is printed here with the kind permission of Ariadne Press.

1. A literal translation of the German title of Canetti's novel would be "The Blinding"; some English editions appear under the title *The Tower of Babel*. Canetti began work on his novel in 1930 and completed it in 1931; it was first published in 1935.

2. Canetti refused to write an introduction for the 1980 Matthes & Seitz reprint of *Geschlecht und Charakter* (personal communication from Gerald Stieg). Allan Janik reports receiving this information from Stieg independently (Janik 1985, 97).

3. The published 1906 translation of Weininger's study is abridged and sometimes inaccurate. I have used the published translation where possible, in some cases, my own translation appears along with the page numbers for the published translation. This will enable the English–speaking reader to look up the context of the quotation. Weininger 1903, 334–35: "Es liegt darin ein derartiger Akt der Projektion aller, das zeitlich Eingeengte des Individuums übersteigenden Werte auf ein an sich gänzlich wertloses Weib, daß man nicht leicht es über sich bringt, die wahre Natur des Vorganges zu enthüllen .... Lieber schwört man auf die weibliche 'Schamhaftigkeit,' entzückt sich am weiblichen 'Mitleid,' interpretiert das Senken des Blickes beim Backfisch als ein eminent sittliches Phänomen, als daß man mit dieser Lüge die Möglichkeit preisgäbe, das Weib als Mittel zum Zweck der eigenen höheren Wallungen zu benützen."

4. The original German is given only for quotations from *Die Blendung* and *Geschlecht und Charakter*, not for other sources.

While Pöder's published article of 1985 does not develop this thought, her unpublished manuscript devotes over thirty pages to Therese as an illustration of "*W*" (Pöder 1984, 64–97). While I cannot summarize all of Pöder's results here, the four main areas she investigates are sexuality as the focus of Therese's memory; Therese's lack of boundaries and her constant sexual arousal; the polarization of motherhood and prostitution, with Therese as the embodiment of prostitution; and Therese's narcissism and degradation (*Würdelosigkeit*) as shown in her vanity, sensitivity, and self-observation. My interest in this essay is not in proving Weininger's influence, which Pöder has already done, but in questioning the narrative attitude toward Weininger's ideas.

5. Weininger (1903, 288): "Beide [mother and whore] sind eigentlich in Bezug auf die Individualität des sexuellen Komplementes anspruchslos. Die eine nimmt jeden beliebigen Mann, der ihr zum Kinde dienlich ist . . . . Die andere gibt sich jedem beliebigen Manne, der ihr zum erotischen Genusse verhilft."

6. Weininger (1903, 356): "Organische [und] . . . ontologische Verlogenheit des Weibes."

7. Weininger (1903, 288): "Der absoluten Dirne hingegen sind, schon als Kind, Kinder ein Greuel; später benützt sie das Kind höchstens als Mittel, um durch Vortäuschung eines, auf Rührung des Mannes berechneten, Idylles zwischen Mutter und Kind diesen an sich zu locken."

8. Canetti (1985a, 44): "Sie hatte Erbarmen, nicht mit Menschen, da war es keine Kunst, sondern mit Büchern. Sie ließ die Schwachen und Bedrückten zu sich kommen. Des letzten, verlassenen, verlorenen Wesens auf Gottes Erdboden nahm sie sich an. Kien verließ die Küche in tiefer Erregung. Zur Heiligen sprach er nicht ein Wort."

9. Canetti (1985a, 59): "Ein furchtbarer Haß steigt langsam hoch: das hat sie gewagt. Die Bücher! . . . Kien stürzt in langen Sätzen aus dem Zimmer, sperrt sich ins Klosett . . . ein, zieht sich an diesem Ort mechanisch die Hosen herunter, setzt sich aufs Brett und weint wie ein kleines Kind."

10. Canetti (1985a, 47): "Ich werde sie heiraten! Sie ist das beste Mittel, um meine Bibliothek in Ordnung zu halten."

11. Weininger (1903, 306): "Schlürft bis aufs äußerste den Genuß" (not in English version).

12. As Charlotte Perkins Gilman pointed out in her 1906 review: "The real importance of this book lies in its so fully concentrating and carrying to its logical conclusion the andro-centric view of humanity" (Gilman 1906, 417).

13. Although Canetti first met Alma in 1933, two years after completing work on his novel (see note 1), her ubiquitous reputation could still have influenced Canetti's conception of Therese even without personal acquaintance.

14. In her study of Canetti's autobiography, Friederike Eigler places the one-sidedness of Canetti's presentation of Alma in the context of his prejudice against the "seductress" type, which she also sees in the context of Weininger's influence (Eigler 1988, 183–86).

15. Weininger (1903, 283): "aus der Erwerbslosigkeit vieler Frauen, und daraufhin spezielle Anklagen gegen die heutige Gesellschaft erhebt, deren männliche Machthaber in ihrem ökonomischen Egoismus den unverheirateten Frauen die Möglichkeit eines rechtschaffenen Lebens so erschwerten; oder auf

das Junggesellentum rekurriert, das ebenfalls angeblich nur materielle Gründe habe, und zu seiner notwendigen Ergänzung nach der Prostitution verlange"

16. For an almost pathetic literary portrayal of the married woman's economic dependency, see Veza Canetti's short story "Der Oger" (Canetti 1990, 45–82). (Veza Canetti, Elias Canetti's first wife, had greater initial success as a writer than her husband, publishing her short stories in Vienna's *Arbeiterzeitung* in the early 1930s.)

17. Canetti (1985a, 64–65): "Er hat mich wollen, mir war er zuwider. Ich hab' ihn nur zugelassen, damit die Mutter sich ärgert. Die war immer: alles für ihre Kinder. No, die hat Augen gemacht, wie sie von der Arbeit nach Haus kommt und den Kerl bei der Tochter findet! Es war noch gar nicht dazugekommen. Der Fleischer will grad herunterspringen. Ich halt ihn fest, daß er nicht loskommen kann, bis die Alte im Zimmer drin ist, beim Bett. Das gibt ein Geschrei. Mit bloßen Fäusten jagt die Mutter den Mann zum Zimmer hinaus. Mich packt sie, heult und will mich gar küssen. Ich laß mir das nicht gefallen und kratz."

'Eine Stiefmutter bist, ja, das bist!' schrei ich. Bis zu ihrem Tod hat sie geglaubt, der Mann hat mir meine Jungfernehre geraubt. Dabei ist es gar nicht wahr. Ich bin eine anständige Person und hab' mit keinem Menschen noch was gehabt."

18. Weininger (1903, 287): "Prüfstein [des Unterschiedes zwischen Mutter und Dirne] ist am sichersten das Verhältnis zur Tochter: nur wenn sie diese gar nicht beneidet wegen größerer Jugend oder Schönheit . . . sondern sich vollständig mit ihr identifiziert und des Verehrers ihrer Tochter sich so freut, als wäre es ihr eigener Anbeter, nur dann ist sie Mutter zu nennen."

19. Canetti (1985a, 24): "Mit Frauen ist ja doch nicht auszukommen."

20. Canetti (1985a, 406): "Oft wartete er volle fünf Minuten aufs Essen. Dann aber riß ihm die Geduld und er prügelte sie [die Frau], noch bevor er satt war. Sie starb unter seinen Händen. Doch wäre sie in den nächsten Tagen bestimmt und von selbst eingegangen. Ein Mörder war er nicht."

21. "His actions had affected her from the earliest moments of her life" (Canetti 1978a, 369); "Sein Tun wirkte auf sie seit den ersten Augenblicken ihres Lebens" (Canetti 1985a, 408).

22. Canetti (1985a, 405): "Er, der Polizeibeamte, er, der Ehemann, er, der Vater."

CHAPTER 19 *Memory and History:* The Soul of a Jew *by Jehoshua Sobol*

A longer version of this article appeared in *Assaph: Studies in the Theatre* (Rokem 1989) and is reprinted here by kind permission of the Faculty of the Arts of Tel Aviv University. When the 1989 article was published, the Israeli politics were clearly "suicidal," and in my critical response to the play I tried to analyze the discourses Sobol had engaged for his cultural critique of Israeli ideology. Even though the official policies of Israel have changed radically since the play and my article were written, the "arguments" themselves have far from disappeared from the Israeli discourse and its collective consciousness. I want to thank Galit Hasan-Rokem, Jeanette R. Malkin, Paul Mendes-Flohr, and Eli Rozik for their reactions and productive comments during different stages of the work. A special thanks to Jehoshua Sobol for openly discussing the various issues and for making his private archives available to me.

All translations are by the author.

1. Before the 1982 production of *The Soul of a Jew*, several of Sobol's plays had already been produced at the Haifa Municipal Theatre: *The Days to Come* (1971), *Status Quo Vadis* (1973), *Sylvester '72* (1974), *The Joker* (1975), *The Night of the Twentieth* (1976, also produced at the Habima National Theatre in 1990), *The Gog and Magog Show* (1976), *The Tenants* (1977), and *Crisis* (1977, with Sobol as coauthor). In 1984 *Ghetto*, to date Sobol's most popular play, which has been performed in more than thirty theaters all over the world, premiered at the Haifa theater, and after that *Shooting Magda* (*Palestinait*, 1985), *King of Israel* (1985), and *The Jerusalem Syndrome* (1988) were also performed at that theater.

Sobol's plays have also been performed at other Israeli theaters: *Homeward Angel* and *Wedding Night*, the two first parts of a trilogy that also includes *The Next Day* (Habima, Tel Aviv, 1978); *The Last of the Workers* (Beit Lessin, Tel Aviv, 1980); *The Wars of the Jews* (Khan Theatre, Jerusalem, 1981); and *The Sailors' Revolt* (Beit Lessin, 1983). Together with *Ghetto*, *Adam* (first performed at Habima, 1989) and *Basement* (first performed in New Haven, Connecticut, 1990) make up the *Ghetto-triptych*. *Solo*, a play about Baruch Spinoza, premiered at Habima in 1991, and *Aleph-Beth* premiered in Germany in 1992. The Haifa production of *The Soul of a Jew* was performed at the Edinburgh Festival and in London (August 1983), at the Berliner Theatertreffen and other German cities (May 1985), in Chicago and Washington, D.C. (March–April 1986) and in other U.S. cities (November 1988), and in Woodstock, Connecticut (1989). The play has also been produced in a number of European cities such as Düsseldorf and Munich (1985), Odense, Denmark (1986), Hamburg (1986), Bremen (1986), Paris (1986 and 1990), and Vienna (1988, which was filmed in 1990); a radio version was produced by the Swedish Radio Theatre (1989).

For additional discussions of *The Soul of a Jew*, see Feldman (1987) and Ofrat (1983). For a discussion of the *Ghetto-triptych* and *Palestinait*, see my contributions to Ben-Zwi (in press).

2. On narrative strategies see, for example, Rimon-Kenan (1983); on historical drama, see Lindenberger (1975).

3. Sobol (1982, 5). For an English translation of the play, see Sobol (n.d.).

4. See n. 1 above.

5. See, e.g., White (1973, esp. 346ff.).

6. Translated into English from a Hebrew manuscript that served as the basis for the French translation. The private archives of Jehoshua Sobol, Tel Aviv.

7. The words "Fascist" and "Nazi" have been used in Israeli public discourse by both the left and the right to describe their opponents.

8. See also the comment of the writer Chanoch Bartov (1982), who claimed that the play touches a central nerve in the modern Jewish experience. Ben-Ami Feingold (1982), however, in his review of the published play, not the performance, claims that it is more like a dramatization of a situation/conflict than a play.

9. Cf. negative reactions to *The Soul of a Jew* from right-wing intellectuals like

Moshe Shamir (1982) and Israel Eldad (1982), as well as comments in letters to the editors in various newspapers, such as "The arts are all the time against Zionism" (*Ma'ariv*, November 1, 1982), and "A play filled with hatred and hostility toward sacred values" (*Ha'aretz*, November 29, 1982, and December 5, 1982).

10. Additional reviews on which this estimation has been based are Warnecke (1986), May (1986), and Reitter (1986).

11. This issue stands at the heart of the German history debate, where the exceptionality of the Holocaust in history is being discussed. For a summary of some of the basic issues of this debate see, for example, Diner (1987) and Habermas (1987).

12. Sobol often makes substantial changes and textual additions for different productions of his plays, usually to clarify or to contextualize a certain point. One interesting example is the London production of *Ghetto* in which passages alluding to Shakespeare's *The Merchant of Venice* were added.

13. The Fassbinder debate has received considerable critical attention because of its sensitive position in Germany. See, for example, Lichtenstein (1986) and Markovits, Benhai, and Postone (1986).

Works Cited ✦

Abrahams, Israel. 1898. *Jewish Life in the Middle Ages.* Reprint, 1981. New York: Atheneum.

Abrahamsen, David. 1946. *The Mind and Death of a Genius.* New York: Columbia University Press.

Adams, Robert M. 1972. *Surface and Symbol: The Consistency of James Joyce's "Ulysses."* New York: Oxford University Press.

Adorno, Theodor; Frenkel-Brunswik, Else; Levinson, Daniel J.; and Sanford, R. Nevitt. 1950. *The Authoritarian Personality.* New York: Harper.

Amery, Jean. 1976. "Deutschland—Frankreich: Mißverständnisse und Voruteile." *Neue Rundschau* 87:429.

Anderson, Harriet. 1992. *Utopian Feminism: Women's Movements in Fin-de-Siècle Vienna.* New Haven and London: Yale University Press.

Andree, Richard. 1881. *Zur Volkskunde der Juden.* Bielefeld and Leipzig: Verlag von Velhagen & Klasing.

Anonymous. 1904. *Kölnische Volkszeitung.* Literarische Beilage, no. 21.

Anonymous. 1943. "Berliner Mädel im Kriegseinsatz: Sie bewähren sich überall." *Völkischer Beobachter* (Berlin), no. 295 (October 22); 6.

Anonymous. 1943. "Nationaler Ehrendienst: Die Stabshelferin des Heeres—Ein Heim für Führerinnen." *Völkischer Beobachter* (Berlin), no. 297 (October 24), 8.

Apollinaire, Guillaume. 1902. "Le Passant de Prague." *La Revue blanche:* 216.

———. 1965. *Oeuvres poétiques.* Edited by M. Adema and M. Decaudin. Paris: Gallimard.

———. 1971. *Alcools.* Edited by R. Lefèvre. Paris: Larousse.

Appignanesi, Lisa. 1973. *Femininity and the Creative Imagination: A Study of Henry James, Robert Musil and Marcel Proust.* London: Vision.

Arendt, Hannah. 1946. "Privileged Jews." *Jewish Social Studies* 8:7–30.

Arens, Katherine. 1985. "Mach's 'Psychology of Investigation.'" *Journal of the History of the Behavioral Sciences* 21(2):151–68.

———. 1986. "Arthur Schnitzler and Characterology: From Empire to Third Reich." *Modern Austrian Literature* 19(3–4):97–127.

———. 1989a. "Characterology: Hapsburg Empire to Third Reich." *Literature and Medicine* 9:128–55.

———. 1989b. *Structures of Knowing: German Psychologies of the Nineteenth Century.* Dordrecht and Boston: Reidel/Kluwer Academic Publishers.

Arieti, Silvano. 1950. "New Views on the Psychology and Psychopathology of Wit and the Comic." *Psychiatry* 13:43–62.

———. 1976. *Creativity: The Magic Synthesis.* New York: Basic Books.

———. 1977. *New Views of Creativity*. New York: Geigy.

———. 1979. *The Parnas*. New York: Basic Books.

Artaud, Antonin. 1956. *Oeuvres complétes*. Vol. 7, *Les Nouvelles Révélations de l'Être* (1937). Paris: Denöel.

———. 1967. *Héliogabale ou l'anarchiste Couronné. Ouevres complètes*. Vol. 7. Paris: Denöel.

———. 1971. *Oeuvres complètes*. Vol. 9, *Les Tarahumaras*. Paris: Gallimard.

Aspetsberger, Friedbert, and Stieg, Gerald, eds. 1985. *Blendung als Lebensform: Elias Canetti*. Königstein/Ts.: Athenäum.

Auerbach, Elias. 1905. "Zur Psychologie des Mutes." *Jüdische Turnzeitung*, February–March, 20–26.

Augustine. (1963). *Confessions*. Translated by Rex Warner. New York: New American Library.

Bahr, Hermann. 1906. *Wien*. Stuttgart: C. Krabbe.

———. 1993. "The Overcoming of Naturalism (1891). In *The Vienna Coffee House Wits, 1890–1938*, edited and translated by Harold Segal, 48–51. West Lafayette, IN: Purdue University Press.

Barthes, Roland. 1979. "From Work to Text." In *Textual Strategies: Perspectives in Post-Structuralist Criticism*, edited by Josué V. Harari, 73–81. Ithaca, NY: Cornell University Press.

Bartov, Chanoch. 1982. ["*The Soul of a Jew*—A celebration for 'Good Souls' "]. *Ma'ariv*, November 19.

Bass, Joseph. 1913. "Die Darstellung der Juden im deutschen Roman des zwanzigsten Jahrhunderts." *Monatschrift für Geschichte und Wissenschaft des Judentums* 57:641–65.

———. 1915. "Die Darstellung der Juden im deutschen Roman des zwanzigsten Jahrhunderts." *Monatschrift für Geschichte und Wissenschaft des Judentums* 59:13–33.

Bataille, Georges. 1957. *L'Erotisme*. Paris: Editions de Minuit.

Baudelaire, Charles. 1975a. "Fusees." In *Oeuvres complètes*, vol. 1, edited by Claude Pichois, 649–667. Paris: Pleiade.

———. 1975b. "Mon coeur mis à nu." In *Oeuvres complètes*, vol. 1, edited by Claude Pichois, 676–708. Paris: Pleiade.

———. 1976. "Exposition universelle (1855)." In *Oeuvres complètes*, vol. 2, edited by Claude Pichois, 575–597. Paris: Pleiade.

Baum, Oskar. 1922. "Otto Weininger." In *Juden in der deutschen Literatur: Essays über zeitgenössische Schriftsteller*, edited by Gustav Krojanker, 121–38. Berlin: Welt-Verlag.

Beck, Evelyn Torton. 1986. "Kafka's Triple Bind: Women, Jews and Sexuality." In *Kafka's Contextuality*, edited by Alan Udoff, 343–88. Baltimore: Gordion.

Belke, Ingrid, ed. 1971–86. *Moritz Lazarus und Heymann Steinthal: Die Begründer der Völkerpsychologie in ihren Briefen*. 2 vols. Tübingen: Mohr.

Beller, Steven. 1989a. "The Hilsner Affair: Nationalism, Anti-Semitism and the Individual in the Habsburg Monarchy at the Turn of the Century." In *T. G. Masaryk (1850–1937)*. Vol. 2, *Thinker and Critic*, edited by R. J. Pynsent, 52–76. London: Macmillan.

————. 1989b. *Vienna and the Jews, 1867–1938: A Cultural History.* Cambridge: Cambridge University Press.

Benedikt, Klaus-Ulrich. 1986. *Emil Dovifat: Ein katholischer Hoschschullehrer und Publizist.* Veröffentlichungen der Kommission für Zeitgeschichte, Series B: Forschungen, 42. Mainz: Matthias-Grünewald-Verlag.

Benjamin, Walter. 1969. *Illuminations.* New York: Schocken.

Ben-Zwi, Linda, ed. (in press). *Israeli Theatre.* Ann Arbor: University of Michigan Press.

Berg, Alban. 1987. "Letter to Arnold Schoenberg of May 21, 1915." In *The Berg-Schoenberg Correspondence:Selected Letters,* edited by Juliane Brand et al, 242–44. New York: W. W. Norton.

Biale, David. 1986. *Power and Powerlessness in Jewish History.* New York: Schocken Books.

Bieder, Joseph. 1947. "Quand Apollinaire se défendait d'être juif." *Le Monde juif,* September.

Billington, Michael. 1983. "Haifa's Box of Tricks." *The Guardian,* August 24.

Binder, Hartmut. 1966. *Motiv und Gestaltung bei Kafka.* Bonn: Bouvier.

————. 1976. *Kafka in neuer Sicht: Mimik, Gestik und Personengefüge als Darstellungsformen des Autobiographischen.* Stuttgart: Metzler.

Biró, Paul. 1927. *Die Sittlichkeitsmetaphysik Otto Weiningers; eine geistesgeschichtliche Studie.* Dissertation. Leipzig and Vienna: F. Jasper.

Blei, Franz. 1903. "Kundry: Eine Bemerkung zu Geschlecht und Charakter." *Freistaat,* no. 30.

Bloch, J. S. 1884. "Wie gebieten wir Einhalt dem rapiden Verfall des religiösen Geistes?" *Österreichische Wochenschrift,* (October 15):3–5.

Blomster, Wesley W. 1969. "The Documentation of a Novel: Otto Weininger and Günter Grass' 'Hundejahre.' " *Monatshefte* 61:122–38.

Bödecker, Karl-Bernhard. 1974. *Frau und Familie im erzählerischen Werk Franz Kafkas.* Bern and Frankfurt: Herbert Lang & Peter Lang.

Bogart, Leo. 1991. "The Pollster & the Nazis." *Commentary,* 92(2) August:47–9.

Bohm, Ewald. 1930. "Antisemitismus im Lichte der Psychoanalyse." *Menorah* 8:312–19.

Boring, Edwin G. 1950. *A History of Experimental Psychology.* New York: Appleton-Century-Crofts.

Bottomore, Tom, and Goode, Patrick, eds. and trans. 1978. *Austro-Marxism.* Oxford: Clarendon Press.

Boyer, John W. 1981. *Political Radicalism in Late Imperial Vienna: Origins of the Christian Social Movement, 1848–1897.* Chicago: University of Chicago Press.

Brann, Helmut Walter. 1924. *Das Weib in Weiningers Gechlechtscharakterologie.* Bonn: Marcus and Weber.

Brantzeg, N. 1949. "Otto Weininger og 'Peer Gynt.' " *Vindvet* 3.

Braun, Christina von. 1990. " 'Und der Feind ist Fleisch geworden': Der rassistische Antisemitismus." In *Der ewige Judenhass: Christlicher Antijudaismus, Deutschnationale Judenfeindlichkeit, Rassistischer Antisemitismus,* edited by Christina von Braun and Ludger Heid, 149–213. Stuttgart and Bonn: Burg Verlag.

———. 1992. " 'Der Jude' und 'Das Weib': Zwei Stereotypen des 'Anderen' in der Moderne." *Metis* 2:6–28.

———. 1993. "Antisemitismus und Misogynie: Vom Zusammenhang zweier Erscheinungen." In *Von einer Welt in die andere: Jüdinnen im 19. und 20. Jahrhundert*, edited by Jutta Dick and Barbara Hahn, 179–96. Vienna: Verlag Christian Brandstätter.

Breuer, Josef. 1902. "Die Krise des Darwinismus und die Teleologie." Lecture held May 2, 1902. *Wissenschaftliche Beilage zum 15. Jahresbericht der Philosophischen Gesellschaft an der Universität zu Wien*. Vienna:44–64.

Bridenthal, Renate; Grossmann, Atina; and Kaplan, Marion; eds. 1984. *When Biology Became Destiny: Women in Weimar and Nazi Germany*. New York: Monthly Review Press.

Broch, Hermann. 1914. "Ethik." *Der Brenner* 8 (March–August):684–90.

———. 1957. *Gesammelte Werke*. Vol. 7, *Briefe*. Zurich: Rhein-Verlag.

———. 1969. *Bergroman: Die drei Originalfassungen*. Edited by Frank Kress and Hans Albert Maier. Frankfurt: Suhrkamp.

———. 1987, 1988. *The Spell*. Translated by H. F. Broch de Rothermann. New York: Farrar Straus Giroux; London: Pan Books, Picador Classics.

Brod, Max. 1937. *Franz Kafka: Eine Biographie, Erinnerungen und Dokumente*. Prague: Heinr. Mercy Sohn.

———. 1960. *Franz Kafka: A Biography*. Translated by G. Humphreys Roberts with Richard Winston. New York: Schocken.

Broich, Ulrich, and Pfister, Manfred, 1985. *Intertextualität; Formen, Funktionen, anglistische Fallstudien*. Tübingen: Max Niemeyer.

Brosseder, Johannes. 1972. *Luthers Stellung zu den Juden im Spiegel seiner Interpretation: Interpretation und Rezeption von Luthers Schriften und Äußerungen zum Judentum im 19. und 20. Jahrhundert vor allem im deutschsprachigen Raum*. Beiträge zur ökomenischen Theologie, 8. Munich: Max Hueber Verlag.

Brude-Firnau, Gisela. 1979. "Wissenschaft von der Frau? Zum Einfluß von Otto Weininger auf den deutschen Roman." In *Die Frau als Heldin und Autorin. Neue kritische Ansätze zur deutschen Literatur*, edited by Wolfgang Paulsen, 136–49. Bern and Munich: Francke Verlag.

Bubeniček, Hanna, ed. 1986. *Rosa Mayreder oder Wider die Tyrannei der Norm*. Vienna, Cologne, and Graz: Böhlau.

See also Schnedl-Bubeniček, Hanna.

Burckhardt, S.W. 1979. "Closing the Door on Lord Morton's Mare (The Rise and Fall of Telegony). *Studies in the History of Biology* 3:1–21.

Buresch-Riebe, Ilse. 1942. *Frauenleistung im Kriege*. Deutsche Arbeit, vol. 6. Berlin: Zentralverlag der NSDAP, Franz Eher Nachfolger.

Byrnes, Robert. 1990. "Bloom's Sexual Tropes: Stigmata of the 'Degenerate' Jew." *James Joyce Quarterly* 27(Winter):303–23.

Bytwerk, Randall L. 1983. *Julius Streicher*. New York: Stein and Day.

Canetti, Elias. 1969. *Der andere Prozeß: Kafkas Briefe an Felice*. Munich: Carl Hanser Verlag.

———. 1974. *Kafka's Other Trial: The Letters to Felice*. Translated by Christopher Middleton. New York: Schocken. (This is the transl. of Canetti 1969.)

———. 1975. *Das Gewissen der Worte: Essays*. Munich: Carl Hanser Verlag.

————. 1978a. *Auto-da-Fé.* Orig. publ. 1946. Translated under Canetti's supervision by C. V. Wedgwood. London: Jonathan Cape, Ltd., and Pan Books.

————. 1978b. *Die Fackel im Ohr: Lebensgeschichte 1921–1931.* Munich and Vienna: Carl Hanser Verlag.

————. 1979. *The Conscience of Words.* Translated by Joachim Neugroschel. New York: Seabury.

————. 1982a. *The Torch in My Ear.* Translated by Joachim Neugroschel. New York: Farrar Straus Giroux.

————. 1982b. "Rede zur Verleihung des Nobelpreises 1981." *Moderna Språk* 76:1.

————. 1985a. *Die Blendung.* Orig. publ. 1935. Vienna: Herbert Reichner Verlag; Munich: Carl Hanser Verlag.

————. 1985b. *Das Augenspiel: Lebensgeschichte 1931–1937.* Munich and Vienna: Carl Hanser Verlag.

————. 1986. *The Play of the Eyes.* Translated by Ralph Manheim. New York: Farrar Straus Giroux.

Canetti, Veza. 1990. *Die gelbe Strasse.* Munich and Vienna: Carl Hanser Verlag.

Capuana, Luigi. 1903. "Un consulto legale." *Il Marzocco,* November 8. Reprint, 1974, in *Racconti.* Edited by E. Ghidetti. Vol. 3, 126–32. Rome: Salerno Editori.

Catonné, Jean-Marie. 1990. *Romain Gary/Emile Ajar.* Paris: Belfond.

Cavaglion, Alberto. 1982. *Otto Weininger in Italia.* Rome: Carucci Editore.

————. 1985. "Otto Weininger tra Trieste e Firenze." In *Intellettuali di frontiera: Triestini a Firenze (1900–1950),* edited by Roberto Pertici, 661–74. Florence: Olschki.

Centgraf, Alexander. 1939. *Luther und Berlin: Gedenkschrift der Propstei zu Berlin zur 400. Jahresfeier der Einführung der Reformation in Berlin.* Berlin: Propstei.

————. 1940. *Martin Luther als Publizist: Geist und Form seiner Volksführung.* Zeitung und Zeit, Schriftenreihe des Instituts für Zeitungswissenschaft an der Universität Berlin, Neue Folge, Series A, vol. 14. Frankfurt: Verlag Mortiz Diesterweg.

————. 1943. "Ein Jude treibt Philosophie." Berlin: Verlag Paul Hochmuth.

———— [N. Alexander Centurio]. 1953. *Nostradamus, der Prophet der Weltgeschichte.* Berlin: Schikowski Verlag.

————. [N. Alexander Centurio]. 1991. *Die großen Weissagungen des Nostradamus: Prophetische Weltgeschichte bis zum Jahr 2050.* 16th ed. Munich: Goldmann.

Chamberlain, Houston Stewart. 1899. *Die Grundlagen des 19. Jahrhunderts.* 2 vols. Munich: F. Bruckmann.

————. 1913. *The Foundations of the Nineteenth Century.* Translated by John Lees. Introduction by Lord Redesdale. 2 vols. 4th impression. London: John Lane, The Bradley Head; New York: John Lane Company; Toronto: Bell & Cockburn.

Chasseguet-Smirgel, Janine. 1984. *Creativity and Perversion.* New York: W. W. Norton.

Cixous, Helene. 1977. *Die Unendliche Zirkulation des Begehrens.* Berlin: Merve.

————. 1980. *Weiblichkeit in der Schrift.* Berlin: Merve.

Cocks, Geoffrey. 1985. *Psychotherapy in the Third Reich: The Göring Institute.* New York and Oxford: Oxford University Press.

Corino, Karl. 1973. "Ödipus oder Orest? Robert Musil und die Psychoanalyse." In *Vom "Törleß" zum "Mann ohne Eigenschaften,"* edited by Uwe Bauer and Dietmar Goltschnigg, 123–35. Proceedings of the Graz Musil Symposium, 1972. Munich and Salzburg: Fink.

Dallago, Carl. 1912. "Otto Weininger und sein Werk." *Der Brenner* 3 (October):1–17, 49–61; 3 (November):93–109. Also published in same year as a monograph: *Otto Weininger und sein Werk.* Innsbruck: Brenner-Verlag.

Darwin, Charles. 1896. *The Variation of Animals and Plants under Domestication.* Vol. 1. New York: D. Appleton and Company.

Deák, István. 1990. *Beyond Nationalism: A Social and Political History of the Habsburg Officer Corps, 1848–1918.* New York and Oxford: Oxford University Press.

Debenedetti, Giacomo. 1929. "Svevo e Schmitz." *Il Convegno* 10(1–2). Reprint, 1955, in *Saggi critici,* n. s., 49–94. Milan: Mondadori.

Delavenay, Emile. 1969. *D. H. Lawrence, l'homme et la genese de son oeuvre, les années de formation, 1885–1919.* Paris: C. Klincksieck.

———. 1984. "D. H. Lawrence, Otto Weininger and a Rather Raw Philosophy." In *D. H. Lawrence: New Studies,* edited by Christopher Heywood, 137–57. London: The MacMillan Press Ltd.

Delbo, Charlotte. 1970. *Auschwitz et après* (3 vols). Paris: Minuit.

Deuerlein, Ernst. 1959. "Hitlers Eintritt in die Politik und die Reichswehr." *Vierteljahrsschrift für Zeitgeschichte* 7(2)(April):177–203.

Diehl, Guida. 1932. *Die deutsche Frau und der Nationalsozialismus.* Eisenach: Neuland.

Dijkstra, Bram. 1986. *Idols of Perversity: Fantasies of Feminine Evil in Fin-de-Siècle Culture.* New York and Oxford: Oxford University Press.

Diner, Dan, ed. 1987. *Ist der Nationalsozialismus Geschichte? Zu Historisierung und Historikerstreit.* Frankfurt: S. Fischer.

Doderer, Heimito von. 1958. *Die Strudhofstiege: Oder, Melzer und die Tiefe der Jahre.* Munich: Biederstein Verlag.

Dohm, Hedwig. 1900. "Eine Anregung zur Erziehungsfrage." *Die Zeit* 317 (October 27):53.

Doppler, Alfred. 1971. "Georg Trakl und Otto Weininger." In *Peripherie und Zentrum: Studien zur österreichischen Literatur.* Edited by Gerlinde Weiss and Klaus Zelewitz, 43–54. Festschrift for Adalbert Schmidt. Salzburg, Stuttgart, and Zurich: Verlag Das Bergland-Buch.

Doron, Joachim. 1980. "Rassenbewußsein und naturwissenschaftliches Denken im deutschen Zionismus während der wilhelminischen Ära." *Jahrbuch des Institutes für deutsche Geschichte* 9:389–427.

Dovifat, Emil. 1937. *Rede und Redner: Ihr Wesen und ihre politische Macht.* Leipzig: Bibliographisches Institut.

Durzak, Manfred. 1967. "Hermann Brochs Anfänge: Zum Einfluß Weiningers und Schopenhauers." *Germanisch-romanische Monatsschrift* 17:293–306.

———. 1968. *Hermann Broch: Der Dichter und seine Zeit.* Stuttgart: W. Kohlhammer.

Ebner, Ferdinand. 1919. "Fragment über Weininger." *Der Brenner* 6 (October):28–47.

———. 1963. "Das Wort und die geistigen Realitäten. Fragment 16: Otto Weininger. Geist und Sexualität. Die Juden. Christus." In *Schriften.* Vol. 1,

Fragmente Aufsätze Aphorismen, edited by Franz Seyr, 284–305. Munich: Kösel-Verlag.

Eckart, Dietrich. 1923. *Der Bolschewismus von Moses bis Lenin: Zwiegespräche zwischen Adolf Hitler und mir.* Munich: Hoheneichen-Verlag.

Eigler, Friederike. 1988. *Das autobiographische Werk von Elias Canetti.* Tübingen: Stauffenberg Verlag.

Eldad, Israel. 1982. ["Report on Sobol's *The Soul of a Jew*"]. *Kol Ha-Ir,* November 19.

Ellenberger, Henri F. 1970. *The Discovery of the Unconscious: The History and Evolution of Dynamic Psychiatry.* New York: Basic Books.

Ellis, Havelock. 1920. *Studies in the Psychology of Sex.* Vol. 4, *Sexual Selection in Man.* Philadelphia: F. A. Davis.

Ellmann, Richard. 1972; *James Joyce.* Rev. ed. 1982. New York: Oxford University Press.

———. 1977. *The Consciousness of Joyce.* London: Faber & Faber, Ltd.

Emrich, Wilhelm. 1958. *Franz Kafka.* Bonn: Athenäum-Verlag.

Endelman, Todd M. 1987. "Conversion as a Response to Antisemitism in Modern Jewish History." In *Living with Antisemitism: Modern Jewish Responses,* edited by Jehuda Reinharz, 59–83. Hanover, NH, and London: University Press of New England.

Feingold, Ben-Ami. 1982. ["Review of the published version of Sobol's play, *Nefesh Yehudi: Ha-Layla Ha-Aharon shel Otto Weininger.*"] *Yediot Aharonot,* December 31.

Feldman, Yael S. 1987. "Zionism: Neurosis or Cure? The 'Historical' Drama of Yehoshua Sobol." *Prooftexts: A Journal of Jewish Literary History* 7:145–62.

Feller, F. A. 1931. *Antisemitismus: Versuch einer psychoanalytischen Lösung des Problems.* Berlin: Verlag des Archivs für angewandte Psychologie.

Ferriani, Lino. 1900. "Entartete Kinder." *Die Zeit* 282 (February 2):118.

Fishberg, Maurice. 1911. *The Jews: A Study of Race and Environment.* London: The Walter Scott Publishing Company, Ltd.

Fliess, Wilhelm. 1906. *In eigener Sache: Gegen Otto Weininger und Hermann Swoboda.* Berlin: Goldschmidt.

Foell, Kristie. 1994. *Blind Reflections: Gender in Elias Canetti's "Die Blendung."* Riverside, CA: Ariadne.

Fogel, Daniel Mark. 1979. "James Joyce, the Jews, and *Ulysses.*" *James Joyce Quarterly* 16(4) (Summer):498–501.

Franz-Willing, Georg. 1962. *Die Hitlerbewegung.* Munich, Hamburg, and Berlin: R. v. Decker.

Freud, Sigmund. 1894. "Die Abwehr-Neuropsychosen: Versuch einer psychologischen Theorie der akquirierten Hysterie, vieler Phobien und Zwangsvorstellungen und gewisser halluzinatorischer Psychosen." *Neurologisches Zentralblatt* 10–11. Reprint, 1942, in *Gesammelte Werke,* vol. 1, edited by Anna Freud et al., 57–74. London: Imago.

———. 1942a. "Bruchstück einer Hysterie-Analyse." In *Gesammelte Werke,* vol. 5, edited by Anna Freud et al., 161–286. London: Imago.

———. 1942b. "Drei Abhandlungen zur Sexualtheorie (1905)." In *Gesammelte Werke,* vol. 5, edited by Anna Freud et al., 27–145. London: Imago.

———. 1948. "Einige psychische Folgen des anatomischen Geschlechtsunterschieds." In *Gesammelte Werke*, vol. 14, edited by Anna Freud et al. 19–30. London: Imago.

———. 1955–74. *The Standard Edition of the Complete Psychological Works of Sigmund Freud.* Translated and edited by James Strachey. In collaboration with Anna Freud. Assisted by Alix Strachey and Alan Tyson. 24 vols. London: The Hogarth Press and the Institute of Psycho-Analysis.

———. 1963. *Dora: An Analysis of a Case of Hysteria.* New York: MacMillan.

———. 1985. *The Complete Letters of Sigmund Freud to Wilhelm Fliess.* Edited and translated by Jeffrey Moussaieff Masson. Cambridge and London: The Belknap Press of Harvard University Press.

Frevert, Ute. 1991. *Die Ehrenmänner: Das Duell in der bürgerlichen Gesellschaft.* Munich: Verlag C. H. Beck.

Freyenwald, Hans Jonak von. 1941. *Jüdische Bekenntnisse aus allen Zeiten und Ländern.* Nuremberg: Der Stürmer Buchverlag.

Friedell, Egon. 1931. *Kulturgeschichte der Neuzeit.* Vol. 3. Munich: C. H. Beck'sche Verlagsbuchhandlung.

Friedlander, Saul. 1988. "Historical Writing and the Memory of the Holocaust." In *Writing and the Holocaust,* edited by Berel Lang, 66–77. New York: Holmes and Meier.

Fritsch, Sybille. 1986. "Selbstmord im Beethoven-Haus." *Profil* 23, June 2, 60.

Fritsch, Theodor. 1887. *Der Antisemiten-Catechismus.* Leipzig: T. Fritsch.

———. 1919. *Jüdische Selbstbekenntnisse.* Leipzig: Hammer-Verlag.

———. 1929. *Jüdische Selbstbekenntnisse.* Leipzig: Hammer-Verlag.

———. 1930. *Handbuch der Judenfrage: Die wichtigsten Tatsachen zur Beurteilung des jüdischen Volkes.* Leipzig: Hammer-Verlag.

———. 1943. *Handbuch der Judenfrage: Die wichtigsten Tatsachen zur Beurteilung des jüdischen Volkes.* 49th impression. Leipzig: Hammer-Verlag.

Frühwald, Wolfgang. 1989. "Antijudaismus in der Zeit der deutschen Romantik." *Conditio Judaica: Judentum, Antisemitismus und deutsch sprachige Literatur rom 18. Jahrhundert bis zum Ersten Weltkrieg.* Edited by Hans Otto Horch and Horst Denkler. Vol. 2, 72–91. Tübingen: Max Niemeyer Verlag.

Frye, Northrop. 1957. "The Mythos of Winter: Irony and Satire." In *Anatomy of Criticism,* edited by Northrop Frye, pp. 223–39. Princeton: Princeton University Press.

Fuchs, Eduard. 1921. *Die Juden in der Karikatur.* Munich: Albert Langen Verlag.

Gabriel, Gottfried. 1990. "Solipsismus: Wittgenstein, Weininger und die Wiener Moderne." In *Paradigmen der Moderne,* edited by Helmut Bachmaier, 29–47. Amsterdam: Benjamins.

Garrison, Fielding H. 1915. *John Shaw Billings: A Memoir.* New York: G. P. Putnam's Sons.

Gary, Romain. 1967. *La Danse de Genghis Cohn.* Paris: Gallimard.

Gay, Peter. 1978. *Freud, Jews, and Other Germans: Masters and Victims in Modernist Culture.* London: Oxford University Press.

———. 1988. *Freud, A Life for Our Time.* New York: W. W. Norton.

Gedo, John E. 1983. *Portraits of the Artist: Psychoanalysis of Creativity and Its Vicissitudes.* New York: Guilford Press.

Geuter, Ulfried. 1984. *Die Professionalisierung der deutschen Pyschologie im National-sozialismus.* Frankfurt: Suhrkamp Verlag.

Gifford, Don, with Seidman, Robert J. 1988. *Ulysses Annotated: Notes for James Joyce's "Ulysses."* Rev. and enl. ed. Berkeley: University of California Press.

Gilman, Charlotte Perkins. 1906. "Review of Dr. Weininger's Sex and Character." *The Critic* 12:414–17.

Gilman, Sander L. 1969. "Hofprediger Stöcker and the Wandering Jew." *The Journal of Jewish Studies* 19:63–69.

———. 1985. *Difference and Pathology: Stereotypes of Sexuality, Race, and Madness.* Ithaca: Cornell University Press.

———. 1986. *Jewish Self-Hatred: Anti-Semitism and the Hidden Language of the Jews.* Baltimore: Johns Hopkins University Press.

———. 1990a. "Freud Reads Heine Reads Freud." *Southern Humanities Review* 24:201–18.

———. 1990b. " 'I'm Down on Whores': Race and Gender in Victorian London." In *The Anatomy of Racism,* edited by David Theo Goldberg, 146–70. Minneapolis: University of Minnesota Press.

———. 1991a. *Inscribing the Other.* Lincoln and London: University of Nebraska Press.

———. 1991b. *Jew's Body.* New York and London: Routledge.

———. 1993. *Freud, Race and Gender.* Princeton: Princeton University Press.

Goethe, Johann Wolfgang von. 1984. *Faust I & II,* edited and translated by Stuart Atkins. Cambridge, MA: Suhrkamp/Insel Publishers Boston.

Goldmann, Nahum. 1971. *Autobiographie: Une vie au service d'une cause.* Paris: Fayard.

Gomperz, Heinrich, and Kann, Robert A. 1974. *Theodor Gomperz: Ein Gelehrtenleben im Bürgertum der Franz-Josephszeit.* Vienna: Verlag der Österreichischen Akademie der Wissenschaften.

Gomperz, Theodor. 1905. *Essays und Erinnerungen.* Stuttgart and Leipzig: Deutsche Verlags-Anstalt.

Gorsleben. 1934. *Arbeiter Zeitung,* January 16.

Gould, Stephen Jay. 1983. *Hen's Teeth and Horses' Toes.* New York and London: W. W. Norton.

Grass, Günter. 1963. *Hundejahre.* Neuwied am Rhein and Berlin: Luchterhand Verlag.

———. 1989. *Dog Years.* Orig. publ. 1965. Translated by Ralph Mannheim. New York and London: Harcourt Brace & World Inc. and Martin Secker & Warburg Ltd.; Picador Edition.

Green, Martin. 1974. *The von Richthofen Sisters: The Triumphant and the Tragic Modes of Love.* New York: Basic Books.

Greer, Germaine. 1970. *The Female Eunuch.* London: MacGibbon & Kee Ltd.

Griesinger, Wilhelm. 1882. *Mental Pathology and Therapeutics.* Translated by C. Lockhart Robertson and James Rutherford. New York: William Wood.

Groddeck, Georg. 1966. "Das Zwiegeschlecht des Menschen." In Georg Groddeck, *Psychoanalytische Schriften zur Psychosomatik,* edited by Günter Clauser, 256–63. Wiesbaden: Limes.

Groller, Balduin. 1900. "Die Feigheit der Juden." *Die Welt*, vol. 4, no. 52 December 28:2–5.

———. 1901. "Die körperliche Minderwertigkeit der Juden." *Die Welt* vol. 5, no. 16 (April 19):3–5.

Günther, Hans F. K. 1930 and 1931. *Rassenkunde des jüdischen Volkes*. 2nd ed. Munich: J. F. Lehmanns Verlag.

Gystrow, Ernst. 1899. "Neue Ideen in der Psychologie." *Die Zeit* 256 (August 8):133.

Habermas, Jürgen. 1987. *Eine Art Schadenabwicklung*. Frankfurt: Suhrkamp.

Hahn, Fred. 1978. *Lieber Stürmer! Leserbriefe an das NS-Kampfblatt 1924–1945*. Stuttgart: Seewald.

Haller, Rudolf, and Stadler, Friedrich, eds. 1988. *Ernst Mach: Werk und Wirkung*. Vienna: Hölder-Pichler-Tempsky.

Handelsaltz, Michael. 1982. ["An encouraging and a distressing phenomenon"]. *Ha'aretz*, October 17.

Hanly, C. M. 1986. "Psychoanalytic Aesthetics: A Defense and an Elaboration." *Psychoanalytic Quarterly* 55:1–22.

Hare, Edward. 1987. "Creativity and Mental Illness." *British Medical Journal* 295:1587–89.

Harrowitz, Nancy A. 1994a. *Antisemitism, Misogyny, and the Logic of Cultural Difference: Cesare Lombroso and Matilde Serao*. Lincoln and London: University of Nebraska Press.

Harrowitz, Nancy A., ed. 1994b. *Tainted Greatness: Antisemitism and Cultural Heroes*. Philadelphia: Temple University Press.

Hayman, David. 1970. "The Empirical Molly." In *Approaches to Ulysses: Ten Essays*, edited by Thomas F. Staley and Bernard Benstock, 103–35. Pittsburgh: University of Pittsburgh Press.

Heinemann, Marlene E. 1986. *Gender and Destiny: Women Writers and the Holocaust*. New York, Westport, CT, and London: Greenwood Press.

Heller, Peter. 1978. "A Quarrel over Bisexuality." In *The Turn of the Century: German Literature and Art, 1890–1915*, edited by Gerald Chapple and Hans H. Schulte, 87–116. Bonn: Bouvier.

Hensel, Paul. 1905. "Review of Otto Weininger, *Geschlecht und Charakter* (1903); *Über die letzten Dinge* (1904); Emil Lucka, *Otto Weininger, sein Werk und seine Persönlichkeit* (1905)." *Biologisches Centralblatt*:588–92.

Hering, Ewald. 1870. "Über das Gedächtniss als eine allgemeine Function der organisirten Materie." *Almanach der Kaiserlichen Akademie der Wissenschaften* 20:253–78.

Hermann, Armin, ed. 1978. *Deutsche Nobelpreisträger*. Munich: Heinz Moos.

Hernádi, Miklós. 1990. *Otto*. Budapest: Magvetö Könyvkiadó. Revised German edition: 1993. *Weiningers Ende*. Translated by Erika Bollweg. Frankfurt: Eichborn Verlag.

Herzl, Theodor. 1902. *Altneuland*. Leipzig: Seemann Nachf.

———. 1983. *Briefe und Tagebücher*. 6 vols. Berlin: Propyläen

Hirsch, Wilhelm. 1894. *Genie und Entartung: Eine psychologische Studie*. Berlin: Coblentz.

Hirschfeld, Magnus, ed. 1899. *Jahrbuch für sexuelle Zwischenstufen*. Vol. 1. Leipzig.

Hitler, Adolf. 1934. "Speech to the Nationalsozialistische Frauenschaft. 8 September 1934, Nuremberg." Reprint, 1962, in *Hitler, Reden und Proklamationen*, vol. 1, edited by Max Domarus, 449–54. Würzburg: Translated and reprinted, 1983, in *Women, the Family, and Freedom: The Debate in Documents*, vol. 2, edited by Susan Groag Bell and Karen M. Offen, and translated by Susan Groag Bell, 373–78. Stanford: Stanford University Press.

Hofmannsthal, Hugo von. 1966. "Ein Brief" In *Ausgewählte Werke in zwei Bänden*, edited by Rudolf Hirsch. Vol. 2, *Erzählungen und Aufsätze*, 34. Frankfurt: S. Fischer.

Hofstadter, Douglas. 1985. *Metamagical Themas: Questing for the Essence of Mind and Pattern*. New York: Basic Books.

Homans, Peter. 1989. *The Ability to Mourn: Disillusionment and the Social Origins of Psychoanalysis*. Chicago: University of Chicago Press.

Horney, Karen. 1967. "The Flight from Womanhood: The Masculinity Complex in Women as Viewed by Men and by Women (1926)." In *Feminine Psychology*, edited by Harold Kelman, 54–70. New York: W. W. Norton.

Hueffer, Ford Madox. 1918. "Women and Men." *The Little Review* 4 (March):36–51.

Hyman, Louis. 1972. *The Jews of Ireland from Earliest Times to the Year 1910*. London and Jerusalem: The Jewish Historical Society of England and Israel Universities Press.

Irigaray, Luce. 1985. *This Sex Which Is Not One*. Translated by Catherine Porter with Carolyn Burke. Ithaca: Cornell University Press.

Iser, Wolfgang. 1993. *The Fictive and the Imaginary: Charting Literary Anthropology*. Baltimore and London: Johns Hopkins University Press.

Jaffe, William Walter. 1979. "Studies in Obsession: Otto Weininger, Arthur Schnitzler, Heimito von Doderer." Ph.D. dissertation, Yale University.

Jakubowski, Jeanette. 1991. "Antisemitismus und Antifeminismus von Johann Andreas Eisenmenger bis Houston Stewart Chamberlain." Master's thesis, Freie Universität, Berlin.

Janik, Allan. 1981. "Therapeutic Nihilism: How Not to Write about Otto Weininger." In *Structure and Gestalt: Philosophy and Literature in Austria-Hungary and Her Successor States*, edited by Barry Smith, 263–92. Amsterdam: John Benjamins.

———. 1985. *Essays on Wittgenstein and Weininger*. Studien zur österreichischen Philosophie, 9. Amsterdam: Rodopi.

———. 1986. "Therapeutic Nihilism: How Not to Write about Otto Weininger." Reprinted in *How Not to Interpret a Culture: Essays on the Problem of Method in the "Geisteswissenschaften,"* by Allan Janik, 19–48. Stensilserie, 73. Bergen: Universitetet i Bergen, Filosofisk Institutt.

———. 1987. "Viennese Culture and the Jewish Self-Hatred Hypothesis: A Critique." In *Jews, Antisemitism and Culture in Vienna*, edited by Ivar Oxaal, Michael Pollak, and Gerhard Botz, 75–88. London and New York: Routledge and Kegan Paul.

———. 1988. "Tacit Knowledge, Working Life and Scientific Method." In *Knowledge, Skill and Artificial Intelligence*, edited by Bo Göranzon and Ingela Josefson, 53–66. London: Springer.

———. 1989a. "Tyst kunskap, regelföljande och mening." *Dialoger* 10:6–17.

————. 1989b. "Wittgenstein's revolutionäre Auffassung von Sprache." *Wissen-schaftliche Nachrichten* 80 (April):5–7.

Janik, Allan, and Toulmin, Stephen. 1973. *Wittgenstein's Vienna*. New York: Simon and Schuster (Touchstone).

Janssen-Jurreit, Marielouise. 1976. *Sexismus: Über die Abtreibung der Frauenfrage*. Munich: Carl Hanser Verlag.

————. 1982. *Sexism: The Male Monopoly on History and Thought*. Translated by Verne Moberg. New York: Farrar Straus Giroux.

Jaques, Heinrich. 1859. *Denkschrift über die Stellung der Juden in Österreich*. Vienna: C. Gerold's Sohn.

Jellinek, Adolf. 1938. *Bet Ha-Midrash*. 6 vols. Jerusalem: Bamberger and Wahrmann.

Jenny, Urs. 1985. "Moses, Jesus, Otto!" *Der Spiegel*, vol. 39, no. 51 (Dec. 16):168.

Jeremias, Dr. Med. 1901. "Die Fragen der körperlichen, geistigen und wirtschaftli-chen Hebung der Juden." *Die Welt* 18 (May 3):3–5.

Jerusalem, Wilhelm. 1896. *Die Psychologie im Dienste der Grammatik und Interpreta-tion*. [Lecture.] Vienna: A. Hölder.

————. 1903. *Der Bildungswert des altsprachlichen Unterrichts und die Forderungen der Gegenwart*. [Lecture of January 25, 1902.] Vienna: A. Hölder.

————. 1904. *Kant's Bedeutung für die Gegenwart*. [Memorial speech of February 12, 1904.] Vienna and Leipzig: W. Braumüller.

Jodl, Friedrich. 1872. *Leben und Philosophie David Hume's*. Rev. ed. Dissertation, University of Vienna.

————. 1903. ["On Otto Weininger's death"]. *Neues Wiener Journal*, October 25.

Jodl, Margarete. 1920. *Friedrich Jodl: Sein Leben und Wirken, dargestellt nach Tagebüch-ern und Briefen*. Stuttgart and Berlin: Cotta.

Johnston, William M. 1972. *The Austrian Mind: An Intellectual and Social History 1848–1938*. Berkeley and Los Angeles: University of California Press.

Joly, Ralph Robert. 1973. "The Jewish Elements in James Joyce's *Ulysses*." Ph.D. Dissertation, North Carolina.

————. 1982. "Chauvinist Brew and Leopold Bloom: The Weininger Legacy." *James Joyce Quarterly* 19(2) (Winter):194–98.

Jones, Ernest. 1953. *The Life and Work of Sigmund Freud*. Vol. 1, *The Formative Years and the Great Discoveries 1856–1900*. New York: Basic Books.

————. 1955. *The Life and Work of Sigmund Freud*. 3 vols. New York: Basic Books.

Joyce, James. 1961a. *Scribbledehobble: The Ur-Workbook for Finnegans Wake*. Edited by Thomas E. Connolly. Evanston: Northwestern University Press.

————. 1961b. *Ulysses*. New York: Vintage Books.

————. 1966. *Letters of James Joyce*. Vols. 2 and 3. Edited by Richard Ellmann. New York: The Viking Press.

————. 1975. *Selected Joyce Letters*. Edited by Richard Ellmann. New York: The Viking Press.

————. 1978. *James Joyce Archive: Finnegans Wake—A Facsimile of the Buffalo Notebooks IV, C. 7–267*. New York: Garland Press.

————. 1986. *Ulysses: The Corrected Text*. Edited by Hans Walter Gabler with Wolfhard Steppe and Claus Melchior. New York: Vintage Books; Viking Penguin.

Kafka, Franz. 1948. *The Diaries of Franz Kafka*. Vol. 1, *1910–1913*. Edited by Max Brod. Translated by Joseph Kresch. New York: Schocken.

———. 1949. *The Diaries of Franz Kafka*. Vol. 2, *1914–1923*. Edited by Max Brod. Translated by Martin Greenberg with the cooperation of Hannah Arendt. London: Secker & Warburg.

———. 1953. *Letters to Milena*. Edited by Willi Haas. Translated by Tania and James Stern. New York: Schocken.

———. 1954. *Tagebücher 1910–1923*. Frankfurt: Fischer.

———. 1958a. *Briefe 1902–1924*. Frankfurt: Schocken.

———. 1958b. *Letters to Friends, Family and Editors*. Translated by Richard and Clara Winston. New York: Schocken.

———. 1966. *Letter to His Father*. New York: Schocken. Translated by Ernst Kaiser and Eithne Wilkins.

———. 1968. *Das Schloß*. Frankfurt: Fischer.

———. 1974. *The Castle*. Translated by Willa and Edwin Muir. With added material translated by Eithne Wilkins and Ernst Kaiser. New York: Vintage Books.

———. 1976. Orig. publ. 1949. *Gesammelte Werke*. Vol. 6, *Hochzeitsvorbereitungen auf dem Lande*. Frankfurt: S. Fischer.

———. 1982. *Das Schloß: Apparatband zur Kritischen Ausgabe*. Edited by Malcolm Pasley. Frankfurt: Fischer.

———. 1983. *Briefe an Milena*. Rev. and enl. ed. Edited by J. Born and M. Müller. Frankfurt: Fischer.

Kahn, Lothar, with Hook, Donald D. 1993. *Between Two Worlds: A Cultural History of German-Jewish Writers*. Ames, IA: Iowa State University Press.

Kainz, Friedrich. 1976. "Nachruf auf Victor Kraft." *Almanach der Österreichischen Akademie der Wissenschaften* 125:519–57.

Kant, Immanuel. 1900. *Metaphysische Anfangsgründe der Naturwissenschaft*. Edited by Alois Höfler. Leipzig: C.E.M. Pfeffer.

———. 1903. *Metaphysische Anfangsgründe der Naturwissenschaft*. In *Gesammelte Schriften*, edited by Alois Höfler, 465–565; Commentary, 636–52. Series edited by Wilhelm Dilthey, vol. 4. Berlin: Königliche Preußische Akademie der Wissenschaften.

Kaplan, D. M. 1988. "The Psychoanalysis of Art: Some Ends, Some Means." *Journal of the American Psychoanalytic Association* 36:259–93.

Kaplan, Marion A. 1991. *The Making of the Jewish Middle Class: Women, Family, and Identity in Imperial Germany*. New York and Oxford: Oxford University Press.

Karl, Frederick R. 1985. *Modern and Modernism: The Sovereignty of the Artist 1885–1925*. New York: Atheneum.

Kassner, Rudolf. 1902. *Der Tod und die Maske: Gleichnisse*. Leipzig: Insel.

———. 1938. *Buch der Erinnerung*. Leipzig: Insel.

Katz, Jacob. 1973. *Out of the Ghetto: The Social Background of Jewish Emancipation 1770–1870*. Cambridge: Harvard University Press.

———. 1980. *From Prejudice to Destruction: Anti-Semitism, 1700–1933*. Cambridge: Harvard University Press.

Katz, Leon. 1978. "Weininger and 'The Making of Americans.' " *Twentieth-Century Literature* 24(1):8–26.

Keen, Maurice. 1984. *Chivalry*. New Haven and London: Yale University Press.

Kenny, Anthony, 1982. "Wittgenstein on the Nature of Philosophy?" In *Wittgenstein and His Times*, edited by Brian McGuinness, 1–26. Chicago: University of Chicago Press.

Kernan, Alvin B. 1965. *The Plot of Satire*. New Haven: Yale University Press.

Klaren, Georg. 1924. *Otto Weininger, der Mensch, sein Werk und sein Leben*. Vienna and Leipzig: W. Braumüller.

Klein, Dennis. 1981. *Jewish Origins of the Psychoanalytic Movement*. New York: Praeger.

Klein, Viola. 1946. *The Feminine Character: History of an Ideology*. Foreword by Karl Mannheim. Reprint, 1971. London: Routledge & Kegan Paul.

Klossowski, Pierre. 1963. "Nietzsche, le poythéisme, et la parodie." In *Un Si Funeste Désir*. Paris: Gallimard.

Klüger, Ruth. 1992. *weiter leben: Eine Jugend*. Göttingen: Wallstein Verlag.

Koch, Friedrich. 1986. *Sexuelle Denunziation: Die Sexualität in der politischen Auseinandersetzung*. Frankfurt: Syndikat.

Koebner, Thomas. 1989. "Feindliche Brüder: Stereotypen der Abgrenzung jüdischen und deutschen Wesens." In *Jüdische Identität im Spiegel der Literatur vor und nach Auschwitz*, edited by Eveline Valtink, 40–85. Hofgeismar: Evangelische Akademie.

Koestenbaum, Wayne. 1989. *Double Talk: The Erotics of Male Literary Collaboration*. New York: Routledge.

Koestler, Arthur. 1971–73. *The Case of the Midwife Toad*. New York: Vintage Books.

Kofman, Sarah. 1988. *The Childhood of Art: An Interpretation of Freud's Aesthetics*. Translated by Winifred Woodhull. New York: Columbia University Press.

Kohn, Hans. 1961. "Eros and Sorrow: Notes on the Life and Work of Arthur Schnitzler and Otto Weininger." *Publications of the Leo Baeck Institute. Yearbook VI*, 152–69. London, Jerusalem, and New York.

———. 1962. *Karl Kraus, Arthur Schnitzler, Otto Weininger; aus dem jüdischen Wien der Jahrhundertwende*. Tübingen: Mohr.

Kolleth, Sabina. 1986. "Gewalt in Ehe und Intimpartnerschaft." In *Glücklich ist, wer vergisst . . . ? Das andere Wien um 1900*, edited by Hubert Ch. Ehalt, Gernot Heiss, and Hannes Stekl, 145–71. Vienna: Böhlau.

Koonz, Claudia. 1987. *Mothers in the Fatherland: Women, the Family, and Nazi Politics*. New York: St. Martin's Press.

Körber, Robert, and Pugel, Theodor, eds. 1935. *Antisemitismus der Welt in Wort und Bild*. With Benno Imendörffer and Erich Führer. Dresden: Verlag M. D. Groh.

Kraft, Werner. 1956. *Karl Kraus: Beiträge zum Verständnis seines Werkes*. Salzburg: O. Müller.

Kraus, Karl. 1903. "Otto Weininger." *Die Fackel* 144 (October 17):15.

———. 1906. "Weib und Kultur." *Die Fackel* 213 (December 11):5.

———. 1907. "Kehraus. [with comments on Otto Weininger]." *Die Fackel* 229 (July 2):14.

Krizmanic, Helga. 1969. "Emil Lucka und Otto Weininger." Ph.D. dissertation, University of Graz.

Kuhn, Annette. 1988. "Der Antifeminismus als verborgene Theoriebasis des deutschen Faschismus: Feministische Gedanken zur nationalsozialistischen 'Biopolitik.' " In *Frauen und Faschismus in Europa: Der faschistische Körper*, edited by Leonore Siegele-Wenschkewitz and Gerda Stuchlik, 39–50. Pfaffenweiler: Centaurus-Verlag.

Kurz, Otto. 1967. *Fakes.* Orig. publ. 1948. 2nd ed. London: Faber.

Kuttner, Erich. 1930. *Pathologie des Rassenantisemitismus.* Berlin: Philo.

Labanyi, Peter. 1985. " 'Die Gefahr des Körpers' ": A Reading of Otto Weininger's *Geschlecht und Charakter.*" In *Fin-de-Siècle Vienna*, edited by Gilbert J. Carr and Eda Sagarra, 161–85. Dublin: Trinity College.

Lawrence, D. H. 1946. *Apocalypse.* Paris: Confluences.

Lazarus, Moritz. 1862. "Über das Verhältnis des Einzelnen zur Gesammtheit." *Zeitschrift für Völkerpsychologie und Sprachwissenschaft* 2:437.

Lazarus, Moritz, and Steinthal, Heymann. 1860. "Einleitende Gedanken über Völkerpsychologie." *Zeitschrift für Völkerpsychologie und Sprachwissenschaft* 1:1–73.

Lederer, Gerda. 1993. "Elisabeth Noelle-Neumann und die verletzte Nation." *Journal für Sozialforschung* 33(1):55–58.

Le Rider, Jacques. 1982. *Le Cas Otto Weininger: Racines de l'antiféminisme et l'antisémitisme.* Paris: Presses Universitaires de France.

———. 1983. "Réponses à Allan Janik." *Austriaca* 16:190–93.

———. 1985. *Der Fall Otto Weininger: Wurzeln des Antifeminismus und Antisemitismus.* Translated by Dieter Hornig. Rev. ed. Vienna and Munich: Löcker.

———. 1986a. "Actualité d'Otto Weininger." *Austriaca* 23:93–99.

———. 1986b. "Heimito von Doderer und Otto Weininger." In *L'Actualité de Doderer*, edited by Pierre Grappin and Jean-Pierre Christophe, 37–45. Proceedings of an International Doderer Colloquium in Metz, November 1984. Metz and Paris: Université de Metz and Didier-Erudition.

———. 1990a. *Modernité viennoise et crises de l'identité.* Paris: Presses Universitaires de France.

———. 1990b. *Das Ende der Illusion: Zur Kritik der Moderne.* Translated by Robert Fleck. Vienna. Österreichischer Bundesverlag.

———. 1990c. "Wittgenstein et Weininger." In *Tradition et rupture: Wittgenstein et la critique du monde moderne*, 43–65. Brussels: Ante Post (Le Lettre Volée).

———. 1993. *Modernity and Crises of Identity: Culture and Society in Fin-de-Siècle Vienna.* Translated by Rosemary Morris. Cambridge: Polity Press.

Le Rider, Jacques, and Leser, Norbert, eds. 1984. *Otto Weininger: Werk und Wirkung.* Vienna: Österreichischer Bundesverlag.

Lesky, Erna. 1976. *The Vienna Medical School of the Nineteenth Century.* Translated by L. Williams and I. S. Levij. Baltimore: Johns Hopkins.

———. 1978. *Die Wiener Medizinische Schule im 19. Jahrhundert.* Orig. publ. 1965. 2nd ed. Studien zur Geschichte der Universität Wien, 6. Graz and Cologne: Böhlaus Verlag.

Lessing, Theodor. 1930. *Der jüdische Selbsthaß.* Reprint, 1984, with a foreword by Boris Groys. Munich: Mattes & Seitz.

Lévy-Valensi, Éliane Amado. 1962. *Les Niveaux de l'être et de la connaissance dans leur relations au problème du mal.* Paris: Presses Universitaires de France.

Lewinter, Roger. 1973. "Georg Groddeck: (Anti)judaïsme et bisexualité." *Nouvelle Revue de psychanalyse* 7:199–203.

Lichtenstein, Heiner, ed. 1986. *Die Fassbinder-Kontroverse oder das Ende der Schonzeit.* Königstein: Athenäum.

Liebermann von Wahlendorf, Willy Ritter. 1988. *Erinnerungen eines deutschen Juden 1863–1936.* Munich and Zurich: Piper.

Lilienthal, Georg. 1985. *Der Lebensborn e.V.: Ein Instrument nationalsozialistischer Rassenpolitik.* Forschungen zur Neueren Medizin und Biologiegeschichte, 1. Stuttgart and New York: Gustav Fischer.

Lombroso, Cesare. 1894. *L'antisemitismo e le scienze moderne.* Turin and Rome: L. Roux e C. Editori.

———. 1895. *The Man of Genius.* London: Scott; New York: Scribner's.

Lombroso, Cesare, and Guglielmo Ferrero. 1893; 1903. *La donna delinquente, la prostituta e la donna normale.* Turin: Fratelli Bocca Editori.

———. 1894. *Das Weib als Verbrecherin und Prostituierte: Anthropologische Studien, gegründet auf eine Darstellung der Biologie und Psychologie des normalen Weibes.* Translated by Hans Kurella. Hamburg: Verlagsanstalt und Druckerei.

Lombroso-Ferrero, Gina, ed. 1972. *Criminal Man.* Montclair, NJ: Patterson Smith.

Lucka, Emil. 1905, 1921. *Otto Weininger, Sein Werk und Seine Persönlichkeit.* Vienna and Leipzig: W. Braumüller; Berlin: Schuster & Loeffler.

Lukács, Georg. 1962. *Die Zerstörung der Vernunft.* Vol. 2, *Irrationalismus und Imperialismus.* Darmstadt and Neuwied: Luchterhand.

Luther, Martin. 1971. "On the Jews and Their Lies." In *Luther's Works.* Vol. 47, *The Christian in Society IV,* edited by Franklin Sherman and translated by Martin H. Bertram, 121–306. Philadelphia: Fortress Press.

Lützeler, Paul Michael. 1973. *Hermann Broch: Ethik und Politik.* Munich: Winkler.

Mach, Ernst. 1882. "Die ökonomische Natur der physikalischen Forschung." *Almanach der Kaiserlichen Akademie der Wissenschaften* 32:[316ff.]

———. 1900. *Die Principien der Wärmelehre, historisch-kritisch entwickelt.* 2nd ed. Leipzig: J. A. Barth.

———. 1922. *Die Analyse der Empfindungen und das Verhältnis des Physischen zum Psychischen.* 9th ed. Reprint, 1987. Darmstadt: Wissenschaftliche Buchgesellschaft.

Maddox, Brenda. 1988. *Nora: The Real Life of Molly Bloom.* Boston: Houghton Mifflin Company.

Mahler, Alma. 1973. *Gustav Mahler: Memories and Letters.* 3rd ed. Seattle: University of Washington Press.

Major, René. 1986. *De l'élection: Freud face aux ideologies americaine, allemande et sovietique.* Paris: Aubier.

Malcolm, Norman. 1982. "Wittgenstein: The Relation of Language to Instinctive Behavior." *Philosophical Investigations* 5(1):3–22.

Manor, Giora. 1982. ["The unavoidable death of a sick genius"]. *Al Hamishmar,* October 14.

Markovits, Andrei; Benhai, Seila; and Postone, Moishe. 1986. "Symposium on Rainer Werner Fassbinder's *Garbage, the City and Death.*" *New German Critique* 38:3–27.

Markus, Georg. 1984. *Der Fall Redl*. Vienna: Amalthea.

Marlock, Ingeborg E. 1993. *Otto Weininger's "Geschlecht und Charakter" and Hermann Broch's "Die Schlafwandler."* Ph.D. Diss. Washington University (St. Louis, MO).

Marschall, Brigitte. 1987. "Obsession des Ich: *Weiningers Nacht* von Joshua Sobol." *Maske und Kothurn* 33(3–4):89–105.

Marsky, A. 1900. "Unsere Kinder." *Neuzeit*, March 9, 95–96.

Mason, John Hope. 1988. "The Character of Creativity: Two Traditions." *History of European Ideas* 9:697–715.

Masson, Jeffrey. 1985. *The Assault on Truth: Freud's Suppression of the Seduction Theory*. 2nd ed. New York: Penguin Books.

Mattenklott, Gerd. 1985. *Bilderdienst: Ästhetische Opposition bei Beardsley und George*. 2nd ed. Frankfurt: Syndikat.

May, Rolf. 1986. "Wer hat Angst vor Otto Weininger." *Münchener Tageszeitung*, October 17.

Mayer, Hans. 1975, 1981. *Aussenseiter*. Frankfurt: Suhrkamp.

———. 1982. *Outsiders: A Study in Life and Letters*. Translated by Dennis M. Sweet. Cambridge: MIT Press.

Mayer, Sigmund. 1918. *Die Wiener Juden: Kommerz, Kultur, Politik 1700–1900*. Vienna: R. Löwet.

Mayr, F. K. 1970. "Ludwig Wittgenstein und das Problem einer Philosophischen Anthropologie." *Tijdschr Filosof* 32:214–89.

Mayreder, Rosa. 1905. *Zur Kritik der Weiblichkeit*. Jena and Leipzig: E. Diederichs.

———. 1913. *A Survey of the Woman Problem*. Translated by Herman Scheffauer. New York: G. H. Doran; reprint 1982. Westport, CT: Hyperion Press.

Mayrhofer, Manfred. 1991. "Ein indogermanistischer Versuch Otto Weiningers." *Historische Sprachforschung/Historical Linguistics* 104(2):303–6.

Mecke, Günter. 1982. *Franz Kafkas offenbares Geheimnis: Eine Psychopathologie*. Munich: W. Fink.

Mehlman, Jeffrey. 1974. *A Structural Study of Autobiography: Proust, Leiris, Sartre, Lévi-Strauss*. Ithaca, NY: Cornell University Press.

———. 1983. "Literature and Collaboration: Benoist-Méchin's Return to Proust." In *Lacan and Narration: The Psychoanalytic Difference in Narrative Theory*, edited by R. C. Davis. Baltimore: Johns Hopkins University Press.

Meinong, Alexius von. 1914. "Nekrolog und Porträt von Friedrich Jodl." *Almanach der Kaiserlichen Akademie der Wissenschaften* 64:446–52.

Meisel-Hess, Grete. 1904. *Weiberhaß und Weiberverachtung*. Vienna.

Mendoza, Ramon G. 1986. *Outside Humanity: A Study of Kafka's Fiction*. Lanham, MD, and London: University Press of America.

Miller, Alice. 1984. *Thou Shalt Not Be Aware: Society's Betrayal of the Child*. Translated by Hildegard and Hunter Hannum. New York: Farrar Straus Giroux.

Moll, Albert. 1900. "Die angebliche Minderwertigkeit des Weibes." *Die Zeit* 314 October 6:5.

———. 1900a. "Die Behandlung der Homosexualität." *Jahrbuch für sexuelle Zwischenstufen* 1900:1–29.

Monk, Ray. 1990. *Wittgenstein: The Duty of Genius.* New York: Free Press.

Morgenstern, Christian. 1965. "Die Unmögliche Tatsache." In *Gesammelte Werke in einem Band,* 262–63. Munich: R. Piper.

Morgenstern, Matthias. 1989. "Eine jüdische Seele: Joshua Sobol's *Weiningers Nacht* als Spiegel moderner jüdischer Identitätskonflikte." *Forum Modernes Theater* 4:3–15.

Morton, Lord. 1893. Letter reprinted in *The Philosophical Transactions of The Society of London* 1:20.

Mosse, George L. 1964. *The Crisis of German Ideology: Intellectual Origins of the Third Reich.* New York: Grosset & Dunlap.

———. 1970. Universal Library paperback ed. 1971. *Germans and Jews: The Right, The Left and The Search for a "Third Force" in Pre-Nazi Germany.* New York: Grosset & Dunlap.

———. 1985. *Nationalism and Sexuality: Middle-Class Morality and Sexual Norms in Modern Europe.* Madison: University of Wisconsin Press.

Mosse, George L., ed. 1966. *Nazi Culture: Intellectual, Cultural and Social Life in the Third Reich.* Translated by Salvator Attanasio et al. New York: Grosset & Dunlap.

Mulligan, Kevin. 1981. "Philosophy, Animality and Justice: Kleist, Kafka, Weininger and Wittgenstein." In *Structure and Gestalt: Philosophy and Literature in Austria-Hungary and Her Successor States,* edited by Barry Smith, 293–311. Amsterdam: John Benjamins.

Musil, Robert. 1970. *Der Mann ohne Eigenschaften.* Edited by Adolf Frisé. Special ed. Hamburg: Rowohlt.

———. 1979. *The Man Without Qualities.* Orig. publ. 1954. Translated by Eithne Wilkins and Ernst Kaiser. 3 vols. London: Martin Secker & Warburg (Picador Classics).

Nabbe, Hildegard. 1984. "Parodie und literarische Satire in Carl Sternheims *Die Hose.*" *Neophilologus* 68(3):421–35.

Nadel, Ira. 1989. *Joyce and the Jews: Culture and Texts.* London: The Macmillan Press.

Nerlich, Michael. 1977, *Kritik der Abenteuer-Ideologie.* 2 vols. Berlin: Akademie-Verlag.

———. 1987. *Ideology of Adventure.* Translated by Ruth Crowley. Minneapolis: University of Minnesota Press.

Nicolino, Franco. No date. *Indagini su Freud e sulla Psicoanalisi.* Naples: Liguori editore.

Niehoff, Karena. 1985. "Totentanze aus Israel." *Süddeutsche Zeitung,* May 23.

Nietzsche, Friedrich. 1980. "Der Fall Wagner." In *Sämtliche Werke: Kritische Studienausgabe,* vol. 6, Pt. 3, 3–47. Edited by Giorgio Colli and Mazzino Montinari. Berlin and New York: De Gruyter.

Nitzsche, Bernd. 1980. *Männerängste, Männerwünsche.* Munich: Matthes und Seitz.

Nordau, Max. 1900. "Muskeljudenthum." *Die Welt* 24:2.

———. 1902a. "Rede Dr. Max Nordaus." *Die Welt* 1:2–4.

———. 1902b. "Was bedeutet das Turnen für uns Juden?" *Die Welt* 31:2.

Nordhausen, R. 1903. "Der Schuss im Nebel." *Münchner Neueste Nachrichten,* November 5.

Nunberg, Herman, and Federn, Ernst, eds. 1975–76. *Protokolle der Wiener Psycho-analytischen Vereinigung*. 4 vols. Frankfurt: S. Fischer.

Oden, Robert. 1987. "Religious Identity and the Sacred Prostitution Accusation." In Robert Oden, *Bible Without Theology*, 131–53. Cambridge: Harper and Row.

Oettinger, Eduard. 1879. *Moniteur des dates*. Supplement to vol. 48 (April). Leipzig: L. Denicke.

Ofrat, Gideon. 1983. "Modern Hebrew Drama: Sobol's Night of 1903." *Modern Hebrew Literature* 9(1–2):34–41.

Olender, Maurice. 1989. *Les Langues du Paradis: Aryens et Semites—un couple providentiel*. Paris: Gallimard.

Ostow, M. 1983. "A Contribution to the Study of Anti-Semitism." *Israeli Journal of Psychiatry and Related Sciences* 20:95–118.

Pankau, Johannes G. 1990. "Körper und Geist: Das Geschlechtsverhältnis in Elias Canettis Roman *Die Blendung*." *Colloquia Germanica* 23(2):146–70.

Pawel, Ernst. 1984. *The Nightmare of Reason: A Life of Franz Kafka*. New York: Farrar Straus Giroux.

Perrelli, Franco. 1983. "Strindberg e Weininger." In *Strindberg nella cultura moderna*, edited by Franco Perrelli, 59–70. Rome: Bulzoni.

Pfennig, Richard. 1906. *Wilhelm Fliess und seine Nachentdecker: O. Weininger und H. Swoboda*. Berlin: Emil Goldschmidt.

Philosophical Society. 1902–3. [Remembrance of Otto Weininger.] *Bericht der Philosophischen Gesellschaft an der Universität zu Wien 16*.

Pichl, Eduard. 1942. "Hundert Jahre Schönerer." *Der getreue Eckart: Kulturelle Monatsschrift der Schaffenden* 19:10 (July): 301–4.

Picker, Henry. 1989. *Hitlers Tischgespräche im Führerhauptquartier*. Unrev. new ed. Stuttgart: Seewald; Frankfurt and Berlin: Ullstein.

Pöder, Elfriede. 1984. " 'Männlichkeit' und 'Weiblichkeit' in Canetti's *Blendung: Weininger-Rezeption an den Beispielen Kien und Therese*." Unpublished ms. University of Innsbruck.

———. 1985. "Spurensicherung: Otto Weininger in der 'Blendung.' " In *Blendung als Lebensform: Elias Canetti*, edited by Friedbert Aspetsberger and Gerald Stieg, 57–72. Königstein/Ts.: Athenäum.

Politzer, Heinz. 1965. *Franz Kafka, der Künstler*. Frankfurt: S. Fischer.

———. 1966. *Franz Kafka: Parable or Paradox*. Ithaca, NY: Cornell University Press.

Pontalis, Jean-Bertrand. 1973. "Bisexualité et différence des sexes (L'insaisissable entre-deux)." *Nouvelle Revue de psychanalyse* 7:13–23.

Popp, Adelheid. 1909. *Jugend einer Arbeiterin*. Munich: E. Reinhardt.

———. 1912. *Autobiography of a Working Woman*. London: T. F. Unwin.

———. 1929. *Der Weg zur Höhe: Die sozialdemokraitsche Frauenbewegung Österreichs; Ihr Aufbau, ihre Entwicklung und ihr Aufstieg*. Vienna: Frauenzentralkomitee der Sozialdemokratischen Arbeiterpartei Deutschösterreichs.

Pourtalès, Guy de. 1927. *Louis II de Bavière ou Hamlet-Roi*. Paris: Gallimard.

Praag, Siegfried E. van. 1939. "Essai d'une typologie juive (IV)." *Revue juive de Genève* vol. 4, no. 64 (January):168–172.

Probst, Ferdinand. 1904. *Der Fall Otto Weininger: Eine psychiatrische Studie*. Wiesbaden: Bergmann.

Proust, Marcel. 1961. *Sodome et Gomorrhe*. Paris: Gallimard.

Puff-Trojan, Andreas. 1986. "Im Zeichen des Androgynen: Weininger, Serner und die Folgen einer Bewegung." In *Das lila Wein um 1900: Zur Ästhetik der Homosexualitäten*, edited by Neda Bei, Wolfgang Förster, Hanna Hacker, and Manfred Lang, 97–107. Vienna: Edition Spuren, Promedia.

Pugel, Theodor. 1936. *Die arische Frau im Wandel der Jahrtausende: Kulturgeschichtlich geschildert*. Vienna: Österreichische Verlagsanstalt.

Pultzer, Peter. 1964. *The Rise of Political Anti-Semitism in Germany and Austria*. New York: Wiley.

———. 1988. *The Rise of Political Anti-Semitism in Germany and Austria*. Rev. ed. London: Peter Halban.

Pusch, Luise F. 1984. *Das Deutsche als Männersprache: Aufsätze und Glossen zur feministischen Linguistik*. Frankfurt: Suhrkamp.

Quinn, Susan. 1987. *A Mind of Her Own: The Life of Karen Horney*. New York: Summit Books.

Rabinbach, Anson. 1983. *The Crisis of Austrian Socialism: From Red Vienna to Civil War, 1927–1934*. Chicago: University of Chicago Press.

Rappaport, Moriz. 1907. "Vorwort zur zweiten Auflage." In Otto Weininger, *Über die letzten Dinge*, V–XXIII. Vienna and Leipzig: Wilhelm Braumüller.

Rathenau, Walther. 1965. "Höre, Israel!" In *Schriften*, 89–93. Orig. publ. 1897. Berlin: Berlin Verlag.

Raymond, Marcel. 1969. *De Baudelaire au surréalisme*. Paris: Corti.

Reitter, Bärbel. 1986. "Biographie eines antisemitischen Juden." *Mittelbairische Zeitung*, October 28.

Reizbaum, Marilyn. 1982. "The Jewish Connection, Cont'd." In *The Seventh of Joyce*, edited by Bernard Benstock, 229–237. Bloomington: Indiana University Press.

———. 1985. "James Joyce's Judaic 'Other': Text and Context." Ph.D. dissertation. University of Wisconsin-Madison.

———. 1990. "Swiss Customs: Zurich's Sources for Joyce's Judaica." *James Joyce Quarterly* 27 (Winter):203–18.

Rhees, Rush. 1981. *Ludwig Wittgenstein: Personal Reflections*. Totowa, NJ: Rowman & Littlefield.

Rodlauer, Hannelore. 1987. "Von 'Eros und Psyche' zu 'Geschlecht und Charakter': Unbekannte Weininger-Manuskripte im Archiv der Österreichischen Akademie der Wissenschaften." Anzeiger der phil.-hist. Klasse der Österreichischen Akademie der Wissenschaften, 124 (So. 7):110–39.

———. 1990. *Otto Weininger: Eros und Psyche; Studien und Briefe 1899–1902*. Vienna: Verlag der Österreichischen Akademie der Wissenschaften.

Rogge-Börner, Sophie. 1934. "Akte Sophie Rogge-Börner und Deutsche Frauen an Adolf Hitler." Leipzig: Berlin Document Center.

Rohracher, Hubert. 1934. *Kleine Einführung in die Charakterkunde*. Leipzig and Berlin: B.G. Teubner.

———. 1948. *Kleine Charakterkunde*. 5th rev. and enl. ed. Vienna: Urban & Schwarzenberg.

Rokem, Freddie. 1989. "Memory and History: *The Soul of a Jew* by Jehoshua Sobol." *Assaph: Studies in the Theatre* 5:139–64.

Rosenberg, Alfred, ed. 1928. *Dietrich Eckart: Ein Vermächtnis.* Munich: Verlag Frz. Eher Nachf.

———. 1930. *Der Mythus des 20. Jahrhunderts: Eine Wertung der seelisch-geistigen Gestaltenkämpfe unserer Zeit.* Munich: Hoheneichen-Verlag.

———. 1933. *Unmoral im Talmud.* Munich: Deutscher Volksverlag.

Rosenberg, Saul. 1928. "Friedrich Nietzsche und Otto Weininger." Ph.D. dissertation, University of Vienna.

Roth, Marie-Louise. 1972. *Robert Musil: Ethik und Ästhetik.* Munich: List.

Roudinesco, Elisabeth. 1990. *Jacques Lacan & Co.: A History of Psychoanalysis in France, 1925–1985.* Translated by Jeffrey Mehlman. Chicago: University of Chicago Press.

Rougemont, Denis de. 1965. *The Meaning of Europe.* New York: Stein and Day.

Rozenblit, Marsha L. 1983. *The Jews of Vienna, 1867–1914: Assimilation and Identity.* Albany: State University of New York Press.

Saar, Ferdinand von. 1987. *Seligmann Hirsch.* Edited by Datlef Haberland. Tübingen: M. Niemeyer.

Sachisthal, Kraft. 1943. "Die leichteren Arbeiten den Frauen: Nur am rechten Arbeitsplatz der günstigste Arbeitserfolg." *Völkischer Beobachter* (Berlin), no. 274 (October 1), 3.

Sachs, Franz. 1916–17. "Von deutschen Jüdinnen." *Der Jude 1:* 662–64.

Samuel, Maurice. 1929. "Bloom of Bloomusalem." *The Reflex* 4 (February):10–16.

Sartre, Jean-Paul. 1965. *Anti-Semite and Jew.* Orig. publ. 1946. New York: Schocken Books.

Scandiana, Giuseppe. 1983. "Svevo, Weininger e la donna." *Humanitas* 38(4): 551–58.

Scheichl, Sigurd Paul. 1987. "The Contexts and Nuances of Anti-Jewish Language: Were All the "Antisemites" Antisemites?" In *Jews, Antisemitism and Culture in Vienna,* edited by Ivar Oxaal, Michael Pollak, and Gerhard Botz, 89–110. London and New York: Routledge and Kegan Paul.

Schmiedebach, Heinz-Peter. 1988. "Die Völkerpsychologie von Moritz Lazarus (1824–1903) und ihre Beziehung zur naturwissenschaftlichen Psychiatrie." *XXX Congrès International d'Histoire de la Médicine 1986.* 311–21.

Schnedl-Bubeniček, Hanna. 1981. "Grenzgängerin der Moderne: Studien zur Emanzipation in Texten von Rosa Mayreder." In *Das ewige Klischee: Zum Rollenbild und Selbstverständnis bei Männern und Frauen,* edited by Autorengruppe Uni Wien, 179–205. Vienna: Böhlau.

See also Bubeniček, Hanna.

Schneemann, Wilhelm. 1966. "Juden und Leibesübungen [1938]." In *Nationalsozialistische Leibeserziehung.* Stuttgart: Verlag Karl Hoffmann.

Schnitzler, Arthur. 1927. *Der Geist im Wort und der Geist in der Tat: Vorläufige Bemerkungen zu zwei Diagrammen.* Berlin: S. Fischer.

———. 1972. *The Mind in Words and Actions: Preliminary Remarks Concerning Two Diagrams.* Translated by Robert O. Weiss. New York: Ungar.

———. 1982. "Leutnant Gustl (1900)" In *Arthur Schnitzler: Plays and Stories,* edited by Egon Schwarz, 249–79. The German Library, 55. New York: Continuum.

Schoenberg, Barbara Z. 1987. " 'Woman-Defender' and 'Woman-Offender': Peter

Altenberg and Otto Weininger: Two Literary Stances vis-à-vis Bourgeois Culture in the Viennese 'Belle Epoque.' " *Modern Austrian Literature* 20(2):51–69.

Schopenhauer, Arthur. 1976. "Parerga und Paralipomena." In *Sämtliche Werke*, vol. 5, edited by Wolfgang von Löneysen. Darmstadt: Wissenschaftliche Buchgesellschaft.

Schorske, Carl E. 1980. *Fin-de-Siècle Vienna: Politics and Culture*. New York: Knopf.

———. 1982. *Wien: Geist und Gesellschaft im Fin de Siècle*. Translated by Horst Günther. Frankfurt: S. Fischer.

Schott. Georg. 1927. *Das Lebenswerk Houston Stewart Chamberlains in Umrissen*. Munich: J. F. Lehmanns Verlag.

Schrader, George. 1972. "Kant and Kierkegaard on Duty and Inclination." In *Kierkegaard*, edited by J. Thompson, 321–41. Garden City: Doubleday.

Schur, Max. 1975. *La Mort dans la vie de Freud*. Translated by Briggite Bost. Paris: Gallimard.

Schwarz, Egon. 1979. "Melting Pot or Witches' Cauldron? Jews and Anti-Semites in Vienna at the Turn of the Century." In *Jews and Germans: From 1860 to 1933*, edited by D. Bronsen, 262–87. Heidelberg: Winter.

Segel, Binjamin. 1910. *Die Entdeckungsreise des Herrn Dr. Theodor Lessing zu den Ostjuden*. Lemberg: Verlag "Hatikwa."

Seidenfaden, Ingrid. 1988. "Nachruf auf den Otto." *Abendzeitung: München*, October 17.

Shamir, Moshe. 1982. ["Report on Sobol's 'The Soul of a Jew' "]. *Ha'aretz*, October 14.

Showalter, Dennis E. 1982. *Little Man, What Now? "Der Stürmer" in the Weimar Republic*. Hamden, CT: Archon Books.

Shteir, Rachel. 1990. "In Search of Sobol." *Theater* 21(3) (Summer–Fall):39–42.

Skasa, Michael. 1986. "Nichts dämmert in die Nacht." *Süddeutsche Zeitung*, October 17.

Skloot, Robert. 1989. "Theatre Notebook: Vienna, 1988." *Theatre Three*, Fall.

Sloterdijk, Peter. 1983. *Kritik der zynischen Vernunft*. Frankfurt: Suhrkamp.

Smith, Barry. 1985. "Weininger und Wittgenstein." *Teoria* 5:227–37.

Sobol, Jehoshua [also Joshua or Yehoshua]. 1982. *Nefesh Yehudi: Ha-Layla Ha-Aharon shel Otto Weininger*. Or-Am, Tel Aviv.

———. 1984. "The 'Last Night of Otto Weininger'—Scene 6 from the Play." Translated by Betsy Rosenberg and Miriam Schlesinger. *Modern Hebrew Literature* 9(1–2):42–46.

———. 1987. "Theatricality of Political Theater." *Maske und Kothurn* 33(3–4):107–12.

———. 1988. *Weiningers Nacht*. Translated by Ingrid Rencher and adapted by Paulus Manker. With two essays by Joachim Riedl and Nike Wagner; texts by Jean Amery, Sigmund Freud, Artur Gerber, Adolf Hitler, Jacques Le Rider, Emil Lucka, Karl Lueger, Jonny Moser, Hannelore Rodlauer, Felix Salten, Arthur Schopenhauer, August Strindberg, and Stefan Zweig; and an appendix containing unpublished texts by Otto Weininger. Vienna: Deutsches Volkstheater Program Edition (Europa Verlag).

———. 1989. "Excerpt from: *The Soul of a Jew* [Act I, Scenes 9–12]." Translated by

Betsy Rosenberg and Miriam Schlesinger. *Assaph: Studies in the Theatre* 5:139–64.

———. n.d. The *Soul of a Jew: The Death of Otto Weininger: Weininger's Last Night.* Translated by Betsy Rosenberg and Miriam Schlesinger. Tel Aviv: The Israeli Centre of International Theatre Institute.

Soergel, Albert, and Hohoff, Curt. 1963. *Dichtung und Dichter der Zeit: Vom Naturalismus bis zur Gegenwart.* Vol. 2. Düsseldorf: A. Bagel.

Sokel, Walter H. 1964. *Franz Kafka: Tragik und Ironie.* Munich: A. Langen.

———. 1966. *Franz Kafka.* New York: Columbia University Press.

Sokol, Lech. 1987. "The Metaphysics of Sex: Strindberg, Weininger and S. I. Witkiewicz." *Theatre Research International* 12 (Spring):39–51.

Sombart, Werner. 1962. *The Jews and Modern Capitalism.* Orig. publ. 1911. New York: Collier Books.

Sorkin, David. 1988. *The Transformation of German Jewry, 1780–1840.* Oxford: Oxford University Press.

Spackman, Barbara. 1989. *Decadent Genealogies: The Rhetoric of Sickness from Baudelaire to D'Annunzio.* Ithaca, NY: Cornell University Press.

Spengler, Oswald. 1922. *Der Untergang des Abendlandes.* Vol. 2, *Welthistorische Perspektiven.* Munich: C. H. Becksche Verlagsbuchhandlung.

———. 1928. *The Decline of the West.* Authorized translation with notes by Charles Francis Atkinson. Vol. 2, *Perspectives of World-History.* New York: Alfred A. Knopf.

Spire, André. 1913. *Quelques Juifs: Israël Zangwill, Otto Weininger, James Darmesteter.* Paris: Société du Mercure de France.

Springer, Otto, ed. 1974. *New Muret-Sanders Encyclopedic Dictionary, German-English.* 2 vols. Berlin, Munich, Vienna, and Zurich: Langenscheidt.

Stach, Rainer. 1987. *Kafkas erotischer Mythos: Eine ästhetische Konstruktion des Weiblichen.* Frankfurt: Fischer Taschenbuch Verlag.

Steegmuller, Francis. 1963. *Apollinaire: Poet among the Painters.* New York: Farrar Straus Giroux.

Steinberg, Erwin R. 1969. ". . . The Steady Monologue of the Interiors; the Pardonable Confusion . . . ." *James Joyce Quarterly* 6 (Spring):185–200.

Steiner, Rudolf. 1967. *Die Wissenschaft vom Werden der Menschen.* Dornach: Verlag der Rudolf Steiner-Nachlassverwaltung.

———. 1978. *Das Rätsel des Menschen: Die geistigen Hintergründe der menschlichen Geschichte.* 2nd ed. Dornach: Verlag der Rudolf Steiner-Nachlassverwaltung.

Stieg, Gerald. 1976. *Der Brenner und Die Fackel.* Salzburg: O. Müller.

———. 1983. "Elias Canetti und Karl Kraus: Ein Versuch." *Modern Austrian Literature* 16(3–4):197–210.

———. 1987. "Kafka und Weininger." In *Dialog der Epochen: Studien zur Literatur des 19. und 20. Jahrhunderts,* Festschrift for Walter Weiss. Edited by Eduard Beutner, Josef Donnenberg, Adolf Haslinger, Hans Höller, Karlheinz Rossbacher, and Sigrid Schmid-Bortenschlager, 88–99. Vienna: Österreichischer Bundesverlag.

Stölzl, Christoph. 1975. *Kafkas böses Böhmen.* Munich: Edition Text and Kritik.

Streicher, Julius. ed. 1924–45. *Der Stürmer: Nürnberger Wochenblatt zum Kampfe um die Wahrheit.* Nuremberg.

Strindberg, August. 1903. "Idolatrie, Gynolatrie. Ein Nachruf . . ." *Die Fackel* 144 (October 17):1ff.

———. 1921. "Brief an Karl Kraus vom 12. Oktober 1903." *Die Fackel* 568–71 (May):48.

Sturm, Bruno. 1912. *Gegen Weininger: Ein Versuch zur Lösung des Moralproblems.* Vienna: Braumüller.

Sullerot, Evelyne, ed. 1978. *Le Fait féminin.* Paris: Fayard.

Sulloway, Frank J. 1979. *Freud, Biologist of the Mind: Beyond the Psychoanalytic Legend.* New York: Basic Books.

Svevo, Italo. 1986. *La coscienza di Zeno.* Edited by B. Maier. Pordenon: Studio Tesi.

Swoboda, Hermann. 1906. *Die gemeinnützige Forschung und der eigennützige Forscher.* Vienna and Leipzig: Wilhelm Braumüller.

———. 1923. *Otto Weiningers Tod.* 2nd ed. With previously unpublished letters by Otto Weininger. Vienna and Leipzig: H. Heller.

Taguieff, Pierre-André. 1988. *La Force du préjugé: Essai sur le racisme et ses doubles.* Paris: La Découverte.

Thaler, Leopold. 1935. *Weiningers Weltanschauung im Lichte der Kantischen Lehre.* Vienna: H. Glanz.

Thalmann, Rita. 1984. *Être femme sous le IIIᵉ Reich.* Editions Robert Laffont, S.A.

———. 1984. *Frausein im dritten Reich.* Munich and Vienna: Carl Hanser Verlag.

Theweleit, Klaus. 1977. *Männerphantasien.* 2 vols. Frankfurt: Verlag Roter Stern.

———. 1989. *Male Fantasies.* 2 vols. Translated by Stephan Conway in collaboration with Erica Carter and Chris Turner. Minneapolis: University of Minnesota Press.

Thieme, Ulrich, and Becker, Felix, eds. 1942. *Allgemeines Lexikon der bildenden Künstler von der Antike bis zur Gegenwart.* 37 vols. Leipzig: Seeman.

Thornton, E. M. 1984. *The Freudian Fallacy: An Alternate View of Freudian Theory.* Garden City, NY: Dial Press/Doubleday.

Tögel, Christfried. 1989. "Freud und Wundt: Von der Hypothese bis zur Völkerpsychologie." In *Freud und die akademische Psychologie: Beiträge zu einer historischen Kontroverse,* edited by Bernd Nitzsche, 97–106. Munich: Psychologie Verlags Union.

Tönnies, Ferdinand. 1901. "Die schöpferische Synthese: Ein philosophisches Résumé" [Review of Wilhelm Wundt's *Logik* II]. *Die Zeit* 338 (March 23):183.

Trachtenberg, Joshua. 1983. *The Devil and the Jews: The Medieval Conception of the Jew and Its Relation to Modern Anti-Semitism.* Philadelphia: The Jewish Publication Society of America.

Troll-Borostyáni, Irma von. 1893. *Das Recht der Frau: Eine Soziale Studie.* Berlin: S. Fischer.

———. 1903. *Kathechismus der Frauenbewegung.* Leipzig: Frauen-Rundschau.

Unglaub, Erich. 1988. "Strindberg, Weininger and Karl Kraus: Eine Überprüfung." *Recherches Germaniques* 18:121–50.

Unkeless, Elaine. 1982. "The Conventional Molly Bloom." In *Women in Joyce,* edited by Suzette Henke and Elaine Unkeless, 150–68. Urbana: University of Illinois Press.

Vaerting, Mathilde. 1931. *Wahrheit und Irrtum in der Geschlechterpsychologie.* 2nd rev. ed. Weimar: E. Lichtenstein.

Wagenbach, Klaus. 1964. *Franz Kafka*. Reinbek bei Hamburg: Rowohlt.

———. 1983. *Franz Kafka: Bilder aus seinem Leben*. Berlin: Verlag Klaus Wagenbach.

———. 1984. *Franz Kafka: Pictures of a Life*. Translated by Arthur S. Wensinger. New York: Pantheon.

Wagner, Nike. 1981. *Geist und Geschlecht: Karl Kraus und die Erotik der Wiener Moderne*. Frankfurt: Suhrkamp.

Walden, Oskar. 1896. "Was ist aus uns geworden?" *Die Neuzeit*, April 3:139.

Waldenburg, Alfred. 1911. "Jüdische Rassenhochzucht." *Die Welt*, pp. 976–78.

Warnecke, Klare. 1986. "Tod in der Schwarzspaniergasse." *Die Welt*, April 8.

Weininger, Leopold. 1903. "Zuschrift an Karl Kraus." *Die Fackel* 150 (December 23):28–29.

———. 1904. "Der Fall Otto Weininger. Erklärung und Berichtigung. (Mit Fußnotenkommentar von Karl Kraus)" *Die Fackel* 169 (November 23):6–14.

Weininger, Otto. 1903. *Geschlecht und Charakter: Eine prinzipielle Untersuchung*. 1st ed. Vienna and Leipzig: W. Braumüller.—Reprint, 1980. With an appendix containing Weininger's *Taschenbuch*, selections from Weininger's correspondence, letters from August Strindberg to Artur Gerber, and new essays by Annegret Stopczyk, Gisela Dischner, and Roberto Calasso. Munich: Matthes & Seitz.

———. 1904. *Über die letzten Dinge*. With a biographical preface by Moriz Rappaport. 1st ed. Vienna and Leipzig: W. Braumüller.—Reprint, 1980. Munich: Mattes & Seitz.

———. 1906. *Sex and Character*. Authorized anonymous translation from the 6th German ed. London: William Heinemann; New York: A. L. Burt Company.

———. 1906a. *Geschlecht und Charakter: Eine prinzipielle Untersuchung*. 9th ed. Vienna and Leipzig: W. Braumüller.

———. 1907. *Über die letzten Dinge*. With a biographical preface by Moriz Rappaport. 2nd rev. ed. Vienna and Leipzig: W. Braumüller.

———. 1910. *Geschlecht und Charakter: Eine prinzipielle Untersuchung*. 13th ed. Vienna and Leipzig: W. Braumüller.

———. 1919. *Taschenbuch und Briefe an einen Freund*. Edited by Artur Gerber. Vienna and Leipzig: E. P. Tal.

———. 1922. *Geschlecht und Charakter: Eine prinzipielle Untersuchung*. 25th ed. Vienna and Leipzig: W. Braumüller.

———. 1923. Verse. *Die Fackel* 613–21 (April):158.

———. 1927. *Sex and Character*. 23rd ed. New York and Chicago: A.L. Burt Company.

———. 1992. *Sesso e carattere: Una indagine sui principi*. Edited and translated by Giovanni Sampaolo. Introduction by Alberto Cavaglion. Pordenone: Edizione Studio Tesi.

Weininger, Richard. 1978. *Exciting Years*. Edited by Rodney Campbell. New York: Exposition Press.

WeltDienst: Die Judenfrage/Internationale Korrespondenz. 1945. 12(1–2) (January 1–2): "Das jüdische Wesen," 5–7 and "Juden zeichnen sich selbst," 10–11.

Westenrieder, Norbert. 1984. *Deutsche Frauen und Mädchen!: Vom Alltagsleben 1933–1945*. Düsseldorf: Droste Verlag.

White, Hayden. 1973. *Metahistory*. Baltimore and London: Johns Hopkins University Press.

Wickham, Harvey. 1929. *The Impuritans: A Glimpse of That New World Whose Pilgrim Fathers Are Otto Weininger, Havelock Ellis, James Branch Cabell, Marcel Proust, James Joyce, H. L. Mencken, D. H. Lawrence, Sherwood Anderson, Et Id Genus Omne.* New York: Dial Press.

Widdig, Bernd. 1992. *Männerbünde und Massen: Zur Krise männlicher Identität in der Literatur der Moderne.* Opladen: Westdeutscher Verlag.

Wittgenstein, Ludwig. 1922. *Tractatus Logico-Philosophicus.* Translated by C. K. Ogden. Introduction by Bertrand Russell. Reprint, 1990. London and New York: Routledge.

————. 1967. *Philosophical Investigations.* Translated by G.E.M. Anscombe. 2nd ed. New York: Macmillan.

————. 1969. *On Certainty.* Edited by G.E.M. Anscombe and G. H. von Wright. Translated by D. Paul and G.E.M. Anscombe. New York: Harper.

————. 1974. *Letters to Russell, Keynes and Moore.* Edited by G. H. von Wright, Ithaca: Cornell University Press.

————. 1977. *Vermischte Bemerkungen.* Edited by G. H. von Wright. Frankfurt: Suhrkamp.

Wolff, Lutz-Werner. 1969. *Wiedereroberte Außenwelt: Studien zur Erzählweise Heimito von Doderers am Beispiel des Romans.* Göppingen: A Kümmerle.

Wundt. Wilhelm. 1916. *Elements of Folk Psychology: Outlines of a Psychological History of the Development of Mankind.* Translated by Edward Leroy Schaub. London: George Allen & Unwin.

Wyss, Dieter. 1973. *Psychoanalytic Schools from the Beginning to the Present.* Translated by Gerald Onn. Introduction by Leston L. Havens. New York: Jason Aronson.

Yaron, Elyakim. 1982. ["A Jewish soul is yearning"]. *Ma'ariv*, October 21.

Young, Robert M. 1970. *Mind, Brain and Adaptation in the 19th Century.* Oxford: Clarendon.

Ziegler, Theodor. 1899–1900. [Reviews of H. S. Chamberlain's *Die Grundlagen des 19. Jahrhunderts*.] *Die Zeit*, October 7, 1899, 262; October 14, 1899, 263; November 3, 1900, 318.

Zilboorg, Gregory, and Henry, George W. 1941. *A History of Medical Psychology*. New York: Norton.

Zinik, Zinovy. 1983. "The Origins of Self-Hatred." *Times Literary Supplement,* September 9: 960.

Zohn, Harry. 1971. *Karl Kraus.* New York: Twayne.

Zunzer, Johann. 1924. "Philosophische Erläuterungen zu Otto Weininger." Ph.D. dissertation, University of Vienna.

Zweig. Stefan. 1960. "Vorbeigehen an einem unauffälligen Menschen: Otto Weininger (1926)." In Stefan Zweig, *Europäisches Erbe*, 223. Frankfurt: S. Fischer.

Notes on the Contributors ✦

KATHERINE ARENS is Associate Professor of Germanic Languages at the University of Texas at Austin. She has published on the history of German psychology, intellectual history, literary theory, and second language acquisition.

STEVEN BELLER is the author of *Vienna and the Jews, 1867–1938: A Cultural History* (1989), and *Herzl* (1991). He was a research fellow at Peterhouse, Cambridge University and has taught at Georgetown University. He is writing a book on Francis Joseph and the nature of power in nineteenth-century absolutist/constitutional monarchies.

GISELA BRUDE-FIRNAU is Professor of German at the University of Waterloo, Waterloo, Ontario, Canada. She has published on *völkisch* and National Socialist literary theory and on, among others, Hermann Broch, Heinrich and Thomas Mann, Theodor Herzl, Johann von Goethe, and Alexander von Humboldt. She has just completed a book on literary interpretations of Emperor Wilhelm II, 1889–1989.

ALBERTO CAVAGLION is the author of several books, including *Otto Weininger in Italia* (1982) and a biography of Felice Momigliano (1988). He has also coauthored a book on the racial laws in Italy during Fascism (*Le interdizioni del Duce*), which appeared in 1988.

KRISTIE A. FOELL received the B.A. from Yale University and the Ph.D from University of California at Berkeley, both in German Literature, and was a Fulbright scholar at the University of Vienna. She currently teaches German language, literature, and film at Vassar College, and has also taught at Gustavus Adolphus College. Her book on gender in Elias Canetti's *Auto-da-Fé* appeared in 1994 with Ariadne Press.

SANDER L. GILMAN is Professor of German, the History of Science, Psychiatry and a member of the Program in Jewish Studies at the University of Chicago. A long-time faculty member at Cornell University, he is an intellectual and literary historian and the author or editor of over forty books, including the widely cited study *Jewish Self-Hatred*, which was published by the Johns Hopkins University Press in 1986.

NANCY A. HARROWITZ is Assistant Professor of Italian Literature at Boston University. She has written *Antisemitism, Misogyny, and the Logic of Cultural Difference: Cesare Lombroso and Matilde Serao* (1994), and has edited *Tainted Greatness: Antisemitism and Cultural Heroes* (1994). She is writing a book on the relationship of criminology and racialist discourse to the development of detective fiction in the nineteenth century, and is a Visiting Scholar in the Women's Studies Program at Brandeis University.

JOHN M. HOBERMAN is Professor of Germanic Languages at the University of Texas at Austin. He has published *Sport and Political Ideology* (1984), *The Olympic Crisis* (1986), and *Mortal Engines: The Science of Performance and the Dehumanization of Sport* (1992). He is currently at work on a book entitled *Kafka's Body: Masculinity, Sport, and the Jews*.

BARBARA HYAMS is Lecturer with the rank of Assistant Professor of German at Brandeis University. She has also taught at Boston University and the University of Tulsa. Shortly after German reunification she was Resident Director of the American Institute for Foreign Study Program at Humboldt University in Berlin. She has published articles on modern Austrian literature and New German Cinema. She is currently writing about Leopold Sacher-Masoch.

ALLAN JANIK is Visiting Professor of German at Innsbruck University, Adjunct Professor of Philosophy at Vienna University, and Adjunct Professor for Technology and Culture at the Royal Institute of Technology, Stockholm. His major publications include *Essays on Wittgenstein and Weininger* (1985), *Style Politics and the Future of Philosophy* (1989), *Cordelias Tysnad* (1991), *How Not to Interpret a Culture* (1986), and *Varför Wittgenstein?* (Why Wittgenstein; forthcoming) as well as *Wittgenstein's Vienna* (1973, with Stephen Toulmin). He is currently working on a study of the development of the concepts of dialogue and irony in practical philosophy from Montaigne to Ebner and Buber.

JACQUES LE RIDER is a member of the Institut Universitaire de France and Professor at the Université de Paris VIII in Saint-Denis in the department of Germanics. He has published extensively on Weininger, including *Le Cas Otto Weininger: Racines de l'antiféminisme et de l'antisémitisme* (1982; German translation, 1985), and *Otto Weininger: Werk und Wirkung* (1984, coedited with Norbert Leser). His most recent book is *Modernity and Crises of Identity: Culture and Society in Fin-de-Siècle Vienna* (1993).

JEFFREY MEHLMAN is Professor of French Literature at Boston University and the author of *Legacies of Anti-Semitism in France* (1983) and *Walter Benjamin for Children: An Essay on his Radio Years* (1994). A volume of twenty years of his essays is forthcoming from Cambridge University Press.

ELFRIEDE PÖDER holds a Ph.D. in German Literature from the University of Innsbruck. She is a research associate for a bibliographical project on Austrian periodicals of the 1930s that is sponsored by the *Österreicher Fonds zur Förderung der wissenschaftlichen Forschung* and directed by Professor Sigurd Paul Scheichl of the University of Innsbruck. She has taught German literature and is the co-founder of *Effie Biest, Verein zur Förderung feministischer Literatur, Kunst, und Wissenschaft.* She is the author of several articles on Austrian literature and a book entitled *Interpretation zwischen Theorie und Praxis* (1993).

MARILYN REIZBAUM is Associate Professor of English at Bowdoin College. Her two most recent articles are "The Minor Work of James Joyce" (*James Joyce Quarterly,* Winter 1992), and "What's My Line: The Contemporaneity of Eavan Boland" (*Irish University Review,* forthcoming). She is currently completing a book on James Joyce's Judaic 'Other.'

HANNELORE RODLAUER has specialized in Franz Kafka and the culture of his time since completing her Ph.D. at the University of Vienna. She has taught at the University of Salzburg and the University of Klagenfurt. She has published on Kafka's autobiographical writings and personal relationships, and is the co-editor, with Malcolm Pasley, of the two-volume *Max Brod/Franz Kafka: Eine Freundschaft.* She has also edited Otto Weininger's early writings, including his correspondence with Hermann Swoboda.

FREDDIE ROKEM is the author of *Tradition and Renewal in Swedish Drama and Theatre: 1914–1922* (in Swedish), and *Theatrical Space in Ibsen, Chekhov, and Strindberg: Public Forms of Privacy,* as well as several articles on modern European and Israeli theater. He is Senior Lecturer (Associate Professor) in the Department of Theatre Arts at Tel Aviv University, and is currently writing a book on the representations of the human body in the theater. He also translates Hebrew literature into Swedish.

NATANIA ROSENFELD received her Ph.D. in English from Princeton University in 1992 and is currently writing *Outsiders Together: Virginia and Leonard Woolf.* She is Visiting Assistant Professor at Duke University and is Consulting Editor of *The American Poetry Review.* Her own poetry has appeared in several journals.

GERALD STIEG is Professor of German and Austrian Literature and Area Studies at the Sorbonne Nouvelle (Paris III) and Editor in Chief of the scholarly journal *Austriaca.* His most important publications are *Der Brenner und Die Fackel* (1976) and *Frucht des Feuers* (1990); his *Rilke: POESIE* is scheduled to appear with Gallimard (Paris) in 1996.

Index ✦

Philosophy / Literature / Gender Studies

In 1903 Otto Weininger, a Viennese Jew who converted to Protestantism, published *Geschlecht und Charakter (Sex and Character)*, a book in which he set out to prove the moral inferiority and character deficiency of "the woman" and "the Jew." Almost immediately, he was acclaimed as a young genius for bringing these two elements together. Shortly thereafter, at the age of twenty-three, Weininger committed suicide in the room where Beethoven had died. Weininger's sensationalized death immortalized him as an intellectual who expressed abject misogyny and antisemitism.

This collection of essays, many translated into English for the first time, examines Weininger's influence and reception in Western culture, particularly his impact on important writers such as Ludwig Wittgenstein, Sigmund Freud, Franz Kafka, and James Joyce. One essay considers the ways Weininger's ideas were used to further Nazi ideology, and several offer feminist approaches to interpreting the intersection of antisemitism and misogyny. The concluding essay explores Weininger's surprising role in ... iopolitical self-definition through the bold produc- ... lay, "The Soul of a Jew (Weininger's Last Night)."

This volume's close examination of Weininger's ideas, and their subsequent appearance in other well-known texts, suggests how the legacies of prejudice affect Western culture today.

The contributors are Katherine Arens, Steven Beller, Gisela Brude-Firnau, Alberto Cavaglion, Kristie A. Foell, Sander L. Gilman, John Hoberman, Allan Janik, Jacques Le Rider, Jeffrey Mehlman, Elfriede Pöder, Marilyn Reizbaum, Hannelore Rodlauer, Freddie Rokem, Natania Rosenfeld, Gerald Stieg, and the editors.

NANCY A. HARROWITZ is author of *Antisemitism, Misogyny and the Logic of Cultural Difference: Cesare Lombroso and Matilde Serao* and editor of *Tainted Greatness: Antisemitism and Cultural Heroes* (Temple). BARBARA HYAMS is Lecturer with the rank of Assistant Professor of German at Brandeis University.

UNIVERSITY PRESS ![T] Philadelphia

ISB-N-1 ...
24 441 ...
JEWS ...ene Putterman
09/18 ... U.S.A.

cloth ISBN 1-56639-248-9
paper ISBN 1-56639-249-7

ISBN 1-56639-249-7

90000

9 781566 392495